CADOGANguides

BRUSSELS

ANTONY MASON

About the author

Antony Mason is the author of some 40 books, which include biographies of great artists, children's atlases, and books on exploration, great civilizations, the Wild West, houseplants, volleyball, spying – as well as travel guides. He has also written (with Felicity Golden) the Cadogan Guide to Bali, a book inspired by sitting on a beach in Bali and wondering if there was any way he might be able to make a living out of doing just that (he couldn't). Having travelled to most parts of the world, he now lives and works in London, but for many years has been a frequent visitor to Brussels and Belgium. So convinced is he of the virtues and charms of the Belgians that he has married one, and has since felt sufficiently qualified to write *The Xenophobe's Guide to the Belgians* (1995), designed to cure xenophobes of any misguided prejudices.

About the contributors

James Alexander and **Caroline Mudd** have contributed to and updated a number of Cadogan Guides. James' next big project is writing a guide to Malaysia, while Caroline juggles travelling with an acting career. When they're not travelling the world together, they live in London.

Cadogan Guides
Network House, 1 Ariel Way, London W12 7SL
cadoganguides@morrispub.co.uk
www.cadoganguides.com

The Globe Pequot Press
246 Goose Lane, PO Box 480, Guilford, Connecticut
06437–0480

Copyright © Antony Mason 1995, 1998, 2002
Updated by James Alexander and Caroline Mudd 2002

Series design: Andrew Barker
Series cover design: Sheridan Wall
Art Direction: Sarah Rianhard-Gardner
Photography: © Tim Mitchell 2001
Victor Horta images (pp.8 and 22) courtesy of Sofam-Belgium
Maps created by the XYZ Digital Map Company and
customized by Map Creation Ltd
Map Co-ordinator: Angie Watts

Editorial Director: Vicki Ingle
Series Editor: Claudia Martin
Editors: Philippa Reynolds and Joss Waterfall
Proofreading: Susannah Wight
Indexing: Isobel McLean
Production: Book Production Services
Printed in Italy by Legoprint
A catalogue record for this book is available from the British Library
ISBN 1860118518

Contents

Introduction

Ever since Brussels emerged from a bog in the Dark Ages (Brussels means 'settlement in the marshes'), the city has skulked in the shadow of Europe's ruling powers, and has been occupied and regurgitated time and again, until finally the Belgian nation was formed in 1831. Not surprisingly, 'Brussels' has never had the same ring to it as many of Europe's great cities, but today, as nominal 'Capital of Europe', you might expect the city to be laughing. And, yes, Brussels is proud of its grand new sobriquet, but it has served as a mixed blessing: the city's role as a legislative and administrative centre has given it an unfair reputation for being unassertive, colourless, or just plain boring.

Part of the problem is that Brussels' many graces are not served up on a plate and many fly-by visitors come away with an impression that the magnificent Grand' Place is the city's sole selling point. But uproot Brussels and relocate it anywhere else in the world and heads would turn. It is a progressive city of multiple attractions, a multilingual metropolis shaped not so much as the capital of a nation, but as a centre of middle-class affluence: after all, the architectural high point is not the cathedral, but the arena of guildhouses that forms the Grand' Place.

Within easy walking distance of one another, the city's different quarters each have their attractions. Wander the maze of medieval lanes; settle down in an Art Nouveau café; admire the work of Surrealist masters in a world-class museum or shop in cutting-edge fashion boutiques. For those with a taste for more, catch a tram out to the city's halo of primeval beech forest; experience the energetic nightlife, sipping on one of hundreds of beers brewed to perfection by generations of thirsty monks; and dine on cuisine cooked with such obsessive attention that you wonder at the barbarism of your own culinary skills. Then come away and consider whether you reckon Brussels is boring.

Brussels is also perfectly situated for exploring those other great Flemish cities, Bruges, Ghent and Antwerp. Each has its own distinct flavour, but they all reflect their common heritage as prosperous trading cities through their great collections of art, and sparkling, ornamented squares.

The Neighbourhoods

3 Shopping at Galeries Royales de St-Hubert, p.84

1 The Grand' Place, pp.74–81

North Central Brussels

Around the Grand' Place

Coudenberg and Parc de Bruxelles

7 Gorging on chips and chocolate on medieval Rue de l'Etuve, p.81

Marolles and Sablon

5 Jeu de Balle fleamarket, p.106

6 The cafés of Sablon, p.230, and the bars of Marolles, p.238

2 Musées Royaux des Beaux-Arts, p.91

8 Wining and dining at De Ultieme Hallucinatie, p.122

4 The Art Nouveau splendour around Square Ambiorix, p.132

9 The Centre Belge de la Bande Dessinée, p.119

Quartier Léopold:
Heart of Europe

10 A concert at the Palais des Beaux-Arts, p.97

In this guide, the city is divided into the five neighbourhoods outlined on the map above, each with its own sightseeing chapter. This map also shows our suggestions for the Top Ten activities and places to visit in Brussels. The following colour pages introduce the neighbourhoods in more detail, explaining the distinctive character and highlights of each, and there are also introductions to sights outside the centre of Brussels and to the popular day trips of Bruges, Ghent and Antwerp.

Clockwise from top left: Manneken-Pis, Hôtel de Ville, street scene and bar around the Grand' Place.

Around the Grand' Place

Tucked away in the heart of old Brussels, the Grand' Place is one of Europe's great architectural show-pieces, a dazzling arena of Gothic and Flemish Baroque. The surrounding mesh of cobblestone streets has been prettified and pack-aged for tourists – here you'll find grand 19th-century arcades, lace, chocolate, *moules et frites*, beer and that small naked boy peeing with happy abandon, the Manneken-Pis.

Around the Grand' Place
Around the Grand' Place chapter p.71
Hotels p.212 Restaurants p.224 Bars p.237
Medieval Centre walk p.157 »

Clockwise from top left: Palais des Beaux-Arts, Galerie Ravenstein, Palais Royal, Du Mim Café at the Musée des Instruments de Musique.

Coudenberg and Parc de Bruxelles

Perched regally above the medieval heart of town, Coudenberg was the perfect site for Brussels' ruling classes. From the safety of their palaces they could look down on the action below without dirtying their feet. Though the dukes and governors have gone, this is still an area of stately architecture and sweeping vistas, linked with the lower town by the wide stone stairway and formal gardens of the Mont des Arts. At the heart of Coudenberg are the magnificent Musées Royaux des Beaux-Arts, while to the north is the attractive Parc de Bruxelles, flanked by the solemn bulk of the Palais Royal and the Palais de la Nation.

Marolles and Sablon

The whiff of privilege hangs in the air in Sablon, an old residential quarter centred on two charming squares and a Gothic church. Antiques shops display their treasures, sports cars hum about, and wealthy Bruxellois take it easy over oysters at upper-crust cafés. A mere five-minute walk down the hill into Marolles and it's chips, waffles and the daily exchange of *brocante* ('junk') at the Jeu de Balle flea-market. This is the city's old artisan quarter: a gritty, vibrant area with a scruffy edge and a fierce pride – listen out and you'll hear the unique twang of the Marollien dialect.

From top: Place du Grand-Sablon, Place du Petit-Sablon, Marollien shop windows and street.

Marolles and Sablon

Marolles and Sablon chapter p.101
Hotels p.213 Restaurants p.229 Bars p.238

From top: Cité Administrative, Jardin Botanique, Théâtre de la Monnaie.

North Central Brussels

The northern sector of central Brussels has its finger on the pulse. It is the commercial heart of the city, a varied sprawl of mainstream shops, bohemian enclaves and random architectural gems. The streets that run off from Place Ste-Cathérine are where the trends are set: many of the dilapidated buildings have been given sassy makeovers to house hip bars or designer boutiques. Swing round to the east and you run up against the cathedral, which wears a proud new face after decades of restoration work. The vibrant contrasts of this sector are typified by the ornate façade of Eglise St-Jean-Baptiste au Béguinage, and the Centre Belge de la Bande Dessinée.

Quartier Léopold: Heart of Europe

Quartier Léopold is an unsettled mix of old and new. Peeking over the treetops of Parc Léopold is the bulk of the Parlement Européen, while to the north a wasteland of offices fades into elegant 1870s Square Ambiorix.

Despite the uncompromising presence of the EU, there's plenty to do in this part of town: enter the mind of a megalomaniac at the Musée Wiertz; stretch your legs in Parc du Cinquantenaire; or explore the wealth of treasures and artefacts housed in the palatial halls of the Musées Royaux d'Art et d'Histoire.

Clockwise from top left: Maison Van Eetvelde, Parlement Européen, Parc Léopold, Parc du Cinquantenaire, Square Ambiorix.

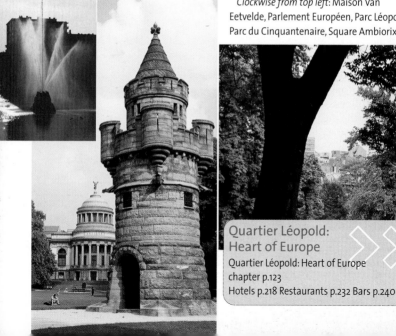

Quartier Léopold: Heart of Europe

Outside the Centre

Step outside the central pentagon and Brussels' charms are bound to grow on you. Leafy suburban pockets rub shoulders with scruffy workaday enclaves and an expanse of accessible beech forest. Then there are some surprises: the delightful Musée David et Alice Van Buuren in Uccle, the Maison d'Erasmus and the lambic brewery in Anderlecht, and the Musée Magritte in Jette. Not to be missed are the swirling façades of the Art Nouveau district in St-Gilles and Ixelles, and the Atomium, cast like a jack into the suburb of Heysel.

Clockwise from top: Atomium, Tour Japonais, Musée Bruxellois de la Gueuze, Place Fernand Cocq in Ixelles.

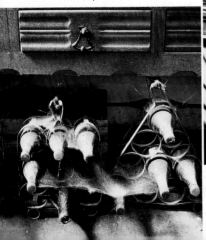

Outside the Centre
Outside the Centre chapter p.133
Hotels p.218 Restaurants p.233 Bars p.241
Art Nouveau walk p.150

Bruges

The undisputed jewel in Belgium's medieval crown, Bruges is a remarkable urban heirloom, unspoilt since its days of prosperous trading activity. Crooked streets, turretted guildhouses, picture-perfect stone bridges over mirror-still canals are all almost as they were in the 15th century. The medieval art collections in the Groeningemuseum and the Memlingmuseum are the key sites, and the hospitality and cooking of the town's many fine restaurants are also widely celebrated.

All photos: Patisserie, bar, canal and street scenes of Bruges.

Bruges

Ghent

Dignified splendour sets this great Flemish city apart from its neighbours and makes it a rewarding choice for a day trip from Brussels. Ghent's gilded spires, stately façades and tranquil canals reflect its noble past, reinvigorated today by the university. Textiles still dominate the city's industry and commerce flourishes in fashionable new boutiques. The city's cathedral is home to Jan van Eyck's masterpiece, *Adoration of the Mystic Lamb*, and its folk museum and *begijnhof* are the most impressive of their kind in Belgium.

From top: Canal-boat figurehead, Sint-Baafskathedraal (*twice*), Sint-Michielsbrug.

Ghent
Ghent chapter p.187
Hotels p.190 Restaurants p.191

Antwerp

There's a seductive energy in Antwerp, born of a proud, powerful past and a more recent adventurous rejuvenation. The old city centre exhibits the traditional Belgian charms of delicate spires, a fine cathedral and an impressive Grote Markt flanked by ornate guildhouses. Antwerp's artistic heritage is evident in its richly endowed galleries, churches and museums. Industry retains a strong presence, but is largely removed from Antwerp's medieval centre, where the international diamond trade thrives. Vibrant, young clothes designers have added a fashionable edge to a city where the bars and clubs are buzzing with music and the literary cafés are alive with discussion.

Clockwise from top left: Diamond District, Onze Lieve Vrouwe Kathedraal, fountain in the Grote Markt, Steen.

Antwerp

Antwerp chapter p.197
Hotels p.200 Restaurants p.201 Bars p.201

Days Out in Brussels

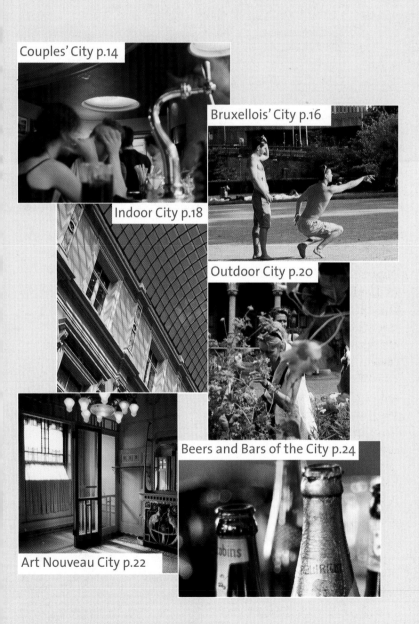

Couples' City p.14

Bruxellois' City p.16

Indoor City p.18

Outdoor City p.20

Beers and Bars of the City p.24

Art Nouveau City p.22

COUPLES' CITY

Forget about eurocrats and the Manneken-Pis: packed tight inside the phantom perimeter of the old city walls are a wealth of activities suitable for two, while the green buffer of beach forest on the fringes is a perfect getaway for an afternoon. The many gardens, the splendid Grand' Place and its neighbouring maze of medieval streets, the Art Nouveau cafés, the fish restaurants and slow-paced bars with a penchant for candlelight – all make the city ideal for a romantic weekend.

One

Start: Metro Gare Centrale.

Breakfast: A coffee at **Le Roy d'Espagne** on the Grand' Place (*photo top left*).

Morning: Have a sniff in the **flower market on the Grand' Place**, then wander up through the fountains and lavender beds of the **Mont des Arts** towards Coudenberg.

Lunch: The top-floor café, **Du Mim** (*photo above, top*), of the **Musée des Instruments de Musique** for cake, a glass of wine and the best views of old Brussels.

Afternoon: Head back across town to the designer boutiques and bars of **Ste-Cathérine**, via the elegant **Galeries Royales de St-Hubert** and the medieval lanes of the **Ilôt Sacré**.

Dinner: Oysters and lobster at **La Belle Maraîchère**.

Evening: A night of opera at the grand **Théâtre de la Monnaie**.

the **Place du Grand-Sablon** (*photo above right*). Peek inside Brussels' most beautiful Gothic church, **Eglise Notre-Dame du Sablon**.

Lunch: Indulge your tastebuds at famous chocolatier **Wittamer**.

Afternoon: Catch the tram down to the **Bois de la Cambre** and hire a rowing boat on the lake. Round off the afternoon with a visit to the **Musée David et Alice Van Buuren**, a wonderful Art Deco home with a landscaped garden.

Dinner: Candlelit tables and an excellent wine list at **L'Amadeus**, in Ixelles.

Evening: A night of jazz and blues music at **Sounds**.

Two

Start: Metro Porte de Namur or Gare Centrale.

Breakfast: A croissant at the country-style **Le Pain Quotidien**.

Morning: The upmarket antiques shops and galleries surrounding

Food and Drinks

L'Amadeus, p.233
La Belle Maraîchère, p.230
Du Mim, p.228
Le Pain Quotidien, p.230
Le Roy d'Espagne, p.238
Wittamer, p.252

Sights and Activities

Bois de la Cambre, p.137
Eglise Notre-Dame du Sablon, p.109

Galeries Royales de St-Hubert, p.84
Flower market on the Grand' Place, p.74
Ilôt Sacré, p.84
Mont des Arts, p.99
Musée David et Alice Van Buuren, p.138
Musée des Instruments de Musique, p.94
Place du Grand-Sablon, p.109
Ste-Cathérine, p.114

Nightlife

Sounds, p.246
Théâtre de la Monnaie, p.117

BRUXELLOIS' CITY

As 'capital of Europe' and the city where Flanders and Wallonia meet, Brussels is a place of many tongues, a hotchpotch of traditions. But ask anyone to point you in the direction of the true heart of Brussels and they will send you to Marolles, the shabby artisan quarter, where old men sit around playing draughts in *brocante*-strewn bars. Brussels' citizens share a passion for food and drink – even the humble chip is venerated, while the beer needs no introduction. If anywhere, the city's soul bides its time in the endless bars and restaurants.

Three

Start: Metro Porte de Hal.
Breakfast: A newspaper and croissant at **De Skieven Architek** in Place du Jeu de Balle.
Morning: Sift through the junk of the lively **fleamarket in Place du Jeu de Balle** (*photo below*) and snap up the early bargains. Stop for refresh-

ment at **Brocante**, among thoroughbred Marolliens.
Lunch: Head towards Sablon, via the restaurant-strewn **Rue de Rollebeek**. Join a different breed of Bruxellois – wealthy business lunchers – for a light meal at **Chez Richard**.
Afternoon: Catch the tram to Ixelles and the excellent **Musée Communal d'Ixelles**, containing interesting works by Belgian artists and the great masters.
Dinner: Treat yourself to top-class French cuisine at **La Maison du Cygne**, just off the Grand' Place.
Evening: Drink beer or fruit wine to the sounds of Jacques Brel at eccentric **Goupil le Fol**.

Four

Start: Metro Botanique.

Breakfast and morning: Grab a coffee in the Art Nouveau **Brasserie Horta** at the **Centre Belge de la Bande Dessinée** (*photo top right*), where you can acquaint yourself with that quintessentially Belgian achievement, the comic strip.

Lunch: Walk down to the **Bourse** and fill your belly with chips and a glob of mayonnaise from **Fritland**.

Afternoon: The **Porte de Hal**, where you can learn a little of the Belgian love of food at the colourful **food market**.

Dinner: Appease your hunger back in town with some meaty Belgian cuisine at **Le Cerf**.

Evening: **Mappa Mundo**, one of the hip bars on nearby **Place St-Géry**.

INDOOR CITY

Brussels is no stranger to rain, so there's more than enough to do indoors. Elegant arcades such as the Galeries Royales de St-Hubert were built more than 150 years ago to protect the bedraggled shopper – though today you'll have to dodge a few leaks. Then there's the wide range of museums, with the world-class Musées Royaux des Beaux-Arts at their helm, and the high-quality restaurants and hip bars to provide sanctuary throughout the day.

Five

Start: Metro Gare Centrale.
Morning: Escape the elements in the vast interlinking exhibition spaces of the **Musées Royaux des Beaux-Arts** – there's enough modern and ancient Belgian art to keep you going for days.

Lunch: Cross the **Place Royale** to **Pablo's** for a fiery Mexican lunch or a few snacks at the long bar.
Afternoon: A high-tech tour at the **Musée des Instruments de Musique** (*photo top*) in the Old England building, then wander around newly renovated **Cathédrale St-Michel** nearby.
Dinner: **In 't Spinnekopke** for *waterzooi*, and other hearty Belgian specialities.
Evening: Relax over drinks in the trendy bars around **Place St-Géry**, such as **Java**.

Six

Start: Metro Trône.

Breakfast: A pastry at **Le Bentley**, overlooking the Place du Luxembourg.

Morning: **Musée Wiertz**, the high-ceilinged studio of over-ambitious artist Antoine Wiertz, then check out the iguanodon skeletons in the **Musée des Sciences Naturelles** across the road.

Afternoon: Catch the metro back to the centre of town and seek shelter in the dazzling **Galeries Royales de St-Hubert** (*photo above left*). Before browsing the shops have lunch at traditional **Taverne du Passage** in the centre of the arcade – then the antiques, books, chocolates, clothes and accessories can receive your full attention.

Dinner: **Aux Armes de Bruxelles**, for warming old-fashioned Belgian cuisine and impeccable service.

Evening: Watch a traditional puppet show at **Théâtre Toone**, then slip downstairs for a few beers in the puppet-hung bar, **Chez Toone**.

OUTDOOR CITY

Not many people know that Brussels is Europe's greenest city – largely due to the Fôret de Soignes, a vast swathe of primeval woodland at the city's southern fringes. The abundance of rain probably plays its part, too. When the weather's fine, outdoor attractions are legion: in the centre of the city there's the fine architecture of the Grand' Place and its surrounding cobbled streets; to the north that outsized model from a school physics lab, the Atomium, and the surrounding Parc de Laeken; to the south the Bois de la Cambre; and to the east a procession of parks with interweaving trails.

Seven

Start: Metro Gare du Midi.

Morning: Explore Brussels' biggest **market** on Sunday mornings, outside the **Gare du Midi**. If it's not Sunday, follow our **Medieval Centre walk**.

Lunch: **Le Lion St-Géry** in Place St-Géry, for a liquid lunch in a peaceful courtyard setting.

Afternoon: Set off north for the **Parc de Laeken**, containing the **Pavillon Chinois** (*photo left*), the **Tour Japonaise** and the **Serres Royales**. If it's hot (or if you're dragging round impatient kids), head for the swimming complex at **Océade**.

Dinner: Dine on Belgian standards at the Bruparck branch of famous **Chez Léon**.

Evening: Relax with a beer outside **La Best Toffe** in leafy **Place de la Liberté**.

Eight

Start: Metro Montgomery.

Morning: Hilly **Parc Woluwe**, a popular picnic spot with pedalos for hire (or iceskating in the winter). If you're feeling more adventurous, catch the historic tram (44) down to **Tervuren** and wander around the extensive grounds of the **Musée Royale de l'Afrique Centrale**. Alternatively, head into the **Forêt de Soignes** for some serious walking.

Lunch: If you stay in Woluwe, lunch in style at **Moulin de Lindekemale**, set in an old watermill.

Afternoon: Head eastwards to leafy **Parc du Cinquantenaire** to see the **Arcade du Cinquantenaire** and the Neoclassical exterior of Victor Horta's **Pavillon Horta**.

Dinner: Dine al fresco on adventurous Spanish seafood at **Jardin d'Espagne**.

Evening: Watch a film at the **outdoor cinema** in Parc du Cinquantenaire (July and August).

ART NOUVEAU CITY

Art Nouveau took Brussels by storm at the turn of the 20th century. Right angles were outlawed, as architects, led by Victor Horta and encouraged by a wealthy literati, applied the sensual 'new art' to townhouses, municipal buildings and cafés, leaving a trail of lovely homes in St-Gilles and Ixelles. Attention to detail is paramount – keep an eye out for the lovingly shaped doorknob or the twisted grillwork of balcony railings.

Nine

Start: Metro Horta.
Brunch: Brunch at **Sisisi**, a whole-some venue on the St-Gilles–Ixelles border.
Morning: **Musée Horta** – the architect's former home and studio is now justifiably considered an Art Nouveau shrine. Contrast this with the lofty salons at **Hôtel Hannon** (*photo above*) nearby.
Lunch: **Café Le Perroquet**, a genuine Art Nouveau venue for the trendy set of the Sablon.
Afternoon: Head up to Square Ambiorix and track down Brussels'

most outlandish example of Art Nouveau, the **Maison St-Cyr** (*photo far left*). Two nearby Horta designs on Avenue Palmerston, **Maison Van Eetvelde** and **Maison Deprez-Van de Velde**, seem tame in comparison. Relax beside the huge sunken pond in adjoining **Square Marie Louise**.

Dinner and evening: If you've booked in advance, dine at Brussels' finest restaurant, **Comme Chez Soi**.

Ten

Start: Metro Louise then tram 81 or 82.

Breakfast: **La Kartchma**'s Art Nouveau mirrors provide a beautiful setting for a morning pastry.

Morning: Return to **St-Gilles and Ixelles** to admire the Art Nouveau façades in our **Art Nouveau walk**, such as **Hôtel Solvay** and **Hôtel Tassel**.

Lunch: A hearty meal at trendy **L'Ultime Atome**.

Afternoon: Head back into the centre of town for a tour of some stunning Art Nouveau cafés, including **Le Falstaff**.

Dinner: A special meal among the sinuous furnishings of **De Ultieme Hallucinatie** (*photo below*).

Evening: **Fin de Siècle** bar, for your final sampling of Art Nouveau sophistication.

BEERS AND BARS OF THE CITY

If you need just one reason to come to Brussels, let it be beer. Belgium produces over 400 varieties – and as many matching glasses – while Brussels provides a limitless choice of bars, from dingy dives to grand *fin de siècle* cafés and Art Nouveau landmarks. A few days is all it will take to acquire a taste for some of the more unusual brews – the fresh coriander tang of Hoegaarden, the round port-like flavours of a Chimay Bleu, or the musty bite of lambic, a beer with an aftertaste that clings like crushed apple pips.

Eleven

Start: Metro Gare Centrale.

Breakfast: One of the grand café-bars that ring the Grand' Place, such as **La Chaloupe d'Or**.

Morning: **La Maison des Brasseurs**, headquarters of the brewers' guild, is one of the most striking buildings on the square. Visit the **Musée de la Brasserie** inside and claim your free beer.

Lunch: Eat seafood or traditional Belgian cuisine at **La Roue d'Or**, a chandelier-hung brasserie just off the Grand' Place.

Afternoon: Buy a selection of beers and matching glasses (or simply taste a few brews) at **Beer Mania** in Ixelles.

Dinner: Those brave enough to mix beer with wine will appreciate **Les Foudres** for its excellent cuisine and fine wines.

Evening: Track down two serious beer-drinking havens in St-Gilles,

Chez Moeder Lambic and **Verschueren**.

Twelve

Start: Metro Lemonnier.

Morning: A fascinating tour of the last brewery to produce naturally fermented gueuze and lambic, the **Musée Bruxellois de la Gueuze** (or Cantillon Brewery) in Anderlecht.

Afternoon: Having bought a bottle or two direct from the brewery, gather a few other morsels for a picnic and head for the tranquil **Parc de Bruxelles** in the centre of town.

Dinner and evening: Seek out some of Brussels' most outstanding café-bars. Begin with eccentric **Le Fleur en Papier Doré**. Then head for the three ornate turn-of-the-century bars that surround the Bourse and serve food: **Le Falstaff**, **Le Cirio** and **P. P. Café**. Finish the evening at the atmospheric **Greenwich**.

Food and Drinks
La Chaloupe d'Or, p.237
Les Foudres, p.233
La Roue d'Or, p.225

Sights and Activities
Beer Mania, p.256
La Maison des Brasseurs, p.79
Musée de la Brasserie, p.79
Musée Bruxellois de la Gueuze, p.138

Parc de Bruxelles, p.95
Nightlife
Chez Moeder Lambic, p.242
Le Cirio, p.237
Le Falstaff, p.237
Le Fleur en Papier Doré, p.237
Greenwich, p.239
P. P. Café, p.238
Verschueren, p.242

Roots of the City

Belgium has been in existence for only 160 years. Forged as an independent state in 1830, it's had a hard time establishing deep historical roots to its nationhood. Before 1830 it had barely seen itself as a nation at all, more the haphazardly constructed filling in a sandwich of powerblocks.

History, however, has a hunger for labels. It likes neatly defined borders, dynasties and empires, big dates and strong storylines. Belgium can provide few of these. Its tale is complex; it has been busy in the wings of mainstream European history, but seldom centre stage. It might be tempting to pretend that Belgium has no history at all – but of course it does, written into the worn bricks of the step-gables of Bruges, into the gilded cornucopia of Brussels' Grand' Place, and into the battlefield of Waterloo.

The Bravest of the Gauls

By about 400 BC much of northern Europe was occupied by the Celts, a loosely knit federation of iron-working tribes who had spread out from their original base in southern Germany and Switzerland. The Celts were gifted horsemen and fearless warriors, who would enter into battle naked except for a bronze torque around their necks.

The Romans lived in dread of the Celts, whom they called the **Gauls**. The Gauls hemmed them in across the northern borders of Italy and represented the very opposite of what their civilization stood for. Worse, in 390 BC the Gauls poured into Italy and sacked Rome. The Romans had to wait for the greatest leader of their history, **Julius Caesar** (100–44 BC) to see the Gauls finally subdued. After 59 BC he waged a campaign that pushed the Roman Empire to the North Sea. However, on the eastern fringes of Gaul he came up against furious resistance from the **Belgae**, causing him to comment, '*Horum popularum omnium fortissimi sunt Belgae.*' ('Of all these people [the Gauls], the Belgae are the most courageous.')

The Belgae were subsequently ruled as a part of Roman Gaul, which had its eastern border along the Rhine. After AD 15 Gaul was subdivided, and **Gallia Belgica** became a separate province, which stretched south-wards from the North Sea coast and included much of modern Switzerland. As elsewhere in the Roman Empire, the Pax Romana brought a prolonged period of stability and prosperity to the region, once its people had accepted subjugation.

The Franks and Charlemagne (5th–8th Centuries)

After the collapse of the Roman Empire, a Germanic tribe called the **Franks**, who had settled as Roman mercenaries in northern Belgium around Tournai, pushed the remnants of the Romans out of Gaul. Their leader, **Clovis I** (r. AD 481–511), founded the Christian Merovingian dynasty (c. 500–751).

Throughout the Merovingian period, Tournai was the hub of an empire covering much of France and Germany. Brussels, by contrast, was merely a twinkle in the eye of a bishop. According to legend, **St Géry**, Bishop of Cambrai, built a chapel on one of the islands in the swampy River Senne in the late 6th century AD. A settlement may then have grown up around it. However, the name Bruocsella, meaning 'house in the swamp', is not recorded before AD 966.

The Merovingian kings ruled until AD 751, when they were ousted by Pepin the Short, who founded the Carolingian dynasty

(AD 751–987). Pepin the Short's son, born in Liège in AD 742, was one of the great kings of this transitional period of European history. He was called **Charlemagne** ('Charles the Great', r. AD 768–814). Under his rule the Moors were pushed back from northern Spain, and the Frankish kingdoms extended into Italy and southern Germany.

Charlemagne saw himself as the heir to the Roman Empire, and the Pope obliged by crowning him Emperor of the West in AD 800. But after his death his heirs squabbled and the Frankish Empire splintered. Under the Treaty of Verdun in AD 843 the River Scheldt, which flows across the middle of Belgium between Tournai and Antwerp, marked the border between lands assigned to rival grandsons of Charlemagne – the German king **Lothair I** (AD 795–855), and the French king **Charles the Bald** (AD 823–77). Charles took West Francia to the west and north of the Scheldt, and Lothair took lands to the south and east. His kingdom became known as Lotharingia, later Lorraine.

Flanders and Lorraine (9th–11th Centuries)

The division of the Frankish Empire along the Scheldt was not simply geographical. In late Roman times, when the Franks had settled in the north of Belgium, the south was occupied by Romanized Celts called the Wala. The language of the Romanized Celts evolved out of Latin to become French, and this was the language of the Wala – later the Walloons. This was a political and linguistic divide which, broadly speaking, still exists today. Paradoxically, however, the part assigned to France was Flemish-speaking, while the French-speaking half fell into the orbit of East Francia, which evolved into Germany.

History now follows two different threads for five centuries. Flanders in the north became powerful under a series of notable leaders called Baldwin (Baudouin in French, Boudewijn in Flemish). The first of these, **Baldwin Iron-Arm**, challenged the authority

of the French king, Charles the Bald, and eloped with his daughter, Judith. The couple fled to Rome where Pope Nicholas I managed to bring about a reconciliation of all parties; as a result Charles appointed Baldwin the first Count of Flanders. Although strictly owing allegiance to France, Baldwin and his successors were powers in their own right. **Bruges** and **Ghent** developed and prospered as their main strongholds.

Meanwhile, in East Francia, ruled by German kings, Lorraine became a separate duchy, subdivided into powerful feudal princedoms: Hainaut, Limburg, Namur, Liège and Brabant. In AD 977 **Charles, Duke of Lorraine**, took up residence on the island of St Géry (**Brussels**) in AD 979 – the year given as the official foundation of the city. In 1041 these estates passed into the hands of the **Counts of Leuven** (Louvain), who ruled the surrounding county (subsequently duchy) of Brabant.

The Battle of the Golden Spurs (1302)

With the decline of feudalism, a powerful merchant class emerged in the towns and cities of Flanders, which were well placed to exploit the trading links that now spread right across northern Europe. The principal trade was in textiles: **wool** from England was imported and made into cloth by Flemish weavers.

Ghent, Bruges and Ypres became virtually independent city states, which put them constantly at odds with the Counts of Flanders. After violent confrontations and disputes over succession in the 12th century, the French reasserted their grip on Flanders;

12th–13th Centuries

Béguinage d'Anderlecht, for the development of these communities of single women in the Low Countries, p.140

Tour d'Angle, a rare survivor of the first set of city walls, p.104

Tour Noire, for the best-preserved remnant of the 12th-century city walls, p.114

Timeline

59 BC	Julius Caesar begins his campaign against the Gauls (Celts).
57 BC	Caesar comes close to defeat by the Belgic tribe, the Nervii.
54 BC	Revolt against the Romans by the Eburones under Ambiorix. After its suppression by Caesar, the Belgae are subdued.
AD 15	Creation of Roman province of Gallia Belgica.
Late C5th	Collapse of the Roman Empire.
c. 500–751	Merovingian dynasty of the Franks, ruling from Tournai.
Late C6th	According to legend, St Géry builds a chapel on an island in the River Senne – the origin of the settlement that is to become Brussels.
c. 751–987	Carolingian dynasty of the Franks.
768–814	Reign of Charlemagne, centring upon Aachen.
843	Treaty of Verdun splits Frankish Empire along the line of the River Scheldt: first division of Belgian lands into what will become Flanders and Wallonia.
979	The date of the official foundation of Brussels.
Late C11th	Count Lambert of Leuven builds first fortress on the Coudenberg, Brussels.
1100	First ring of defensive walls raised around Brussels.
1302	Tension in French-dominated Flanders develops into a revolt in Bruges led by Pieter de Coninck and Jan Breydel, culminating in victory at the Battle of the Golden Spurs.
1337	Start of the Hundred Years' War (to 1453).
1338	Revolt in Flanders against French, led by Jacob van Artevelde.
1356	The Flemish under Count Louis de Male seize Brabant but are removed from Brussels after two months by rebels led by Everard 't Serclaes.
1379	Completion of the massive new set of city walls around Brussels.
1384	Philip the Bold, Duke of Burgundy inherits Flanders through his marriage to Louis de Male's daughter.
1406	The Dukes of Burgundy inherit Brabant through marriage, and go on to take over most of the Low Countries.
1419–67	Reign of Philip the Good, high point of the Burgundian period. (First) construction of Grand' Place and Hôtel de Ville, Brussels. Era of Jan van Eyck.
1477	Mary of Burgundy marries Maximilian I of the German–Austrian Habsburg family; beginning of Habsburg rule of the Low Countries (until 1794).
1506–55	Reign of Charles V: Brussels is at the hub of his mighty empire.
1556–98	Philip II rules from Spain.
1568	Execution of Counts Egmont and Hornes in Brussels.
1579	United Provinces (modern Netherlands) declare independence.
1585	Capitulation of Antwerp and Brussels to the Spanish under the Duke of Parma leads to the creation of the Spanish Netherlands (approximately equivalent to modern Belgium; lasts until 1713), with Brussels as the capital.
1598–1633	Beginning of rule of the Infanta Isabella and Archduke Albert. Period of prosperity; the age of Rubens.
1648	Spain formally recognizes United Provinces through the

	Peace of Münster. Closing of the River Scheldt by the Dutch (until 1794) cripples Antwerp.
1695	During the War of the Grand Alliance, French troops under Marshal de Villeroy bombard Brussels, destroying the Grand' Place and city centre.
1713	At the end of the War of the Spanish Succession, the Treaty of Utrecht assigns the Spanish Netherlands to Austria. Belgium is known as the Austrian Netherlands until 1794.
1719	Execution of François Anneessens puts an end to resistance to Austrian rule.
1741–80	Rule by Charles of Lorraine: a period of prosperity and stability.
1780–90	Unpopular rule from Vienna by reformist Emperor Joseph II.
1790	French Revolution of 1789 triggers the Brabançon Revolt; the United States of Belgium declared independent; the revolt is crushed by the Austrian army.
1794	The French Revolutionary Army defeats the Austrians at Fleurus.
1795	Belgium is incorporated into France.
1815	Final defeat of Napoleon at Waterloo. The Congress of Vienna makes Belgium a part of the United Kingdom of the Netherlands (until 1831).
1830	On 25 August a performance of the opera *La Muette de Portici* in Brussels incites the audience to revolt. Dutch troops finally forced out of Brussels on 27 Sept. Provisional government declares Belgium independent on 4 Oct.
1831	At the London Conference the international community accepts Belgium's independence. Léopold of Saxe-Coburg becomes King Léopold I (r. 1831–65).
1865–1909	Reign of King Léopold II, marked by rapid economic and industrial development, grand building projects and the modernization of Brussels, and the acquisition of the Congo (in the 1880s).
1909	Accession of King Albert I (r. 1909–34).
1914–18	First World War: Germany ignores Belgian neutrality to overrun much of the country. King Albert I leads spirited resistance in northwest Belgium.
1934	Death of Albert I in a climbing accident; accession of Léopold III (r. 1934–51).
1940–45	Second World War: Germany again ignores Belgian neutrality.
1951	Violent controversy leads to the abdication of Léopold III in favour of his 21-year-old son, Baudouin I (r. 1951–93).
1958	The European Economic Community (EEC) is created; Belgium is a founder member, and Brussels is established as the EEC headquarters.
1962	The Belgian Congo (now Zaire) wins its independence.
1993	The 'Saint-Michel Accords' formalize the ongoing devolution of government to the three regional governments: Flanders, Wallonia and Brussels. The death of Baudouin I and subsequent accession of Albert II reveal the breadth of popular support for the preservation of Belgian unity against increasing federalization.

but the disdainful behaviour of the Frenchified élite and the cloth merchants, who lorded it over weavers and other workers, became the source of increasing resentment. A mood of rebellion set in, resulting in an uprising against the French in Bruges in 1302, led by **Pieter de Coninck** and **Jan Breydel**, during which anyone unable to speak Flemish was slaughtered.

Later that year, Flemish workers led by Jan Breydel – and armed with little more than lances and staves – took on the full might of the French king, Philip IV (Philip the Fair), near Kortrijk (Courtrai). The French had massively superior and better equipped forces, but the Flemish prepared the marshy ground well, laying branches that acted as traps for the heavily armoured French knights. The French became completely bogged down and were picked off, one by one. This humiliating rout became known as the Battle of the Golden Spurs, because the Flemish victors collected 700 pairs of golden spurs and exhibited them triumphantly in Kortrijk Cathedral. As a result of this battle, Philip the Fair granted Flanders its independence. However, the aristocracy, still loyal to the French, gradually reasserted their power, and by 1329 Flanders was under French rule once more.

Events in Brussels followed a similar pattern. Lying on the main trade route between Cologne and Bruges, it too had prospered, and it developed its own flourishing industries, particularly weaving and goldsmithing. In 1225 work on the **Cathédrale St-Michel** was begun. The city also had its share of unrest, as workers rose up against the merchants. The Guild of Weavers, Dyers

and Fullers won some political power after the Battle of the Golden Spurs, but in 1306, after continuing turmoil, the rebels were defeated by Duke Jean II of Brabant at the Battle of Vilvoorde. To show he meant business, Duke Jean had the leaders buried alive outside the city gates.

The Hundred Years' War (1337–1453)

English claims to French territory, plus their trading interests in Flanders, led to a protracted series of military confrontations with France known as the Hundred Years' War. The trigger was the death of the last French Capetian king, who died in 1328. The English king, **Edward III** (r. 1327–77), the maternal grandson of Philip the Fair of France, reckoned he had a good claim to the French throne – as least as valid as Philip's nephew, Philip de Valois, who became Philip VI. The aristocracy of Flanders naturally sided with the French – so England responded with sanctions: all wool exports to Flanders ceased. This had a rapid and profound effect and the wealthy Flemish wool merchants were faced with ruin. In 1338 a brewer from Ghent called **Jacob van Artevelde** led a successful rebellion against the French authorities, and invited Edward the Black Prince (1330–76), son of Edward III, to become Count of Flanders. Edward III arrived in Flanders with an army, and was proclaimed king of France in Ghent in 1340.

The weavers (as opposed to the wool merchants) had other views. In 1345 they murdered Jacob van Artevelde and seized control of the Flemish cities. It was a unilateral move guaranteed to antagonize other craftsmen. The result was civil war, which ended with the reassertion of the power of the (real) Count of Flanders, with the support of France.

Events in Brabant, further south, now brought the people of Brussels into conflict with Flanders. In 1355 Duke Jean II of Brabant died without a male heir, and the succession fell to his daughter **Jeanne**, who was married to Wenceslas of Luxembourg. In 1356 **Louis de Male**, Count of Flanders, seized the opportunity to invade and took Brabant for himself, although the Flemish were driven out of Brussels by rebels led by the leader of the guilds, **Everard 't Serclaes**. So matters rested until 1381–2, when **Philip van Artevelde** (son of Jacob) led an uprising, defeating Louis de Male before himself coming to grief in a battle against the French. Meanwhile Jeanne and Wenceslas transferred their centre of power from Leuven to Brussels.

In 1384 the throne of Flanders passed to **Philip the Bold of Burgundy** by virtue of his marriage to Louis de Male's daughter, Margaret (the Dukes of Burgundy were part of the Valois family: Philip was the brother of Charles V of France). Bit by bit, the Burgundians took control of most of what is Belgium today: in 1406 the Duchy of Brabant also passed into their hands through marriage, when Jeanne (the last of the Leuven line) died and inheritance passed through the line of her sister.

Meanwhile the Hundred Years' War rumbled on. Charles VI (r. 1380–1422) succeeded his father to the French throne: known as Charles the Mad, he was indeed of unsound mind, and power in France seemed up for grabs. The Dukes of Orleans and Burgundy entered into bitter rivalry to take control. In 1407 the Duke of Burgundy, **John the Fearless**, had Louis, Duke of Orleans murdered, plunging France into civil war. John then negotiated with the English, offering to support **Henry V**'s claim to the French throne. Henry thereupon opened up a new campaign with his famous victory over the French at Agincourt in 1415.

As the English laid siege to Paris, John the Fearless got cold feet. He attempted to negotiate with the new Duke of Orleans, but was

himself murdered. In revenge, his son, **Philip the Good** (r. 1419–67), now gave his open support to the English, and had soon forced Charles VI to sign the Treaty of Troyes, in which Henry V was named as Charles's successor to the French throne.

But it was not to be. Henry V died just two months before Charles, and the throne went to Charles' son, Charles VII (1422–61). The French then launched a new campaign, inspired by Joan of Arc (1412–31), and eventually pushed the English out of their lands.

The Burgundian Period (15th Century)

Philip the Good's Burgundian empire covered two distinct areas: the Burgundy region of central eastern France and the area covering most of modern Belgium plus the Netherlands – the 'Low Countries'. Philip took up residence in Brussels, by 1430 stealing the limelight from Burgundy's former capital, Dijon. (It was at this time that the **Grand' Place** began to take shape.) Philip was the richest man in Europe and his court was the height of European fashion, attracting composers, writers and painters (including the brothers **Van Eyck**). Philip also created the **Order of the Golden Fleece** in Bruges in 1430, its name acknowledging the continuing importance of the wool trade.

Philip's son, **Charles the Bold** (r. 1467–77), attempted to extend his territory by conquering the rest of Lorraine, but was killed at the Battle of Nancy. Louis XI of France (r. 1461–83) then seized the French part of Burgundy for France. Charles's only heir was his daughter, **Mary**, who was thus left with only the Burgundian lands of the Low Countries. Louis' plan was to coerce Mary into marriage with his own son, but Mary's mother, Margaret of York (sister to Edward IV of England) thwarted him: in 1477 she arranged a marriage between Mary and **Maximilian I**, a member of the ruling German–Austrian **Habsburg** family, and future Holy Roman Emperor. Mary died in

1482, and in 1494 the Burgundian Low Countries were passed on to her son, **Philip the Handsome**. Two years later, he married **Joanna of Castile**, and they ruled Castile (effectively Spain) together for just one year (1506) before Philip died. But this was enough to assure the succession of their son, Charles V, to a vast kingdom.

Emperor Charles V (1500–58)

Charles V was by far the most powerful ruler of Europe in his day. He was born in Ghent, but events and his restless energy took him further afield, and for most of his reign the home countries were governed by his sister, **Mary of Hungary**. In 1517 Charles took over the Spanish throne on the death of his grandfather, and assumed the crown of Holy Roman Emperor (after the death of Maximilian) in 1520 – ruling Austria, Germany, Burgundy and the Low Countries, as well as the kingdoms of Naples and Sicily.

Charles's reign coincided with the remarkable advances of Renaissance learning and art in northern Europe. The great Humanist **Desiderius Erasmus** acted as his adviser and went on to play a leading role in the development of Leuven/Louvain University; **Christopher Plantin** set up his famous printing workshop in Antwerp in the 1570s; and Charles's own physician, **Andreas Vesalius** (1514–64) is now regarded as the father of modern anatomy.

16th Century

However, the new thinking promoted by the Renaissance smacked to some of subversion. Martin Luther posted his 95 theses to the church door of Wittenberg in 1517, and thereafter the course was set: the Reformation rapidly spread among the dissident German states and in the northern Netherlands. It was the one challenge that Charles was not equal to.

In 1555, exhausted by his struggles, Charles announced from his palace in Brussels that he was abdicating. He gave his Spanish crown to his son Philip and the crown of the Holy Roman Empire to his brother, Ferdinand.

Suppression in the Spanish Low Countries (Late 16th Century)

Brussels and the rest of the Low Countries did not take kindly to the fact that, shortly after the beginning of his reign, Philip II decided to rule at arm's length, from Spain. 'I would prefer to lose all my domains and die 100 times than rule over heretics,' Philip, a fanatical Catholic, is quoted as saying. He meant it. The Inquisition was sent to the Low Countries in order to apply its ruthless answer to **Protestantism**; all unconventional thinking came under its scrutiny.

When heavy taxes were imposed to finance Philip's extravagant wars, resentment in the Low Countries boiled over into rebellion. A champion was found in **William of Orange** ('the Silent'), whose forebear had been rewarded for his loyalty to Charles V with substantial estates in the Netherlands. William formed a League of Nobility, appealing for moderation in the treatment of Protestants. Their petition was rejected.

In 1566 the resentment of Calvinist Protestants turned to violence. Throughout the Low Countries they vented their pious wrath on the churches, vandalizing them in an orgy of **iconoclasm**. William of Orange and the Governor of Flanders, Count Egmont, tried to find a compromise, but as events slipped out of control William withdrew to

Germany. Philip sent the **Duke of Alva** with 10,000 troops to restore order, also assisted by the Inquisition. Among those executed were **Counts Egmont** and **Hornes**, left to carry the can in William's absence.

From this year on, William began a military campaign against Spanish rule. After several false starts, William gained the upper hand, and took the towns of the Low Countries one by one. Facing mutinous troops and angry creditors, the Duke of Alva fled in 1573. William entered Brussels in triumph in 1576 and won Amsterdam in 1578.

However, not everyone in the Low Countries was overjoyed. The problem was that the south – essentially modern Belgium – was primarily Catholic, and did not believe it shared a destiny with the Protestant provinces of the north – the modern Netherlands. Indeed, Catholics were now being persecuted in the north.

In 1578 Philip of Spain sent Alexander Farnese, **Duke of Parma**, into the south at the head of a large army; he was rewarded by a series of capitulations in the French-speaking provinces. Many of these then signed the Union of Arras in 1579, declaring their allegiance to Spain. In response, the Protestant northern provinces – called the **United Provinces** – declared their independence and appointed William of Orange as their *stadhouder* (governor). The Duke of Parma pressed on north, taking Antwerp after a year-long siege and Brussels in 1585. Most of Flanders and the French-speaking provinces were now back in Spanish hands, and these lands became known as the **Spanish Netherlands**, with Brussels as the capital.

Just before his death in 1598 Philip II handed the Spanish Netherlands over to his daughter, the **Infanta Isabella** (1566–1633), and her husband, **Albert, Archduke of Austria** (1559–1621). The Spanish, however, still aspired to regain the United Provinces – but they insisted that only Catholicism would be tolerated. The Twelve Years' Truce of 1609 sealed independence for the United Provinces, and 100,000 Protestants from Flanders emigrated across the border.

Europe's Battleground: the Spanish Netherlands (1579–1713)

For a while the Spanish Netherlands, and Brussels in particular, enjoyed a period of peace and prosperity, a mood caught by the ebullient paintings of **Rubens**, who was court painter to Isabella and Albert. But Europe was overshadowed by the Thirty Years' War (1618–48), in which Protestants contested the power of the Catholic Habsburgs. Isabella and Albert took the opportunity to take up the cudgels once more against the United Provinces, who entered an alliance with the French in 1633. The lasting result was that Philip IV of Spain (r. 1605–65), desperate to be able to turn all his military strength on France, signed the **Peace of Münster**, which gave formal recognition to the independence of the United Provinces. The terms of the treaty allowed the United Provinces to stop all traffic through the mouth of the River Scheldt, which ran through territory now controlled by them. Antwerp's access to the sea was sealed off and its fortunes doomed until Napoleon lifted the ban 150 years later.

Spain's conflict with France was a running sore throughout the 17th century. When William III of Orange, *stadhouder* of the United Provinces, became king of England in 1689 by virtue of his marriage to Mary, Protestant daughter of James II, the stage was set for a major bust-up.

The first phase was the **War of the Grand Alliance** (1690–7), designed to put an end to the expansionist exploits of Louis XIV of France. Louis took Namur in 1692. This was then besieged by forces under William.

17th Century

Grand' Place, for guildhouses such as Le Sac, hit during the 1695 bombardment, p.76
La Maison des Boulangers in the Grand' Place, for its bust of Charles II, p.76
Musées Royaux des Beaux-Arts, for ebullient paintings by Rubens, p.92

When **Marshal de Villeroy**, commanding 70,000 French troops, failed to lift the siege, he marched on Brussels in a fit of pique, and bombarded the city throughout the night of 13 August 1695. The city centre was flattened and some 4,000 houses were burned to the ground. The French then dusted their hands and withdrew. (The citizens of Brussels re-erected the buildings within five years.)

Louis's antics were not over yet. In 1700 Charles II of Spain died heirless, and the crown of Spain was passed to Philip, Duke of Anjou, grandson of Louis XIV. Louis leaned upon Philip to hand over the Spanish Netherlands to France, but such a solution was unacceptable. The result was the **War of the Spanish Succession** (1701–13). England, the Netherlands, Austria and many German states formed an alliance against France, and the brilliant generalship of the Duke of Marlborough and Prince Eugene of Savoy drove the French out of the Spanish Netherlands. At the end of the war France was left in ruins. In the **Treaty of Utrecht** it renounced its claims to the Spanish Netherlands, which passed into the hands of **Charles VI**, the Habsburg Emperor of Austria, becoming the Austrian Netherlands. In Brussels the leader of the guilds, **François Anneessens**, led a revolt, but it was short-lived, and he was beheaded in 1719.

The Austrian Netherlands (1713–94) and the Age of Napoleon

Charles VI of Austria had no male heir, so in 1713 he announced a 'pragmatic sanction' that the succession would pass into the female line through his daughter, **Maria Theresa**. However, when Charles died in 1740, the European powers disregarded this arrangement and Maria Theresa had to contend with the **War of the Austrian Succession** (1740–8), a complex conflict that was fought across most of Europe as well as in North America. Nevertheless, she emerged

from it with her succession affirmed, and a period of prosperity followed.

In 1741 Maria Theresa put the Austrian Netherlands in the hands of her enlightened brother-in-law, **Charles of Lorraine** (1712–80), who set up a dazzling court in Brussels, famed for its generous and elegant hospitality. But while the aristocracy partied, the poor faced crowded, insanitary conditions exacerbated by high levels of unemployment. With the Age of Enlightenment came also the rumblings of intellectual discontent.

Joseph II, son and successor of Maria Theresa, was a child of the Enlightenment, and introduced reforms in education, administration and religion, allowing Protestants to build churches and to become full citizens. He also wanted to centralize power in Vienna, and in 1784 announced that German was to be the official language of the empire. For all Joseph's good intentions, such reforms were interpreted in Belgium as the meddling of a despot. The Revolution in France inspired an uprising in Belgium, and when this was crushed by the Austrians at Turnhout, the whole country rose to the call in what has become known as the **Brabançon Revolt**. In January 1790 the provinces agreed to form their own Congress, and proclaimed an independent **United States of Belgium**, recognized by England, Holland and Prussia. But in February 1790, Joseph II died and was succeeded by **Léopold II** (r. 1790–2), who despatched troops to crush the revolution. However, in 1792 the French went to war against Austria, securing victory two years later at Fleurus (near Charleroi), ending Austrian rule.

18th Century

La Louve in the Grand' Place, attacked by revolutionary *sans-culottes* in 1793, p.75

Musée Royal de l'Afrique Centrale, where Charles of Lorraine once had a pleasure palace, p.146

Place Royale, for the Chapelle Royale and Palais de Charles de Lorraine, p.90

Tour d'Angle, where François Anneessens was held before his execution, p.104

Immigration

Over a quarter of Brussels' population is of non-Belgian origin – a remarkably high statistic. Many of these people are connected to the EU, diplomatic missions or multinational companies; others are immigrant workers from Spain, Portugal, Italy, Greece, the former Yugoslavia and Zaïre. But when the Bruxellois speak of *les immigrés* they are thinking primarily of the people who make up about one-third of this immigrant population, the North Africans and Turks.

Immigration into Belgium took place on a large scale during the 1960s, when growing prosperity left the nation short of labour. Workers came from all parts of the world, but particularly from Turkey and the Maghreb – Tunisia, Algeria and above all Morocco. As the Bruxellois drifted out of the city towards the leafy suburbs, so the inner-city areas began to fill with immigrant workers and families.

Many of these immigrant populations are now well into their second generation, with well-established communities in Brussels. They have their own shops, restaurants, mosques and language groups – often a closed, exotic world. But most non-EU immigrants are at the mercy of the prevailing winds of the economy. Whenever there is a downturn, unemployment rises, and so does their dependency on state welfare. Belgians are quick to see the immigrant population as a problem, a drain on national resources, a source of crime; and in times of recession, calls for repatriation all too predictably appear on the platforms of the extreme political parties.

Where one might hope for a will towards integration, one encounters rather suspicion and mutual contempt. Middle-class Belgians will happily bang on about *les immigrés* as if racism was a perfectly acceptable attitude. The gulf widens: many of the immigrants have a poor grasp of the Belgian languages, and send their children to immigrant-dominated schools. Due partly to high levels of unemployment, a class of alienated youth is growing up and, with little to lose, they are becoming increasingly confrontational. It is a measure of the potential seriousness of this situation that Belgians often express admiration for the level of racial integration they perceive in Britain – which itself is not a model for racial tolerance.

The French were welcomed by many Belgians as an army of liberation – one that heralded the advent of a modern state in which merit, not family connections and wealth, would be rewarded. But to many of the more radical French revolutionaries Belgian Catholicism was anachronistic and a hindrance to change. In October 1795 Belgium was absorbed into France and religion was suppressed. The churches were closed; many were vandalized and appropriated as stables, warehouses and factories.

Despite his charisma as leader of the young French state, Napoleon failed to win over the Belgians. In 1815, when he was finally defeated by the allies (Britain, Prussia, Austria and Russia) at **Waterloo**, just south of Brussels, the majority of Belgians celebrated his downfall too. They thought their hour had come.

The United Kingdom of the Netherlands (1815–31) and the 1830 Revolution

It hadn't. The Congress of Vienna in 1815 decided instead to create the United Kingdom of the Netherlands, tacking Belgium on to the Netherlands and entrusting it to the care of **William of Orange** (William I). It was an insensitive decision: all the historic resentments about big-power carve-ups and about Protestant Netherlands, all the aspirations to Belgian nationhood, gave William I an impossible task.

In 1830 the July Revolution in France removed the revisionist King Charles X (r. 1824–30) and put the more egalitarian Louis Philippe (r. 1830–48) in his place.

19th Century

In Brussels too revolt was in the air. On 25 August an opera called *La Muette de Portici* (The Dumb Girl of Portici) by the contemporary French composer Daniel-François-Esprit Auber, was performed in Brussels. The story concerns a revolutionary called Masaniello who led an uprising in Naples against the Spanish in 1647. The audience was incited to a ferment. The people ran out to join a workers' demonstration already taking place in the Place de la Monnaie, stormed the Palais de Justice, drove out the Dutch garrison and raised the flag of Brabant over the Hôtel de Ville. Barricades were erected and uprisings spread throughout the provinces. William of Orange responded by sending in the troops, which defeated the rebels at **Hasselt**. On 23 September the Dutch troops advanced on Brussels, but gradually, by the 28th, they had simply melted away. Brussels was free. Ghent and Antwerp finally

fell from Dutch rule in 1832, with the support of the French.

The New Nation Flourishes

Independence was accepted by the international community at the **London Conference** of 1831, largely because Belgium's revolution was widely supported by the nobility. The European powers insisted on Belgian neutrality. Since constitutional monarchy was in vogue, the Belgians then looked for a king, and Prince Léopold of Saxe-Coburg, an uncle of Queen Victoria, agreed to take the throne as **King Léopold I** (r. 1831–65). William of Orange eventually accepted the division of his nation in 1839. In 1832 Léopold married **Louise-Marie**, daughter of King Louis Philippe of France, thus sealing the friendship between the two nations.

Brussels looked to its future as the new nation's capital with enthusiasm. Continental Europe's **first public railway line**, connecting Brussels to Mechelen, was inaugurated in 1834, and **Brussels University** was founded that same year. The medieval city walls were replaced by wide boulevards and the **Galeries Royales de St-Hubert** opened in 1847. Belgium's 1830 constitution embodied numerous jealously guarded liberties, such as freedom of speech, of the press, and of association. As a result it became a refuge for numerous writers and intellectuals, such as Karl Marx and Victor Hugo, and something of a cultural and artistic melting pot.

Léopold I was succeeded by his son **Léopold II** (r. 1865–1909), a man with great ambitions. During his reign Belgium was transformed into a modern industrial state, drawing on its great reserves of coal to fuel its new factories, producing iron and steel, textiles and pottery. The population of Brussels more than doubled, from 250,000 at Léopold's coronation to 600,000 at his death. Léopold II wanted to place Belgium among the big league of European nations, and that meant acquiring colonies. In the 1880s with the help of the British–American explorer Henry

Morton Stanley, Léopold personally took charge of a vast slice of Central Africa, the **Belgian Congo**. This brought not only status but also considerable wealth through the exploitation of the Congo's raw materials – copper, tin, diamonds, rubber and cotton.

The Two World Wars

By the early 20th century the European nations were again jostling dangerously with each other for pre-eminence, both within Europe and across the continents that they had carved up between them. In June 1914 the assassination in Sarajevo of the Archduke Ferdinand triggered off a complicated system of alliances that dragged all the great powers of Europe into war. Germany invaded Belgium, breaching its neutrality, and came to a grinding halt close to the Belgian border with France. Three years of devastatingly costly trench warfare ensued.

The German occupying powers treated the Belgians harshly, brutally suppressing opposition, confiscating property, and commandeering labour to work in Germany. Meanwhile the King of Belgium, **Albert I** (r. 1909–34), nephew of Léopold II, led the Belgian army in a spirited defence from the polders (reclaimed land) around the River

---

Brussels the Euro-bogeyman

Since the beginning of 1993 the European Community has been called the European Union (EU) – much to the alarm of many dissenters in the UK and elsewhere, to whom the word 'union' seems like a misnomer laden with a bagful of unwelcome associations. To many Euro-sceptics, 'Brussels' is a kind of abstract concept, signifying centralism, loss of national sovereignty and the gradual eradication of national identity towards a bland Euro-culture.

EU rules of product standardization appear to threaten the livelihoods of traditional ham-smokers in the Jura, olive-stuffers in Spain, cheese-makers in Devon, and to jeopardize the existence of outside loos in British country pubs. The EU's Common Agricultural Policy edicts have provoked enraged farmers to dump cartloads of turnips in rural market squares, fishermen to hold protests, and there is widespread tension over European Monetary Union.

In short, to some, 'Brussels' has become a dirty word. In Brussels itself such reservations about the EU are seldom heard. Belgians are, by and large, enthusiastically pro-European. Their cars proudly display European Union stickers; you can buy flags, labels, postcards, even umbrellas, bearing the EU symbol, a neat circle of stars on a deep blue background.

Of course, Brussels has much to gain from being the 'Capital of Europe', in terms of both status and financial benefit. But the pro-European fervour of the Belgians is not simply self-seeking. A vision of a united Europe grew directly out of Belgium's unique historical experience, particularly during the Second World War when the country was overrun and mutilated by the Germans for the second time in a quarter of a century.

Paul-Henri Spaak, who was Socialist prime minister just before the war and foreign minister thereafter, battled tirelessly to turn this vision into a reality – a Europe that could build on its many common interests and create a structure through which to settle its age-old differences in a peaceful and constructive fashion.

Brussels was a natural choice for the EC's headquarters. The city is centrally located in a country committed to European ideals. Furthermore, Belgium itself is a kind of microcosm of Europe, struggling to promote harmony within its own frontiers between its two main communities. It may be that Belgium owes its very survival to the EU, which has allowed it a broader field upon which to play out its national conflicts. It is hardly surprising, therefore, to find Belgians championing the EU – and to find them incredulous when they see other member nations dragging their heels.

Divide and Rule

On 1 April 1992, *The Times* of London announced the start of secret talks between the leaders of Belgium's two main linguistic blocks in an effort to resolve their differences once and for all. The proposal was for the realignment of Flanders with the Netherlands and Wallonia with France, effectively resulting in the dismantlement of Belgium after 162 years of independence. This would, of course, have serious implications for the European Community, although the report mentioned that Brussels itself might become a neutral territory as the capital of Europe, rather like Washington DC.

The article was, of course, a cunning *poisson d'avril*, an April Fool's joke. But the joke was about a subject that is no laughing matter for many Belgians. In recent years the term 'Belgian' has taken on a new significance. '*Il n'y a plus de Belges,*' is a common complaint, '*il n'y a que des Flamands et des Wallons.*' ('There are no more Belgians, only Flemings and Walloons.')

There is a car sticker that announces '*Belge et fier de l'être*' ('Belgian and proud of it'). Such sentiments are expressed widely in both Flemish- and French-speaking communities. There are many Belgians who want to preserve the historic union between Flemings and Walloons, and there are plenty of intercommunal, bilingual marriages, friendships and working partnerships to underpin this.

Nonetheless, there are deep historical, social and political reasons for tension between the Flemish and the Walloons (*see* History), which emerge in the common unflattering stereotypes that one community holds of the other. In a situation heading towards polarization, some unpleasant extremist political groups have emerged – on both sides of the divide – and from time to time otherwise tranquil Belgian communes erupt into unedifying outbursts of violence.

The headlong dash towards federalism within the country has caused increasing dismay to those who still regard themselves above all as Belgian. Those who have married someone from another community and are bringing up their children bilingually suddenly find themselves compromised and their aims called into question. The Belgium that was once considered to be a model for multi-linguistic unity now seems on the verge of disintegration.

In 1993 the nation was taken by surprise at the sudden death of King Baudouin I. Baudouin had been a symbol of Belgian unity, widely respected by all, and a quiet, dignified campaigner for harmony within his nation. A tide of public emotion was unleashed: not just of grief, but also an expression of support for what he represented. Belgians (and proud of it) stood up and were counted for the first time, and were found to represent a substantial force that had been overlooked by federalism.

However, today there are sadly few signs of change. 'Divide and rule' still remains the easier option among the politicians, and many Belgian people are gloomy about the long-term prospects of maintaining a unified country.

Yser in northwest Belgium, causing havoc to the Germans by opening the sluice gates to flood the land. His persistence and fortitude endeared this 'Soldier King' to his nation.

After the First World War Belgium was left to pick up the pieces. Like the rest of Europe it faced the huge task of reconstruction against the background of the Depression. Belgium had acquired the German-speaking provinces of Moresnet, Eupen and Malmédy as compensation after the war. It had also renounced its neutrality, but in the early 1930s the rise of Adolf Hitler in Germany began to send shudders through the nation. Belgium reasserted its neutrality in 1936, but to little avail. On 10 May 1940 Germany invaded the Netherlands and Belgium, led by Léopold III (r. 1934–51), surrendered.

The Belgian government found exile in England, but Léopold III stayed on. The German army of occupation gradually turned the screws on the Belgian people, meeting any activity of the **Belgian Resistance** movement with harsh reprisals. It was a time of immense bravery: Jews were concealed by non-Jewish families for years, and downed Allied pilots were spirited back across the Channel by clandestine Resistance networks. The Nazis were happy to exploit tensions between the French- and Flemish-speaking populations, and accorded Flanders a special status.

Belgium was liberated in September 1944, but Allied progress very nearly came unstuck in December. As the nation settled down to enjoy its first Christmas in freedom for five years, German tank divisions under Field Marshal von Rundstedt launched a last-ditch counter-offensive across the Ardennes (the **Battle of the Bulge**), and bombed Antwerp and Liège. American troops under General MacAuliffe were trapped at Bastogne. Invited to surrender, MacAuliffe came up with the famous response: 'Nuts!' – and eventually the Germans were pushed back.

Post-war Prosperity and Federalization

Belgium was free again, but immediately encountered a constitutional crisis about the controversial role of Léopold III during the war. Some argued that he had spared the nation a calamity by surrendering; and that he had suffered as an effective prisoner of the Germans. Many British military analysts argue that, by holding out against massive odds for 18 days, Léopold's 60,000 troops had allowed the Allied evacuation at Dunkirk. In

Belgium, however, Léopold's performance was compared unfavourably with that of his father, Albert I, in the First World War, and many hinted darkly at collaboration. His wartime marriage to a commoner, Mary Lilian Baels, in 1941 didn't help.

Léopold's brother Charles stood in as regent from 1944 to 1950, and during this period Socialists and Communists (mainly from Wallonia) campaigned actively to form a republic. While Léopold III remained in self-imposed exile in Switzerland, a referendum showed that 57 per cent of the nation favoured his return – but the fact that the majority of Walloons voted against it was effectively a thumbs-down. He returned to Belgium nonetheless, but the mood soon turned ugly, as Belgium seemed on the brink of civil war. In 1951, under pressure from Walloon socialists, Léopold III abdicated in favour of his son, **Baudouin I** (r. 1951–93), hoping thereby to restore unity. These hopes were justified: Baudouin, although only 21 years old, demonstrated an exceptional ability to heal the nation's rifts.

Since the war, Belgium has once again found its historic form as a major industrial and trading nation. Like other European countries, it had to give up its colonial economy, and it granted independence to the Congo (now Zaire) in 1960 – although it was much criticized for its haste. It also had to go through the painful transition from heavy industry towards the light and service industries. This effectively removed the trump cards from the hands of the French-speaking south in favour of the Flemish north. The language divide, exploited successfully by politicians from both communities, has resulted in an increasingly devolved, federal system of government, with an undercurrent of tension that arcs sporadically across Brussels. Under the 'Saint-Michel Accords' of 1993, Belgian federalization was further reinforced, with the result that Belgium is now effectively ruled by three regional governments (Wallonia, Flanders and Brussels), overseen by a national government.

1945 Onwards

Album, for an introduction to key themes of Belgian history, culture and daily life, p.86

Musée de la Dynastie, for the history of the Belgian royal family, p.95

Musée Royal de l'Afrique Centrale, for the history of the Belgian Congo, p.146

Palais Royal, where the crowds gathered in 1993 to honour King Baudouin I's death, p.94

Parlement Européen, for the Brussels headquarters of the European Parliament, p.126

In its post-war history, the **European Community/Union** has proved a godsend to Belgium in two ways. Belgium was a founder member of the EEC, and Brussels, geographically at its heart, became its headquarters in the 1960s, with all the attention, status and income that it entails. In addition, Belgium's view of itself within the political framework of Europe – a Europe seen as a confederation of nations – has allowed it to accommodate a confederation within its own boundaries. By defining itself in terms of Europe, there is less pressure to define itself as a nation.

Throughout so much of its history, Belgium has stood between competing nations, earning itself the sobriquet 'the cockpit of Europe'. History has taught it to be flexible, and given it the ability to accept with grace what has become respectfully known as the 'Belgian Compromise'. It remains an essential characteristic of the nation.

Art and Architecture

Belgian art? Because this concept does not fit a convenient slot in the history of European art, it may invite the conclusion that it is somehow second-rate. Nothing could be further from the truth. The fact that Belgium has only existed as a nation since 1830 obscures a much longer history of great Flemish art to which it can legitimately lay claim. The European tradition of oil painting was born on Belgian soil, perfected by Jan van Eyck, and later applied with unique charm by Pieter Bruegel. Antwerp produced Rubens, one of the great geniuses of 17th-century art. After independence, the liberal atmosphere in Belgium fostered an interest in the avant-garde, out of which the Symbolists developed, as well as the fever-ishly eccentric talents of James Ensor. Belgium was also home to two of the leading Surrealists of the 20th century: René Magritte and Paul Delvaux.

As a result, Brussels, Bruges, Ghent and Antwerp contain some of the most rewarding art galleries in Europe – rich with surprises. They have the distinction of containing collections that are high quality, but also almost entirely home-grown.

The Middle Ages

For over 700 years, until the Renaissance, the main inspiration for European art and architecture was the Church. Charlemagne's court in Aachen in the late 8th century attracted the leading manuscript illustrators of the day. Illuminated books remained one of the chief fields of artistic endeavour in the Low Countries for five centuries. One of the best-known series of illuminations, the *Très Riches Heures du Duc de Berry*, was produced by friars from Limburg province around 1411.

Manuscript illuminations were highly detailed, brightly coloured and demonstrated great technical skills in portraiture and the depiction of textiles and artefacts. These same talents were put to work when oil painting was developed in the 15th century. Previously any large-scale paintings had had to be done on the walls, but although fresco

painting might have been appropriate in Italy, it was not a suitable technique for the damp conditions of northern Europe. Oil paints, however, were ideal: a broad range of rich colours could be manufactured and applied to wooden panels with great control to give the kind of detail and intense coloration that were achieved in illuminated manuscripts. Furthermore, the paintings were now easily portable, which helped to create a new kind of art market.

Jan van Eyck (1390–1441), based in Bruges, was the first artist to demonstrate the full potential of oil painting, and he produced some of the most dazzling work of the late medieval period. *The Adoration of the Mystic Lamb* (painted with his brother Hubert in 1426–32) in Ghent Cathedral is one of the great treasures of European art, full of saint-liness and sensuality and luminescent detail. Jan van Eyck is one of the earliest Flemish painters known to us by name, as he signed his work. At that time painters worked in guilds, usually remaining anonymous, hence titles such as the Master of Hoogstraaten.

Jan van Eyck was official painter to Philip the Good, Duke of Burgundy, who presided over an economic boom in the Low Countries. Paintings of this era are primarily religious, but also offer a fascinating insight into the life of the well-to-do at that time, from their sumptuous textiles and encrusta-tions of jewellery, to the ornately carved choir stalls and the glazed floor tiles.

Another speciality of this period was the retable, a large, screen-like altarpiece which contained a mixture of elaborate high-relief woodcarving (usually gilded) and painting. Retables are usually divided up as folding triptychs, depicting complex religious scenes enacted by dozens of carved charac-ters, often within a framework of miniaturized Gothic church architecture. There were celebrated workshops producing retables in Brussels, Mechelen and Antwerp.

The achievements of architecture during the Middle Ages were likewise principally ecclesiastical. The chief influences came from France, and for about 150 years after the 11th century the Romanesque style predominated. **Romanesque** churches were robust and solid, with massive supporting columns and semicircular arches. They were supposedly influenced by Roman architecture, hence the name.

If you look at the cross-section of two intersecting rounded arches, you will see a pointed arch. This became the leading motif of the next phase of architecture, which evolved in the mid-12th century and was later dubbed **Gothic** by Renaissance architects, who considered it a barbarian perversion of the classical ideal. Architects now attempted to create magical illusions of space and light, filling walls with huge, elongated windows held in place by delicate columns and supported by external buttresses. During the 15th century the increasingly flamboyant Gothic style was adopted by secular architecture. The Hôtel de Ville in Brussels was rebuilt after 1402, with its towering spire a potent symbol of the growing strength and confidence of the merchant classes. But perhaps the most stunning secular manifestation of Gothic architecture is the town hall of Leuven (built 1439–69), a wedding-cake building in cream-white stone.

Jan van Eyck's place at Philip the Good's court was later taken by his pupil, **Rogier van der Weyden**, called Rogier de la Pasture in French (c. 1400–64). His religious paintings are emotionally charged and full of stress, as in his great triptych, *The Seven Sacraments*. He was closely involved in the decoration of the new Hôtel de Ville in Brussels, but his paintings for it were destroyed in the French bombardment of 1695. Like many other painters over the next 300 years, he also designed for the famous tapestry workshops of Brussels. Other major names of this late medieval period include **Hugo van der Goes** (?1435–82); **Hans Memling** (?1430–94); and **Dirk Bouts** (1415–75), perhaps best known for his *The Justice of Otto* (1471–3). As with Van Eyck, a distinctive mark of the work of these artists was a limited understanding of space: perspective is not rendered with complete confidence, landscapes are often naïve, and groups of people are packed slightly too close together. These problems were addressed by the next great phase of painting in the Low Countries.

The Renaissance

The Renaissance was a watershed between the medieval and the modern world, a long and gradual phenomenon which began in Italy in the 13th century and lasted for some 300 years. It was triggered by the rediscovery of classical learning and literature – and the gradual realization that not only had the Greeks and Romans achieved rather more than the medieval world in terms of science, medicine, architecture and philosophy but they had done so without the assistance of Christianity. The Renaissance effectively freed people from the straitjacket of purely Christian teaching and encouraged them to approach all questions with an open mind.

Italian art and architecture were the leaders of fashion during the Renaissance, and accomplished artists from northern Europe travelled to Italy to admire and learn from the likes of Leonardo da Vinci, Michelangelo, Titian and Tintoretto. The Italian Renaissance, however, was only partially assimilated in the Low Countries. Although architects were happy to borrow Renaissance motifs, such as classical columns and garlands of flowers, their application of these was mainly cosmetic: Renaissance façades were essentially adaptations of the traditional step-gable (which had been around since the 11th century) tacked on to traditional Flemish houses. Ecclesiastical architecture, meanwhile, remained Gothic.

Flemish painting now followed two main courses. One set of artists was directly influenced by Italian painting. **Quentin Metsys** (1466–1530) represents the link between the medieval world and the Renaissance, as well as the shift from Bruges to Antwerp as the main centre of art in the southern Low Countries. Metsys' *The Lineage of St Anne*

(c. 1508) shows a real understanding of architectural perspective, and Metsys also uses the kind of hazy, distant blue landscape so beloved of Leonardo da Vinci. **Bernard van Orley** (c. 1499–1541) brought the Renaissance to Brussels, in painting and in his designs for tapestry and stained glass. Other 'Romanists' include Van Orley's pupil **Michiel Coxie** (1499–1592), who lived in Rome in the 1530s, and **Jan Gossaert** of Mauberge (1478–1532) (also known as Mabuse), who painted the first classically inspired nudes in Flemish art.

Other painters, however, developed a more independent Flemish style of painting, reflecting the distinctive outlook and heritage of the Low Countries. Supreme among them was **Pieter Bruegel the Elder** (c. 1525–69). He trained in Antwerp and made a trip to Italy in about 1551, but this appears to have left him unmoved. His interest lay in the people and landscape of his homeland, so even when painting a classical subject such as his famous *Fall of Icarus* (1567) his main focus is on rural life, leaving poor Icarus's plight virtually incidental. Bruegel was particularly successful in translating religious scenes into Flemish village life, breathing into them a new poignancy and

relevance. Another line of work took him into the realms of bizarre fantasy associated with the Dutch painter Hieronymus Bosch (1450–1516) – as in his *The Fall of Rebel Angels* (1562).

In 1563 Pieter Bruegel moved to Brussels and married. He had two sons late in life, who became painters in their own right well after their father's death. Pieter Bruegel the Younger (1564–1638) painted numerous versions of his father's work; he used a more polished style that somehow lacks the naïve spontaneity of his father's paintings (of which only some 40 examples have survived). His younger brother Jan 'Velvet' Bruegel (1568–1625) is celebrated for his landscapes and his delicate flower paintings.

Another artist in the Flemish tradition is **Joachim Beuckelaer** (1530–74), who produced richly packed market scenes, full of vivid and affectionate details, in a confident, flowing style somewhat in advance of his times.

During the Renaissance, painters found extra outlets for their work among the newly rich middle classes. The full flowering of the Renaissance, however, was cut short by the religious troubles that swept through northern Europe in the second half of the

16th century, disrupting patronage. There was no stability until the following century, when the Counter-Reformation brought its own flourish in both arts and architecture.

The Age of Rubens

It was largely because of **Pieter Paul Rubens** (1577–1640) that Antwerp remained a cultural centre in the Low Countries during the 17th century. Born of well-to-do Flemish parents, Rubens started training as an artist when just thirteen years old. In his twenties, he lived and worked in Italy for eight years, and was strongly influenced by the work of Michelangelo, Titian and his contemporary Caravaggio. Rubens returned to Antwerp in 1608 with a glittering reputation; the following year he became court painter to Archduke Albert and the Infanta Isabella, married Isabella Brant and bought his fine house in the city. His *Raising of the Cross* (1610) and *Descent from the Cross* (1612) for Antwerp Cathedral caused a sensation, and commissions rolled in. Rubens' ability to handle vast paintings on dramatic subjects was unsurpassed. His compositions carry the eye through the paintings with a unique vigour, assisted by his deft, virtuoso touch, often applied in thin, almost sketchy layers of paint. Throughout almost all his work there is a lusty, life-enhancing quality, very Flemish in nature. This is typified by his predilection for the sensuous, buxom nudes which are virtually his trademark.

After his wife died in 1625, Rubens entered the diplomatic service. He travelled to Spain and England in an effort to broker peace, for which he was rewarded in England by a knighthood. He also won several major commissions in both countries (including the ceilings of the Banqueting House in Whitehall, London). In 1630, at the age of 53, he married Hélène Fourment, the 17-year-old daughter of a wealthy tapestry merchant. He painted her in a series of charming portraits, full of life and flirtatiousness. He also maintained a flow of work right up to the end of his life, bringing his total *œuvre* to over 2,000 major paintings.

The other two great Antwerp painters of this era were both closely associated with Rubens. **Antoon (Anthony) van Dyck** (1599–1641) was celebrated for his sedate portraits which capture the solemnity and dignity of the affluent – notably after he became court artist to Charles I of England in 1632. **Jacob Jordaens** (1593–1678) painted in a vigorous style in the manner of Rubens and specialized in joyous, bacchanalian scenes.

During this period Flemish 'genre' painting also thrived – portraits of ordinary rural and town life in inns, markets and kitchens, often spiced with gentle humour. Two of the leading genre painters of the period were **David Teniers the Younger** (1610–90) and **Adriaen Brouwer** (1605–38).

The fecund, flowing style of Rubens and his followers is typical of the Baroque period, which can be most readily identified in architecture. Baroque architecture was essentially a lavish, curvaceous interpretation of classical style: pediments became broken pediments, columns became barley-sugar twists, façades became embellished with *œil de bœuf* windows. The principal Flemish architects were also sculptors, such as Rubens' pupil **Luc Fayd'Herbe** (1617–97), who may have been responsible for Brussels' most successful Baroque church, St-Jean-Baptiste au Béguinage. Baroque can become overbearing, but with the right balance it is joyous and delicate, elegant and swanky, befitting the ostentatious lifestyles of the wealthy merchant classes of the 17th century. Nowhere is the Flemish version of the Baroque better expressed than in Brussels' Grand' Place, a festival of individualistic design and gilded ornamentation.

The religious troubles of the 16th century had left numerous churches in ruins, their statues shattered by the iconoclasts. During the 17th century they were restored, and the statues of the saints were replaced by new works in the Baroque style of Bernini – vigorously moulded and expressive, but often out of keeping with the Gothic architecture on to which they were grafted. Among the most noted sculptors in this line were **Jérôme**

Duquesnoy the Younger (1602–54), son of the original sculptor of the Manneken-Pis (*see* p.81), and Luc Fayd'Herbe. This was also the era of the fantastically elaborate wooden pulpits, as seen for example in the Cathédrale St-Michel in Brussels.

Classical Revival

During the 18th century fashions imitated the French once more, and in particular the styles associated with Louis XV. During this period architects reassessed the lessons of classical architecture and pressed for more stringent, sober adherence to these models, with emphasis on well-modulated proportions and symmetry. Both churches and mansions took on the outward appearance of Greek temples. In the Brussels of Charles of Lorraine several major building projects were undertaken in this new mould, notably the Place Royale and the Palais de la Nation, designed by **Barnabé Guimard** (*active* 1765–92), and what is now the Place des Martyrs, designed by **Claude Fisco** (1736–1825). The sculptor **Gilles-Lambert Godecharle** (1750–1835) worked in corresponding Neoclassical style, but this mood was not as successfully translated to painting.

The end of the 18th century was marked by the turbulence of the Brabançon Revolt and the French occupation, and the prevailing style was again Neoclassical. The French Neoclassical painter Jacques-Louis David (1748–1825) spent the last years of his life in Brussels and had a number of disciples in Belgium, but – with the possible exception of **François-Joseph Navez** (1787–1869) – they lacked David's ability to inject a sense of noble drama into their classical scenes.

Truly Belgian Art

Belgian independence in 1830 gave fresh impetus to artists, sculptors and architects. The new nation needed to make its own statements about its role in the world and to glamorize its heritage. Sculptors such as **Willem Geefs** (1805–85) were called in to evoke the Belgian past through historical sculptures. In painting, a wave of Romanticism – passionate, vigorous and poetic – swept Neoclassicism before it. **Gustave Wappers** (1803–74) painted his huge *Day in September 1830* to the glory of the Belgian Revolution in the style of Delacroix; while the morbid works of **Antoine Wiertz** (1806–65) attempted to convey profound messages through erotic and macabre images. After the 1850s a Realist school evolved in the fashion of the French painter Gustave Courbet (1819–77), in which ordinary scenes such as peasants at work and cowbyres were depicted with the Romantics' eye, but unprettified and (in principle) devoid of interpretation. **Hippolyte Boulenger** (1837–74), **Jan Stobbaerts** (1838–1914) and **Henri de Braekeleer** (1840–88) are the best-known exponents of this trend. The social implications of Realism were taken up with greater vigour by the painter and sculptor **Constantin Meunier** (1831–1905), who focused on the misery and dignity of industrial labour.

In the latter part of the century, architecture ranged from the Neo-Gothic to the Neoclassical, which were seen as complementary rather than contradictory. The famous architect Joseph Poelaert (1817–79), produced Neo-Gothic churches, such as Notre-Dame de Laeken, as well as the mighty Neoclassical Palais de Justice. For public projects, stately grandeur based on well-tried principles was the essential criterion.

However, Belgium was also noted as a liberal country, a refuge for artists from repressive regimes, notably France, and this fuelled a taste for the avant-garde. Societies were formed to promote contemporary work. One of these was Le Cercle des Vingt (**Les XX**), founded by Octave Maus in 1883. It held controversial exhibitions of invited artists, many of whom were unknown at the time. Paul Cézanne, who was later dubbed the 'father of modern art', was exhibited by Les XX long before he was recognized in his own country. Despite the influence of such innovative groups, Belgian art essentially

Finding Brussels' Art

The Middle Ages

Groeningemuseum in Bruges, for its dazzling medieval art, including Jan van Eyck, Dirk Bouts and Hans Memling, p.184

Memlingmuseum in Bruges, for its Hans Memling collection, p.185

Musée Communal de la Ville de Bruxelles in Maison du Roi, for superb retables, p.76

Musée du Livre, for its illuminated manuscripts, p.99

Musées Royaux d'Art et d'Histoire, Salle aux Trèsors, for its medieval treasures, p.130

Sint-Baafskathedraal in Ghent, for Jan van Eyck's *Adoration of the Mystic Lamb*, p.192

Sint-Pieterskerk in Leuven, for Dirk Bouts' triptych *Last Supper*, p.168

The Renaissance

Cathédrale St-Michel, for its stained-glass windows, p.120

Musée d'Art Ancien, for Pieter Bruegel the Elder's *Fall of Icarus*, p.91

Musée Communal de la Ville de Bruxelles in Maison du Roi, for its Bernard van Orley tapestries, p.76

Musées Royaux d'Art et d'Histoire, for its Bernard van Orley tapestries, p.130

Museum Plantin-Moretus in Antwerp, for its tapestries, paintings and printing presses, p.206

Onze Lieve Vrouwekerk in Bruges, for its fine altarpiece, p.184

The Age of Rubens

Musée d'Art Ancien, for stirring paintings by Rubens, p.92

Musées Royaux d'Art et d'Histoire, for the 'Arts Décoratifs' on Level 1, p.130

Onze Lieve Vrouwe Kathedraal in Antwerp, famous for Rubens' triptychs, p.203

Rubenshuis in Antwerp, for Rubens' home and studio, p.207

Classical Revival

Musée d'Art Moderne, for Jacques-Louis David's *Marat Assassiné*, p.92

Palais de la Nation, for Godecharle's sculptured pediment, p.96

Truly Belgian Art

Musée d'Art Moderne, for some fascinating Symbolist work on Level 2, p.92

Musée Constantin Meunier, for Meunier's studio and a collection of his paintings, p.136

Musée de l'Hôtel Charlier, for paintings by James Ensor, Fernand Khnopff and Léon Frédéric, and sculpture by Rik Wouters, p.96

Musée Wiertz, for the artist's home and studio, p.127

The 20th Century

Musée Communal d'Ixelles, for Belgian artists such as Léon Frédéric, Magritte, Spilliaert and Wouters, p.137

Musée René Magritte in Jette, for the artist's home and studio, p.141

followed the patterns of French painting in the late 19th century. Artists such as **Théo van Rysselberghe** (1862–1926) adopted a form of pointillist Impressionism; **Emile Claus** (1849–1924) created a kind of late Impressionism called 'Luminism', depicting rural scenes with famously fetching charm.

Belgium also produced more individualistic talents, notably the bizarre **James Ensor** (1860–1949). He began his painting career with well-made Postimpressionist paintings of interiors and portraits. In the mid-1880s, however, his palette suddenly became charged with intense, clashing colours, which he applied with vigour to increasingly

oddball subject matter, such as dead fish, and animated skeletons. His great masterpiece is the carnival-like *Entry of Christ into Brussels* (1888).

At the same time a loosely defined group of painters called the **Symbolists** began to explore the world of suggestion and mystery. Many of their works are fascinating for their idiosyncrasy, such as the visionary fantasy world of **Jean Delville** (1867–1953). By contrast **Léon Frédéric** (1856–1940) painted triptychs of social realism infused with the kind of saintly clarity found in the works of the medieval Flemish masters. Perhaps the most haunting Symbolist is **Fernand Khnopff**

(1858–1921), who used a polished style to bring a dreamlike quality even to his group of tennis players (*Memories*, 1889). Another highly individual painter associated with Symbolism is **Léon Spilliaert** (1881–1946), who brought a strong sense of design to his stylized interiors and unmistakable landscapes – often brooding silhouettes set against empty twilight coastlines, filled with the abstract shapes of cloud and reflected patches of water.

Les XX was superseded by **La Libre Esthétique** (1894–1914) as Brussels' leading artistic circle. It encouraged cooperation between artists, architects and craftsmen and fostered the emerging decorative style, Art Nouveau. Belgium was at its forefront, with figures such as **Victor Horta** (1861–1947), **Gustave Serrurier-Bovy** (1858–1910) and **Henri van de Velde** (1863–1957), who became director of the Art and Crafts School in Weimar in 1901, which in 1919 evolved into the Bauhaus. Art Nouveau remained fashionable until the First World War.

The 20th Century

Out of Impressionism and Postimpressionism grew Fauvism, whose name was based on a critic's term of abuse meaning 'wild beast', and reflecting an unbridled use of colour. Belgium's most successful exponent was **Rik Wouters** (1882–1916), also a gifted sculptor, who used bright but carefully modulated colours to produce work of charm and subtlety, usually featuring his wife Nel.

Meanwhile a school of painters developed in the village of Sint-Martens-Latem, near Ghent. The first wave, founded in around 1904, included mystic, Symbolist-style painters such as **Valerius de Saedeleer** (1867–1941) and **Albert Servaes** (1883–1966). The second wave developed in around 1909 and in the post-war period; it was centred upon **Constant Permeke** (1886–1952), who painted emotional, blocky portraits with thick colours – a unique combination of social realism, Cubism and Expressionism.

Two of Belgium's best-known 20th-century painters are Surrealists. Surrealism developed in Paris in the 1920s as an effort to unveil a reality in the subconscious through spontaneous behaviour and events, usually of a highly unconventional nature. The term was applied to the dreamworld evoked by painters such as Salvador Dali. **René Magritte** (1898–1967) lived in Paris in the 1920s then returned to Belgium to begin producing his small-scale paintings of witty absurdities, such as floating men in bowler hats. Meanwhile, **Paul Delvaux** (1897–1994) painted countless versions of his obsessions: trams and stations by night, peopled by sleepwalkers, skeletons and reclining nudes, all suffused with a haunting, quality and latent eroticism.

During most of the 20th century, architecture in Belgium followed the same course as in the rest of the Western world. The angular, machine-age style of Art Deco was in vogue during the early interwar years, then was gradually superseded by the functionalism of the International Style. This led to the soulless high-rise urban developments of the post-war years, sad perversions of Bauhaus ideals, and then the prettified eclecticism of Postmodern architects over the last 20 years.

In art, too, recent Belgian work has reflected movements elsewhere in the world. In the immediate post-war years, a group called **La Jeune Peinture Belge** (1945–8) attempted to gather together the various strains of contemporary art. Its members produced abstract work, influenced by the mechanistic abstractions of **Victor Sevranckx** (1897–1965). **Anne Bonnet** (1908–60), **Louis van Lint** (1909–89) and **Gaston Bertrand** (b. 1910) are the best known of these today. In 1948 an international group called **Cobra** formed around a common interest in children's painting and primitive art, free of the encumbrance of Western painting traditions. Belgium's most famous participant in Cobra is **Pierre Alechinsky** (b. 1927), whose poetic works have reached the international stage. The more recent trend towards non-gallery art and installations has left the Belgian art world in a state of confusion, and generally it looks to the USA and the past for guidance.

Travel

GETTING THERE

By Air

Brussels, 'the capital of Europe', is well served by the world's airlines, jostling to harness the ceaseless ebb and flow of Eurocrats, multinational business travellers and a large population of expatriates – as well as tourists. There are many flights from all points of the globe, and they tend to be packed; if you are on a tight schedule, book early. International flights arrive at Belgium's main airport at Zaventem, just 14km from the centre of Brussels (see 'Arrival').

From the UK and Ireland

The main carriers to Brussels each offer up to seven flights daily from London Heathrow, and there are also daily flights from London Gatwick, Bristol, Manchester, Birmingham, Leeds, Newcastle, Glasgow, Edinburgh and Dublin. The full London–Brussels fare for unrestricted economy travel is around £330 return. However, if your journey includes a Saturday night, prices for APEX fares drop to about £120–150.

The flight from London to Brussels takes about 60 minutes. An airport tax of £18 is payable when you purchase your ticket.

Scheduled Flights

Aer Lingus, **t** Dublin (01) 866 8888, **w** www .aerlingus.ie. Up to five flights a day direct from Dublin. Ticket prices vary enormously so shop around. For under-25s, a fully flexible unrestricted ticket is available for £152 (when bought within seven days of departure). Apex prices, on the other hand, start at £110 if your stay includes a Saturday night. Add IR£10 to all fares to cover airport tax.

British Airways, reservations **t** 0845 77 333 77, **w** www.britishairways.com. Look out for their occasional 'World Offers': return tickets for as little as £56 (plus tax), which must be booked at least a month in advance. Tickets and other travel products available at BA Travelshops, **t** 0845 606 0747, located throughout the country (open daily 6–6).

Flights on the Internet

The best place to start looking for flights is the Web – just about everyone has a site where you can compare prices (see the airlines listed), and booking online usually confers a 10–20% discount.

In the UK and Ireland

w www.airtickets.co.uk
w www.cheapflights.com
w www.flightcentre.co.uk
w www.lastminute.com
w www.skydeals.co.uk
w www.sky-tours.co.uk
w www.thomascook.co.uk
w www.trailfinder.com
w www.travelocity.com
w www.travelselect.com

In the USA

w www.air-fare.com
w www.airhitch.org
w www.expedia.com
w www.flights.com
w www.orbitz.com
w www.priceline.com
w www.travellersweb.ws
w www.travelocity.com
w www.smarterliving.com

In Canada

w www.flightcentre.ca
w www.lastminuteclub.com
w www.newfrontiers.com

British Midland, **t** 0870 607 0555, **w** www .flybmi.com. Direct flights from Heathrow and Birmingham.

Sabena, **t** 08456 010933, **w** www.sabena .com. The Belgian national airline also runs a daily service (except Saturdays) from London City Airport.

Low-cost Airlines

The cheap no-frills low-cost carriers can offer astonishingly low prices if you book well in advance (usually 2 months at peak travel times). You can book directly over the Internet and a discount is usually offered if you do. Prices go up the closer you get to your leaving date; fares booked last minute are often not much cheaper than those of the major carriers. Each ticket has various conditions attached, for example whether you can get a refund or whether the date of the flight can be changed. All services may be less frequent in the winter.

Ryanair, *t 08701 569569*, **w** *www.ryanair.com*. Operates three flights daily from London Stansted and Dublin and one flight a day from Glasgow Prestwick to Charleroi, one hour's drive from Brussels. Flights can be supercheap if you take advantage of their frequent deals.

Virgin Express, *t (020) 7744 0004*, **w** *www.virgin.express.com*. There are nine flights daily from London Heathrow. Tickets are non-transferable and cost from £82.

From the USA and Canada
Scheduled Flights

There are direct flights to Brussels from just about all the major gateway cities of the USA. Prices vary enormously but, to give some kind of yardstick, the round-trip price quoted by airlines for New York–Brussels is around US$350–500 in the low season (winter), and rises to at least US$800 in the high season (summer). All fares are subject to additional airport taxes, which amount to about $40. Canadians are rather less well served: travellers have to take a two-stage journey, changing in the USA or in Europe to continue to Brussels.

Airline Offices in Brussels

Aer Lingus, *98 Rue du Trône*, *t 02 548 9848*.
Air France, *149 Av Louise*, *t 02 541 4251*.
American Airlines, *98 Rue du Trône*, *t 02 714 4916*.
British Airways, *Centre International Rogier*, *t 02 548 2111*.
British Midland, *15 Av de Pléiades*, *t 02 771 7766*.
Delta Airlines, *Sabena House, Brussels National Airport, 1930 Zaventem*, *t 02 723 8260*.
Lufthansa, *1 Bvd Anspach*, *t 02 212 0922*.
Sabena, *35 Rue Cardinal Mercier*, *t 02 511 9030*.

Air Canada, *t 888 247 2262*, **w** *www.aircanada.com*. Flies via London from Montreal, Toronto, Vancouver, Calgary, Winnipeg and Halifax.

British Airways, *t 800 403 0882*, **w** *www.britishairways.com*. Flights through Heathrow and Gatwick from a host of US cities.

Continental Airlines, *t 800 231 0856*, **w** *www.continental.com*. From New York JFK, Boston, Los Angeles and many other major US and Canadian cities.

Delta Airlines, *t 800 241 4141*, *t 800 221 1212 (in Montreal dial 337 5520)*, **w** *www.delta.com*. From New York JFK and Atlanta, with connections to many of their US destinations.

Sabena, *t 800 955 2000*, **w** *www.sabena.com*. Flights from US cities direct to Brussels. Canadians must change in the USA.

Charter Flights

Numerous agencies in the USA offer competitive prices through charter flights or consolidated fares on scheduled flights; look in the travel pages of your newspaper. The Sunday *New York Times* has the most listings. Major charter companies and consolidators include:

Council Travel, *205 East 42nd St, New York, NY 10017*, *t 800 2COUNCIL*, **w** *www.counciltravel.com*.

TFI, *34 West 32nd St, New York, NY 10001*, *t 800 745 8000*, *t (212) 736 1140*.

By Sea

The ferry can be a good option if you're travelling by car or with young children (under 4s free; under 14s reduced rates). For people in Scotland and the north of England wishing to travel to Brussels, the ferry may still be the most convenient option.

Dover to Ostend

Hoverspeed, *t 0845 674 6006*, **w** *www.hoverspeed.com*. Operates a fast-ferry 'SeaCat' service. In summer there should be three crossings a day at 7am, 3pm and 8pm. For the early morning ferry, you'll pay £150 for a 5-day return for a car and two passengers.

Peak mid-afternoon rates for a similar ticket are closer to £200. Apex fares are around £110 and foot passengers pay £28 on all crossings. The journey takes about 2hrs and Ostend is just over an hour's drive from Brussels. Unfortunately, because the boat is particularly light, this service is often liable to cancellation in poor weather.

Dover to Calais

Thanks to improved road links on the continent following completion of the Channel Tunnel, it is well worth considering this route. The E40/A18 is now open all the way from Brussels to Calais; the drive should take around two hours. This sector of the market is particularly competitive and prices are constantly being revised. A standard return should set you back something in the region of £150, whilst a day return can be bought for as little as £10.

P&O Stena Line, t *0870 600 0600,* **w** *www .posl.com.*

Sea France, t *08705 711711,* **w** *www.seafrance .com.* Up to 15 departures a day.

Hull to Zeebrugge

P&O North Sea Ferries, t *08701 296002,* **w** *www.mycruiseferries.com,* runs the overnight service. Standard foot passenger fares range from £44–310 depending on accommodation. For those with a car, a five-night return, which must include a Saturday night, can be bought in summer for £86 (with passenger fares on top of this). Brussels is a further hour's drive away on the motorway.

By Train

By far the quickest and most convenient way to reach Brussels is on the foot passenger train service through the Channel Tunnel run by **Eurostar**.

There are usually 11 departures a day which, following the completion of the new high-speed line between Lille and Brussels, should take about 2–3 hours to travel from London Waterloo to the Gare du Midi/Zuid Station in Brussels. If travelling from the International Station in Ashford, Kent, the journey time is cut to just 1hr 40mins. Prices are on a par with Eurostar's direct competitor air travel and vary between £70 and £300 depending on how far in advance you book. It is, however, well worth asking about any special deals that might be running. In the winter a weekend day return can be bought for as little as £69 (rising to £79 if your stay includes a Saturday night). Passengers need to check in at least 20mins before departure.

Brussels has three interlinked mainline stations: Gare Centrale/Centraal Station, Gare du Midi/Zuid Station and the Gare du Nord/Noordstation, and two others, Schuman and Quartier Léopold, serving the European Parliament. It is well connected with other European capitals with frequent departures to Amsterdam and Cologne and a TGV (Train à Grande Vitesse) link to Paris. The Belgian railway service (SNCB) is run with the kind of dedication and efficiency that will render most British travellers quite nostalgic.

Eurostar, *UK* **t** *0870 160 6600, USA* **t** *800 EUROSTAR,* **w** *www.eurostar.com.*

Rail Europe, *179 Piccadilly, London W1,* **t** *08705 848848,* **w** *www.raileurope.co.uk; in North America, US* **t** *877 456 RAIL, Canada* **t** *800 361 RAIL,* **w** *www.raileurope.com.* For rail tickets to Belgium from England, or vice versa.

By Bus

The main carrier between London and Brussels is Eurolines. Coaches depart from Victoria Coach Station in central London and arrive at the Gare du Nord. There are usually three departures a day and the journey will take around 12 hours. Crossings are via Calais and cost £52 all year. There are discounts for anyone under 26, senior citizens and children under 12.

Information and booking:

UK: *Eurolines, 4 Cardiff Rd, Luton,* **t** *0990 143219,* **w** *www.eurolines.com.*

Republic of Ireland: *Bus Eireann,* **t** *(01) 836 6111.*

By Car

The other Channel Tunnel option is **Eurotunnel** (*t (01303) 273300, w www.euro tunnel.co.uk*), which transports cars on purpose-built carriers between Folkestone and Calais. The journey time is a mere 35 minutes platform to platform. The standard economy fare between 6am and 10pm rises to £299 in the summer months. There are cheaper rates for travelling between 10pm and 6am, and special rates for 5-day breaks (£180 in August). Day-trip return crossings can cost as little as £49 (non-refundable), though the standard fare is £170. The fare is for car space only regardless of the number of passengers. It is advisable to reserve space in advance although it is possible just to turn up and wait.

If you want to hire a car to travel around Belgium you will probably get a much better deal if you arrange this in your own country before departure.

If you take your own car to Belgium you'll need a valid EU driving licence or an international driving licence – plus a valid insurance document and your vehicle registration documents. It is advisable to take out an insurance policy to cover your car against the cost of breakdown and rescue while abroad. You are required by law to carry a warning triangle and a first-aid kit. Your headlights should be adjusted for driving on the right-hand side of the road, but they do not need to be yellow.

The roads in Belgium are well maintained, and the free motorway network can whisk you from one end of the country to the other in about three hours. However, Belgium still ranks highly among European countries with the most dangerous roads. Belgian drivers seem to have no concept of stopping distance and will chase each other nose-to-tail at high speed.

Another warning: *priorité de droite* (priority for vehicles coming from the right) is alive and unwell in Belgium. On unmarked roads (but not on major thoroughfares and motor-ways) vehicles may quite legally come shooting out from the right, off a minor road, without looking – provided they do not hesitate. Junctions where this is not permissible have white dog-tooth marks across the road at which drivers must give way. Beware, in particular, of drivers who still apply this rule on roundabouts.

Finally, do not flash your lights as a signal in Belgium, because you are liable to be misunderstood. In the UK this means, 'Go ahead, I'm allowing you to pass.' However, in Belgium this signal means, 'Get out of my way, I'm coming through.' The official speed limits are 120km/hr (75mph) on the motorway, 90km/hr (55mph) on major country roads and 50km/hr (30mph) in built-up urban areas.

Be aware that seatbelts must be worn in cars and also that children under 12 years old are not allowed to sit in the front seat of a car if other seats are available.

TOUR OPERATORS

Various travel companies offer weekend breaks in Brussels and other parts of Belgium, including several of the ferry companies and Eurotunnel. The only UK company specializing exclusively in Belgium is the Belgian Travel Service (*see* contact details on the next page). The Belgian Travel Service offers a broad range of holidays to all the most popular Belgian destinations and can also book accommodation for tailor-made trips.

There are a number of tour operators offering specialist tours of Brussels as well as more general tours of Flanders and the cities of the north. The themes on offer include river and canal cruising, gourmet tours, beer festivals, battlefield tours (Ypres, Waterloo, Passchendaele, the Ardennes), fine arts and even country-and-western weekends.

In the UK

Ace Study Tours, *Babraham, Cambridge CB2 4AP*, **t** *(01223) 835055*, **f** *837394*, **w** *www.study-tours.org*. Cultural and garden tours.

Belgian Travel Service, *Bridge House 55–58 High Road, Broxbourne, Herts EN10 7DT*, **t** *(01992) 456156*, **e** *belgian@bridge-travel.co.uk*.

British Museum Traveller, *46 Bloomsbury St, London WC1B 3QQ*, **t** *(020) 7323 8895*, **f** *7580 8677*, **w** *www.britishmuseumtraveller.co.uk*. Guest lectures, art and architecture tours.

City Breaks Online, **t** *0800 542 2282*, **w** *www.citybreaks-online.com*.

City Holidays, *14 City Business Centre, Basin Road, Chichester, West Sussex PO19 2DU*, **t** *(01243) 775770*.

Compass Agencies, *669 Honeypot Lane, Stanmore, Middlesex HA7 1JE*, **t** *(020) 8537 6156*, **f** *8930 2283*, **w** *www.compassagencies.com*.

Cox and Kings, *4th Floor, Gordon House, 10 Greencoat Place, London SW1P 1PH*, **t** *(020) 7873 5027*, **f** *7630 6038*, **w** *www.coxandkings.co.uk*. Short breaks, gourmet and escorted cultural tours with guest lecturers.

Cresta Holidays, *Tabley Court, Victoria Street, Altringham, Cheshire WA14 1EZ*, **t** *0870 161 0909*.

Crystal Holidays, *King's Place, Wood St, Kingston, Surrey KT1 1JY*, **t** *0870 848 7015*, **f** *0870 848 7031*, **w** *www.crystalholidays.co.uk*.

Driveline, *Greeleaf House, Darkes Lane, Potters Bar EN6 1AE*, **t** *0870 757 7575*, **w** *www.drive-line.co.uk*.

Eurobreak, *Inghams Travel, Gemini House, 10–18 Putney Hill, London SW15 6AX*, **t** *(020) 8780 7700*, **f** *8780 7705*, **w** *www.eurobreak.com*.

Eurotours, *St George's House, 34–36 St George's Road, Brighton, East Sussex BN2 1ED*, **t** *(01273) 883838*, **f** *383123*, **w** *www.eurotours.co.uk*.

Great Escapes, **t** *0800 731 2929*, **w** *www.greatescapes.co.uk*.

Holts Battlefield Tours, *The Old Plough, High Street, Eastry, Kent CT13 0HF*, **t** *(01304) 612248*, **f** *614930*, **w** *www.battletours.co.uk*.

Inn Travel, *Hovingham, York YO62 4JZ*, **t** *(01653) 629000*, **f** *628741*, **w** *www.inntravel.co.uk*.

Insight International Tours, *26–28 Paradise Road, Richmond, Surrey TW5 1SE*, **t** *(020) 8332 2900*.

Leisure Direction, *Image House, Station Rd, London N17 9LR*, **t** *0870 442 8945*, **w** *www.leisuredirection.co.uk*.

Lupus Travel, *Triumph House, 189 Regent St, London W1B 4JS*, **t** *(020) 7306 3000*, **f** *7287 2142*.

Martin Randall Travel, *10 Barley Mow Passage, Chiswick, London W4 4PH*, **t** *(020) 8742 3355*, **f** *8742 7766*, **w** *www.martinrandall.com*. Cultural tours accompanied by a lecturer.

Off 4 the Weekend, **w** *www.off4theweekend.com*.

Page & Moy, *135–140 London Road, Leicester LE2 1EN*, **t** *08700 106212*, **w** *www.pagemoy.com*.

Prospect Music and Art Tours Ltd, *36 Manchester Street, London W1M 5PE*, **t** *(020) 7486 5704*, **f** *7486 5868*. Cultural breaks including an 'Art Nouveau' tour.

Saga Holidays, *The Saga Building, Enbrook Park, Sandgate High St, Folkestone CT20 3SE*, **t** *0800 300500*, **f** *01303 771010*, **w** *www.saga.co.uk*. Holidays for the over-50s.

Shortbreaks Ltd UK, **t** *(020) 8402 0007*, **w** *www.short-breaks.com*. All-inclusive Eurostar breaks.

Sovereign, *Groundstar House, London Road, Crawley, West Sussex RH10 2TB*, **t** *08705 768373*, **f** *(01293) 457760*, **w** *www.sovereign.com*.

Travelscene, *11–15 St Ann's Road, Harrow, Middlesex HA1 1LQ*, **t** *0870 777 4445*, **f** *(020) 8861 4154*, **w** *www.travelscene.co.uk*.

Voyages Jules Verne, *21 Dorset Square, London NQ1 6QG*, **t** *(020) 7616 1010*, **f** *7723 8629*, **w** *www.vjv.co.uk*. Speciality tours including food and drink, art and history and the single traveller.

Where 2 Break, *Cresta Holidays Ltd, Tabley Court, Victoria Street, Altrincham, Cheshire W14 1EZ, **t** 0870 169 0708, **w** www .where2break.com.*

In Ireland

Go Holidays, *28 North Great George's Street, Dublin 1, **t** (01) 874 4126, **f** 872 7958.*
United Travel, *Stillorgan Bowl, Stillorgan, Co. Dublin, **t** (01) 283 2555, **f** 283 1527, **w** www .unitedtravel.ie.*

In the USA

Contiki Travels, *300 East Katella Ave, 450 Anaheim, CA 92806, **t** (888) CONTIKI, **f** (714) 935 2556, **w** www.contiki.com.* Bus tours for 18–35-year-olds.
Europe Through the Back Door, *109 4th Av N, Box C-20009, Edmonds, WA 98020, **t** (425) 771 8303, **f** 771 0833, **w** www.ricksteves.com.* Fully guided and more independent bus tours.
Jet Vacations, *880 Apollo St, Suite 243, El Segundo, CA 90245, **t** 800 JET 0999, **f** 310 640 1700, **w** www.jetvacations.com.* Independent travel packages and customized group packages.
Kesher Tours, *347 Fifth Ave, Ste 706, New York, NY 10016, **t** (212) 481 3721, **f** 481 4212, **w** www.keshertours.com.* Fully escorted kosher tours.
Worldwide Classroom, *P O Box 1166, Milwaukee, W1 53201, **t** (414) 251 6311, **f** (800) 276 8712, **w** www.worldwide.edu.* Database listing worldwide educational organizations.

ENTRY FORMALITIES

Passports and Visas

EU citizens just need a valid passport or visitor's card for stays of up to 90 days. Americans, Canadians, Australians and New Zealanders need valid passports, but no visa is required. Strictly speaking you are supposed to be able to produce your passport or identity card at any time, so keep it with you.

If you plan to stay longer than 90 days you will need to apply for registration (*see* 'Working and Long Stays' in the Practical A–Z chapter, p.68).

Customs

Since July 1999, duty-free goods have been unavailable on **journeys within the European Union**, but this does not necessarily mean that prices have gone up, as shops at ports, airports and the Channel Tunnel do not always choose to pass on the full cost of the duty. It does mean that there is no limit on how much you can buy, as long as it is for your own use. Guidelines are issued (e.g., 10 litres of spirits, 800 cigarettes, 90 litres of wine, 110 litres of beer) and, if they are exceeded, you may be asked to prove that it is all for your own use. Goods bought on a ferry crossing will include duty, but food and drink consumed whilst aboard are still duty-free.

Non-EU citizens flying from an EU country to a non-EU country (e.g., flying home to the USA from Belgium) can still buy duty-free. Americans can take home 1 litre of alcohol, 200 cigarettes and 100 cigars, etc. Canadians can take home 200 cigarettes and 1.5 litres of wine or 1.14 litres of spirits or 8.5 litres of beer.

ARRIVAL

Zaventem Airport

Zaventem Airport is 14km from Brussels' city centre and has all the facilities. The airport is divided into five levels, with shops, bars, restaurants and a viewing gallery on level 4; departures on level 3; arrivals on level 2; buses and taxis on level 0; and trains on level –1. You can pick up a detailed plan of the airport at the main information point beside the escalators on level 2 (arrivals). Also in the arrivals hall is a bureau de change, a bank, a post office (open Mon–Fri 8am–7pm and Sat

8.30am–1.30pm) and a tourist information point. Flight information and transport details are listed on the airport Web site, **w** *www.brusselsairport.be.*

Getting to and from Zaventem Airport

Taxis from Zaventem airport to the city centre cost approximately €25, but taxis with an orange and white aeroplane sticker in the top right-hand corner of the windscreen offer reduced rates, usually 25 per cent off.

It is, however, far cheaper to travel by **train**. Special train services (**t** *02 753 4221*) run three times an hour throughout the day from around 4.45am to 11.40pm, and connect with the Gare du Nord and the Gare Centrale (some trains go on to the Gare du Midi). The train journey takes 20 minutes to the Gare du Nord and a second class ticket costs €2.25.

There is an hourly **bus** service to the Gare du Nord which takes 35 minutes; tickets cost around €2.

If you are travelling with **Sabena**, the airline will pick up your luggage at your hotel for the return flight (**t** *070 222242*). The service costs about €40.

Arrival by Eurostar

The Eurostar service terminates at the Gare du Midi, in a downbeat part of town just south of the city centre. There are several bureaux de change dotted about the station, though the commission charges are relatively high. The numerous cash machines in the station all accept credit cards and Cirrus/Maestro debit cards.

Though you can hop straight on to the Métro or catch a tram to any destination within Brussels, there is always a long queue of taxis outside the main entrance. Taxi charges within central Brussels should be no more than €7.50, but do confirm this first with the driver. There is a tourist information kiosk located in the centre of the station concourse.

GETTING AROUND

Maps

This book should provide you with sufficient maps for your stay. The Brussels Tourist Office includes a useful fold-out map in its booklet 'Brussels Guide and Map' (€2). For more detail, Eurocart publishes an excellent book-form map, while Girault Gilbert produces a large single-sheet fold-out map with street index, called 'Nouveau Plan de Bruxelles et Grande Banlieue'. The best public transport map is issued free by the transport authority STIB (Société des Transports Intercommunaux Bruxellois), available from their information offices (at Métro stations Porte de Namur, Rogier and Midi), and tourist offices (*see* p.68).

On Foot

Brussels is a compact city and most of the museums and sights are within walking distance of the Grand' Place. There's good public transport around the centre, but walking is often quicker and more rewarding.

One word of warning: do not assume cars will stop at pedestrian crossings for you. Given enough distance, drivers will reluctantly give way once you are on the crossing – but don't count on it. Foreign drivers also take note: other drivers do not expect you to stop at pedestrian crossings. If you do so in traffic, you are liable to incur the wrath of the driver behind you, if not an accident.

By Tram

Brussels was once a city of trams: it grew with the tram age. Over the last two decades, however, the trams have been savagely axed and replaced by buses. This process has now largely abated, and those tram routes that have survived look set to stay. It is a speedy and efficient way to travel and has the novelty of its historic tradition.

The STIB public transport map (see 'Maps', p.58) shows the tram routes. Trams can be boarded only at designated tram stops (red signs). Note that you must signal that you want to get off at the next stop by pressing a bell button on the wall of the tram. Trams, buses and the Métro system, operate from about 5.30am to midnight, but weekend services are much reduced after 6pm.

By Bus

The bus network is now far more extensive than the tram network that it has largely usurped. Buses operate on the same ticket system as trams, and you have to validate your ticket on the bus at the start of your journey. Once you have got the hang of it, the bus system is a very effective way of getting around. The STIB public transport map marks all the routes and the stops, so it is easy to plan your journey and to feel confident about where to board and where to get off.

By Métro

The Métro system in Brussels, constructed since 1965 and still being extended, has the fresh look of something new, and remains both clean and efficient. It has two lines: Line 1 crosses town on an east–west axis and Line 2 curls around the centre of the city. An additional service called the Pré-métro, which in fact is part of the tram network, runs underground in the 'tram tunnel' on a north–south axis, beneath the Boulevards Adolphe Max and Anspach.

To find your way around the Métro system you really need to consult a Métro map (there are maps posted in the stations). The direction of a train is indicated by the terminus towards which it is travelling, and this will be signalled on the platform and by signs inside the carriages.

By Taxi

Taxis in Brussels are ordinary saloon cars with 'Taxi' written on the top. They can be hired only at a designated taxi rank (or by

Tickets for Public Transport

Public transport tickets can be used on the tram, bus and Métro, which all form part of STIB. The price of an *aller simple*, for a single continuous journey, is €1.50; this permits changes and is valid for one hour.

If you are making several journeys by public transport there is a five-journey card (*carte de cinq voyages*) for €6, but the best buy is the 10-journey card (*carte de dix voyages*), which costs €9. Alternatively, for €4, you can buy a card that is valid for 24 hours (*carte de vingt-quatre heures*), during which time you can make as many journeys as you like. Also available from the Tourist Information Office in the Grand' Place is the Tourist Passport which will give you 24 hours' unrestricted travel and reduced admission to the city's museums; it costs about €6. It is worth remembering that children over six years old have to pay adult prices. Single tickets and multiple journey cards are available from bus and tram drivers or at Métro stations and Brussels railway stations, at STIB information offices (see 'Maps', p.58), at tourist offices (see p.68), and at newsagents displaying the STIB sign. When travelling with an STIB card you have to validate it – which is to say, have it stamped with the time and date at the start of each part of a journey. As you board your tram or bus, or as you enter a Métro station, drop the ticket into the machine with the strip towards you, arrow downwards. The machine can tell if you are using your card to continue your journey on the same unit, or beginning a new journey. Don't assume that other passengers are not validating their tickets: they may well have passes.

telephone), and cannot be hailed from the street. The fact that someone is registered as a taxi driver in Brussels does not guarantee that they know any more than just the key destinations and streets in the city: it helps to be able to supply as much information as possible yourself.

A short journey will cost about €5 or €6: this comprises the initial fee of €3 and then

€1 per kilometre (it is advisable to check the meter on departure). It is normal to add 10–15 per cent as a tip, or round up to the nearest euro.

Major Brussels taxi companies:
ATR, t *02 242 2222,* **t** *02 647 2222.*
Autolux, t *02 411 1221.*
Taxis Bleus, t *02 268 0000.*
Taxis Oranges, t *02 349 4343.*
Taxis Verts, t *02 349 4949.*

By Car

Driving in Brussels there are two things to watch out for; *priorité de droite* (*see* p.55) and trams. Trams have priority and you have to get out of their way if you can. These days there are fewer roads where trams and cars jostle for position, but where they do, beware!

Parking is comparatively easy, especially in outlying districts. In the centre of town there is a fair number of underground car parks and parking meters.

By Bicycle

Although cycling is a national sport and you will see pelotons of sleek cyclists on the open road, cyclists in Brussels are a rarity. This is probably an example of evolutionary adaptation: cyclists simply do not survive long enough to reproduce. Not recommended. If, however, you are determined to cycle, you could make use of a network of 'green' car-free routes devised by the green party Ecolo (*12 Rue Charles VII, 1030 Brussels*). Bicycles can be hired from Pro Velo (*15 Rue de Londres, t 02 502 7355, closed Mon*) for about €12 per day. Pro Velo also organizes guided cycling tours in groups of up to 23 persons, visiting the city centre, Art Nouveau houses, the parks and outlying woods and castles.

By Horse-drawn Carriage

During the summer months, and at weekends at either end of the season, authentic horse-drawn carriages are available for short tours of the city centre. Starting from Rue Charles Buls (off the Grand' Place), the usual tour goes to the Manneken-Pis, then around to the Bourse and across the Grand' Place itself. A 20-minute journey costs around €15 (for the carriage, irrespective of the number of passengers).

Guided Tours

Several companies offer guided tours of Brussels, ranging from a quick sweep around the highlights in a coach to walks with a guide focusing on special themes. For €70, De Boeck offers a walk in the Grand' Place followed by a coach trip past the Atomium, Palais de Justice, Colonne du Congrès and Parc du Cinquantenaire, all of which is achieved in about two and a half hours flat. ARAU, an excellent, highly professional, non-profit-making organization, has a list of more specialist trips, such as Art Nouveau (including private houses otherwise inaccessible), parks and gardens, and industrial archaeology, all for around €13 per person.

The Brussels Tourist Office (*see* p.68) has its own expert guides who can take you on walking tours of the centre or on tailor-made tours (about €25 per hour per group). In general they like at least two weeks' notice to arrange group tours but it is always worth asking if something can be arranged at shorter notice. Their list of organized walks includes such themes as 'Brussels in the footsteps of famous women', 'Brussels through the eyes of famous people', 'Brussels... Cheers' (beer), and Jewish history in Brussels.

Arcadia, *38 Rue du Métal (off maps),* **t** *02 534 3819.*
ARAU, *55 Bvd Adolphe Max (E3–F2),* **t** *02 219 3345,* **e** *tourville@wol.be.*
De Boeck, *8 Rue de la Colline (E5),* **t** *02 513 7744.*
Itinéraires, *14 Rue de l'Aurore (off maps),* **t** *02 715 9120.*

Practical A–Z

Climate

Belgium shares a similar weather pattern to the UK – there are glorious summers of endless sunshine, and there are summers when it never ceases to rain. In winter, however, temperatures can be noticeably colder than in Britain, sometimes dropping to −20°C if the wind is blowing from the Baltic; the north of the country can be shrouded in an eerie cold fog for days.

All the seasons have their merits, even winter. Clear, ice-cold winter days can be invigorating; the lakes and canals are thronged with skaters and sprawling children, like a winter scene from Bruegel, and in filthy weather you can always eat well. Autumn is perhaps the most spectacular season, when the huge beech woods (especially to the south of Brussels) are transformed into visions of shimmering gold.

Average daily temperatures (°C)

Jan	April	July	Oct
1	11	19	12

Average rainfall (mm)

Jan	April	July	Oct
66	60	95	83

Crime and the Police

Crime in Brussels, and in Belgium generally, is no worse than it is in the rest of Europe. As everywhere, common-sense **precautions** should see you through, such as avoiding the parks late at night and parts of the north and west of the city. Pickpockets operate among the crowds on public transport, and the Métro has its own breed of nimble handbag slashers who can extricate wallets in a single swipe. If you have lost your property or are the victim of crime, go straight to the **police**, many of whom speak English. Remember that you have to report theft to the police at their headquarters (*Rue du Marché au Charbon*, *t* 101) in order to claim insurance. Note also that you are obliged to carry your passport or another form of identity at all times, and this is the first thing the police will ask to see. (They can check it, but they are not allowed to take it away from you.) If you are arrested for any reason, you have the right to insist that your consul is informed (*see* 'Embassies and Consulates'). Proper legal representation can then be arranged.

Disabled Travellers

Brussels isn't an easy city for the disabled, with its busy cobbled streets, narrow pavements and hills. That said, people generally show greater respect towards the disabled than many of their European counterparts, and their offers of assistance may compensate for the absence of lifts and ramps in museums and restaurants.

An excellent publication is available (in French) called *Guide Touristique et des Loisirs à l'Usage des Personnes à Mobilité Réduite* (Tourist and Leisure Guide for People with Reduced Mobility). This is a thorough compilation of restaurants, sports facilities and shops in Brussels, with an assessment of accessibility. To receive a copy, contact AWIP (*Agence Wallonne pour l'Intégration des Personnes Handicappées, 21 Rue de la Rivelaine, 6061 Charleroi, t 071 205711*).

In our **museum** entries throughout this book, we use the term 'wheelchair accessible' for those places that are most accessible for disabled travellers. Note that most museums are only partially accessible: bathrooms and cafeterias are often located in inconvenient spots, so calling ahead is the safest bet. In our 'Eating Out' chapter we list those **restaurants** with wheelchair access and/or equipped with a wheelchair-accessible toilet, though they are few and far between. In the 'Where to Stay' and 'Entertainment' chapters, we also list those hotels, cinemas, theatres, etc., that are wholly or partly accessible – but, as before, call ahead.

Organizations in Brussels

Croix Rouge de Belgique (Belgian Red Cross), *98 Chaussée de Vleurgat (I12), t 02 645 4411*. General advice about facilities, loan of wheelchairs and other equipment. For emergencies call **t** 105.

International Organizations

Accessible Europe, *Promotur-Mondo Possibile, Piazza Pitagora 9, 10137 Turin, t (39) 011 309 6363, f 011 309 1201, w www.accessible europe.com*. Network of specialist European travel agencies, providing detailed information on major sites and transport, as well as organizing assistance for disabled travellers.

Mobility International, *w www.mobility-international.org*. This organization produces country guides that cover access and facilities for transport, accommodation, tourist attractions and sites, as well as information on personal assistance schemes and key travel contacts.

Organizations in the UK and Ireland

Holiday Care Service, *2nd Floor, Imperial Buildings, Victoria Rd, Horley, Surrey RH6 9HW, t (01293) 774535, f 771500, w www .holidaycare.org.uk*. Up-to-date information on destinations, transportation and suitable tour operators.

Irish Wheelchair Association, *Blackheath Drive, Clontarf, Dublin 3, t (01) 833 8241, w www.iwa.ie*. They publish a range of guides with advice for disabled holiday-makers.

RADAR (Royal Association for Disability and Rehabilitation), *Unit 12, City Forum, 250 City Rd, London EC1V 8AF, t (020) 7250 3222, f 7250 0212, w www.radar.org.uk*. Publishes several books with information on everything travellers with disabilities need to know.

Royal National Institute for the Blind, *224 Great Portland Street, London W15 5TB, t (020) 7388 1266*. Its mobility unit offers a 'Plane Easy' audio cassette which advises blind people on travelling by plane. They also advise on accommodation.

Tripscope, *Alexandra House, Albany Rd, Brentford, Middx TW8 0NE, t 08457 585641, f (020) 8580 7022, w www.justmobility.co.uk/ tripscope*. Practical advice and information on travel and transport for elderly and disabled travellers. Information can be provided by letter or tape.

Web Sites for Disabled Travellers

w *www.accesstourism.com*: information on hotels and specialist tour operators.

w *www.sasquatch.com/able-info*: travel tips for disabled travellers.

w *www.emerginghorizons.com*: travel newsletter for disabled people.

w *www.geocities.com*: network with information and links on travel guides for disabled travellers.

Organizations in the USA

American Foundation for the Blind, *15 West 16th Street, New York, NY 10011, t (212) 620 2000, toll free t 800 232 5463*. The best source for information in the USA for visually impaired travellers.

Federation of the Handicapped, *211 West 14th Street, New York, NY 10011, t (212) 747 4262*. Organizes summer tours for members; there is a nominal annual fee.

Mobility International USA, *PO Box 3551, Eugene, OR 97403, t (503) 343 1248*. Offers a service similar to that of its sister organization in the UK.

SATH (Society for the Advancement of Travel for the Handicapped), *Suite 610, 347 5th Av, New York, NY 10016, t (212) 447 7284, w www.sath.org*.

Travel Information Center, *Moss Rehab. Hospital, 1200 West Tabor Road, Philadelphia, PA 1914/3099, t (215) 456 9600*.

Electricity, Weights and Measures

The current is 220 volts, 50 hertz. Standard British equipment requiring 240 volts will operate satisfactorily on this current. Plugs are the standard European two-pin type. Adaptors are available locally, but it is easier to buy a multi purpose travelling adaptor before you leave home. Visitors from the US will need a voltage converter in order to use their electrical appliances.

For continental clothing and shoe sizes it's best to ask in the shop and get an assistant to measure you.

Belgium uses the metric system; below is a conversion chart for quick reference.

1 cm = 0.3937 inches
1 metre = 3.094 feet
1 kilometre = 0.6214 miles
1 kilogramme = 2.2 pounds
1 litre = 0.264 gallons
1 inch = 2.54 centimetres
1 foot = 0.3048 metres
1 mile = 1.6 kilometres
1 pound = 0.4536 kilogrammes
1 liquid pint = 0.4732 litres
1 gallon = 3.7853 litres

Embassies and Consulates

In Brussels

Canada: *2 Av de Tervuren, t 02 741 0611.*
Ireland: *89 Rue Froissart, t 02 230 5337.*
UK: *85 Rue Arlon, t 02 287 6211.*
USA: *27 Bvd du Régent, t 02 508 2111.*

Abroad

Canada: *4th Floor, 80 Elgin St, Ottawa, Ontario K1P 1B7, t (613) 236 7267.*
Ireland: *2 Shrewsbury Rd, Ballsbridge, Dublin 4, t (01) 269 2082.*
UK: *103–105 Eaton Square, London SW1W 9AB, t (020) 7470 3700.*
USA: *330 Garfield St, Washington DC 20008, t (202) 333 6900.*

Health, Emergencies and Insurance

Accident emergency/ambulance/fire/rescue: *t 100.*
Police emergency: *t 101.*
Red Cross Ambulance: *t 105.*
Emergency anti-poisoning centre: *t (070) 245245.*
Paediatric emergency (Hôpital Universitaire des Enfants Reine Fabiola): *t 02 477 3100.*
Dental emergencies (non-surgery hours): *t 02 426 1026.*
Brussels standby emergency services: *t 02 479 1818, t 02 648 4014.*

Belgium has an excellent **medical service**, with first-class modern hospitals, well-trained staff and a nursing profession founded on the high standards set by Edith Cavell (*see* 'Edith Cavell', p.108). Funded by the state, national insurance and private medical insurance, it has suffered less from growing constraints on government finance than other European nations, notably Britain.

Under the Reciprocal Health Arrangements, visitors from EU countries are entitled to the same standard of treatment in an emergency as Belgian nationals. To qualify you should travel with the E111 form; application forms are available from UK post offices. However, the E111 does not cover all medical expenses, and you are well advised to take out health insurance as well. Those who are not from the EU should take out full insurance as a matter of course.

Travel insurance packages for Europe are not expensive compared with the cost of replacing stolen goods or paying any medical bills yourself. Standard packages include insurance to cover all unrefundable costs should you have to cancel, compensation for travel delays, lost baggage, theft, third-party liabilities and medical cover.

Hotels have a list of **doctors** and dentists to whom their guests can apply, but a trip to a pharmacy may be sufficient for minor complaints. Pharmacists have a good knowledge of basic medicine and are able to diagnose: if in doubt they will recommend that you visit a doctor, and can provide you with details.

A list of 24-hour duty **pharmacies** is posted on every pharmacy door, together with a list of doctors on call. To get hold of a dentist in Brussels, call **t 02 426 1026**.

You will be expected to pay for all medicine and treatment. With an E111 you can claim back about 75 per cent of the cost at the local Belgian sickness office; if you have separate health insurance you can claim the entire cost on your policy, but make sure that you ask for the correct documentation to make your claim.

Internet

There are plenty of cybercafés dotted around Brussels, which come and go as more people get hooked up at home. The emergence of the enormous easyEverything café has put pressure on the smaller places, but dozens of tiny cybercafés remain in the Matonge district of Ixelles, frequented by the African community. To find more try the 'Pot-au-Lait' Web site, **w** *www.cybercafe .potaulait.be*.

easyEverything, *Place de Brouckère (E3)*, **w** *www.easyeverything.com; metro De Brouckère. Open 24hrs daily*. Hundreds of terminals and the cheapest connection charges. Minimum payment of €2.50 for 1hr 20mins online. You get a ticket with an ID number, so you don't have to use all of your minutes at once. Coffee bar downstairs.

Cyber Théâtre, *45 Av de la Toison d'Or (D9–G8); metro Porte de Namur*. About 30 terminals. Internet access costs around €3.50 per hour, plus initial fee of €3.

Useful Web Sites

These official and unofficial tourist sites provide a good starting point for your holiday research:

w *www.art-events.be*
w *www.belcast.be*
w *www.belgique-tourisme.net*
w *www.bru.com*
w *www.brugge.be*
w *www.brusselstourism.com*
w *www.bruxelles.irisnet.be*
w *www.bruxelles-j.be (information on Brussels for young people)*
w *www.dma.be*
w *www.frites.be (webzine for everything Belgian)*
w *www.noctis.com*
w *www.pim.be/pimfichier/bruxelles.html*
w *www.tib.com*
w *www.toervl.be*
w *www.virtualbruges.be (a virtual tour of Bruges)*
w *www.visitantwerpen.be*
w *www.webguidebrussels.com*

Media

The Belgian media is divided into the two main language communities, but this is a cosmopolitan society and **newspapers** are widely available in just about every language. The main French-language newspapers in Belgium are *Le Soir, La Libre Belgique* and *La Dernière Heure;* the main Flemish ones are *Het Laatste Nieuws, De Standaard* and *De Morgen*.

An excellent locally produced weekly English magazine , *The Bulletin* (€2.50), is worth looking out for. Designed mainly for English-speaking residents of Brussels, it contains a thorough what's-on guide, including film, theatre and restaurant reviews.

Another useful source of listings is *Le Soir* newspaper, which produces a supplement called *MAD* (Magazine des Arts et du Divertissement) every Wednesday and *Kiosque*, a listings magazine in French.

Belgian **TV** not only has Flemish and locally produced French channels, but also those from France, Germany, the Netherlands and the UK.

The main Belgian TV and **radio** stations are run by state-owned RTBF (Radio Diffusion Télévision Belge), which broadcasts in French, and BRT (Belgische Radio en Televisie), which broadcasts in Flemish. It's also possible to receive BBC radio and BBC World Service, as well as numerous other European stations.

Money, Banks and Taxes

On 1 January 1999, the euro became the official currency of Belgium (at the rate of 40.34 BF to the euro), and franc notes and coins became obsolete on 28 February 2002.

Banking hours are not absolutely rigid but are usually Mon–Fri 9.15–3.30, although some branches stay open until 5pm. Some branches close for lunch between 12 and 2, and a number of banks in the centre of Brussels are open on Saturday mornings. You will find no shortage of banks offering exchange facilities. **Exchange bureaux** have extended opening hours, including weekends, but tend to charge higher commission rates than banks. There are exchange bureaux at:

Crédit Général, *7 Grand' Place (open 24hrs)*.
Gare Centrale *(open daily 7am–9pm)*.
Gare du Midi *(open daily 7am–10pm)*.
Gare du Nord *(open daily 7am–10pm)*.

Travellers' cheques are widely accepted not only for exchange, but also in lieu of cash. Eurocheques, backed by a Eurocheque card, can be used in the same way up to a limit of €175 per transaction.

Credit cards (Visa, Mastercard/Eurocard) can be used to draw cash from banks, but usually only through **automatic cash dispensers**, which means you must come armed with your PIN number. Visa, Mastercard/Eurocard, Diners Club, American Express and a handful of other leading cards are all widely accepted in shops, restaurants, hotels and petrol stations, but you should always check this first.

Amex, *100 Vorstin (off maps)*, **t** *02 676 2121 (lost cards:* **t** *02 676 2323 or* **t** *02 676 2121)*.

Diners Club, *1 Bvd du Roi Albert II (off maps)*, **t** *02 206 9511 (lost cards:* **t** *02 206 9800)*.

Mastercard/Eurocard/Visa, *159 Bvd Emile Jacqmain (E2)*, **t** *02 205 8585 (lost cards:* **t** *(070) 34 4344)*.

All shop prices include **Value Added Tax** (TVA/BWT) where applicable. At the time of writing this stands at 21 per cent. Non-EU visitors may claim a refund on purchases in excess of €175 made in any one shop. This is a fairly complex procedure, most effectively dealt with if you are departing from Brussels international airport (Zaventem).

When making your purchase, ask the shop for a form called a 'Tax-free Shopping Chèque'. At the airport, have it stamped by customs (who may wish to inspect the goods), then take it to the refund office in the departure hall.

Refunds are also available at the Interchange offices in central Brussels (88 Rue du Marché aux Herbes) and in Antwerp

(36 Suikerrui). If you prefer, you can apply for a refund by post through Interchange. For further information ask at any major shop or tourist office.

Opening Hours and Public Holidays

For bank and post office hours, *see* 'Money, Banks and Taxes' or 'Post and Fax'. The standard opening hours for **shops** are 9–5.30, but many boutiques open 10–6 or 7. Department stores have late-night shopping on Fridays, when they stay open to 8 or 9pm. On Sundays, supermarkets and high-street shops are closed but pâtisseries and other specialist food shops open in the morning to cater for the traditional Sunday lunchtime indulgence.

The large public **museums and galleries** are generally open over the weekend but closed on Mondays; other museums are often open on Mondays but closed at other times.

Belgium has a generous number of **public holidays**, when all banks and post offices and most shops, bars , restaurants and museums are closed. Where a public holiday falls on a Sunday, the following Monday is taken as a holiday in lieu. Public offices and institutions are also closed on 15 November (Dynasty Day) and 26 December (Boxing Day).

1 Jan	New Year's Day (Nouvel An)
Mar/Apr	Easter Monday (Pâques)
1 May	Labour Day (Fête du Travail)
May	Ascension Day (6th Thurs after Easter) (Ascension)
	Whit Monday (7th Mon after Easter) (Pentecôte)
21 July	Independence Day (Fête Nationale)
15 Aug	Assumption (Assomption)
1 Nov	All Saints' (Toussaint)
11 Nov	Armistice Day (Armistice)
25 Dec	Christmas Day (Noël)

Packing

Due to the changeability of Belgian weather, pack for all weathers. Keep warm by wearing several layers – in winter, Belgian homes, hotels and restaurants can be heated to hothouse temperatures. The dress code is fairly relaxed. People tend to dress casually, but with attention to detail, and they appreciate elegance. Jackets and ties are required only in the smartest restaurants – where most Belgians don't normally eat anyway.

Photography

Camera film is widely available in Brussels – even newsagents sell it – and there are hundreds of places that will develop your pictures. Minit Colors has several chains around the centre of town (3 Rue de la Madeleine and in the Centre Monnaie) and more in Anderlecht, Auderghem, Uccle and Waterloo. Specialist film processors for professionals include:

Campion, *13 Rue St-Boniface, 1050 Ixelles*, *t 02 512 1331*.

Contraste, *122 Rue de Haerne, 1040 Etterbeek, t 02 640 9440*.

Le Labo, *62 Rue de l'Arbre Bénit, t 02 513 3530*.

Post and Fax

Post offices are generally open Mon–Fri 9–5, but the following branches have extended opening hours:

Brussels X, *Gare du Midi, 48a Av Fonsny*, *t 02 538 4000*. **Open** *24 hrs daily*.

Centre Monnaie, *Place de la Monnaie*. **Open** *8.30–7, Sat 9–3*. Also offers an expensive fax service. It is Brussels' main poste restante address (Poste Restante, 1000 Brussels 1, Belgium).

Stamps are also available from tobacconists; however, for reliable information about the cost of postage, ask at a post office.

Smoking

In Brussels it is illegal to smoke in confined public spaces (i.e. in stations, on public transport and in municipal buildings). However, the attitude is pretty relaxed; smoking is permitted in virtually all restaurants and only some of them have no-smoking sections.

Students

Université Libre de Bruxelles (ULB), *50 Av Franklin Roosevelt, t 02 650 2111*. The city's largest university, founded in 1834.

Vrije Universiteit Brussel (VUB), *2 Pleinlaan*, *t 02 629 2505*. The Dutch-speaking counterpart of the ULB, founded in 1970.

Bibliothèque Royale de Belgique, *4 Bvd de l'Empereur, t 02 519 5311, w www.kbr.be*. **Open** *Mon–Fri 9–8, Sat 9–5*. The state library built to hold every Belgian publication.

ULB Bibliothèque, *50 Av Franklin Roosevelt, t 02 650 4700*. **Open** *Mon–Fri 8am–10pm, Sat 10–5*. The library at Brussels' main university. Non-students can use it for a fee.

Socrates and Youth (formerly Erasmus), *70 Rue Montoyer, t 02 233 0111*. **Open** *Mon–Fri 9–5.30*. European student exchanges.

Telephones

There's a wide network of public phone booths in Brussels. Local calls are relatively cheap and it's easy to place international calls from any booth showing a row of foreign flags on the window. If you intend to make a lot of calls a **Telecard** is a good investment. They are available from newsagents, post offices and public transport ticket offices and cost either €5 for 20 units or €25 for 105 units.

There is a specialist telephone centre at the head office of Belgacom at 17 Bvd de l'Impératrice, open daily 8am–10pm, from where you can make or receive phone calls, send faxes, telexes or telegrams. Expect to pay a big surcharge if you do any telephoning from your hotel.

The country code for Belgium is 32 and if you are calling Brussels you should then dial 2 instead of 02. Note that you must use the area code for every Belgian city even when calling from within the city. To make an international call from Belgium dial 00, then the country code, then the area code without the initial 0, then the number. The country code for the UK is 44, for Ireland 353, for the USA and Canada 1.

For national directory enquiries, call **t** 1307; European directory enquiries, **t** 1304; international directory enquiries, **t** 1324 and for reverse charge calls, **t** 1324.

Time

Belgium is an hour ahead of Greenwich Mean Time, and six hours ahead of Eastern Standard Time in the USA.

Tipping

Tips in Brussels are welcome but not really expected. In restaurants a 16 per cent service charge is usually included in the bill, along with 21 per cent TVA (Value Added Tax). If you have had table service at a bar or café, it is usual to leave any small change, but this is not essential.

Service is included in hotels, so there is no need to tip porters or staff providing room service. In taxis it is usual to round up the total by 10 per cent, but note that in metered taxis the tip is included in the fare. Cinema ushers and cloakroom and public toilet attendants will expect a tip of about €0.50.

Toilets

Public toilets are usually kept scrupulously clean by dedicated women with their own brand of hearty chat. There is not a huge number of public toilets: in their absence most Belgians will freely make use of bar and café facilities, but it is considered polite to buy a drink in passing.

Tourist Offices

Abroad

Before you go, pick up more information from a Belgian National Tourist Office:

UK: *31 Pepper Street, London E14 9RW,* **t** *(020) 7867 0311,* **f** *7458 0045.*

USA: *Suite 1501, 780 Third Av, New York 10017,* **t** *(212) 758 8130,* **f** *355 7675.*

In Brussels

The tourist offices in Brussels offer all kinds of advice about what to see and when, and about special activities and guided tours; they will also make hotel and theatre reservations for you. They publish various annual brochures, including their useful 'Guide and Map' (€2), and a free weekly programme of events. Ask about the discounts available with their 'tourist passport'.

Brussels International Tourism and Congress (BITC): *Hôtel de Ville, Grand' Place (D–E5),* **t** *02 513 8940,* **f** *02 514 8320,* **e** *tourism .brussels@tib.be,* **w** *www.tib.be.* **Open** *daily 9–6, Sun in winter 10–2.*

Commissariat Général au Tourisme/ Commissariat General voor Toerisme: *63 Rue du Marché aux Herbes/Grasmarkt (E5),* **t** *02 504 0390,* **f** *02 504 0270.* **Open** *Mon–Sat 9–6 (until 7pm in summer), Sun 1–5 (9–7 in summer).* Offers copious literature about the various regions of Flemish Belgium.

Zaventem Airport: *t 02 725 5275.* **Open** *daily 6am–10pm.*

Women Travellers

Amazone, *10 Rue du Méridien (I3),* **t** *02 229 3800; metro Madou.* **Open** *Mon–Fri 9–6.* This women's centre is home to a long list of women's organizations. They also provide information for the general public on women's issues.

British and Commonwealth Women's Club, *509 Rue du Bois (off maps),* **t** *02 772 5313.*

Working and Long Stays

Getting permission to live and work in Belgium requires plenty of stamina and perseverance. If you come from a country within the EU, the hurdles are lower and further apart, but there are hurdles nonetheless.

The Paperwork

EU passport holders have the right to stay in Belgium and take up work without a work permit, but only for 90 days. After this you have to register with the police to acquire a three-month residence card (*certificat d'immatriculation*), renewable for a further three months if you have found work. It is advisable to register at the local town hall (*maison communale*) as soon as you arrive in Brussels, if you intend to find work. You will need to have done so before applying to a recruitment agency (*see* 'Finding a Job'). All you will need is three passport-style photos and you will have to pay a charge (about €25) each time you register, and may be asked also to give your fingerprints. After your first or second three-month visa you can apply for a five-year identity card (*certificat d'inscription au registre des étrangers*, CIRE).

If you are from outside the EU your passport entitles you to a visit of 90 days or whatever visa restriction applies. For non-EU nationals hoping to work in Belgium the application process can be quite complicated. Rising unemployment has drastically reduced the number of jobs available to those from outside the EU. Not only must your prospective employer apply for a work permit on your behalf (as well as any accompanying family) before you enter the country, but he or she must also be able to prove that the job you intend to do could not be performed by a Belgian or other EU national. It is best to apply to the Belgian consulate in your home country as early as possible; the process can take several months and there will be various documents to be gathered from home.

Once in Brussels, for clarification about legal formalities (such as permit renewal), you can apply to the **Service des Etrangers**, Square de Meeüs, **t** 02 514 2270.

Finding Somewhere to Live

Rents average €500–1,250 and it may be worth staying in an apartment hotel (*see* p.219) to begin with, while you find your way around. Certain areas of the city – Ixelles, Uccle, St-Gilles, Woluwe and Watermael-Boitsfort – seem to be most popular with Western foreigners. (Note, however, that the following municipalities do not grant residence permits to non-EU nationals: Anderlecht, Forest, Molenbeek, Saint-Gilles, Saint-Josse and Schaerbeek.) Properties for rent are advertised in the national newspapers such as *Le Soir* and *De Standaard*, and there are also useful listings in *The Bulletin*. By far the best, however, are to be found in the weekly journal *Vlan*, which reaches newspaper shops first thing on Monday morning. Alternatively, you can apply to any of the estate agencies (*agence immobilière*) or property agencies that offer a scouting service in return for a fee.

Finding a Job

With over a quarter of the Brussels population of foreign extraction, and half of these from EU countries, it goes without saying that foreigners can get jobs in Brussels. The majority of job vacancies fall into two categories: executive, governmental posts, largely arranged from abroad, and temporary work for experienced personnel. Note that the construction industry is forbidden by law to employ temporary staff. Executive posts are advertised in the newspapers, such as *Le Soir*, *La Libre Belgique*, *De Standaard*, and also in *The New York Herald Tribune*. *The Bulletin* also lists vacancies, primarily for secretaries, PAs and other office staff.

The Office Régional Bruxellois de l'Emploi (government job agency) will help EU citizens find employment and offer advice.

A major employer is the European Union, and many of its staff are recruited locally. Apply to The Commission of the European Communities, Recruitment Unit – Sc 41 00–16, 200 Rue de la Loi, **t** 02 299 3131 or **t** 02 299 1111. Recruitment agencies in Brussels include:

Creyf's Interim, *21–23 Rue de l'Ecuyer*, **t** *02 218 8370*.

Focus Career Services, *23 Rue Lesbroussart*, **t** *02 646 6530*. Offers not just the services of a recruitment agency, but also training programmes to help newcomers find paid employment or voluntary work. It is particularly valued by families who have relocated but where one spouse, for whatever reason, cannot pursue his or her normal career. The agency also publishes a document called *Getting Started Legally*, which offers advice on setting up a business in Belgium.

Manpower, *523 Av Louise (G11)*, **t** *02 639 1070*. Specializes in secretarial work, especially for those with language skills.

Vedior Interim, *Riverside Business Park, 55 Bvd International (off maps)*, **t** *02 555 1611*. One of the largest agencies with everything from administrative to technical positions.

Survival Guides

There are several publications that anticipate the concerns of the expatriate community, including the free biannual *Newcomer*, which is produced as a supplement to *The Bulletin* in March and September. It contains numerous addresses and advertisements for schools, clubs, removal companies and employment agencies. *Newcomer* is also available from major relocation agencies (*see* opposite). Another similar publication, produced annually, is called *Living in Belgium* (€12), which is available in English-language bookshops such as Waterstone's (*see* p.252).

The Belgian Embassy in London supplies a useful document called *Working in Belgium*, and it's worth consulting the Web site **w** *www.xpats.com*.

The annual Brussels Welcome Fair – a dynamic event organized by *The Bulletin* is an opportunity for property agencies, tax consultants, insurance brokers, schools, associations, and even restaurants to promote themselves to the expatriate community. For information, contact The Welcome Fair, 1038 Chaussée de Waterloo, **t** 02 373 8329.

Addresses and Contacts

American Chamber of Commerce, *50 Av des Arts (H7)*, **t** *02 513 6770*, **f** *02 513 3590*.

British Chamber of Commerce, *15 Rue d'Egmont (H7–8)*, **t** *02 540 9030*, **f** *02 540 8363*.

British Council and Library, *15 Rue de la Charité (off maps)*, **t** *02 227 0840*.

Brussels Language Studies, *8 Rue du Marteau (I–J5)*, **t** *02 217 2373*.

Bruxelles-Accueil, *6 Rue de Tabora (D4–5)*, **t** *02 511 8178*. Catholic organization offering advice to anyone of any denomination (incl. students and refugees) about the law, accommodation, acclimatization, courses, etc.

Linguarama, *19 Av des Arts (H7)*, **t** *02 217 9055*.

Around the
Grand' Place

Around the Grand' Place

The Grand' Place is the jewel in Brussels' crown – and such a splendid jewel that the rest of the crown might just as well be made of iron. Nothing can quite prepare you for the elation you feel when you emerge from the warren of surrounding streets into this spacious, gilded arena. The French dramatist Jean Cocteau described the Grand' Place as '*un riche théâtre*', and that is what it is: a splendid stage for the public.

The Grand' Place is Brussels' top tourist attraction, so it is almost permanently overrun by tourists, and the neighbouring streets are tacky with tourist tat; despite all this, the area has an atmosphere of infectious, easy-going pleasure, suggesting the more sedate pace of bygone eras and providing as convincing a link with the past as its medieval street plan. Despite being at the heart of one of Europe's great cities, it's barely bothered by traffic or by the intrusion of modern business and its architecture.

1 Lunch

La Maison du Cygne, *2 Rue Charles Buls or 9 Grand' Place*, **t** *02 511 8244*; **metro** *Bourse*. **Open** *Mon–Fri noon–2.30 and 7–11, Sat 7–11; closed Aug*. **Expensive**. Sumptuous and justly famous restaurant in one of the Grand' Place guildhouses, serving top-notch French cuisine.

2 Tea and Cakes

La Roue d'Or, *26 Rue des Chapeliers*, **t** *02 514 2554*; **metro** *Bourse*. **Open** *daily 12.30pm–midnight*. An old brasserie with elaborate chandeliers and a high painted ceiling.

3 Drinks

Le Roy d'Espagne, *1 Grand' Place*, **t** *02 513 0807*; **metro** *Bourse*. **Open** *daily 10am–1am*. An institution: a wonderfully atmospheric bar-restaurant, magnificently positioned in the Grand' Place, with waiters in starched, medieval aprons.

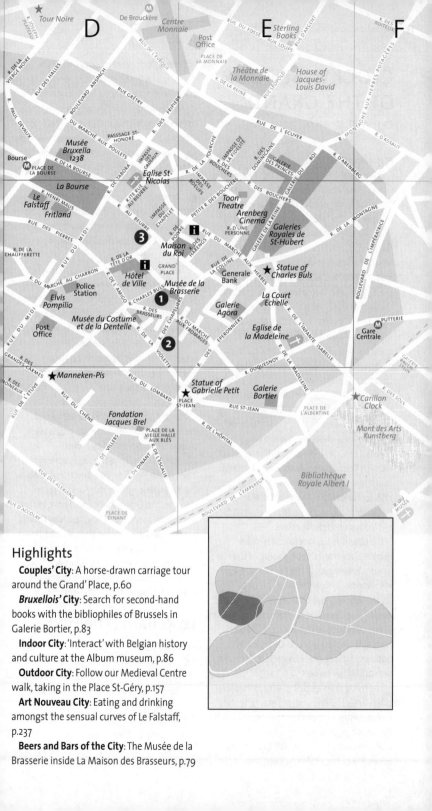

Highlights

Couples' City: A horse-drawn carriage tour around the Grand' Place, p.60

Bruxellois' City: Search for second-hand books with the bibliophiles of Brussels in Galerie Bortier, p.83

Indoor City: 'Interact' with Belgian history and culture at the Album museum, p.86

Outdoor City: Follow our Medieval Centre walk, taking in the Place St-Géry, p.157

Art Nouveau City: Eating and drinking amongst the sensual curves of Le Falstaff, p.237

Beers and Bars of the City: The Musée de la Brasserie inside La Maison des Brasseurs, p.79

CLOCKWISE TOUR OF THE GRAND' PLACE

Metro *Bourse.*

Quite what Brussels would be without the Grand' Place does not bear thinking about. The good burghers of Brussels looked this prospect in the face in 1695. Having failed to raise the siege of Namur by William III of England, Marshal de Villeroy, leading the French troops of Louis XIV, issued an ultimatum: Brussels would be bombed unless the English and Dutch lifted their blockade of the French ports. He gave the authorities just six hours to consult all parties, then on the night of 13 August his troops opened up a great barrage, demolishing the Grand' Place along with nearly 4,000 houses and 16 churches. The splendid tower of the Hôtel de Ville was practically the sole survivor – something of a paradox, since this was what the artillery had used as their principal target. What you see, then, is not quite what it seems. The Grand' Place looks like a perfect Flemish Renaissance–Baroque square, but much of it was built at the very end of the 17th century, within five years of the bombardment, in a style that was already outmoded and retrospective.

The Grand' Place was Brussels' main marketplace from the beginning of the city's history. The names of the streets that lead into it today bear witness to this past: Rue au Beurre (butter), Rue Chair et Pain (meat and bread), Rue des Harengs (herrings), and so on. These streets once threaded past various halls and covered markets occupied by butchers, bakers, cheesemongers, fishmongers and other traders.

The rising stars of civic power in medieval times were the *échevins*, assistants to the burgomaster. In the 1390s they permitted the formation of corporations, guilds of craftsmen and traders which became the backbone of the economy. Then during the

15th century the *échevins* organized the building of a grand Hôtel de Ville – a bold statement of the city's wealth and pride which confirmed the Grand' Place's central role in the public life of Brussels. This was where all important public decrees would be announced. It was the setting for colourful pageants and jousting tournaments – and also the scene of public executions. The guilds wanted to be near the seat of civic authority, and during the 16th century the borders of the old market square started to fill up with their guildhouses, first in wood, then in stone.

The Grand' Place was now less a market and more the city's gathering place, busy with ladies and gentlemen parading in their finery, gilded carriages, carts, stray dogs, mobile theatres, hawkers, quacks and charlatans. The centre of Brussels earned a reputation for lively taverns, reckless spending and licentiousness – and the *échevins* were soon struggling to formulate legislation to curb this behaviour.

The role of the Grand' Place as the city centre survived even after the guilds were disbanded in the 1790s by French Revolutionaries. With the large-scale renovations to the Hôtel de Ville and the Maison du Roi during the 19th century and in recent decades, the Grand' Place could have become a museum piece, but it hasn't: today the old guildhouses are occupied by cafés, banks, hotels and lace shops. Now that all traffic has been outlawed, a daily plant and flower 'market' (actually just a couple of stallholders) occupies the centre stage.

Le Renard (The Fox)

7 Grand' Place.

Our clockwise tour of the Grand' Place starts in the northwest corner, where the Rue du Marché au Charbon (coal-market street) enters the square. Like most of the buildings lining the Grand' Place, No.7 has a picturesque name, Le Renard. Many of the guildhouses' names date back to the earliest building occupying the site and have no link

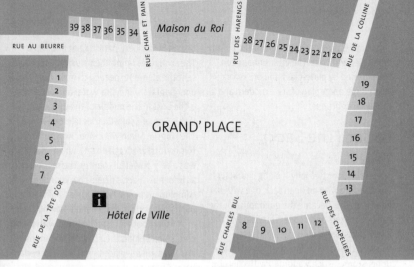

Map Key

with the guilds themselves. The name Le Renard (in Flemish, De Vos) predates the acquisition of the building by the haberdashers' guild in the 15th century; it was later elaborated by the carving of the fox over the doorway. A statue of St Nicholas, patron saint of haberdashers as well as of merchants generally, stands on the crest of the gable. As with almost all the guildhouses, each storey is decorated by a different style of classical column or pilaster: Doric, Ionian (topped by a scroll) and Corinthian (with an ornate capital incorporating foliage, such as acanthus leaves).

Le Cornet (The Horn)

6 Grand' Place.

This is the most successful of the buildings designed by one of the main architects of the Grand' Place, Antoon Pastorana. This was the boatmen's guildhouse and is encrusted with marine symbols. The gable resembles the stern of a galleon, and the horn that gives the building its name can be seen over the central window.

La Louve (The She-wolf)

5 Grand' Place.

This building is so named because there is a statue over the entrance of Romulus and Remus suckling the wolf. This was the house of the archers, a kind of city militia raised to the rank of a corporation. This connection made the house the target of assault in 1793 by sans-culottes inspired by the French Revolution, who pulled down the statues on the third storey. Since restored to their plinths, these represent Truth, Falsehood, Peace and Discord; the medallions set high on the façade show Emperors Trajan, Tiberius, Caesar Augustus and Julius Caesar, who are held to be symbols of each of these properties. The gable is topped by a phoenix rising out of the ashes.

La Louve is now occupied by a branch of the Crédit Général bank. The interior has been transformed by plate-glass and brickwork into a large open-plan office – modern and totally incongruous.

Le Sac (The Sack)

4 Grand' Place.

Over the door two jolly-looking characters are standing with an open sack, one with his head in it. This became the guildhouse of the cabinet-makers and coopers in 1444, and the lower two storeys, constructed in 1644, survived the bombardment of 1695. The later upper storeys – richly adorned with cherubs, barley-sugar balustrades, cornucopiae, garlands and urns – are another example of the work of Antoon Pastorana, who was by training a cabinet-maker.

La Brouette (The Wheelbarrow)

3 Grand' Place.

Here you'll see the forerunners of the modern wheelbarrow pictured over the door. This building belonged to the tallow merchants – demonstrating their power in the days before petrol-based lubricants and electric lighting. A statue (1912) of their patron saint, St Gilles, stands over the gable. Although the building is dated 1697, a reference to the restoration work carried out by the architect–sculptor Jan Cosyns, but in fact much of the original façade survived the bombing of 1695.

La Maison des Boulangers (The Bakers' House)

1 and 2 Grand' Place.

Jan Cosyns is also thought to be the designer of La Maison des Boulangers, the grandest of the guildhouses, and distinguished by its elegant domed lantern in place of a gable. The golden head over the

door is St Lambert, patron saint of bakers. The six figures lining the balustrade represent the elements needed to make bread: energy, grain, wind, fire, water and prudence.

The bust in the middle of the upper storey is the King of Spain, Charles II (r.1661–1700). The kings of Spain were effectively rulers of this country from 1517 to 1713, when Spain was a very powerful country. Their reputation as imperial rulers is given a backhanded compliment by the two figures flanking the bust; an American Indian and a North African in a turban, both looking dejected with their hands tied behind their backs. The canons and flags are misplaced symbols of imperial glory: Charles II was mentally and physically handicapped and furthermore had no direct heir. During his reign the Spanish empire began to falter. Medallions of the Roman emperors were used for decorative effect and to imply a moral message: here Antoninus Pius and Trajan represent long and just rule; Nerva and Decius, by contrast, had dubious claims to power and ruled for only a couple of years. The gilded figure of Fame, perched on top of the dome, is one of the most delightful statues in the square. This building now houses the celebrated bar, Le Roy d'Espagne (*see* p.238).

Le Chêne (The Oak)

37 Grand' Place.

The Rue au Beurre enters the Grand' Place at the northern corner. To the right there is a series of less elaborate houses, dated 1696–7 and now occupied by cafés and lace shops. Le Chêne was once the guildhouse of the weavers, the most powerful guild of the medieval period.

Maison du Roi (Musée Communal de la Ville de Bruxelles)

*1 Rue de Poivre; **metro** Bourse. **Open** Tues–Fri 10–5, public hols 10–1; **adm** €2.*

Moving clockwise, you come to the Rue Chair et Pain. For over a century now the

Maison du Roi has housed the city museum. The building is a bizarre construction, a confection of arches and loggias, crockets and steep-pitched roofs topped by statues of knights waving banners and swords. This is 19th-century Gothic run riot, now blackened by city grime. It should not belong, but somehow it does.

This building has changed its skin at least five times. It was initially a centre for the bakery trade; then in the 15th century a new building was erected on this site to house the Duke of Brabant's high court, hence it became known as the Duke's House. The high court was supplanted in the 16th century by the Royal Assizes, so it became known as the King's House. (The loaf and crown on the weathervane refer to this history.) The Counts Egmont and Hornes (see p.108) were held here before their execution in the Grand' Place in 1568. In the 1870s, the present building was constructed, its design modelled on etchings of the 16th-century building.

The Museum

The Musée Communal de Bruxelles is an oddball collection of painting, pottery, tapestry, historical documents, models showing the evolution of Brussels, and – its most famous possession – the vast wardrobe of clothes tailormade around the world for the Manneken-Pis. Its sombre, neo-medieval halls are rewarding for anyone interested in Brussels' history.

On the ground floor are some superb retables (the ornate, sculpted and painted altarpieces for which Brussels was renowned) dating from 1480 to 1510. In the same room is a delightful painting attributed to Pieter Bruegel the Elder, who lived in Brussels from 1563 to 1569: *Le Cortège de Noces* (The Wedding Procession) is an affectionate caricature of peasant life. Neighbouring rooms contain fine examples of Brussels' tapestries from the 16th and 17th centuries, and porcelain, which was produced in Brussels from 1767 to 1953.

The historical models on the first floor show how Brussels has developed through the ages. In the model of the old walled city, for instance, you can see the old path of the River Senne, the Ile St-Géry (the site of the original settlement), the Grand' Place, the city walls, and the Coudenberg. A good collection of paintings serves to illustrate notable historical landmarks, such as the magnificent Coudenberg Palace, destroyed by fire in 1731.

The second floor includes a series of displays relating to the traditional crafts of Brussels – lacemaking, printing, and weaving. A further large room has been devoted to the costumes of the Manneken-Pis, where about 100 of his 650 or so outfits are on display. The earliest here dates from the 1920s, but most are modern. They include regimental uniforms, the costume of the Gilles de Binche (see p.268), sporting kits (including a sub-aqua outfit), tradesmen's working clothes (plumber, beekeeper, etc.) and samurai armour – all carefully designed so the little chap can continue the activity for which he is so well known.

An Embarrassing Virginity

As you leave the Maison du Roi you might picture the dejection of the great French poet Charles Baudelaire (1821–67) as he too left the building in 1863, after a literary disaster. In one of his meet-the-poet seminars here, he addressed a large and enthusiastic audience, including a contingent from a highly respected girls' school. Seeking to thank his audience for helping him to overcome his nerves, he said: '*Votre grâce m'a bien vite fait connaître que cette virginité de parole n'est, en somme, pas plus difficile à perdre que toute autre*' ('Your kindness has quickly made me realize that this virginity of words is in fact no more difficult to lose than any other'). The schoolgirls were hastily ushered out, followed by the rest of the audience. Baudelaire's standing as a celebrity had been eradicated in a single phrase, and he became increasingly embittered towards the Belgians thereafter.

La Chambrette de l'Amman (The 'Little Room' of the Amman)

28 Grand' Place.

Next on this clockwise tour is La Chambrette de l'Amman, beside the Rue des Harengs. The Amman was the Duke of Brabant's representative to the council of *échevins*, and also a senior legal officer. His main office was over the other side of the square, at L'Etoile (*see* below).

Le Pigeon (The Pigeon)

26–27 Grand' Place.

Le Pigeon was acquired by the Guild of Painters in 1510 and reconstructed after 1695. Plaques on either side of the door of No.26 announce the fact that Victor Hugo lived here in 1852. A bitter critic of Louis Napoleon, who had just declared himself Emperor Napoleon III, Victor Hugo had been forced to flee from France. He stayed in this house for several months, protected from the intrusions of an admiring public by his landlady who owned the tobacconist's on the ground floor. When Victor Hugo, by his continued vitriolic outpourings against Napoleon III, became a security risk and embarrassment to the Belgian government, he went to live in the British Channel Islands, but returned frequently to Brussels. His long-suffering wife, Adèle, took up residence in the Place des Barricades, while his unhappy mistress of the past 18 years, Juliette Drouet, found lodgings nearer at hand in the Galeries Royales de St-Hubert. Hugo himself, however, directed his formidable amorous energies towards a string of servant girls and prostitutes.

La Maison des Tailleurs (The Tailors' House)

24–25 Grand' Place.

This building was designed by another of the great architects of the Grand' Place,

Willem de Bruyn. It has a bust of the patron saint of tailors, St Barbara, over the entrance, and St Boniface on the gable, beneath whom you can see a plaque bearing tailor's shears. This pair of houses is now another celebrated bar/restaurant called La Chaloupe d'Or (*see* p.237).

Anna-Joseph and Le Cerf (The Stag)

20–22 Grand' Place.

The ground floor of this pair is a shop selling Godiva chocolates (*see* p.252). The two houses are known as Anna-Joseph from the inscription over the lower windows. (The reference is to Joseph, husband of the Virgin Mary, and Anne, her mother.) The iron pulley on the gable is a survivor from the days when stores and furniture were raised to the upper storeys on ropes, rather than up the internal stairs. No.20 is known as Le Cerf and houses an expensive restaurant (*see* p.224); the stag in question can be seen sculpted in relief around the corner in the Rue de la Colline.

La Maison des Ducs de Brabant

13–19 Grand' Place.

The entire southeast corner of the Grand' Place is occupied by this series of six houses unified by a single façade and designed as a whole in 1698 by Willem de Bruyn. The building was conceived in palatial style, and is decorated by the busts of the dukes of Brabant (which gave the building its grand name). Recently restored, it glistens with scrubbed-up stonework and newly painted gilding.

Mont Thabor (Mount Thabor) and La Rose (The Rose)

11 and 12 Grand' Place.

The last stretch of gabled buildings begins with Nos.12 and 11, dating from 1699 and 1702 respectively and called Le Mont Thabor (Mount Thabor) and La Rose (The Rose) – so named because it belonged to the Van der Rosen family and was used as a private house. The buildings are now occupied by a restaurant and a jewellers.

La Maison des Brasseurs (Musée de la Brasserie)

10 Grand' Place, w www.beerparadise.be. Museum open daily 10–5; adm €2.50.

This was the headquarters of the brewers' guild, and is the only house in the Grand' Place still occupied by the guild that built it, now called the Confédération des Brasseries de Belgique. It houses a small museum of brewing.

This is one of the most striking buildings of the Grand' Place – a reflection of the wealth and standing of brewers since medieval times. Beer was the most common drink in Europe before the development of safe piped water in the late 19th century. The crew of a man-of-war in Napoleonic times, for example, were given 4.5 litres of the stuff as part of their daily rations. Statistics for the Belgian brewing industry today are no less impressive: the industry's total annual output is 14,000 million litres, more than 1,000 litres per head of population.

Designed by Willem de Bruyn, the Maison des Brasseurs is unusual in that the columns rise right through the second and third floors to a simple but effective semicircular pediment. Note the hop vines and grain stalks entwined around the lower sections of the columns.

The Museum

Although brewing is one of Belgium's great art-forms (*see* Nightlife, p.240), this museum is not essential viewing: if you want to visit only one brewing museum during your visit to Brussels, the unique Musée de la Gueuze (*see* p.138) is a more interesting option.

The museum consists of two rooms: the first contains a variety of traditional

Marx in Brussels

Karl Marx used to hold meetings of the Deutscher Arbeitverein (German Workers' Union) in a café in Le Cygne in the Grand' Place. Marx's antagonism to the Prussian government, expressed in a series of articles in a German paper produced in Brussels, made the authorities nervous, and his meetings were regularly infiltrated by spies. Matters came to a head on 24 February 1848 following the revolution in France. Like most European capitals, Brussels was alive with revolutionary fervour, and the Grand' Place filled with an excited crowd fuelled by rumours of the abdication of Leopold I. The police intervened, with sabres drawn, and made a number of arrests. Following this, the authorities thought it prudent to expel all foreign subversives, and so on 2 March Marx was given 24 hours to leave the country. He and his wife, Baroness Jenny von Westphalen, were taken to a police station not far from the square; Jenny was scandalized to be held in the same cells as common prostitutes. They later sought refuge in England.

paraphernalia from the old days of brewing, while the second gives a flavour of the hi-tech, squeaky-clean world of modern brewing. Touch-screen computers offer a breakdown of statistics about the Belgian brewing industry.

Le Cygne (The Swan)

9 Grand' Place.

This building is so named after the sculpture of a swan, wings outstretched, over the door. The elegant, classical-style house was rebuilt as a private dwelling in 1698 but became the butchers' guildhouse in 1720. It differs from others in the Grand' Place by having a dome-shaped roof pierced by dormer windows in place of a gable. Le Cygne is now an expensive restaurant, an ironic twist of fate given that Karl Marx used to hold meetings of the German Workers' Union in a café on this site whilst he was writing the Communist Manifesto with Friedrich Engels.

L'Etoile (The Star)

8 Grand' Place.

Built over the arched arcade that leads into the Rue Charles Buls, this was the main office and residence of the Amman, one of whose duties was to oversee executions as the king's representative. It is said that his balcony gave him a good view of executions taking place in the Grand' Place. The original building was demolished in 1850 to give better road access to the Grand' Place, and the present building was erected over an arcade in the 1890s, to redress the lost sense of architectural balance.

Monument to Everard 't Serclaes

Turn left into the arcade beneath L'Etoile. Stand for a moment and observe passers-by rubbing their hands along the bronze statue fixed to the wall. Over the years his limbs have been polished to a shine. This is the 19th-century monument to Everard 't Serclaes, the alderman and leader of the guilds who, in 1356, led a rebellion that repulsed the Flemish occupation of Brussels. The Duke of Flanders, Louis de Male, had invaded the city while laying claim to the vacant Duchy of Brabant. In 1388 Everard 't Serclaes was captured during an attack by troops from Gaasbeek loyal to Flanders, and his tongue was cut out. He was brought to the building on this site, L'Etoile, where he died. In revenge the furious citizens of Brussels attacked and demolished the castle of Gaasbeek – during which they fed robustly on chickens and so, according to some theories, earnt the Bruxellois their nickname kiekerfretters (chicken-eaters). Stroking his limbs is said to bring good fortune. However, some Flemish activists see this tradition as provocative and have made equally provocative calls for the monument's removal.

The Art Nouveau monument to the left of the statue is rather more endearing. It is dedicated to Charles Buls, burgomaster of Brussels from 1891 to 1899. A goldsmith by training, but also an artist, reformer and man of letters, Buls was the political force behind the restoration of much of old Brussels, including the Grand' Place.

Hôtel de Ville

Grand' Place, t 02 279 4365; metro Bourse. Open Tues–Fri 9.30–5, Sun 10–4; adm €2.50. Guided tours in English, German, Dutch or French last about 45 mins; English tours Tues and Wed 3.15, plus April–Sept Sun 12.15.

Although it was originally built in the early 15th century, what you see now is really what 19th-century romantics thought a medieval town hall should look like – for almost all the arches, statues, crocketed spires, turrets and balustrades date from a restoration programme that was begun in 1821. The building's real glory, however, is the vast tower, which stood alone amid the rubble after the French bombardment of 1695.

Buildings on this site were used as a town hall as early as 1327, but after 1380 the area was cleared to make way for a grand new building. Work proceeded on an ever more ambitious scale during the 15th century, culminating in the tower, by Jan van Ruysbroeck. It rises 96m and is topped by the splendid, primitive 15th-century gilded statue of St Michael (the patron saint of Brussels) killing the devil.

You can enter the inner courtyard of the Hôtel de Ville through the arched gateway at the base of the tower. After the destruction of 1695, a new town hall was built around a central courtyard in the Neoclassical style associated (ironically) with Louis XIV of France. The star in the cobbles in the middle of this courtyard marks the official centre of Brussels, from which all measurements are made. The 18th-century marble statues set against the west wall represent the two main rivers of Belgium, the Meuse (by Jean de Kinder) and the Scheldt (by Pierre-Denis Plumier).

The Interior

Although mostly 19th century, the interior of the Hôtel de Ville is worth a visit if you can manage to slot into the limited schedule of guided tours on offer. The tour takes you through just one level of the building, which consists mainly of grand public rooms. The 18th-century Council Room is a dazzling confection of tapestries, gilt mirrors and ceiling paintings, and seems like a cross between a royal bedchamber and a funfair roundabout. In the Antechamber of the Burgomaster there is a series of interesting oil paintings by Jean-Baptiste van Moer, dated around 1874. They were based on his earlier watercolours depicting the River Senne flowing through Brussels before it was covered over. Most of the remaining rooms are grandiose examples of municipal Neo-Gothic.

SOUTHWEST OF THE GRAND' PLACE

The cobbled streets to the southwest of the Grand' Place, such as Rue de l'Etuve, Rue du Marché au Charbon and Rue des Grands Carmes retain their medieval layout and can be a pleasant place to wander, though few of the original buildings remain. During the day Rue de l'Etuve is often a river of tourists passing between the Grand' Place and the Manneken-Pis, while the intersection of streets around the statue is riddled with shops selling souvenirs. You'll find that the poor Manneken has been put to countless debased uses, such as corkscrews and drinks-dispensers.

The Manneken-Pis D6

Corner of Rue de l'Etuve and Rue du Chêne; ***metro*** *Bourse.*

Manneken is bruxellois for little man; Pis speaks for itself. This bronze statue of a little naked boy peeing with happy abandon has long been held in great affection by the people of Brussels and has become a symbol of their city. No one can quite explain why – which must be part of his charm.

Endless legends have evolved to fill this gap in human knowledge. One is that the statue celebrates a little boy who prevented a great fire during the time of the Burgundian dukes by extinguishing a fire-bomb in this manner. Another relates how a wealthy citizen lost his son in the carnival crowds. When the child was found, his grateful father decided to have a statue made of the boy in the pose – and erected in the place – in which he was discovered. In another version, dating back to the 12th century, the infant Godfrey, future Duke of Brabant, was taken to the battlefield where Brussels was fighting against Mechelen. He was placed in the branches of an oak tree to watch the battle, where he was discovered by one of the enemy. Godfrey's response was to piss in his face, a gesture of scorn that so demoralized the whole Mechelen army that it fled.

Here's another idea. One day the infant son of Duke John III of Brabant exposed himself to a company of women in the Rue de l'Etuve. This coincided with a period during which the 14th-century mystic philosopher Jean de Ruysbroeck was having a great public debate with another Brussels mystic called Bloemaerdinne. Bloemaerdinne argued that there was no sin involved in fulfilling the natural impulses of love – an idea that appealed to the hedonistic Bruxellois. A statue of the child served as an apt symbol of Bloemaerdinne's cause.

Perhaps, more prosaically, it was just a rather apt and charming adornment for a public fountain in a district where there were public baths during medieval times (*étuve* means 'steam-bath').

Whatever, when the first bronze statue was cast by Jérôme Duquesnoy the Elder in 1619, it was probably based on an earlier model. Duquesnoy's version was already held in great affection when French soldiers tried to carry it off in 1747. The citizens of Brussels were furious, and to make amends Louis XV had a brocaded suit made for the Manneken-Pis – the first in his splendid collection of costumes. In 1793 he was given a Revolutionary bonnet by the Paris Convention. When an ex-convict stole the Manneken-Pis in 1817 the town was distraught; the culprit was caught and branded in the Grand' Place, then sentenced to eleven lifetimes' hard labour. But the statue was in ruins and had to be recast. This, then, is the statue you see today. He is much smaller than you expect, perched on his plinth behind high railings. A programme listing which costume he'll be wearing over the current period is posted on the railings.

Eglise Notre-Dame de Bon Secours C5

*91 Rue du Marché au Charbon; **metro** Bourse; wheelchair accessible. **Open** July–Sept 9–6, Oct–June 9–3; closed Oct–June Sun pm.*

With the coat of arms of Charles of Lorraine over the door, this modest little gem was built between 1664 and 1694 in Flemish Baroque style. The body of the church is based on an octagonal plan soaring to a domed ceiling, made all the more impressive by a nave that has been compressed to virtual non-existence. As in many Brussels churches, recorded sacred music is played here during visiting hours, demonstrating the church's remarkable acoustics.

SOUTHEAST OF THE GRAND' PLACE

Take a wander around the streets to the southeast of the Grand' Place. The street plan has changed little since medieval times and many buildings have preserved their 17th-century gables. A typical street is Rue du Marché aux Fromages, with a pleasantly animated atmosphere. Rue des Eperonniers nearby is a mildly grubby street lined with tatooists, grungy jewellers and quirky gift-

Gabrielle Petit

In Place St-Jean is a statue of Gabrielle Petit (1893–1916), a resistance worker during the First World War who helped to conceal Allied soldiers and usher them across the border to the Netherlands. She was arrested in 1916 and sentenced to death. The Germans were sensitive to the international outcry over the execution of Edith Cavell in 1915 (*see* p.108), and made it clear that her sentence would probably be commuted if she appealed. She refused, and faced the firing squad on 1 April 1916 after making the declaration inscribed (in French) on this monument: 'I have just been condemned to death. I shall be shot tomorrow. Long live the King, long live Belgium...and I shall show them that a Belgian woman knows how to die.'

shops. This is the principal entry point into the characterless Galerie Agora. The streets around Rue de la Violette are lined with lace shops. Rue St-Jean is the street of print-sellers and booksellers, while Rue de la Madeleine has an attractive jumble of art galleries, bookshops and antique shops.

Musée du Costume et de la Dentelle D5

*6 Rue de la Violette, t 02 512 7709; **metro** Bourse or De Brouckère; wheelchair accessible. **Open** Mon, Tues, Thurs and Fri 10–12.30 and 1.30–5, Sat, Sun and public hols 2–4.30; closes Oct–Mar at 4pm; **adm** €2.*

This small museum, housed in an 18th-century building, contains a small but rich collection of lace (*see* p.254) and clothing accessories from the 17th century to the present day and hosts well-presented temporary exhibitions about the history of fashion. If you want to make some sense of all the lace that fills so many of the shops in the surrounding streets, this a good place to start. The museum's extensive costume collection forms the basis of a rolling series of temporary exhibitions.

Fondation International Jacques Brel D6

11 Vieille Halle aux Blés, **t** *02 511 1020,*
e *fondation.jacques.brel@skynet.be,* **w** *www
.jacquesbrel.be;* **metro** *Gare Centrale; wheelchair accessible.* **Open** *Tues–Sat 11–6;* **adm** *€5.*

The foundation was established in 1980 by
the great *chansonnier's* daughter, France Brel,
in response to the flood of requests from
fans for information about her father (*see*
box below). As well as cataloguing Brel's
recordings and publishing a newsletter, the
foundation hosts a permanent exhibition
called *Avec Brel, un Soir de Tournée* (A Night
on Tour with Brel), which opened to the
public in 1999. It attempts to sketch a typical
evening on the road with Brel in the 1960s,
reproducing spaces in which Brel spent much
of his adult life: dressing room, backstage
areas, stage and bar. Ashtrays overflow with
butts, a guitar rests on the dressing table, a
vintage juke box offers the entire selection of
Brel's singles, and TV screens show recordings of Brel in action. Obviously, the appeal of
all this is limited to fans.

Galerie Bortier E6

17–19 Rue St-Jean; **metro** *Gare Centrale;
wheelchair accessible.* **Open** *Mon–Sat 9–6.*

This cavernous 19th-century shopping
arcade was designed (like the far more glamorous Galeries Royales de St-Hubert) by J. P.
Cluysenaar. Beneath a canopy of glass and
ornate ironwork, it is now a dimly lit shrine
for bibliophiles, lined with shops selling
second-hand books (mainly in French), prints
and postcards.

Eglise de la Madeleine E5

21 Rue de la Madeleine, **t** *02 511 2845;* **metro**
Gare Centrale; wheelchair accessible. **Open**
*Mon–Fri 7am–7.30pm, Sat 8.30–12.30 and
4–8, Sun 7–12.30 and 5–8.*

This pretty, 15th-century brick church had a
Baroque chapel, the chapel of Ste-Anne,
tacked on to its northern side in 1957, when it

Jacques Brel

In Belgium, a person who can write and
perform truly well-made songs acquires a
status equivalent to that of a poet. Among
this small handful of great chanteurs-
compositeurs of the last century stands one
of the heroes of modern Belgium,
Jacques Brel.

Everyone in Belgium, France and the
Netherlands can sing excerpts from their
favourite Brel songs. He sang passionately,
his rich, mellifluous voice usually accompanied by a simple band consisting of piano,
guitar, bass, drums and accordion. His songs
paint powerful, unforgettable images, drawn
from everyday experiences. In his most
famous songs he evokes the rough and ready
atmosphere of sailors' dives in Amsterdam,
inebriated drinking companions in the small
hours of the morning, the awkwardness of
impassioned lovers and the ridiculous atti-
tudes of the bourgeoisie. He is perhaps best

remembered for his portraits of Belgium,
tender but not always flattering.

Brel rose to stardom in Paris in the 1950s
and was always greatly admired by the
French, but he never forgot his Belgian
origins. Born in 1929 of Flemish-speaking
parents in Brussels, he is celebrated first and
foremost for his French songs, but he made
Flemish versions of many of these.

In 1966 Brel abandoned his solo tours and
thereafter he worked in the cinema and took
on a series of ambitious projects, including a
musical about Don Quixote which became
the Broadway hit *The Man of La Mancha*.
However, Brel became increasingly disen-
chanted with stardom, and spent more and
more of his time in retreat in the Marquesas
Islands in French Polynesia. Here he fell ill
with lung cancer. Returning to Europe for
treatment, he cut a final album in 1977, and
died near Paris in 1978. Brussels gave him an
unusual accolade for a popular singer: it
named a Métro station after him.

was transferred from the nearby Rue de la Montagne to make room for a car park. Radical modern restoration has made the interior rather soulless – but beggars encountered in the dim entrance lobby during Mass restore some of its lost medieval mood.

NORTH AND WEST OF THE GRAND' PLACE

Immediately to the north of the Grand' Place, surrounding the Galeries Royales de St-Hubert, is a lively tangle of narrow medieval streets known as the **Ilôt Sacré** (sacred isle). During the 1960s any original architecture in this area was protected and restored (though most Bruxellois will enjoy telling you that historical accuracy was forfeited for the sake of tourist revenue). At the centre of the Ilot Sacré is Rue des Bouchers, a colourful street lined with restaurants and musicians who serenade tourist as they pick through bucket-loads of mussels.

Rue du Marché aux Herbes (grass or hay market) was once a busy thoroughfare on the trade route between Bruges and Cologne. Rue de la Montagne, behind the striking statue of Charles Buls, is lined with gabled houses. Baudeleire once lived at No.26, with his pet bat. Rue du Midi, running west of the Grand' Place, is lined with philatelists' shops.

Galeries Royales de St-Hubert E5

Rue des Bouchers/Rue du Marché aux Herbes; metro Bourse; wheelchair accessible.

This beautiful marbled shopping arcade was designed by J. P. Cluysenaar and built in 1847. It was the first of its kind in mainland Europe. It is divided into two halves, the Galerie de la Reine and the Galerie du Roi (with a further spur called the Galerie des

Princes), intersected by the Rue des Bouchers. It is a celebrated shopping precinct, with ostentatiously expensive clothes shops, dainty chocolatiers, and elegant cafés. With their air of 19th-century elegance, the Galeries Royales de St-Hubert are the picture of established calm. Yet their construction was highly controversial. It involved the destruction of a considerable swathe of traditional housing, leading to the eviction of both inhabitants and businesses. A famous barber called Pameel was driven to kill himself in protest by slitting his throat in his own salon.

Rue des Bouchers E4–5

Metro Bourse or De Brouckère.

The Rue des Bouchers (butchers' street) is a visual feast: wall-to-wall restaurants with gaily painted awnings, fronted by spectacular displays of fish, shellfish and fruit laid out on ice-strewn trestles – and patrolled by importuning waiters. Pretty it may be, but no self-respecting Bruxellois would dream of eating in such places: the displays, in their view, are in inverse proportion to the quality of the cooking.

From the Petite Rue des Bouchers you have an excellent view of the statue of St Michael on the top of the tower of the Hôtel de Ville. Halfway down the Petite Rue des Bouchers, on the left-hand side, is the Impasse Schuddeveld. At the bottom of this atmospheric little alleyway is the remarkable **Toone puppet theatre** (*see p.248*) in a house built in 1696. It only opens for performances in the evening.

Eglise St-Nicolas D4–5

Place St-Nicolas; metro Bourse or De Brouckère; wheelchair accessible. Open daily 8–6.30, Sat, Sun and public hols 9–7.30.

This is one of the oldest and most atmospheric churches in Brussels, with its dim, candlelit interior and quaintly crooked aisle. A church has been on this site virtually since Brussels' foundation, closely linked to the market activities on the Grand' Place. St Nicholas, said to be a 4th-century bishop of Myra in Turkey, is the patron saint of merchants – although he is better known as Santa Claus. Most of the present structure dates from the 14th and 15th centuries.

The church suffered from vandalism at the hands of Protestant iconoclasts during the 1570s and was damaged in the 1695 bombardment. A cannonball is still preserved in one of its walls as a reminder of these more tempestuous times. Restoration gave it its Baroque flourishes. The impressive reliquary of the Martyrs of Gorcum dates from 1868; the martyrs were tortured to death by the Protestant '*gueux*' (rebels) in 1572.

La Bourse D4–5

*2 Rue Henri Maus; **metro** Bourse or De Brouckère. **Open** Mon–Fri on request.*

The former stock exchange is an impressive rectangle in Neoclassical style but with little sense of Neoclassical restraint. Decked with garlands of stone flowers and cherubs playing at horticulture, it is typical of the retrospective style used for many of the grand buildings in the Brussels of Léopold II. Though it looks much earlier, the Bourse dates from 1873.

The Bourse is now used to mount temporary exhibitions. Even when no exhibition is taking place, you can glimpse the interior and its ornate stucco ceiling by going through the entrance into a glass-canopied walkway.

Musée Bruxella 1238 D4

*Rue de la Bourse, t 02 279 4355; **metro** Bourse or De Brouckère; **adm** €2.50. Guided **tours** in English on Wed 10.15, 11.15, 1.45. 2.30 and 3.15. They start from Maison du Roi, Grand' Place, prior reservation required.*

In 1988 work on the roads around the Bourse uncovered the remains of a 13th-century Franciscan convent, destroyed in the religious wars of the 16th century. The excavation site has been turned into a small museum, with pottery, medieval bones and the grave of Duke John I of Brabant on display. You can glimpse a meagre section of the convent beneath the pavement on the north side of the Bourse, where part of the foundations have been glassed over for public viewing.

Place St-Géry C4–5

***Metro** Bourse.*

Off Place de la Bourse, Rue Jules van Praet is a mini-Chinatown of restaurants and oriental food suppliers. Continue to Place St-Géry, a square that once stood in the middle of the **Ile St-Géry**, one of a cluster of islands formed by the River Senne. Some time in the late 6th century, as tradition has it, St Géry (Bishop of Cambrai) founded a chapel here. This became the focus of a small settlement which remained obscure for 400 years until AD 977, when Charles, Duke of Lorraine, built a castle on the island, and the history of Brussels began. St Géry's original chapel was destroyed in about AD 800, but a succession of churches stood on this spot until 1798, when the last became a victim of French Revolutionary zealots. The red-brick covered market, Les Halles de St-Géry, which now occupies the middle of the square, was built in 1881 as a meat market. It was restored as a shopping arcade, but the venture failed and it is now used instead as an unusual setting for corporate functions.

Ile St-Géry has now become fashionable, and the developers have moved in to subject the area to what is jocularly referred to as 'façadisme': the façade of an old building is propped up and preserved while everything behind it is demolished to make way for rebuilding.

Notre-Dame aux Riches Claires C5

*Rue de la Grande Ile; **metro** Bourse.*

Just off the square is this small, red-brick church that once stood on the northern tip of one of the larger islands, overlooking the bridge that connected it to the Ile St-Géry.

This is one of Brussels' finest Baroque churches, designed by Luc Fayd'Herbe (1617–97) – a pupil of Rubens and a noted sculptor – and built in 1665.

Album C4

25 Rue des Chartreux, t 02 511 9055; metro Bourse. Open Thurs–Tues 1–6; sliding adm charges according to time spent in museum €1.25–5.

Established in 1997 by French Brussels enthusiast Oliver Guilbaud, Album is an excellent introduction to the city and to key themes of Belgian history, culture and daily life. It is called an 'interactive' museum because visitors are invited to explore the themes through video films, headphones, cupboards containing old photos, and real old newspapers and magazines to browse through. Set in a sympathetically refurbished 17th-century *maison-de-maître*, it makes light work of a great weight of information on Belgian history, the royal family, beer, comic strips, song, film and so on. There is something for everyone here, including Belgian cartoons on video for younger visitors. Much, though not all, is in English.

As you come out of Album look at the window of Maurice Demarteau, the horloger (clock-mender) at No.42 opposite, which usually contains an array of supremely ornate mantel clocks. To the left is a black door, and through the fanlight you can see the wall of a stone tower inside, part of the 12th-century city walls that were once linked to the Tour Noire (*see* p.114). You can push the door open, if the horloger is open, to gain a closer look.

Coudenberg and Parc de Bruxelles

Coudenberg and Parc de Bruxelles

No visit to Brussels would be complete without paying a call on the magnificent national art collection at the Musées Royaux des Beaux-Arts, which consist of the Musée d'Art Ancien and the Musée d'Art Moderne. These museums sit on the summit of the Coudenberg, the high ground south of the city centre which was once an enclave for the ruling classes and the aristocracy. It is still a very grand, breezy part of town, with long vistas, stately architecture and the large, formally planned Parc de Bruxelles over-looked by the Palais Royal.

1 Lunch

Pablo's, *51 Rue de Namur,* **t** *02 502 4135;* **metro** *Porte de Namur.* **Open** *Mon–Sat noon–3 and 6–midnight, Sun 6pm–midnight.* **Moderate.** Upbeat Mexican restaurant with a bar the size of a bowling alley. Tacos, enchiladas, *arroz con pollo,* etc., with pitchers of margaritas.

2 Tea and Cakes

Du Mim, *6th Floor, Rue Montagne de la Cour,* **t** *02 502 9508;* **metro** *Gare Centrale.* **Open** *Tues–Sun 9.30am–4.30pm.* One of the best daytime café experiences in Brussels. Perched at the top of a prominent Art Nouveau building, it is the perfect place to acquaint yourself with views of the city.

3 Drinks

Le Coudenberg, *68 Coudenberg,* **t** *02 512 4896;* **metro** *Gare Centrale.* **Open** *daily 11am–8pm.* Somewhere quiet to rest your feet and sample the wide range of beers, away from the crowds after a museum visit.

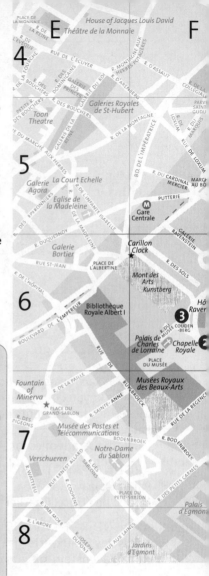

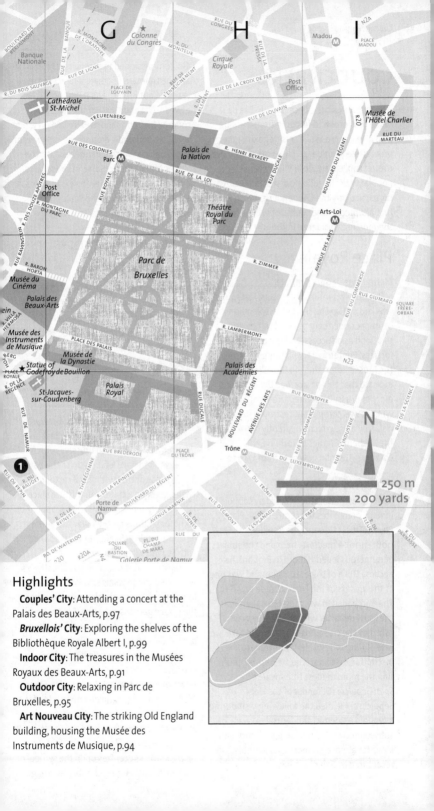

G · H · I

Banque Nationale

Colonne du Congrès ★

Madou Ⓜ

PLACE MADOU

N2A

BOULEVARD DE BRIALMONT

RUE DE LA BANQUE

RUE MONTAGNE DE L'ORATOIRE

RUE DE LIGNE

R. DU MONITEUR

RUE DU CONGRES

RUE DE LA PRESSE

Cirque Royale

Post Office

R. DU BOIS SAUVAGE

PLACE DE LOUVAIN

RUE DE L'ENSEIGNEMENT

Cathédrale St-Michel ✚

TREURENBERG

RUE DE LA CROIX DE FER

RUE DE LOUVAIN

Musée de l'Hôtel Charlier

R20

RUE DU MARTEAU

RUE DES COLONIES

Parc Ⓜ

Palais de la Nation

R. HENRI BEYAERT

R. DU PARLEMENT

RUE DUCALE

BOULEVARD DU RÉGENT

Post Office

R. DES DOUZE APÔTRES

R. MONTAGNE DU PARC

RUE ROYALE

RUE DE LA LOI

Théâtre Royal du Parc

Arts-Loi Ⓜ

AVENUE DES ARTS

RUE RAVENSTEIN

R. BARON HORTA

Musée du Cinéma

Palais des Beaux-Arts

Parc de Bruxelles

R. ZIMMER

RUE DU COMMERCE

RUE GUIMARD

SQUARE FRÈRE-ORBAN

R. VILLA... HERMOSA

Musée des Instruments de Musique

PLACE DES PALAIS

Musée de la Dynastie

R. LAMBERMONT

N23

BERG...

Statue of ★ Godefroy de Bouillon

PLACE ROYALE

St-Jacques-sur-Coudenberg

Palais Royal

Palais des Académies

BOULEVARD DU RÉGENT

AVENUE DES ARTS

RUE MONTOYER

RUE DU COMMERCE

RUE DE L'INDUSTRIE

RUE DE LA SCIENCE

R. DE LA RÉGENCE

RUE DUCALE

RUE DE NAMUR

RUE BREDERODE

PLACE DU TRÔNE

Trône Ⓜ

RUE DU TRÔNE

RUE DU LUXEMBOURG

N

❶

R. THÉRÉSIENNE

R. DE LA PÉPINIÈRE

BOULEVARD DU RÉGENT

RUE D'EGMONT

R. DE L'ESPLANADE

R. DE PARIS

RUE DE FLEUR...

R. DE LA REINETTE

250 m

200 yards

RUE DU BAUDET

Porte de Namur

AVENUE MARNIX

RUE DE HORNES

R20

R20A

N8

BD. DE WATERLOO

SQUARE DU BASTION

PL. DU CHAMP DE MARS

RUE DU...

Galerie Porte de Namur

RUE DE PARNASSE

Highlights

Couples' City: Attending a concert at the Palais des Beaux-Arts, p.97

Bruxellois' City: Exploring the shelves of the Bibliothèque Royale Albert I, p.99

Indoor City: The treasures in the Musées Royaux des Beaux-Arts, p.91

Outdoor City: Relaxing in Parc de Bruxelles, p.95

Art Nouveau City: The striking Old England building, housing the Musée des Instruments de Musique, p.94

COUDENBERG

For centuries the city centre – le Bas de la Ville – was prone to flooding from the sluggish River Senne, while this ridge of higher ground – le Haut de la Ville – was spared. For this reason le Haut de la Ville became popular with the ruling classes and well-to-do, particularly the Coudenberg, which was first adopted by the counts of Leuven for their fortress-residence in the 11th century.

Place Royale F6–7

Metro Trône or Gare Centrale.
This busy yet intimate Neoclassical square was laid out on the site of the splendid 15th-century Coudenberg palace, built by Philip the Good as a successor to the original fortress. Contemporary paintings (notably in the Musée Communal de Bruxelles, *see* p.76) indicate that this palace was the crowning glory of Brussels' architecture – until 1731, when it was completely destroyed in just six hours by a fire which apparently started in the kitchens. Charles of Lorraine, the country's Austrian governor from 1749 to

---

Godefroy de Bouillon

An equestrian statue, erected by Leopold I in 1848, dominates the centre of the Place Royale. This is Godefroy de Bouillon (1061–1100), a medieval hero and the subject of numerous legends. Born in Brabant, he became Duke of Lower Lorraine, and was one of the leaders of the First Crusade (1096–9). This succeeded in wresting Jerusalem from the Muslims, after which Godefroy was asked by the crusading kingdoms to take the title of King of Jerusalem. Contrary to the inscription on this statue, he refused, preferring the more modest title *Avoué du Saint-Sépulcre* (Defender of the Holy Sepulchre). He died the following year during a typhoid epidemic, and Jerusalem was subsequently ruled by a series of European kings for almost a hundred years until it was recaptured by Saladin in 1187.

1780, commissioned the French architect Barnabé Guimard to create a new square over the 'Cour Brûlée', and it was built between 1772 and 1785. For the sake of economy the foundations were laid on top of the cellars and underground passageways of the old palace, which still run beneath the cobbles of the square. Some of these have now been exposed to view by excavations in the northeast corner of the square, but their long-term future remains uncertain.

Eglise St-Jacques-sur-Coudenberg F7

Place Royale, t 02 511 7836; metro Trône. Open Sat 10–6, Sun 10am–11am. Guided tours on written request 2 weeks in advance.
The original 18th-century façade of this church was an uncompromising reconstruction of a Graeco–Roman temple. Perhaps it was too pagan a concept for 19th-century sensibilities, for on to this was grafted an incongruous, squat, octagonal bell-tower.

Despite this mongrel exterior, St-Jacques-sur-Coudenberg is one of the loveliest 18th-century churches in Brussels, with a barrel-vaulted nave leading up to the half-domed apse dotted with floral cartouches. There has been a church on this site since the 12th century, when it served as a stopping-off point for pilgrims on their way to Santiago de Compostela in Spain, hence its connection with St James (Iago, Jacques).

St-Jacques-sur-Coudenberg is directly connected to the Palais Royal next door. Members of the royal entourage can cross the palace gardens, take a seat in the royal box on the left-hand side of the choir and peer at the service from behind glass, rather like looking through a railway carriage window.

Two monumental paintings by Jan Frans Portaels (1818–85) hang on either side of the nave. The one on the right depicts people of all nations gathering around the Cross, while the *Crucifixion and Transfiguration of the Heart* on the left centres upon the symbol of the heart, representing charity – an image

Six Hundred and One Baudouins

During the funeral of King Baudouin I on 7 August 1993, which took place in the Cathédrale St-Michel (see p.120), the service was relayed on to a screen at the church of St-Jacques-sur-Coudenberg, which was packed with 600 men all called Baudouin. This somewhat surreal situation arose from a tradition founded by Léopold I whereby the seventh consecutive son in any family is automatically the godson of the monarch, and takes the monarch's name. (The seventh successive daughter takes the name of the queen, but this occurrence is statistically far rarer.)

explored and celebrated in the remarkable Musée Boyadjian du Cœur in the Musée Royaux d'Art et d'Histoire (see p.131). The beautiful white and gold statue of the Virgin to the right of this painting, surrounded by a gilded filigree tree, was brought here from s' Hertogenbosch in the Netherlands in 1629 as a gift from Archduchess Isabella. It survived both the fire of 1731 and the deconsecration of the church during the Napoleonic era (when the building served as a Temple of Reason and Law), and was restored to its place in 1853.

Musées Royaux des Beaux-Arts F6–7

3 Rue de la Régence for Musée d'Art Ancien (15th- to 18th-century art), 1–2 Place Royale for the Musée d'Art Moderne (19th-century to present day art), t 02 508 3211, e info@fine-arts-museum.be, w www.fine-arts-museum .be; metro Gare Centrale; wheelchair accessible. Open Tues–Sun 10–5; closed public hols; adm €5, free first Wed of every month from 1pm.

This combines two museums, the Musée d'Art Ancien (15th to 18th centuries; blue and brown sections on the museum's colour-coded map) and the Musée d'Art Moderne (19th and 20th centuries; green and yellow sections). By the standards of most major national art collections, the Musées Royaux des Beaux-Arts are refreshingly single-minded. The main focus is squarely on Belgian art – or at least the art of the Low Countries, for those centuries before Belgium came into existence. Italy and Spain, even France, barely get a look in, but nonetheless the collection is a ravishing *tour de force* and a monument to the technical virtuosity and distinctive mood of North European art. What you see here in fact represents only about 20 per cent of the museum's total collection, most of which is in storage.

Musée d'Art Ancien

15th and 16th Centuries

Blue section on the first floor, rooms 10–45. Closed for lunch 12–1pm.

The earliest Flemish 'primitive' paintings concentrate primarily on religious subjects, since the Church was the main patron of the arts up to and during the Renaissance. Early Flemish artists depicted these with intense colour and detail, reminiscent of the illuminated manuscripts that were a major influence on their style. One of the most celebrated paintings of this section is *La Justice d'Othon* (The Justice of Otto) in Room 13, a huge narrative diptych by Dirk Bouts (1415–75), which tells the tragic story of the German Holy Roman Emperor Otto II (r.973–83). Secular art, particularly portraiture, becomes increasingly prominent as the decades progress. The influence of the Italian Renaissance can be detected in the growing prevalence of classical architectural settings, meticulously rendered in perspective, and the introduction of subjects from Roman mythology.

Pride of place in this section is given to Pieter Bruegel the Elder (c.1525–69) (Room 31), who lived in Brussels during the later part of his life. What this collection lacks in quantity it makes up for in quality, with the famous *Fall of Icarus* and *The Census in Bethlehem*, one of Bruegel's most endearing works. There are also numerous examples of the work of Bruegel's son, Pieter Bruegel the Younger (1564–1638), whose subjects, often copied from works by his father, are equally

Finding Your Way Around the Musées Royaux des Beaux-Arts

It is worth stopping for a moment to plan your visit. At the reception desk you can pick up a schematized map, which lays out the colour-coded chronological paths leading from room to room, and through the underground galleries that cleverly link the two buildings. An excellent way to start your visit is with the 35-minute audiovisual in Auditorium B on the ground floor. It introduces the history of Belgian art from the 15th to 17th century, focusing on selected works in the collection. The audiovisual is presented more or less continuously, and you can pick up a set of headphones in the language of your choice at the reception desk beforehand, if you leave some form of identity as security.

powerful but whose more polished style lacks the immediacy of his father's painting.

17th and 18th Centuries

Brown section on the first floor, rooms 50–62. Closed for lunch 1–2pm.

The star of this section is Pieter Paul Rubens (1577–1640) (Rooms 52 and 62). For anyone who knows him mainly for his well-fed, rose-pink nudes, this large collection is a revealing insight into his versatility. The paintings in Room 62 are vast, full of drama, and painted with a swift, dynamic touch. *La Montée au Calvaire* (The Ascent to Calvary) and *Le Martyre de Saint Liévin* (The Martyrdom of St Livincus) are extraordinarily stirring works. A visit to the Musées Royaux des Beaux-Arts is justified by the contents of this room alone.

More representative images of the times are provided by the portraits of the well-to-do, full of solid burgher virtues and gravitas, by Antoon (Anthony) van Dyck (1599–1641) (Room 53) and Cornelis de Vos (1584–1651). The paintings of Jacob Jordaens (1593–1678), by contrast, are brimming with ebullience and *joie de vivre*.

Sculpture Gallery

Orange section on the lower ground floor.

This gallery takes you on a brief and (in contrast to the rest of the museum) undistinguished tour of Belgian sculpture from the mid-18th century to the early 20th century. The tour opens with Baroque sculpture in terracotta and some examples of church furniture, followed by Neoclassical pieces from the turn of the 19th century; Mathieu Kessels' work, acquired by the Belgian state after his death in Rome in 1836, is particularly well represented. Next comes the free expression of Romanticism, which inspired the likes of eccentric artist Antoine Wiertz (*see* p.127). The bronze figures of workers by one of the leading exponents of realism in sculpture, Antoine Meunier (1831–1905), are prominent towards the end of the gallery.

Musée d'Art Moderne

19th Century

Yellow section climbing through six floors, rooms 69–91. Closed for lunch 12–1pm.

This is effectively where Belgian art (i.e. after independence) begins, and it contains some of the most fascinating work of the 19th-century Belgian Postimpressionists and Symbolists. **Level −2** begins with the Neoclassical era, and work by the influential French painter Jacques-Louis David (1748–1825), who died in exile in Brussels. The famous *Marat Assassiné* portrays the French Revolutionary Jean-Paul Marat (1743–93), slumped dead in his bath. There is also work on this level by the French Romantic painters Théodore Géricault (1791–1824) and Eugène Delacroix (1798–1863), and the great Belgian odd-ball Antoine Wiertz (1806–65, *see* p.127).

Level −1 is devoted to Realism and includes some rather gloomy landscapes, typical of the celebrated Brussels-based artist Hippolyte Boulenger (1837–74). There are also a few good works by French realists Jean-Baptiste-Camille Corot (1796–1875) and Gustave Courbet (1819–77).

On the right-hand side of **Level +1** is 'Social Art', heralded at the entrance by the strong social-realist work *A l'Aube* (Dawn) by Charles Hermans (1839–1924), in which young and flushed gentlemen spill out on to the street with their women in the early hours under the pious gaze of a family of labourers on their way to do an honest day's work. On the left-hand side of Level +1 is a section devoted to Belgian Impressionism, which includes work by Théo van Rysselberghe (1862–1926) and Henri Evenpoel (1872–99). The right-hand side of **Level +2** takes you through Luminism, the post-impressionist movement founded by Emile Claus (1849–1924), who has few rivals in his ability to evoke the rural idyll.

Continue around Level +2 in a clockwise direction to reach the first part of one of the great collections of Symbolist painters in Europe. There are several classics here, including *Des Caresses/L'Art/Les Caresses* (The Sphinx) by Fernand Khnopff (1858–1921), in which, in a mood of dreamy sensuality set vaguely in antiquity, a male/female figure stands cheek to cheek with a similarly ill-defined personage, whose head is attached to the body of a cheetah. His *Memories/Lawn Tennis* portrays seven women tennis players in an empty green landscape, calm, silent but filled with unspoken thought and pent-up emotion. By contrast, the unrestrained, psychedelic side of Symbolism can be seen on the landing of Level +2 in *Les Trésors de Satan* (Satan's Treasures) by Jean Delville (1867–1953), in which a demonic figure with octopus tentacles for wings steps over a sub-aqua stream of naked damsels and youths lying in sleepy abandon.

Level +3 has a collection entitled 'Pre-Expressionism' with work by the sculptor and painter Rik Wouters (1882–1916) and the sculptor George Minne (1866–1941). Continue clockwise on Level +3 through a small but good collection of French Impressionists and post-impressionist paintings, including work by Monet, Sisley, Seurat, Signac, Gauguin, Vuillard and Bonnard.

This then brings you into a room devoted to one of Belgium's most extraordinary painters, James Ensor (1860–1949), a fascinating and enigmatic precursor of Expressionism. His early paintings, such as the portraits of his mother and father (1881 and 1882) are well executed in a rapid, grainy, impressionistic style, but comparatively controlled and conformist. Within ten years, however, he had taken the imaginative leap into the bizarre personal world for which he is renowned – a world of masks, skeletons and Punch and Judy characters painted in bright, feverish slabs of paint. The small oil *Squelettes se disputant un hareng-saur* (Skeletons arguing over a pickled herring) shows the drift.

20th Century

Green section in six underground levels. Closed for lunch 1–2pm.

The collection is essentially laid out chronologically and includes a spattering of big names such as Dufy, Rouault, Picasso, Braque, Matisse, Nolde, Kokoschka, Chagall, Ernst, de Chirico, Dali, Francis Bacon and Henry Moore. In the opening section on **Level –3** there is a selection of recent acquisitions by Claus Oldenburg, Robert Rauschenberg, Christo, and Allen Jones.

But take this opportunity to study the Belgians instead. The collection includes more paintings and sculptures by Rik Wouters (1882–1916), Postimpressionist in style, bright, cheering, and with a deft sense of finish. Léon Spilliaert (1881–1946) produced melancholic works, implying a remote and inward-looking world, shot through with a unique sense of design. The extensive selection devoted to work by the Sint-Martens-Latem school includes most notably the earth-toned, thickly pasted Expressionist work of Constant Permeke (1886–1952).

Belgium produced two major Surrealist painters. Paul Delvaux (1897–1994) is well represented here, with several large paintings of tram and railway stations peopled by nudes with body hair, and skeletons. The collection of work by René Magritte (1898–1967), mainly the legacy of his wife, Georgette, is a little disappointing, given his huge output (the bulk of his work is in the

USA). Nonetheless it includes plenty of the usual visual puns and incongruities, in sketches, sculptures and paintings – among which is the famous *L'Empire des Lumières*.

The post-war collection includes work from the 1940s group La Jeune Peinture Belge – a highly disparate movement which included the lyrical abstraction of Louis van Lint (1909–89), and the geometric abstraction of Anne Bonnet (1908–60). The influential group Cobra, founded in 1948, is best represented by the near-abstract expressionism of Pierre Alechinsky (b.1927).

Musée des Instruments de Musique (MIM) F6

2 Rue Montagne de la Cour, t 02 545 0130, w www.mim.fgov.be; metro Gare Centrale. Open Tues, Wed and Fri 9.30–5, Thurs 9.30–8, Sat and Sun 10–5; adm €2.50.

This museum is in a former department store called Old England – a throwback to the late 19th century when the British Arts and Crafts movement and Liberty style were all the rage. The building was designed by Paul Saintenoy (1862–1952) and completed in 1899. The building still shows its cast-iron pillars with characteristic swirling Art Nouveau motifs, and steel joists painted with floral decoration.

The interactive museum contains more than 6,000 items from all over the globe and is the biggest of its kind in the world. The collection is mainly European, dating from the Renaissance onwards, and includes numerous interesting oddities, such as the 18th-century kits or *pochettes* – tiny violins which dancemasters could carry about in their pockets. The vast *tromba marina*, dated 1680, is a single-stringed cello-like instrument that can only produce harmonics – amplified by 20 sympathetic strings inside the triangular body – creating the unearthly sound that gave it its misleading name, 'marine trumpet'. The glass harmonica designed by the American statesman and inventor Benjamin Franklin (1706–90) produces a similarly eerie humming sound

by employing the same principle as running a wet finger around the rim of a wine glass. Beethoven and Mozart wrote music for it.

The building retains its top-floor tearoom, which has been transformed into the museum café, Du Mim (*see* p.228), with views over the lower town as far as the Atomium.

Palais Royal G7

Place des Palais, t 02 551 2020; metro Trône; wheelchair accessible. State rooms open end July–early Sept Tues–Sun 10.30–4.30; adm free.

The Palais Royal is a grand if rather cold-looking building, set too close to the road for comfort and with only a sunken formal parterre garden to relieve the weight of its deadening architecture. The interior is spacious, glittering with chandeliers, brocade curtains and polished marble, but rather soulless. It is no surprise that the royal family prefers to live at their other palace at Laeken (*see* p.144). The two wings date from the 18th century, but the central section was rebuilt in the French 18th-century Neoclassical style of Louis XVI in 1904–12. It looks more impressive at night, under its soft pink floodlights.

On special occasions the royal family presents itself on the balcony to crowds assembled in the Place des Palais. This was the scene of a moving demonstration in support of the royal family – and for a united Belgium – after King Baudouin I's death in 1993. On 5 and 6 August, 125,000 people queued in the rain for seven hours or more to pay their last respects to the king, who lay in state in the palace. A few days later, the Place des Palais was thronged with people who had come to greet the new king, Albert II, as he performed the ancient tradition of *La Joyeuse Entrée* (*see* p.129), after swearing his oaths at the Palais de la Nation (*see* below).

The State Rooms

The state rooms themselves are a stilted display of opulence, dripping with candelabra, chandeliers and 19th-century royal portraits. There's the large Throne Room, where official ceremonies are held

The Royal Family

'The king reigns, but he does not govern.' So runs the summary of the role of the Belgian monarchy. The king has a very similar function to that of the British monarch, as head of state and guarantor of the country's constitution, with little real power but a considerable amount of influence.

Today the influence of the Belgian monarchy is largely due to King Baudouin I, who died in 1993. He took over on his 21st birthday in a moment of constitutional crisis when his father, Léopold III, abdicated after being unfairly vilified for his role during the war. Baudouin won popular affection for his understated manner and his fairhanded treatment of both the Flemish and the Walloons, with whom he could converse fluently in both national languages. He and his family were the embodiment of low-key royalty, promoting family values with the common touch entirely suited to modern European constitutional monarchy. Baudouin showed genuine interest when he talked to the ordinary people whose lives he crossed.

There was a major constitutional crisis in 1990 when Baudouin refused to sign a bill legalizing very limited abortion in Belgium. 'Does freedom of conscience apply to everyone but the king?' he asked. In a classic fudge, he abdicated for 24 hours while parliament passed the law. Most of the nation admired him for having the courage of his convictions, even if they did not share them.

The Belgian royal family's roots go back a mere 160 years, to the accession of Léopold of Saxe-Coburg-Gotha, shortly after independence. Since then the family has married with the aristocracy of just about every European nation except Britain. The current heir, Prince Philippe, married the Belgian Princesse Mathilde recently.

who many consider to be the father of modern art.

Musée de la Dynastie G6

7 Place des Palais, t 02 512 2821; metro Trône. Open Tues–Sun 10–6; closed 1 Jan, 21 July and 25 Dec; adm €6.

The Hôtel Bellevue, which was designed by Barnabé Guimard (who was also responsible for the Place Royale), was incorporated into the Palais Royal by Léopold II and now houses this museum. The Musée de la Dynastie tells the public and private history of the Belgian royal family through a collection of paintings, prints, family photographs, furniture, clothing and other mementoes. Even if you are not an avid royal-watcher, it's at least worth a quick visit, if only to be able to put faces to the names of the Belgian royals through their short history and see them in their historical context.

Palais des Académies H6–7

Place des Palais; metro Trône.

This grandiose Neoclassical building, at the foot of the Place des Palais and east of the Palais Royal, was built in 1823–6 for the Dutch King William of Orange, during his brief reign over Belgium prior to independence. It then served as a picture gallery before becoming the seat of the Académie Royale de Belgique, a society of established figures from the arts and sciences.

AROUND PARC DE BRUXELLES

Parc de Bruxelles G6

Metro Parc or Trône. Open daily 6am–9pm.

This is Brussels' most attractive formal park. Ranks of mature trees stand over the broad avenues, which lead past statues, ornate cast-iron benches and fountains to vistas of the palaces at either end. The Dukes of Brabant once owned a famous

(beneath the palace's most outrageous chandeliers); the Hall of Mirrors and the marble salon with its huge chimney pieces; and a number of smaller rooms, including the Goya salon with tapestries designed by the artist

Renaissance pleasure park on this site, known as the Warande, or warren. It is said that its ingenious fountains inspired the architects of the gardens of Versailles Palace. Following the fire of 1731 the Parc de Bruxelles was neglected and fell into ruin until it was renovated in French style after 1778. The unusual layout has invited speculation that it represents the symbols of freemasonry. Certainly from a map or aerial view it is possible to trace out the shapes of several of the masonic symbols, such as the compass, set square and the bricklayer's trowel. The ornate park was designed during the heyday of freemasonry and, like many of his contemporaries, Charles of Lorraine belonged to a freemason's lodge, and therefore, such speculation may have some basis in fact.

In September 1830, during the Belgian Revolution, troops from the Dutch garrison holed up in the park, surrounded by revolutionary barricades and sniped at by insurgents from the windows of houses in the Rue Royale. On the morning of 27 September, however, a party of revolutionaries crept into the park to find it deserted: the Dutch had fled during the night. A joyous mob assembled and invaded the royal palace, where they inspected the royal wardrobe and destroyed portraits of King William of Orange. They also brought out a marble bust of the king, crowned it with a Dutch cheese, and chanted loudly, 'Down with the first and last King of the Netherlands.' Moderation is a Belgian virtue, even in a revolution.

The avenues of the Parc de Bruxelles converge on the huge round pond and fountain at its northern end.

Théâtre Royal du Parc H5

This late 18th-century theatre still contains its original tiered auditorium. It can only be visited on a group tour, but there is a model of it in the foyer, to help theatre-goers to select their seats. The theatre stages well-respected seasons of French plays, both classical and modern.

Palais de la Nation G–H5

Rue de la Loi, public access to the interior via Rue de Louvain behind the building, t 02 549 8136 (Hse of Representatives), t 02 501 7355 (Senate), e pri@lachambre.be, w www .lachambre.be; metro Parc or Arts-Loi. Public galleries are open while the houses are sitting (mid-Oct–end June); closed Sun and public hols; adm free. Guided tours of 1hr available July–mid-Oct daily 10–4; identity documents must be presented at the entrance; tel reservation recommended at least 2 months in advance.

This Neoclassical building was designed by Barnabé Guimard in 1783 as the seat of the ruling council of the Austrian Netherlands. The sculptured pediment, representing Victory and Justice, is the most notable work of Gilles-Lambert Godecharle (1750–1835), sculptor to Napoleon and William of Orange. Since 1830 the Palais de la Nation has been the main parliament building of Belgium.

The interior contains the Senate and House of Representatives. The central government legislature is divided into two houses, along the lines of most western governments. The Representatives (*députés*) and over half the Senate are elected for a four-year term of office. In recent years the role of these houses has been gradually eroded as increased power has been devolved to the regional governments. Nonetheless, they still have responsibility for legislation that affects Belgium as a whole, in fields such as finance, defence and foreign affairs.

Musée de l'Hôtel Charlier I5

16 Av des Arts, t 02 218 5382, e musee-charlier-museum@yahoo.fr, w www.musee-charlier-museum. be; metro Madou. Open Mon 10–5, Tues–Thurs 1.30–5, Fri 1.30–4.30; closed public hols; adm €2.50; ring on the brass doorbell to gain entry.

The Hôtel Charlier is a grand *maison de maître*, built in the 19th century in Neoclassical style. In 1890 it was bought by the wealthy and cultivated Henri van Curtsem, who commissioned Victor Horta to replan the interior. A great patron of the arts, Van Curtsem effectively adopted a poor young sculptor called Guillaume Charlier, and gave the house to him when he retired to the country. Charlier maintained Van Curtsem's tradition that had made the house a cultural meeting point, and he left the house to the surrounding commune, Saint-Josse-ten-Noode, when he died in 1925. Preserved as a museum since 1928, it offers an exceptional insight into the décor of a house where the well-to-do of the late 19th century entertained their friends.

This was a period in which interest in antique furniture was growing, and the house includes a series of rooms in period style, such as the Salon Louis XV, with its fine marquetry bombé chests, and the Salon Chinois, with coromandel lacquer furniture. The Empire-style bedroom contains an excellent collection of furniture and accessories, decorated with ormolu plaques, sphinxes and caryatids. Contemporary late 19th-century taste is represented by paintings by James Ensor, Fernand Khnopff, and Léon Frédéric, and sculpture by Rik Wouters and Charlier himself. Look out for the glass display case by Victor Horta, an ingenious solution to a design problem.

A room at the top of the house provides a historical perspective on the commune of St-Josse: old prints show the city walls that once ran along the street below.

AROUND RUE RAVENSTEIN

Palais des Beaux-Arts G6

23 Rue Ravenstein, t 02 507 8200; metro Parc; wheelchair accessible. Open Sat–Thurs 10–6, Fri 10–8; closed public hols; adm €6.

This was designed in Art Deco style by Victor Horta (*see* p.155) and completed in 1928. It is now a cultural centre, where major

temporary exhibitions and concerts are staged, and home to the Philharmonique de Bruxelles. Horta had to contend with a highly restrictive brief: in order to preserve the view from the Palais Royal he was not allowed to build above the level of the parapet on the Rue Royale.

Along the Rue Baron Horta (he was made a Baron in 1932) the building presents a bold, angular exterior, very different from those of Horta's Art Nouveau heyday. The Palais des Beaux-Arts was to be part of a grand urban redevelopment plan referred to as the Quartier Ravenstein, stretching from here to the Gare Centrale, but it remained unfinished at Horta's death in 1947.

Until the first decade of the 20th century there was a large house and garden where the Palais des Beaux-Arts now stands. This had once been the Pensionnat Héger, a boarding school for girls from wealthy families, which Charlotte Brontë attended in 1842–3, and where she developed an unrequited passion for the husband of the principal (*see* 'Charlotte Brontë in Brussels' box on the next page).

Musée du Cinéma

9 Rue Baron Horta, underneath Palais des Beaux-Arts, t 02 507 8370, e museeducinema @ledoux.be; metro Gare Centrale. Open daily 5.30pm–10.30pm; adm €2.25, or €1.50 if pre-booked 24 hrs in advance; children under 16 not admitted. Tickets valid for 2hrs and include entrance to auditoriums. You can reserve a seat after 9.30am on the day (or on Fri for the weekend), which must be taken up 15mins before the show. Monthly leaflet gives programme details.

There are two auditoriums, one screening a programme of three 'art films' every evening starting at 6.15pm (most shown in their original language with French subtitles), the other showing old silent films at 7pm and 9pm every evening, accompanied by live piano music.

Laid out in the restful, dimly lit foyer are numerous ingenious exhibits to demonstrate the early history of the moving

Charlotte Brontë in Brussels

In February 1842 Charlotte Brontë and her sister Emily were sent to learn French in Brussels. It was a peculiar move for this strictly Protestant family, but the Reverend Brontë considered it a risk worth taking for the further education of his two daughters, who had now reached the comparatively mature ages of 26 and 24 respectively.

The Pensionnat Héger was run by Madame Héger, whose husband Constantin taught French literature in the school. By all accounts it was a fairly relaxed and friendly place, where girls from respectable families were gently educated to the unambitious standards of women's education of the time.

The sisters had nothing but contempt for the Belgians, whose offensive manners the girls attributed to Catholicism. After nine months Charlotte and Emily were fluent and left Brussels. In January 1843 Charlotte returned to the Pensionnat Héger as a teacher of English. She was no happier in this guise, and left at the end of the year on the pretext that her father's growing blindness called for her presence at home.

Charlotte's experiences in Brussels had a profound effect on her. They provided the inspiration and the thinly veiled setting for her two novels: *The Professor* and *Villette*. Both reveal the inner torment of the protagonists as they fall in love with people who cannot return their affection – in the case of *Villette*, this is the older teacher, Monsieur Paul Emanuel. Neither book paints a very flattering picture of Brussels, which in the latter is renamed Villette, the capital of the kingdom of Labassecour.

The reality was yet stranger, and remains shrouded in mystery. Charlotte had clearly developed a strong passion for Monsieur Héger, and once back at Haworth she began writing highly emotional letters to him. All evidence suggests she developed this passion from afar, and received little or no encouragement from him.

A batch of Charlotte's letters was eventually sold to the British Museum by Monsieur Héger's son, principally to allay rumours that Charlotte had had an affair with his father. Some of these letters had apparently been retrieved from the wastepaper basket by Madame Héger, who had little reason to think highly of Charlotte either then or later: in Villette Charlotte portrayed the headmistress as a vain, manipulative and prying woman who was clearly enough identified with Madame Héger to cause great offence. When Mrs Gaskell went to Brussels after Charlotte's death to research her biography, Madame Héger flatly refused to see her, although Monsieur Héger (who has been identified with the character of Paul Emanuel) spoke kindly to her of Charlotte.

---

image. They include such early wonders as the Phénakisticope (1832) and Zoetrope (1834), in which a series of images pasted to spinning drums and discs appear to move. Eadweard Muybridge's experiments of the 1870s, using multiple cameras triggered by people or animals in motion, demonstrated the potential of photography to show movement, a concept pursued in conjunction with the magic lantern by Emile Reynaud in 1881. But the breakthrough was made ten years later by Thomas Edison with his Kinetograph using celluloid film. This history is succinctly explained through working models and various historic exhibits, many of them set up to operate at the push of a button.

Hôtel Ravenstein F6

*3 Rue Ravenstein; **metro** Parc or Gare Centrale.*

This attractive red-brick building with a stepped gable is the only substantial survivor of the old Coudenberg quarter, dating from the 15th century. It formed part of the palace of the Princes of Cleves-Ravenstein and was the birthplace of Anne of Cleves (1515–57), fourth wife of Henry VIII of England. This was a disastrous political marriage: Henry found her not to his taste and declared that he could 'never in her company be provoked and steered to know her carnally'. Dubbing her the 'Flemish Mare', he divorced Anne of Cleves the same year as he married her, 1540.

The building is now home to the Royal Society of Engineers and a restaurant called Relais de Caprices (*see* p.225).

MONT DES ARTS

This is the area that links the upper and lower towns. A wide stone stairway leads up from the Place de l'Albertine through a formal rectangle of gardens, with lavender beds and fountains, towards the Place du Musée and the art museums. The gardens, which are flanked by the imposing buildings of the royal library and the Palais des Congrés, were laid out in the French style by René Pechère in 1956. At the summit of the Mont des Arts, a sculpture named the 'Whirling Ear' stands in the middle of a fountain, from where there are views right across the old town. During the day the Mont des Arts is a busy pedestrian thoroughfare, with weary tourists resting on benches and skateboarders honing their skills. At night the area has a reputation as a gay pick-up point.

Carillon Clock F6

Mont des Arts (on the archway over the lower end of the road); metro Gare Centrale.

The clock has 24 bells and 12 characters, one for each hour. Just before the hour a figure emerges while the bells sing out their tunes – one Walloon, the other Flemish at alternate hours – before the top-hatted burgher strikes the hour. The sculptures represent key figures from Belgian history, such as a Gaul, Godefroy de Bouillon, Philip the Good, Charles V, Count Egmont (holding his severed head under one arm), and a tam-tam player, representing the Belgian Congo.

Carillon clocks, found throughout the Low Countries, were developed around 1500, when sets of small bells, designed to play simple tunes, were attached to town clocks in order to alert the citizens to the coming hour. The carillon on the Mont des Arts is a modern version, erected in the early 1960s.

The surrounding complex of buildings is known collectively as the Albertine, originally planned as a memorial to Albert, but not constructed until 1954–69. The building on the left as you face up the hill is a congress centre, the Palais des Congrès.

Bibliothèque Royale Albert I E6

*4 Bvd de l'Empereur, t 02 519 5311, e serveduc @kbr.be, w www.kbr.be; metro Gare Centrale. **Open** (only to registered cardholders) Mon–Fri 9–7.50, Sat 9–4.50. To become a card-holder you'll need your passport or identity card and it costs €15 per year, €2.50 per week.*

This is Belgium's national library, housing a collection that began in the 15th century with the illuminated manuscripts of the Dukes of Burgundy and containing pretty much everything published in Belgium.

Musée de l'Imprimerie (Printing Museum) E6

*t 02 519 5356. **Open** Mon–Sat 9am–5pm; closed last week in Aug; adm free.*

This is spread out along the marbled corridors of the floor below the entrance to the library. It consists of a collection of old printing presses and equipment, from massive hand-pulled presses and compositors' trays to hot-metal casting machines, bewilderingly complex monotype keyboards and a vast camera on a wooden frame for making early photographic plates. It offers a brief glimpse of the world of printing, which computer technology has rendered archaic in less than two decades.

Musée du Livre (Museum of the Book) E6

*t 02 519 5357. **Open** Mon, Wed and Sat 2–5pm; closed last week of Aug; adm free.*

This is a little gem on the same floor as the Musée de l'Imprimerie, but with frustratingly restricted visiting hours. The museum occupies just one small room – a womb-like interior of dark carpeting and softly lit display cases, containing books of up to 1,200 years old. The 12th- and 13th-century exhibits date from the heyday of the illuminated manuscript, while a printed text from Japan of AD 770 is a salutary reminder that Gutenberg's breakthrough in around 1430 was not so much printing itself but the development of movable type. The earliest European printed book on display, dating from 1474, is so immaculately preserved that it might have been printed 50 years ago, not 500. There are also 16th-century books from Christopher Plantin's famous workshop in Antwerp (*see* p.206), and a priceless manuscript by Matisse illustrating a work by the 15th-century poet Charles d'Orléans.

The short entrance passageway to the museum is lined with a series of reconstructed rooms which show donated collections of books displayed in their original settings. They include a stylish Art Nouveau library with furniture by Henri Van de Velde, the theatrically decorated study of the celebrated Belgian playwright Michel de Ghelderode, and the study of the Belgian poet Emile Verhaeren from his house at St-Cloud.

Palais de Charles de Lorraine F6

1 Place du Musée, t 02 519 5786, w www .kbr.be; metro Gare Centrale. Open Tues–Sun 10–noon and 1–5; adm free.

This 18th-century palace attached to the royal library was built for Charles de Lorraine, the country's Austrian governor from 1749 to 1780. The palace's surviving apartments are now a museum charting intellectual developments in the 18th century. The five salons are each devoted to a different discipline: science, music, cartography, and (believe it or not) the art of table-setting.

Service de Chalcographie

1 Place du Musée, t 02 519 5630; metro Gare Centrale. Open Mon–Fri 9–12.45 and 2–4.45; closed public hols and last week in Aug. Press the bell to gain access, and follow signs that lead down several storeys.

Chalcography is a fancy name for the art of engraving using copper plates. This department of the Bibliothèque Royale Albert I owns a collection of 5,400 engraving plates which include everything from old views of Brussels to abstract art. You can buy prints over the counter or select others from their catalogue, which will then be printed using traditional presses.

Chapelle Royale F6

2 Place du Musée; metro Gare Centrale. Opening times vary, usually Sun pm only.

This small chapel is worth seeing if you are in the right place at the right time. It is a pearl: an ornate Neoclassical sanctuary, full of light. It was built in the 1760s by Charles of Lorraine (you can see the double Cross of Lorraine on the capitals and balustrades), but in the 1790s it was turned into a stable by the French revolutionary army. In 1802, under a decree issued by Napoleon, Protestants were given freedom of worship in Belgium, and the chapel was restored as a Protestant church in 1804. The interior was then pasted with copious layers of whitewash, which preserved the delicate plasterwork until its renovation to pristine condition in 1987. Charlotte Brontë, a fervent Protestant, came to worship here during her stay at the nearby Pensionnat Héger in the 1840s.

Marolles and Sablon

Marolles and Sablon

'Faire du lèche-vitrines' ('window-licking') is an activity indulged in with much relish by the Bruxellois. You can window-shop to your heart's content in the charming Sablon district – an old residential quarter which is now the focus of Brussels' upmarket antiques trade, with a number of chic art galleries thrown in. From here it is only a short walk southeast to the area called Porte Louise (around Place Louise) – Brussels' answer to the Champs-Elysées – a showpiece of Euro-commerce with a roll call of the world's most revered designer names.

This chapter is not entirely dedicated to Mammon, however. It includes Brussels' loveliest Gothic church, the Eglise Notre-Dame du Sablon, and the gargantuan Palais de Justice. In the shadow of the Palais de Justice lies the Marolles district. This is the old artisans' quarter, with a long and ragged history, its own dialect and its own inalienable scruffiness.

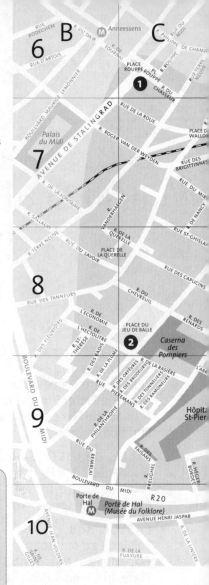

1 Lunch

Comme Chez Soi, *23 Place Rouppe,* **t** *02 512 2921;* **metro** *Anneessens.* **Open** *Tues–Sat noon–2 and 7–10; closed July.* **Expensive.** Brussels' premier restaurant. Exquisite concoctions of eel, truffle and lobster, all beautifully presented in an intimate setting.

2 Tea and Cakes

De Skieven Architek, *50 Place du Jeu de Balle,* **t** *02 514 4369;* **bus** *48.* **Open** *daily 6am–1am.* Welcoming modern bar-café with a sense of Marollien history, views over the market and a good beer and snack menu.

3 Drinks

Chez Richard, *2 Rue des Minimes,* **t** *02 512 1406;* **metro** *Porte de Namur or Gare Centrale;* **tram** *92, 93, 94.* **Open** *Mon–Wed 7am–2am, Thurs–Sat 7am–3am, Sun 9am–midnight.* A lively little drinking den fashionable with rich young people who shout over the music.

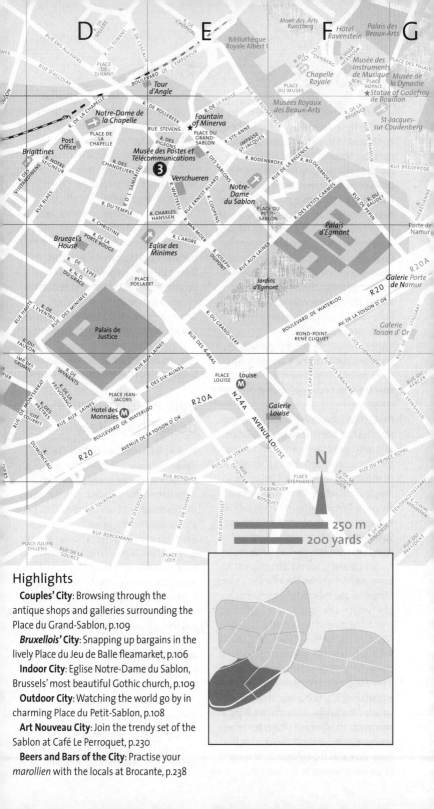

D **E** **F** **G**

RUE DE VILLERS
R. DE DINANT
R. D'ESCALIER
RUE DE L'HÔPITAL
RUE DES ALEXIENS
RUE D'ACCOLAY
PLACE DE DINANT
BOULEVARD DE L'EMPEREUR

Mont des Arts
Kunstberg
Hôtel Ravenstein
Palais des Beaux-Arts
PLACE DES PALAIS
R. DU MUSÉE
MUSENBERG
R. VILLA HERMOSA
Musée des Instruments de Musique
Musée de la Dynastie
Chapelle Royale
PLACE DU MUSÉE
PLACE ROYALE
★ Statue of Godefroy de Bouillon
St-Jacques-sur Coudenberg
Musées Royaux des Beaux-Arts

Bibliothèque Royale Albert I

Tour d'Angle
R. DE ROLLEBEEK
Notre-Dame de la Chapelle
RUE STEVENS
Fountain of Minerva
RUE DE LA PAILLE
R. DE RUYSBROECK
R. DE LA REGENCE

PLACE DE LA CHAPELLE
R. DE LA CHAPELLE
Post Office
Brigittines
R. DES VISITANDINES
R. NOTRE SEIGNEUR
RUE BLAES
R. DES CHANDELIERS
R. D L SAMARITIN
PLACE DU GRAND-SABLON
R. DES PIGEONS
Musée des Postes et Télécommunications
❸
R. STE-ANNE
IMPASSE ST-JACQUES
R. DES SABLONS
R. BODENBROEK
R. DE LA REGENCE
R. BODENBROEK

Verschueren
R. WATTEEU
R. DU TEMPLE
R. CHARLES HANSSEN
R. ERNEST ALLARD
R. COOPENS
Notre-Dame du Sablon
PLACE DU PETIT-SABLON
R. DES PETITS CARMES
R. DE REPIN
R. DU BAUDET
RUE BREDERODE
THERESIENNE

Porte de Namur

Bruegel's House
R. CHRISTINE
R. DE LA PORTE ROUGE
R. DE L'EPEE
R. N D DU GRACE
R. VAN MOER
R. L'ARORE
R. JOSEPH DUFONT
RUE AUX LAINES
Palais d'Egmont

Eglise des Minimes

PLACE POELAERT
Jardins d'Egmont
Galerie Porte de Namur
R20A
R20
BOULEVARD DE WATERLOO
AV. DE LA TOISON D'OR
R. DES CHEVALIERS
Galerie Toison d'Or
RUE DE STASSART

RUE HAUTE
R. DE L'EVENTAIL
RUE DES MINIMES
R. DU FAUCON
Palais de Justice
RUE AUX LAINES
RUE DES 4-BRAS
R. DU GRAND-CERF
ROND-POINT RENÉ CLIQUET

IMP DES GROSEIL
R. DE MONTSERRAT
R. DE WYNANTS
R. DE LA PREVOYANCE
R. DES PRETRES
CITÉ COURBET
R. AUX LAINES
PLACE JEAN-JACOBS
R. DES SIX-AUNES
PLACE LOUISE
Louise Ⓜ
RUE CAP CRESPEL
RUE DES DRAPIERS
RUE SEYNEVELD
RUE DU BERGER

DUMONCEAU
Hotel des Monnaies Ⓜ
BOULEVARD DE WATERLOO
R20A
N24A
AVENUE LOUISE
Galerie Louise

AVENUE DE LA TOISON D'OR
RUE JEAN STRASS
RUE DHONEECK
R. DE SA CROIX OUR
R. DU PRINCE ROYAL

PLACE JULIEN DILLENS
RUE DE LA SOURCE
RUE JOURDAN
RUE D'ECOSSE
RUE DE SUISSE
RUE BOSQUET
RUE CAPOUILLET
PLACE STÉPHANIE
R. DEJONCKER
R. BOSQUET
PLACE LOIX
EENDRACHTSTR
N

RUE BERCKMANS

N

250 m
200 yards

Highlights

Couples' City: Browsing through the antique shops and galleries surrounding the Place du Grand-Sablon, p.109

Bruxellois' **City**: Snapping up bargains in the lively Place du Jeu de Balle fleamarket, p.106

Indoor City: Eglise Notre-Dame du Sablon, Brussels' most beautiful Gothic church, p.109

Outdoor City: Watching the world go by in charming Place du Petit-Sablon, p.108

Art Nouveau City: Join the trendy set of the Sablon at Café Le Perroquet, p.230

Beers and Bars of the City: Practise your *marollien* with the locals at Brocante, p.238

MAROLLES

The term Marolles is often used loosely to describe the area around the Rue Haute and Rue Blaes, but true Bruxellois will put you right: the Marolles lies strictly around the foot of the Galgenberg hill on which the Palais de Justice stands, to the west of the palais and northeastwards to Notre-Dame de la Chapelle. It used to occupy a larger part of the Galgenberg, but some 1,000 houses were forcibly cleared to make way for the Palais de Justice's huge plinth. This caused great outrage, and the architect, Joseph Poelaert (1817–79), became the object of hatred. The expression '*de skieven architek*' ('filthy architect') soon became a term of serious abuse in the Marolles.

The Bruxellois are proud of the Marolles traditions, but what these are today is hard to pin down. This area went into a tailspin after the River Senne was vaulted over in the 1860s, when many of the old industries on its banks closed down or relocated. Once the Marolles had been the home of proud artisans, who spoke their own distinct version of *bruxellois* called *marollien*, incomprehensible to all but themselves. Now it became a marginalized refuge for casualties of the Industrial Revolution, with its own subculture and ready violence, its lively bars and Sunday dancehalls. It still had a certain appeal. The late 19th-century *Guide des Plaisirs à Bruxelles* speaks admiringly of '*les jeunes apaches et leurs fidèles amies*' ('young tearaways and their faithful girlfriends'); however, it warns its readers to be discreet in their admiration of these pretty Marolliennes, 'for these ladies' companions will readily box with any overzealous admirers – outside working hours'.

The Marolles is undergoing redevelopment, encouraging arty bric-a-brac shops, small galleries and design studios which bring a new touch of colour and vitality to the area. However, plenty of detractors deplore this development at the expense, as they see it, of the real character of the Marolles.

Tour d'Angle D–E6

Bvd de l'Empereur; **metro** *Gare Centrale.*

This half-ruined, circular corner tower is a rare survivor of the first set of defensive city walls. It may look solid enough, but it is modest compared with the huge city walls built two centuries later. Note the arrow slits, whose French title *meurtrières* ('killers') graphically describes their function.

The tower stood close to the Steenpoort gate (demolished in 1760), around which the Marollien community was clustered. Both the tower and the gate were used as prisons. During the 15th century the Tour d'Angle became known as the *pyntorre*, because it housed a torture chamber. François Anneessens, a guild leader who led a rebellion against Austrian rule, was apparently held in the tower before his execution in 1719, and hence the Tour d'Angle is sometimes referred to as the Tour d'Anneessens.

Eglise Notre-Dame de la Chapelle D7

Place de la Chapelle; **metro** *Gare Centrale; wheelchair accessible.* **Open** *June–Sept 9–5, Oct–May 11.30–4.30; closed public hols.*

The fortress-like grandeur of this church, with its orbed and black-shingled clock tower and its massive creamy-white stone walls, has made it one of the great landmarks of Brussels. Built originally in the 13th century, the church belongs to that transitional period when the pointed Gothic arch was beginning to emerge from the intersection of rounded Romanesque arches. The choir and transept are essentially Romanesque, whereas the nave and aisles are Gothic, added in the 15th century. The curious clock tower was a later addition by Antoon Pastorana after the church was damaged by the French bombardment of 1695.

The Interior

The interior is an elevating space of arching stone vaults, lit by Gothic windows. The statues of the apostles on the columns of the nave are a typical 17th-century device. The sculptors include Jan Cosyns, Luc Fayd'Herbe and Jérôme Duquesnoy the Younger. The wooden pulpit, dating from 1721, is another example of exuberant Baroque carving by Pierre-Denis Plumier.

Notre-Dame de la Chapelle is noted as the burial place of Pieter Bruegel the Elder (*see* p.46), and the third side chapel of the south aisle is dedicated to his memory. Born in Flanders, he trained in the studio of Pieter Coecke in Antwerp, but moved to Brussels in 1563 and lived on the Rue Haute before his death in Brussels in 1569, at the age of 44.

Eglise des Brigittines C7

From the northwestern corner of the Place de la Chapelle, you can look down the Rue des Brigittines to the red-brick and stone façade of the Eglise des Brigittines. Unfortunately this is as much as you can see of this pretty little Italo–Flemish church, built

in the 1660s for a religious order named after the 14th-century Swedish mystic and saint, Ste Brigitte. The church was damaged in the 1695 bombardment, and the convent was suppressed in 1784, after which the building had a varied career as a prison (1792), a poorhouse (after 1794) then, after the 1850s, a butcher's shop with a dancehall overhead. In a sorry state of neglect, it is now used for periodic cultural events; its crumbling, dilapidated interior provides an intense and dramatic setting for performances on an impromptu scaffolding stage.

House of Pieter Bruegel the Elder D8

132 Rue Haute; **metro** *Louise.* **Open** *Wed and Sun pms, and to groups on written request.*

Pieter Bruegel the Elder apparently lived in this house from 1563 until his death in 1569. This restored, step-gabled house indicates

---

Getting to the Roots of Marolles and Sablon

Brussels first became a walled city in around 1100, when a modest stone curtain was erected around today's city centre and the palace quarter on the Coudenberg hill. Some 250 years later a vast new wall was constructed about 1km further out, gathering into its protective embrace a motley collection of religious foundations, market gardens, and the homes of thousands of the merchants, artisans and labourers who were the key to the city's burgeoning wealth.

A ridge of higher ground lay on the southern perimeter of the city, between the Coudenberg and the Galgenberg ('Gallows Hill'), the place of public execution. On the slopes between these hills was an open space traditionally used as a horse market. It became known in French as the Sablon (*sablon* means fine sand). Around the skirt of the Galgenberg lay a teeming artisans' quarter, the powerhouse of Brussels' textile trade. Here weavers, dyers and bleachers lived, close to the central markets and to the

river on whose banks much of the industry was conducted. During the 17th century the religious foundation, Les Sœurs Marolles, was set up at the southern end of the city, near to the present Rue de Montserrat, and gradually this area took on their name – the Marolles. (Some claim, however, that the term is derived from the Spanish *marrullero*, meaning cunning or wily, a description of its inhabitants.) In the 17th century the Sablon marsh was drained and merchants and the nobility began to build their homes here. The church for the people of the Marolles remained Notre-Dame de la Chapelle, while the daintier folk of the Sablon attended Notre-Dame du Sablon.

The distinction between the two quarters is just as real today. The spacious Sablon, with its step-gabled houses, antiques shops and restaurants, is clearly where the money is. The Marolles is rough and ready, with overcrowded housing, knots of idle youths and a car-boot-sale atmosphere which emanates from the daily market in the Place du Jeu de Balle and pervades the dingy bars.

how this district might have looked in the 16th century when it was a prosperous suburb. So little is known about Bruegel's life that it is not certain that he did live here. However, it does seem that the house belonged to Anne Bruegel, Bruegel's grand-daughter, who probably inherited it through her father, Jan ('Velvet') Bruegel.

Around the Place du Jeu de Balle C8

Metro *Porte de Hal.*

This large square – where a ball game similar to *pelota* used to be played, and known to older Bruxellois for its black market during the war – is now the scene of a daily fleamarket (7am–2pm), which augments considerably on Sunday mornings (*see* p.251). This is the opposite end of the antiques trade from the Sablon. Here stallholders try to shift bits of carpet, brass odds and ends, shop mannequins and execrable oil paintings. But you may also find interesting craftwork among the dross, and some real bargains.

Facing the square, on Rue Blaes, is the **Caserne des Pompiers**, the old red-brick fire station, designed by Joseph Poelaert and built in 1863 as one of the most advanced fire stations of its day. It has been imaginatively renovated and now houses junk shops, small art galleries and book shops.

On Rue de la Rasière, is **Cité de la Rasière**, a public housing complex divided into lateral streets named after guilds, such as Orfèvres (goldsmiths) and Brodeurs (embroiderers). These are folksy names applied when the complex was built in 1912. This could be just another depressing backwater of shabby tenements were it not for the inventive use of polychromatic brick.

Porte de Hal B10

Metro *Porte de Hal. Closed at the time of writing – when it does **reopen**, the times will be Tues–Sun 10–5; closed public hols.*

The isolated, impressively bold Porte de Hal houses the **Musée du Folklore**, a branch of the Musées Royaux d'Art et d'Histoire.

The sheer scale of this bastion gives some idea of the ambitious size of the second perimeter wall that was built around Brussels over three decades after 1357. The wall was 7km long in all, with 72 defensive towers and seven fortified gates. This one is the sole surviving remnant. In 1782 the modernizing Austrian monarch Joseph II decreed the dismantling of all city walls in his empire, as weapons technology had rendered them redundant. The Porte de Hal, however, was retained because it served as a prison. In the 1840s it was once again reprieved, and began its career as a museum. When there was widespread rebuilding in Brussels during the 1860s, it was radically restored and embellished. As a result, what you see today is partly a truncated city gate and partly a Neo-Gothic fantasy castle.

The Interior

In the vaulted hall on the first floor you can look down through glass plates to where a huge portcullis was once lowered. The robust military tone is curiously disarmed by a display of 'folklore' items – a modest collec-tion of Toone puppets and toys. A spiral staircase decorated with sculptures of medieval figures, leads to the upper storey, from where you may be allowed to walk around the parapet. Views extend over the Marolles and across the city to the Atomium.

PALAIS DE JUSTICE AND PORTE LOUISE

Place Poelaert D–E8

Metro *Louise.*

This square stands before the Palais de Justice. The monument on the corner is a tribute from the British to the Belgians who helped wounded British soldiers and pris-oners during the First World War.

There is a vantage point on the northwest side of the square. The view north across

Brussels has been blighted by the intrusion of ugly rooftops. Nonetheless, you can still look across western Brussels to the green copper dome of the 20th-century Basilique Nationale du Sacré Cœur (*see* p.141). Straight ahead is Notre-Dame de la Chapelle, and to the right is the distinctive spire of the Hôtel de Ville. Immediately below stand the modern tenements of the Marolles.

Palais de Justice D8

1 Place Poelaert, t 02 508 6578; metro Louise. Open Mon–Fri 9–3; closed public hols; adm free. Guided tours (€25) on written request.

The Palais de Justice is a monumental hulk of a building. The area that it covers, 180m by 170m, made it the largest construction in continental Europe in the 19th century. Its dome – an elaborate confection of copper and gilt – rises to 105m. It cost 50 million francs to build, a huge sum in its day, contested as sheer folly by many Bruxellois. The plan was initiated under Leopold I in 1833 but was not undertaken until the reign of Leopold II. It was the crowning achievement of Joseph Poelaert, who paid for it with his sanity. Building started in earnest in 1866 and was not completed until 1883, by which time Poelaert had died in a mental asylum – the victim, according to legend, of a witch from the Marolles.

The Interior

You can wander the public hallways of this extraordinary building. Subtlety was not Poelaert's strong card and, using every trick in the Neoclassical book, the ranks of giant columns lining the entrance portico seem designed to belittle anyone who passes between them. But this is nothing compared with the interior, consisting mainly of one colossal atrium, with broad marble stairs rising on either side to the galleries. Two bizarre allegorical canvases by the visionary Symbolist Jean Delville, painted in 1914, hang at either end of the first-floor gallery. The waiting hall is known as the *Salle des Pas Perdus* ('Hall of Lost Footsteps'), particularly appropriate for its disorientating scale.

Almost as an afterthought, there are 25 courtrooms tucked away in the walls of this building, including the *Cour de Cassation*, the highest court in the land. Groups of lawyers and their anxious clients pepper the floor, speaking in hushed tones. All around them, and over the city outside, the architecture booms imperiously: 'Justice Shall Be Done!'

Around Place Louise E9

Metro Louise.

The Boulevard de Waterloo and the Avenue de la Toison d'Or form part of the busy thoroughfare called the *Petite Ceinture*, which rings the city centre along the course of the ancient city walls. The area between the former sites of two city gates – the Porte Louise and the Porte de Namur – forms one of Brussels' most impressive shopping zones, with covered modern galleries leading off the Avenue de la Toison d'Or to the south – the Galerie Louise, the Galerie de la Toison d'Or and the Galerie Porte de Namur. This is where Eurocrats come to spend Euromoney and lounge in smart pavement cafés.

Around the top of the Avenue Louise the concentration of famous names thickens: Chanel, Versace, Gucci. This grand boulevard, shaded by chestnut trees, is considered the smartest street in Brussels. Lining the pavements are galleries, showrooms for exclusive furniture designers, and the kind of couturiers' boutiques where you wonder if the decimal point has been left out of the prices. *See* p.250 for more information on shopping in this area.

Galerie Louise F9

Entrances on Av Louise and Av de la Toison d'Or; wheelchair accessible.

This 20th-century Aladdin's Cave is a showcase of elegant style, packed with shops selling mainly *haute couture*, jewellery, and shoes that smell sweetly of fine leather – all of which will be delicately giftwrapped and emblazoned with prestigious shop names to make you feel especially good about parting with your money.

SABLON

This old residential quarter centres around two charming squares – Place du Grand-Sablon and Place du Petit-Sablon – with Brussels' Gothic centrepiece, the church of Notre-Dame au Sablon, in their midst. At lunch time wealthy Bruxellois discuss auction pieces over a meal at one of the over-priced cafés that line the main square – a far cry from the trade in *brocante* (junk) just down the hill in Marolles. At the lower end of the Place du Grand-Sablon, a fan of cosy streets with restaurants, cafés and antiques leads down towards Rue Haute.

Palais d'Egmont F7–8

Rue aux Laines; gardens accessible from Rue du Grand-Cerf; **metro** *Louise.*

This was the site of Count Egmont's 16th-century mansion. In the 18th century it was replaced by the Neoclassical palace of the Duke of Arenberg, who had married the Egmont heiress. Destroyed by fire in 1891, the palace was rebuilt in the same style, and now belongs to Belgium's Ministry of Foreign Affairs. In 1972, Great Britain, Ireland and Denmark signed the treaty here that brought them into the European Community.

Jardin d'Egmont E–F8

The palace garden is now a slightly forlorn public park, but affords good views of the palace, albeit now over-restored in kitsch shades of pink and grey. The park has a statue of Charles-Joseph, Prince de Ligne (1735–1814). Diplomat, statesman, writer and friend of both Charles of Lorraine and the unpopular Joseph II, he was the personification of the cosmopolitan ruling class of the Austrian Netherlands. Dubbed the 'Prince Charming of Europe', he is remembered for his epigram: '*Chaque homme a deux patries: la sienne et puis la France*' ('Every man has two fatherlands: his own, and France').

Place du Petit-Sablon E–F7

Metro *Louise.*

The formal gardens in the middle of this square were laid out in 1890 by Henri Beyaert (1823–94). They are dedicated to Counts Egmont and Hornes, and to the spirit of the struggle for liberty and enlightenment that marked the medieval and Renaissance periods. During the reign of Charles V both men had distinguished military records and were respected establishment figures by the time William of Orange led a rebellion of nobles against the repressive régime of Philip II. Although they sided with the rebels,

---

Edith Cavell

On 12 October 1915 the Germans executed Edith Cavell in Brussels. They could hardly have made a greater mistake. In the UK it was seen as an act of unbelievable barbarity, and military recruitment surged. Shortly thereafter the Americans joined the war. If Allied propagandists were to be believed, it was a turning point in Germany's fortunes.

Edith Cavell was a rather prim and humourless 49-year-old British nurse – on paper, not obvious material for a heroine. However, she was deeply respected in Brussels even before the war. She had gone there in 1906, and through years of devoted duty had transformed the Belgian nursing

system into a proper profession. Her work was acknowledged by the queen and did much to promote the respectability of careers for women in general.

At the outbreak of war and German occupation, Edith Cavell was directrice of three Brussels hospitals. In the meantime, a Belgian nobleman and his wife, the Prince and Princesse de Croy, had allowed their estate near Mons to become a refuge for Allied soldiers caught behind enemy lines. These men had to be carefully escorted to freedom by crossing the border to the Netherlands. Before long Edith Cavell had been recruited to provide refuge for Allied soldiers at her nursing institute, and at other safe houses in Brussels. She threw herself they were moderates. Notwithstanding, they were singled out, found guilty of treason, and beheaded in the Grand' Place in 1568. This made them heroes to a nation which saw them as unjustly punished for defending the legitimate rights of the people.

Statues of the counts stand over the central fountain. They are joined by sculptures of other luminaries from the same epoch of Belgian history. Such historical statues crop up all over Brussels, reflecting the concerted bid of the Belgian authorities in the 19th century to establish the cultural heritage of their new nation. An endearing feature of these gardens is the series of 48 small statues depicting representatives of the various medieval guilds of Brussels – also noted defenders of their liberties.

Place du Grand-Sablon E7

Metro *Gare Centrale or Louise.*

This large, triangular square was laid out in the late 17th century and is still fronted by old step-gabled façades. At weekends a superior antiques market (*see* p.251) clusters around the foot of the Eglise Notre-Dame du Sablon. To the northwest of the square is the **Rue de Rollebeek**, a sloping, cobbled street lined with step-gabled houses, restaurants and furnishing shops.

Eglise Notre-Dame du Sablon E7
Rue de la Régence. **Open** *Mon–Fri 9–5, Sat 10–5, Sun 1–5; closed during church services.*

Also known as Notre-Dame des Victoires, this is Brussels' most beautiful Gothic church. Unfortunately the grime-blackened external masonry is in a decrepit state, but the interior is like a magic lantern. Soft light filters through the stained glass and the semicircular choir is particularly lovely, lit by 11 towering lancet windows.

The Guild of Crossbowmen (*arbalétriers*) built a chapel on this site in 1304. In 1348 Baet Soetken, a hemp weaver from Antwerp, heard celestial voices instructing her to steal a wooden statue of the Madonna and take it to Brussels. She brought the statue in a boat and it was set up in the crossbowmen's chapel and became the focus of fervent devotion. Margaret of Austria (Regent to Charles V) joined the cult, bringing the church into the ambit of the royal quarter nearby. The Sablon became the starting-point for the city's grand processions, notably the *Ommegang* (*see* p.268), which still sets out from here. The Gothic church of today was built in the 15th and 16th centuries to accommodate the cult. The statue itself, however, was destroyed by iconoclasts in 1580. A large model of the boat sits on top of the entrance porch inside the church.

into this work with little concern for her own safety and was fully aware that the penalties would be severe if she was caught.

When the Germans eventually realized that enemy soldiers were crossing out of Belgium, they used an agent to infiltrate the de Croys' network. Edith Cavell was arrested along with other members of her cell, but not before 200 Allied soldiers had won their freedom. She was held in St-Gilles prison and at a military court she was sentenced to death by firing squad. The international community in Brussels made vigorous protests, to no avail.

Edith Cavell prepared herself for her death with her customary fastidiousness. She said on parting, 'I know now that patriotism is not enough. I must have no hatred and no bitterness toward anyone.' At the shooting range, she apparently conducted herself with such dignity that the firing squad aimed above her head. She fainted, and the commander of the squad walked up and shot her in the head. At the end of the war Edith Cavell's body was repatriated and taken to Norwich for burial. The funeral cortège passed through London, its silent streets lined with crowds numbering tens of thousands.

In Brussels Edith Cavell is remembered with great affection, and one of its most prestigious hospitals is named after her.

The wealth of the congregation can be judged by the elegant family tombs and the coats of arms in the stained glass. Two marbled Baroque chapels were erected in the 17th century by the Turn and Taxis family; the Chapel of St Ursula, contains the family vault and a sculpture of St Ursula by Jérôme Duquesnoy the Younger. Valuable altarpieces that used to adorn this church have since been removed to the safety of the Musée Communal in the Grand' Place (*see* p.76) and the Musées Royaux des Beaux-Arts (*see* p.91). However, next to the Chapel of St Ursula is a triptych of the Resurrection (and donors) by Michiel Coxie (1499–1592), painter to the court of King Philip II.

Musée des Postes et Télécommunications E7
*40 Place du Grand-Sablon, t 02 511 7740. Closed at time of writing, due to **reopen** in 2002 on Tues–Sat 10–4.30, Sun and public hols 10–12.30; **adm** free.*

In 1500 the head of the Turn and Taxis family was made Master of the Posts. Within half a century the family controlled the most effective post and messenger service in Europe. This small museum is worth visiting if only to admire the huge boots – like plaster casts – worn by postillions, and the historic letterboxes (dating from their introduction in 1800). Exhibits in the telecommunications section explain various communications systems that led from the 'visual telegraph' set on hilltops – which linked Brussels to Paris in 1803 – to the first electrical telegraph networks introduced with the railways.

Fountain of Minerva E7

In the centre of the square, is a weather-beaten statue of Minerva, the Roman goddess of war. It replaced an earlier fountain that had drained the water from the Sablon marshes. The new fountain was gifted by an Englishman, Thomas Bruce, second Earl of Aylesbury. He lived on the square during his 45 years in exile in Brussels (1696 to 1741) – the price of supporting James II, who fled the English throne in 1688.

Verschueren E7
16 Rue Watteeu, t 02 511 0444, w www .belgian-lace.com; metro Louise or Gare Centrale. Open daily 9–6.

This commercial enterprise serves as a centre for the Belgian lace industry. Here you can see a lacemaker at work, a video explaining the art of lacemaking and its survival as a cottage industry, and hundreds of samples of real Belgian lace. All these are for sale, at prices ranging from €15 to €1,000.

Eglise des Sts-Jean-et-Etienne aux Minimes D8
62 Rue des Minimes; metro Louise or Gare Centrale. Open daily 10–1.

This church was built between 1700 and 1715 when the Neoclassical style was taking over from Flemish Baroque. Hiding behind an unpromising façade is a church of cool simplicity, as befitted the Minimes, a mendicant order of monks. The Italian order came to Brussels in 1616 and built a convent on this site. The convent was closed down in 1796 during the French occupation, but the church was restored to use in 1819.

The small chapel of Notre-Dame de Lorette to the right of the nave reveals a more surprising Italian connection. In wild contrast to the rest of the church, the walls are painted with naïve murals bright with Mediterranean colour. The chapel was built as a reconstruction of the Santa Casa, Christ's family home in Nazareth, which according to legend was brought to Loreto in eastern Italy by angels in 1294. The earlier murals fell into decay and were replaced in 1987 by scenes depicting Christ at different ages in his house at Nazareth, which evidently looked very similar to a Greek taverna. The black Madonna over the altar is said to date from 1621 and to be made out of wood from the oak tree that grew from a stick planted by St Guidon at Anderlecht (*see* p.140).

North Central Brussels

North Central Brussels

This chapter peels back some of the layers of history across the northern sector of the 'Pentagon' – the heart of Brussels. You'll find narrow medieval passageways and the bustle of some of Brussels' most hectic shopping streets. The Pentagon of Brussels was first created when its great city walls were erected around it in the 14th century. Since then layer upon layer has been added to the space within, and very little is quite what it seems. In a courtyard behind a row of shops stands a pristine 17th-century façade; beneath a sedate, Neoclassical square lie the bodies of hundreds of revolutionaries; what was once an Art Nouveau textile store is now a museum devoted to comic strips.

1 Lunch

De Ultieme Hallucinatie, *316 Rue Royale, t 02 217 0614; metro Botanique. Open Mon–Fri 11am–2am, Sat and Sun 8pm–2am. Expensive.* Famous Art Nouveau restaurant, with chandeliers, fireplace, side cabinets, ceiling mouldings and stained-glass partitions – all of the period – and an adventurous menu.

2 Tea and Cakes

Brasserie Horta, *Centre Belge de la Bande Dessinée, 20 Rue des Sables; metro Botanique. Open Tues–Sun 10am–6pm.* Stylish lunchspot in the Centre Belge de la Bande Dessinée, a popular venue for the design world.

3 Drinks

Greenwich, *7 Rue des Chartreux, t 02 511 4167; metro Bourse. Open daily 11am–2am.* There's something special about this old bar: the walls are wood-panelled, the ceiling high, and the atmosphere – like the beer – cloudy, befuddled and a world apart from the street outside.

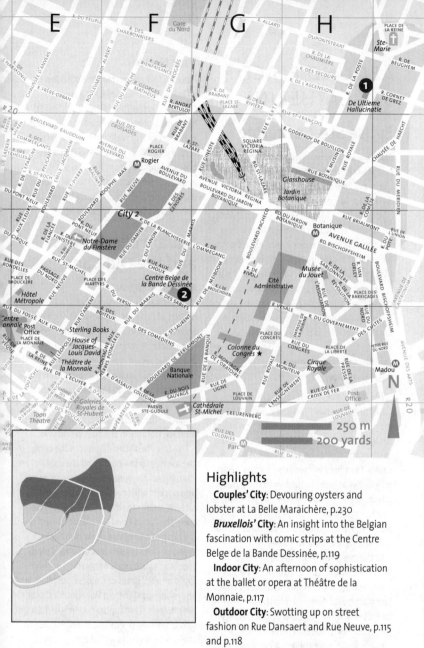

Highlights

Couples' City: Devouring oysters and lobster at La Belle Maraichère, p.230

Bruxellois' City: An insight into the Belgian fascination with comic strips at the Centre Belge de la Bande Dessinée, p.119

Indoor City: An afternoon of sophistication at the ballet or opera at Théâtre de la Monnaie, p.117

Outdoor City: Swotting up on street fashion on Rue Dansaert and Rue Neuve, p.115 and p.118

Art Nouveau City: Early 20th-century elegance at the celebrated restaurant and bar De Ultieme Hallucinatie, p.230

Beers and Bars of the City: L'Archiduc, for its 1930s ambience and jazz concerts, p.239

AROUND PLACE STE-CATHÉRINE

Eglise Ste-Cathérine E4

Place Ste-Cathérine, entrance at west door, t 02 513 3481; metro Ste-Cathérine; wheelchairs available on request. Open Mon–Sat 8.30–5.30, Sun 9–12.

You might be forgiven for thinking that this grime-coated church has been here longer than the old Willebroeck Canal. In fact it is a piece of 19th-century Neo-Gothic designed in 1854 by Joseph Poelaert. After the canal was covered over in 1853 a new church was built over it. An earlier Eglise Ste-Cathérine, dating from the 13th century, was pulled down in 1893, but its ruined belfry can still be seen close to the west door of the new church, on the other side of the street.

The Interior

The interior of the present Eglise Ste-Cathérine now has the air of a neglected greenhouse, with peeling paint, the whiff of decay and the odd pigeon flitting about the vast vacant spaces beneath the roofing vaults. On a grey winter's day it looks decidedly down-at-heel, in tune with the pious gloom of the wooden statues of suffering saints. In contrast it comes to life in bright weather, when light streams in through the pale yellow and blue windows.

At the top of the north aisle there's a famous 'Black Virgin', a 15th-century limestone statue of the Virgin holding her child. The statue was dumped into the River Senne by Protestants in 1744, and by the time it was recovered the stone had turned black.

In the south aisle there is a painted wooden statue of St Catherine, a 4th-century Christian from Alexandria. Although they ended up beheading her, the Romans first attempted to martyr her on a wheel, from which she was miraculously saved – hence the name of the firework called the Catherine wheel. In this statue her wheel can be seen beneath the folds of her dress.

Tour Noire

Place du Samedi; metro Ste-Cathérine.

On the south side of the Eglise Ste-Cathérine is the Tour Noire (Black Tower). This is the best-preserved remnant of the first major set of city walls, built in the 12th century. The Tour Noire was a D-shaped bastion built out from the wall so that archers, hiding behind narrow slits, could pick off enemies approaching the wall. It now houses temporary exhibitions.

Square des Blindés and the Old Canal C3

Metro Ste-Cathérine.

This square lies on the edge of a poor district of Brussels, a glum area of soulless tenement blocks. The square is named after its monolithic monument to armoured cars in the two world wars. Opposite it is one of Brussels' most charming and unusual public monuments: a **bronze statue** of a woman holding a pigeon. It is dedicated '*aux pigeons soldats*' – the messenger pigeons used by the military, notably in the First World War.

The treelined strip of grass in the centre of the avenue to the north and the cobbled area running south were once filled with water and packed with barges, sailing ships and, latterly, small steamships. On either side were the quays lined with warehouses, an antheap of activity as dockers in their wooden clogs loaded and unloaded shipments of salt, barrels of herrings, sacks of grain, timber, cases of Chinese porcelain, and squealing pigs. The old Willebroeck Canal, which, from its inauguration in 1561, brought goods from Antwerp and the North Sea to the city centre, was a vital element in Brussels' burgeoning prosperity.

The canal, however, suffered from repeated flooding, and by the 1850s the railways had begun to usurp its role. So in 1853 it was covered over. The quays retained their old titles from the days when merchants of a kind clubbed together: Quai à la Houille (coal), Quai au Bois de Construction (building timber), Quai au Bois à Brûler (firewood), Quai aux Briques (bricks). The newly created square was occupied by a fishmarket. This was demolished in 1955, but there is still a tang of fish in the air, emanating from the few surviving fishmongers' warehouses and the many restaurants that now line the old quays. Place Ste-Cathérine, often referred to as the Marché aux Poissons, is still the place to eat fish in Brussels.

The **large fountain** south down the Quai aux Briques is an 1897 monument to Jules Anspach for his role in redesigning the city centre in the 1860s. This splendid piece of late 19th-century medievalism depicts a naked St Michael slaying a devil.

Rue de Flandre B3

Metro *Ste-Cathérine.*

Modest though this street now looks, it was once one of Brussels' main thoroughfares, linking the Grand' Place (*see* p.74) to the Flanders Gate and the road to Ghent. Today it is a pleasantly quiet backwater. No. 17 is a butcher's specializing in tripe and other offal – the base ingredients of famous Bruxellois dishes such as *choesels* (*see* p.223). No.28, La Maison de la Casquette, is a hatmaker's, specializing in clergy's headgear, traditional berets and long-peaked student caps; each university has its own design.

Maison du Spectacle la Bellone C3

*46 Rue de Flandre, **t** 02 513 3333; metro Ste-Cathérine. Maison du Spectacle **open** Tues–Fri 10–6; closed July. Maison de la Bellone **open** only during temporary exhibitions; **adm** free, except for temporary exhibitions.*

The Maison du Spectacle (built around the Maison de la Bellone) is a theatre centre, with an archive and library, where workshops, public concerts, small-scale performances and exhibitions, are held. Along a passage and through some glass doors is a courtyard, overlooked by the Maison de la Bellone. In 1913 Charles Buls, the burgomaster celebrated for his efforts to save the historic face of Brussels, persuaded

the city to purchase this old aristocratic residence. It's been a gallery since 1980.

Its beautifully proportioned, honey-coloured façade is a delightful surprise, tucked away behind a row of shops. The house was built in 1697 to designs by Jan Cosyns, who was also engaged in the restoration of the Grand' Place. His signature can be seen over the door, on the plinth of his bust of Bellona, a Roman goddess of war. Stone reliefs of various war trophies and weapons of imperial Rome, and medallion portraits of Roman emperors, take up the theme of power and war; these strike a dissonant chord against the mellow Renaissance–Baroque architecture. The gable is crowned by a pelican plucking her breast (to nourish her young on her own blood), an old symbol for the sacrifice of Christ.

Rue du Rempart des Moines B3–4

Metro *Ste-Cathérine.*

At No.15 is a Boucherie Chevaline, a horse-meat butcher: horsemeat is still eaten in Belgium but is now a rarity. On the right-hand side of the street is a stone arch, dated 1760. This is the entrance to the Rue de la Cigogne (Stork Street), a tiny, crooked passage between cottages, and a survivor of a network of alleyways that threaded through the medieval city. The upper end is the most picturesque part, but unfortunately it's no longer possible to walk along it.

Rue Dansaert B3–C4

Metro *Ste-Cathérine.*

Despite its slightly haggard appearance, Rue Dansaert is still a centre for serious avant-garde fashion in Brussels. The fashion shops include Rue Blanche, Virgin Shoes, Kat en Muis children's clothes and, in the stretch between Marché aux Grains and the Place du Nouveau Marché au Grains, Nathalie Vincent, Idiz Bogum II (second-hand), and Stijl, which carries many of the great Antwerp names (*see* 'Shopping', p.250).

Eglise St-Jean-Baptiste au Béguinage D3

Place du Béguinage, t 02 217 8742; metro Ste-Cathérine; wheelchair accessible. Temporarily closed at the time of writing, but when it reopens times will be Tues–Thurs and Sat 9.30–5, Sun 9.30–12.

The Baroque Eglise St-Jean-Baptiste au Béguinage is one of the city's loveliest churches. It was once the hub of Brussels' largest *béguinage* (see 'The History of Béguinages', p.141) – one of many semi-religious, charitable communities for single women in the Low Countries. This *béguinage* dates from 1250 and in its heyday possessed most of the land in the northwestern corner of Brussels – a self-contained area filled with orchards and dotted with the houses of 1,200 *béguines*. Some lived in style, in large houses with servants; the less well off lived in communal houses and ran a laundry, a windmill and a hospital serving the community at large. By the 14th century the *béguinage* was rich enough to build a large Gothic church.

In 1579 marauding Calvinists laid waste this peaceful community, returning to flatten the church in 1584. The *béguines* were dispersed, but drifted back over the following years. It took over half a century to rebuild the *béguinage*, and only in 1657 was it possible to begin work on the present church. But the *béguinage* was already in decline. Members now had to pay high entrance fees, build their own house and donate it to the community. It became the preserve of the rich, and it soon became out of kilter with contemporary values. The number of *béguines* declined, and in the early 19th century the Conseil des Hospices intervened, handing empty houses out to impoverished aged people. The last *béguine* of this community died in 1833. Only the streetplan and church of the *béguinage* have survived.

The Façade

No one knows who designed Eglise St-Jean-Baptiste au Béguinage, although Luc

Fayd'Herbe has been suggested, mainly for the church's similarities to Notre-Dame aux Riches Claires. The façade is a crescendo of twirls, curls, finials, pediments and *œils de bœuf* – a triumph of the Italian-influenced Flemish Baroque. Over the door is a statue of St Begga, who is thought to have founded the first *béguinages* in the 7th century. The great bronze doors were installed during renovation in the 1850s.

The Interior

The interior is a model of cool, tranquillity, a mixture of massive architectural force and deft stone carving, seen for example in the winged cherubs' heads that fill the intervals between the Romanesque-style semi-circular arches. Many of the flagstones are redeployed tombstones from the earlier church and the surrounding cemetery, commemorating *béguines* and their chaplains. The *béguines* could be buried in the cemetery, nave or choir according to an established structure of fees – an important source of income for the *béguinage*.

The pulpit is a supreme piece of Baroque woodcarving, sculpted in 1757 for a Dominican church in Mechelen. St Dominic can be seen with his foot on a prostrate heretic. The four apostles are represented by their old medieval symbols: the ox for St Luke, the lion for St Mark, the angel for St Matthew and the eagle for St John.

Hospice Pacheco D2–3

12 Rue du Grand Hospice; metro Ste-Cathérine.

This massive building, set around two leafy courtyards, was built in 1824, during the declining years of the *béguinage* (*see* 'Eglise St-Jean-Baptiste au Béguinage', opposite). In 1835 it became the new home of the Hospice Pacheco, founded in 1713 through funds willed by the widow of Don Augustin Pacheco, a governor during the last years of the Spanish Netherlands. Still very much in use today, the Hospice Pacheco maintains a tradition of caring for the old and infirm that has been a feature of this quarter of Brussels for seven centuries.

AROUND THÉÂTRE DE LA MONNAIE

Théâtre de la Monnaie E4

Place de la Monnaie, t 02 229 1211; metro De Brouckère; wheelchair accessible. Open during performances, box office open Tues–Sat 11–6.

In the Place de la Monnaie old and new Brussels come face to face across a cobbled square. In one corner is the vast **Centre Monnaie**, a huge X-shaped block of curving glass and concrete that houses a shopping mall, the central post office and various municipal offices. It stands on the site of the old mint, built in 1420, which has given the square its name. Dwarfed in the other corner is the Théâtre de la Monnaie, built in 1819 to resemble a robust Greek temple. But this contender has form – it was the start of the Belgian Revolution (*see* p.37).

Revolutionary Lyrics

On 25 August 1830 an excitable audience at the Théâtre de la Monnaie was stirred into a frenzy by the provocative text of the opera *La Muette de Portici* (The Mute Girl of Portici), by the French composer Daniel-François-Esprit Auber. The story concerns a revolutionary who led an uprising in Naples against the Spanish in 1647. Such sentiments as 'Far better to die than to live a wretched life in slavery and shame! Away with the yoke before which we tremble; away with the foreigner who laughs at our torment!' incited the audience to a ferment. Dressed in their opera finery, they ran out to join a workers' demonstration already taking place in the Place de la Monnaie, stormed the Palais de Justice, drove out the Dutch garrison and raised the flag of Brabant over the Hôtel de Ville. Barricades were erected and uprisings spread throughout the provinces. It was the start of the Belgian Revolution and led directly to the declaration of Belgian independence just one month later.

There has been a theatre on this site since 1698. After struggling for decades in a moral climate that denigrated all theatre as immoral, this 'Hôtel des Spectacles' began to flourish during the era of Charles of Lorraine (1741–80). In 1766 a company called the Théâtre de la Monnaie was set up, modelled on the Comédie Française in Paris – i.e. with no star system. The theatre was soon all the rage with members of the court: it had gambling tables, and furthermore the cast-list provided the nobility with a string of beautiful and much contested mistresses.

The old building was demolished in 1810 to make way for a new version. The interior of this, however, was gutted by a fire in 1855 and then remodelled to designs by Joseph Poelaert. With only 1,200 seats, this is a small opera house. It has a deliberate policy of not contracting operatic megastars, preferring instead to nurture rising stars and to concentrate on the staging and theatrical qualities of opera, for which it has earned a high reputation. The theatre also maintains a resident ballet company, separate from the opera. For three decades until the late 1980s it was the home of the Twentieth Century Ballet of Maurice Béjart, king of the big spectacle in modern dance. When Béjart left after a series of disagreements, he was replaced for a brief but mercurial spell by the troupe formed by the celebrated American dancer Mark Morris; his effusively camp antics and risqué comments succeeded in ruffling the feathers of crustier season-ticket-holders while delighting the avant-garde. The slot has now been filled by Anne Teresa De Keersmaeker, who has successfully held the middle ground.

House of Jacques-Louis David E4

5 Rue Léopold; metro De Brouckère.

The great French Neoclassical painter Jacques-Louis David (1748–1825) lived and died in this house. Having been First Painter to Napoleon, David feared reprisals in Paris after the final defeat of his master in 1815, and so came to live in Brussels. The house he chose is suitably Neoclassical, with Empire-style Grecian harp motifs on the balcony, but is now in a state of semi-dereliction and covered in graffiti.

Place de Brouckère E3

Metro De Brouckère.

This busy thoroughfare was built over the vaulted River Senne and is lined by some grand 19th-century commercial buildings. The name commemorates Charles de Brouckère (1796–1860), a leading political figure in the Provisional Government set up after the Revolution, and burgomaster from 1848 to 1860.

On the south side is the **Hôtel Métropole**, one of Brussels' famously grand hotels. The lavish, gilded interior was designed in around 1900 and the equally ornate Café Métropole next door dates from 1890.

Close to where the Boulevard Adolphe Max joins Place de Brouckère is the entrance to the **Passage du Nord**. This shopping arcade was built in 1882, and retains a late 19th-century flavour, with its curving iron-work lamps, towering glass vaulting and lines of Grecian ladies propping up the architecture.

Rue Neuve E3

Metro De Brouckère.

This is one of Brussels' busiest shopping streets, with many upmarket chainstores. The narrow pedestrianized thoroughfare is often packed and the shops, bars and boutiques resound to the patter of countless footfalls and the steady throb of imported music: small wonder that it looks a little ragged at the edges. Many of the street names in this area – Rue aux Choux (Cabbage Street), Rue du Persil (Parsley Street) – recall the fact that there were market gardens here until the 15th century.

Place des Martyrs E–F3

Metro De Brouckère.

After the brash hurly-burly of the Rue Neuve this charming Neoclassical square comes as a refreshing surprise. Designed by Claude Fisco (1736–1825), it was built in 1775 and preserves the genteel air that character-ized the rule of Charles of Lorraine.

Its original character was transformed between 1830 and 1840 when it was dedicated to the memory of the 445 'martyrs' killed in the critical days (23–26 September 1830) of the Belgian Revolution. The centre was turned into their mausoleum, a subter-ranean cloister with commemorative marble slabs. The white marble statue depicts 'Belga', and is one of many notable public monuments by Willem Geefs (1805–85).

Having fallen into disrepair the square is undergoing radical renovation, which is the subject of heated contention. The Flemish regional government has established their headquarters, draped in Flemish flags, at the northern end. This has inflamed the majority of Bruxellois, who feel increasingly threatened by Flemish nationalism.

Tintin

Name the most famous Belgian in the world. Tintin! Translated into 40 languages, sold in 140 million volumes worldwide, Tintin's adventures have enthralled children and adults for over half a century.

It's hard to pin down the secret of Tintin's charm, but his influence is profound. The historical and geographical detail of the stories set in exotic worlds is carefully researched: Central America (*Tintin and the Picaros*), Ancient Egypt (*Cigars of the Pharaoh*), even to the moon.

Topped by his peculiar blond quiff and accompanied by his faithful white terrier Milou (Snowy in English), Tintin first appeared in 1929 in *Le Petit Vingtième*, part of the Roman Catholic newspaper *Vingtième Siècle*. His creator was Georges Rémi (1907–83), a self-taught illustrator born in Brussels, and a comic strip pioneer. His pseudonym is his initials in reverse, spelt out in their French pronunciation: R. G. Hergé.

In the 1930s, his adventures became more challenging, inspired by contemporary events that affronted Hergé's sense of justice – such as the bloody Gran Chaco War between Paraguay and Bolivia (*The Broken Ear*), and the Japanese invasion of Manchuria (*The Blue Lotus*). In *King Ottokar's Sceptre* the fascist Iron Guard attempts to seize power in a central European state. It is some wonder that Hergé was vilified during the war, when he produced an inoffensive version of Tintin

for *Le Soir*, a newspaper controlled by the occupying Germans. During this period several new characters arrived, including the English seadog Captain Haddock and Professor Calculus (Tournesol in French). Hergé was imprisoned at the end of the war on charges of collaboration – a label that he was never fully able to shed.

He was rescued from his immediate plight by a respected member of the Resistance called Raymond Leblanc, a publisher and a Tintin fan. With Leblanc's help, Hergé began producing the bimonthly *Journal de Tintin* in 1946, which was an instant success, and the fortunes of Tintin escalated from this point on. After 1950 the adventures began to appear in their now-famous volume form. Tintin's 50th anniversary in 1979 was widely celebrated, but Hergé's health declined, and he died aged 76 on 4 March 1983. Tintin has subsequently been transformed for radio, animated cartoons, models and T-shirts, but the publishers have fortunately resisted the temptation to extend his adventures without the hand of his original creator.

Innocent, brave, foolhardy, illuminated by a clear sense of justice, always polite, and tolerant of foibles of his wayward associates, Tintin no doubt contains much of Hergé himself. The ageless 'boy reporter' makes an unlikely contender among comic book heroes of the modern age, and has never caught on in the USA, but his place in the rest of the world seems assured.

AROUND THE CITÉ ADMINISTRATIVE

Centre Belge de la Bande Dessinée F3

20 Rue des Sables, t 02 219 1980; metro Botanique or Rogier; wheelchair accessible. Open Tues–Sun 10–6; adm €6.

This old Art Nouveau textile megastore designed in 1903 by Victor Horta was stylishly renovated, and opened in 1989 as a

shrine to the comic strip, consisting mainly of a large collection of original drawings.

The comic strip is an art form far better developed and more widely appreciated in Belgium, France and Italy than in any English-speaking nation. However, the Belgians credit an American cartoonist, Winsor McCay, with the origins of the European comic strip tradition. He created 'Little Nemo in Slumberland' for the *New York Herald* in 1905, and when *Les Adventures du Petit Nemo au Pays des Songes* appeared in French in 1908 it proved a wild success.

Belgian artists soon became leaders of this new field and, as their characters became better known, their escapades became more ambitious and the magazines more substantial. By far the most famous of these characters is Tintin (*see* 'Tintin', p.119).

Tintin is accorded a special place in this museum, with original drawings, historical notes and 3D models of famous Tintin scenes. Other characters, such as Lucky Luke the lackadaisical cowboy (by Maurice de Bevere), are only vaguely recognized by the English-speaking public, but are known to every Belgian. There are hundreds more: Gaston Lagaffe (by André Franquin), Petit Biniou (by Dupa), Boule et Bill and the Ribambelle gang (by Jean Roba), the wily Brussels kids Quick et Flupke (by Hergé), and other characters from the popular magazine *Spirou*. Asterix, by the way, is French. More recently, comic strip artists and their publishers have created a new genre of more adult works. The museum bookshop contains thousands of comic strip books, almost all in French or Flemish, and is a measure of the scale of this industry: 850 new titles are published every year in Belgium alone.

This spacious museum is beautifully presented, with pristine Art Nouveau stairways, a superb Art Nouveau lamp in the entrance hall and cantilevered glass roofs; yet it has a strangely serious air, given its subject. The people poring over the comic strips are not children but adults. It is a window on the extraordinary talents of comic strip artists, and rewarding for devotees of Tintin and Victor Horta (the museum includes a section devoted to his work, with an audiovisual on Art Nouveau design). Well worth it if you can overcome the cultural gap (annotation is in French and Flemish only).

Cathédrale St-Michel F5

Parvis Ste-Gudule, t 02 217 8345; metro Gare Centrale; wheelchairs available on request. Open daily 8–6; adm free.

Brussels' cathedral has recently undergone a massive programme of restoration.

However, this is not Brussels' greatest church. Its twin towers struggle to be noticed among the modern buildings and it seems isolated from the real city centre.

If it seems disappointing as Brussels' cathedral, this may be explained by the fact that it was ravaged twice – by Protestant iconoclasts in 1579 and French revolutionaries in 1793. Furthermore, it only became a cathedral in 1962, when the archbishopric of Mechelen-Brussels was created. Previously, it was a collegiate church dedicated to St Michael (the male patron saint of Brussels) and Ste Gudule (the female equivalent).

Ste Gudule, an 8th-century lady of royal blood, was celebrated for her piety. She's often portrayed holding a lamp, since the most famous tale about her concerns her battle with the devil, who kept blowing out her light as she attempted to reach her isolated chapel. Through the power of prayer, she was able to rekindle the flame. Her venerated remains were brought here from the chapel on Ile St-Géry in the 11th century, but when the church became a cathedral, it was named after St Michael alone because Ste Gudule was not on the official papal register. However, the people of Brussels still obstinately refer to it as 'Ste-Gudule'.

The original Romanesque church was replaced after 1226 by the present Gothic one, which then took three centuries to complete. The towers were designed by Jan van Ruysbroeck, the 15th-century architect of the Hôtel de Ville; they contain a 50-bell carillon, most of which was installed in 1975.

The Interior

The interior is light and airy, with some delicate stone tracery in the clerestory and a Gothic chair completed in 1280. The monumental oak pulpit is a supreme riot of figures and foliage. Adam and Eve stand beneath the Tree of Knowledge, berated by St Michael and a skeleton; the serpent's head is crushed with a cross held by the Infant Jesus. Baroque pulpits such as this are found throughout Belgium, and this is one of the most celebrated, created by the sculptor Hendrik Verbruggen (*c.* 1655–1724) in 1699.

The stained-glass windows in the transepts date from 1537 and 1538 and were designed by the gifted painter Bernard van Orley. They depict (north) the king of the day, Charles V (1500–58), and his wife, Isabella of Portugal; and (south) Mary of Hungary, sister of Charles V, and her husband. Stairs in the nave lead down to the recently excavated foundations of the Romanesque church with a few exhibits of 13th- and 14th-century graffiti.

Colonne du Congrès G4

*Place du Congrès; **metro** Botanique; **bus** 29 or 63 from centre of town.*

Designed by Joseph Poelaert and built in 1850–9, the handsome 47m-high Congress Column celebrates the foundation of Belgium's constitutional monarchy after the Revolution of 1830. The statue of Leopold I on top is by Willem Geefs. The inscriptions at the column's base include extracts from the constitution and lists of the members of the Provisional Government (September 1830–February 1831) and the first National Congress (November 1830–July 1831). Between the bronze lions is the flame to the Unknown Soldier of both world wars.

Cité Administrative G–H3

Metro Botanique.

This slice of the modern world filled with monumental architecture is, by its abrupt contrast, a reminder that the charm of central Brussels lies in its human scale. On Rue des Sables is the huge marble-clad Ministry of Finance and Royal Mint, surrounded by a faceless civil service complex.

Musée du Jouet H3

*24 Rue de l'Association, **t** 02 219 6168, **e** museedujouet@iname.com, **w** www .cyber.be\museedujouet; **metro** Botanique. **Open** daily 10–6; **adm** €3.*

The Toy Museum has the one ingredient that the Centre Belge de la Bande Dessinée lacks: joy. Housed in a grand but rather dilapidated 19th-century *maison de maître*

(gentleman's residence), it is crammed with toys of all kinds and ages: dolls, teddy bears, cars, trains and puppets. It's run on a shoestring, but the higgledy-piggledy arrangements and handwritten labels (French and Flemish only) help to create a magical world – a kind of walk-in toy box.

Children are genuinely welcome: there is an area where they can play with numerous larger toys, the display cases have steps so that smaller children can see into them, and the top floor can be hired for children's parties. Grown-ups will be assailed by nostalgia; and there are some unusual curiosities, such as the set of model figures depicting King Baudouin I's visit to the Congo in 1955. If he's there, the owner will be happy to point out some of the toys he invented and built himself – including mechanized puppets (automates) and cars.

Place des Barricades H3

Metro Botanique.

This elegant Regency-style circus commemorates the barricades erected in September 1830 by Belgian Revolutionaries around the Parc de Bruxelles, trapping the Dutch garrison and enforcing their retreat. In the 1850s Victor Hugo rented the house at No. 4, where his wife Adèle held regular soirées, entertaining other French exiles such as Charles Baudelaire and Alexandre Dumas. In 1871, a riotous mob of students caused a commotion at Hugo's door, drawing the attention of the authorities to his support for the Paris Commune. Sensing dangerous subversion, the government forced Hugo to leave Belgium once and for all.

This district was constructed for the administrators of the new nation after 1830. As they left their homes in their top hats, the street names would remind them of the pillars of their constitution: Place de la Liberté, Rue du Congrès, Rue de l'Association (freedom of association), Rue des Cultes (freedom of religion), Rue de la Presse (freedom of the press) and Rue de l'Enseignement (freedom of education).

Glasshouse of the Jardin Botanique H2

Entrance on Rue Royale, t 02 218 7935; metro Botanique; wheelchair accessible. Open daily 11–6; adm free.

The botanical gardens themselves have been transferred outside Brussels. The glasshouse was built for the Brussels Horticultural Society in 1826–9 following drawings by a painter and theatre designer called Pierre-François Gineste (1769–1850). Although the exterior was cleverly preserved, the glasshouse was converted into the Centre Culturel de la Communauté Française Wallonie-Bruxelles (Cultural Centre of the French Community of Wallonia and Brussels) in the early 1980s, and now contains a series of spaces for temporary exhibitions, concerts and plays, as well as a cinema and brasserie. Only the main corridor retains its hothouse atmosphere, with its small fishponds, ferns and papyrus plants. In the huge hollow in front of the glasshouse is a formal garden with box hedges and statuary, some of which is by Constantin Meunier.

Note that the Jardin Botanique has a sinister – and, alas, well-founded – reputation for muggers, but this really refers to the western part, now cut off from the formal garden by the Bvd St-Lazare.

De Ultieme Hallucinatie H1

316 Rue Royale, t 02 217 0614; metro Botanique, then tram 92, 93 or 94. Open Mon–Fri 12–2.30 and 7–10.30, Sat 7–10.30.

This is a celebrated Art Nouveau restaurant and bar (*see* 'Eating Out', p.230). The building dates from 1856, but it was transformed at the start of the 20th century by Paul Hamesse (1877–1956), a pupil of Paul Hankar (*see* pp.153–4). Even the umbrella stand and piano in the hall have had the Art Nouveau wand waved over them, but the real triumph is the small restaurant (which you can poke your head into from the more spartan bar). Nothing has been left to chance: the chandeliers, stencilled wall-hangings, fireplace, side cabinets, ceiling mouldings, stained-glass partitions – all have been redefined with the graceful curves of Art Nouveau. With its dimmed lighting and brooding tones, this restaurant speaks eloquently of the twilight years that preceded the First World War.

Eglise Ste-Marie I1

Place de la Reine; metro Botanique, then tram 92 or 93, or metro Gare du Nord. No fixed opening hours.

At the head of the Rue Royale is the recently restored Eglise Ste-Marie. This is in the quarter called St-Josse-ten-Noode, a rather rundown area.

Eglise Ste-Marie is the most beautiful 19th-century church in Brussels, worth the visit even if you can only see the exterior. It was designed by a 25-year-old architect from Ghent, Louis van Overstraeten (1818–49), who died of cholera just four years after building work commenced in 1845. Its style is best described as Neo-Byzantine: the octagonal ground plan is topped by a star-spangled copper dome and offset by semicircular side-chapels, buttresses, pepperpot spires, rose windows and fretted, receding arches. The builders have used a traditional Brussels mix of stone, cream-coloured for the body of the church and grey for the detailing.

Quartier Léopold:
Heart of Europe

Quartier Léopold: Heart of Europe

Belgium burst upon the economic and world stage in the late 19th century when it began to reap the rewards of its new, coal-driven industries, its reawakened trading links across Europe, and its wholesale pillage of raw materials from the Belgian Congo. No one stamped this era more decisively that the king, Léopold II (r. 1865–1909), who on ascending the throne, promised to create '*une Belgique plus grande et plus belle*'. Brussels boomed and a swathe of wealthy suburbs began to spread out from the old centre, notably in the area east of the Palais Royal, named after Léopold I.

In 1880 Belgium celebrated 50 years of independence with an International Exhibition in the newly laid-out Parc du Cinquantenaire. This now forms a grand setting for a series of museums. The same part of town has been adopted by the head-quarters of the European Union and much transformation has taken place.

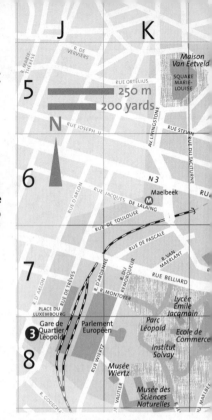

1 Lunch

Jardin d'Espagne, *65–7 Rue Archimède,* **t** *02 736 3449;* **metro** *Schuman.* **Open** *Mon–Fri noon–3 and 7–10, Sat 7–10pm.* **Expensive.** An acclaimed Spanish restaurant with an emphasis on adventurous seafood concoctions. The garden (with fountain) provides an excellent outdoor option for summer.

2 Tea and Cakes

Refresh, *48 Rue Archimède,* **t** *02 230 6911;* **metro** *Schuman.* **Open** *daily 10am–7pm.* Healthy lunches with a Celtic and Nordic influence (reindeer and mushroom quiche).

3 Drinks

Het Ketje, *4 Place du Luxembourg;* **metro** *Trône.* **Open** *Mon–Fri 11am–4am, Sat and Sun 11am–9.30pm.* A good old regular brasserie that will no doubt outlive the pretentions of the flashy new places that have sprung up to cater for the young beer-thirsty Eurocrat.

Highlights

Bruxellois' City: Enjoying the indoor and outdoor delights of the Parc du Cinquantenaire, p.129

Indoor City: The bizarre canvases at the Musée Wiertz, p.127

Outdoor City: Watching a film at the outdoor cinema in Parc du Cinquantenaire, p.246

Art Nouveau City: The spectacular residential façades around Square Ambiorix, p.132

Beers and Bars of the City: Drink with the expats on lively Rue Archimède, p.132

AROUND THE PARLEMENT EUROPÉEN

One of the most noticeable features of this area is the collateral damage – the number of forlorn and empty residential buildings now surrounding it, boarded up and daubed with graffiti. Local residents blame property speculators who want to sell vacant lots when the lucrative Euro-businesses come their way. It causes considerable resentment among those who see the historic intimacy of old residential quarters constantly under pressure from commercial exploitation. Among the ruins are a few admirable survivors – residents or businesses which simply refuse to be driven out. One example is the antique shop 'Au Vieux Magasin'. This Aladdin's cave of miscellaneous *bibelots* (knick-knacks) has been here since 1908.

Parlement Européen J8

Rue Wiertz; metro Schuman. EU citizens wanting a more detailed introduction should contact their MEP. In Britain, this is the European Parliament Office, 2 Queen Anne's Gate, London, WH1H 9AA, t (020) 7227 4300, w www.cec.org.uk. Guided tours allow casual visitors to enter the hemicycle. Headsets (in various languages) available. Tours (Mon–Thurs 10am and 3pm, Fri 3pm, Sat 10am, 11.30am, 2.30pm) begin from the visitors' entrance of the Paul Henri Spaak building on Rue Wiertz, t 02 284 3457.

This glossy building, nicknamed '*caprices des dieux*' ('whims of the gods') – behind a 300m façade of undulating granite, glass and polished steel – is the Brussels head-quarters of the European Parliament. Its 626 Members (MEPs) are elected in the 15 member states of the EU for a five-year term. They spend most of their time in Brussels, where specialist committees discuss proposals for new EU legislation. For one week each month Parliament meets in Strasbourg for a full session (and the bars and restaurants that are the haunt of Brussels' Eurocrats are left eerily quiet). Parliament also meets for a number of two-day mini-sessions back in Brussels. The MEPs also approve appointments to the European Commission which, along with the Council of Ministers, is the other main European insti-tution based in Brussels.

Rue Wiertz drives through the centre of the Parlement Européen buildings. To the west is the 'Mail Building', otherwise known by the code D3. Completed in February 1997 at a cost of £530 million, it contains 2,600 offices for the MEPs and administrators, 16 confer-ence rooms and 52 meeting rooms.

To the east is an oval block called the 'Léopold Building' – D1 and D2. This houses the offices of the President of the Parliament,

Léopold II

Belgium's second king was driven by the ambition to raise his country to the status of a great nation. He was dismissive of the Belgians' natural inclination to modest ambi-tions – '*petit pays, petites gens*' ('small country, small people'), he grumbled. He eventually realised his dream of acquiring colonies when he established the Belgian Congo as a personal fiefdom (*see* p.147). Meanwhile he instigated an ambitious building programme in Brussels and Ostend.

The one cloud in Léopold's life was the fact that he had no male heir. His only son died aged ten. He had three daughters, whom he treated coldly and married off unsuitably, and he finally barred succession through them in favour of his nephew, Albert I. If he was capable of affection it was directed not to his family but to a string of mistresses. In 1899 he became enamoured of 17-year-old Blanche-Caroline Delacroix, la Baronne de Vaughan, and his liaison with her continued after the death of his long-suffering wife in 1902. Caroline gave Leopold two children, and it is still a mystery whether or not he made an honest woman of her on his deathbed, when he was 74.

Artist, Visionary, Megalomaniac

Antoine Wiertz (1806–65) had the misfortune to win the Prix de Rome in 1832, after which he felt he was on course for true greatness. He set about painting a series of vast canvases (11m tall, 8m wide) depicting melodramatic biblical or classical scenes and using ambitious perspectives in the style of Rubens – but unfortunately without his genius. In 1850 he approached the government with a proposal: if the state would build a studio large enough for him to carry out his projects, he would bequeath the studio and his works to the nation as a museum. The state agreed – a measure of Wiertz's standing in Brussels in his day – and here you see the consequences.

Antoine Wiertz saw himself as a visionary, a socialist, a breaker of taboos. He was ruled by obsessive ideas, one of which was inspired by the rejection of a painting by the Paris Salon of 1839. Stung by this, he launched a campaign calling for the development of Brussels as a giant metropolis – a vast, glittering city of magnificent buildings, industry and commerce, arts and literature, which would render Paris a mere *ville de province* by comparison. He wrote a tract entitled 'Bruxelles Capitale et Paris Province' (his hand-written version hangs in the passageway outside the studio). Crackpot or visionary? Antoine Wiertz would have been deeply gratified to see the capital of Europe now blossoming on his very doorstep.

the General Secretariat, press facilities and the 720-seat semicircular assembly chamber. These buildings were designed by a consortium, on the instructions of a committee, and it shows. They are never likely to appear in the annals of great architecture. Incidentally, don't worry about criticizing these buildings to Belgians: they are not Belgian buildings, but EU buildings on Belgian land.

Musée Wiertz K8

62 Rue Vautier, t 02 648 1718, e info@fine-arts-museum.be, w www.fine-arts-museum .be; metro Maelbeek or Schuman. Open April–Oct Tues–Sun 10–12 and 1–5; closed Sat and Sun in July and Aug; adm free.

This museum offers the rare possibility of seeing inside a 19th-century artist's studio. But this was not just any 19th-century artist – this was Antoine Wiertz, who from an early age liked to compare himself to Rubens and Michelangelo. His ambitions and delusions were on a truly epic scale (*see* 'Artist, Visionary, Megalomaniac', above).

The main part of the studio is just high enough to hang several immense canvases. These are rather crudely executed and instantly forgettable. Wiertz's more remarkable works are on a smaller scale, technically very uneven, but stamped with his own peculiar vision. Some are a bizarre

combination of the macabre and erotic; others are loaded with a crushingly blunt moral message. *Le Suicide* graphically illustrates a young man blasting his brains out with a pistol under the covetous gaze of good and bad angels. In *Une Scène d'Enfer* (A Scene from Hell) distraught men and women present severed limbs to a smouldering (literally) figure of Napoleon.

There are some real gems in the smaller rooms to one side of the studio. The criminal laxity of doctors is paraded in *L'Inhumation Precipitée* (The Overhasty Burial), in which a body is seen emerging from a coffin – despite an inscription affirming that doctors had certified the victim well and truly dead. *La Liseuse de Romans* (The Reader of Novels) depicts a woman lies reading in naked abandon, while a horned devil pushes corrupting literature towards her.

Musée des Sciences Naturelles K8

29 Rue Vautier, t 02 627 4238, w www.natural .sciences.net; metro Maelbeek or Schuman; wheelchair accessible. Open Tues–Fri 9.30–4.45, Sat and Sun 10–6; adm €4.50.

Behind a large modern façade, with a statue of a dinosaur in front, is this museum, inaugurated by Léopold II in 1891. The original ornate halls were built to house a major find of iguanodon skeletons at Bernissart (near Mons) in 1870. These have now been joined by a dozen or so life-size, moving, roaring models – the survivors of a temporary exhibition called Dinosaurs & Co. This section really is the only highlight, and particularly appeals to children.

The main body of the museum houses hundreds of stuffed animals and skeletons displayed in a maze of long rooms. There are also some good displays of glittering, gem-like minerals, and an impressive collection of shells. The museum is in a constant state of flux, and even if you invest in a plan of the layout you're likely to find it out of date.

Parc Léopold K8

*Rue Vautier; **metro** Maelbeek or Schuman.*

This park runs along the back of the Parlement Européen buildings and contains a set of elegant 19th-century buildings. These include the Institut Solvay (one of the Solvay family's noble public works, *see* p.150), a former Ecole de Commerce of the Université Libre de Bruxelles, and the Lycée Emile Jacqmain, a handsome mixture of cast-iron and stone, where Neoclassical collided with Art Nouveau in 1895.

AROUND THE PARC DU CINQUANTENAIRE

Council of the European Union L7

*80 Belliard and 175 Rue de la Loi; **metro** Schuman.*

This huge pinkish-brown-marble, plate-glass sprawl was completed in 1995 at a cost of £300 million. It was built to house the offices of the Council of Ministers and their 2,500 officials. The building was named after Justus Lipsius (1547–1606), a Flemish

humanist and philosopher. Unfortunately, it was designed in the days of 12 member states; when it opened there were 15, and it is already too small.

The Council is the main decision-making body of the EU, although the European Parliament is gradually edging into its sphere of action. This therefore remains one of the key forums of the EU, where officials gather to thrash out the burning issues of the day from fish quotas and BSE to immigration policy. The President of the Council changes every six months so each country can have a turn in rotation.

Berlaymont Building L6

*Rond-Point Schuman; **metro** Schuman.*

For two decades after its completion in 1970, the cross-shaped Berlaymont Building with its 12 flags fluttering before it was the very symbol of the European Community. Then in 1991 disaster struck: it was found to be riddled with asbestos, and was thus in breach of the very regulations overseen by the thousands of Eurocrats within it. The building was vacated, and the offices of the European Commission scattered about the district. The asbestos is being removed at vast cost, but it is unclear at the time of writing when the building will reopen.

The European Commission is another key institution, an autonomous body designed to see that the EU functions correctly. It's led by 20 commissioners who are appointed by member states but do not take instructions from their governments: their loyalties, in principle, are to the Community itself. The Commission proposes policies and legislation and ensures the treaties are carried out.

Info Point Europe M6

*12 Rond-Point Schuman; **metro** Schuman. **Open** Mon–Fri 9–5.30, Sat 10–4.*

This information centre – spattered with EU flags – has been set up by the Commission to disseminate literature about the workings of the EU. Here you can get up to date with European health and safety regulations, or the latest edict of the Common Agricultural Policy. It's also a good place to gauge something of the supra-national idealism that was the original inspiration of the EU and still informs its activities. But it won't be able to tell you how the various branches of the EU slot together, only the Commission's view of it. No single body possesses this overview, which can give the whole enterprise something of a Kafka-esque quality.

Parc du Cinquantenaire N7

Metro Schuman or Mérode.

During the late 19th century there was a succession of great international exhibitions, beginning with the Great Exhibition of 1851 in London's Crystal Palace. These fairs were designed to promote industry and trade, and above all to trumpet the prestige of the host nation. Huge halls were built to house comprehensive displays of the latest inven-tions and manufactured products, from porcelain to steam engines. Brussels played its part. The year 1880 marked the Cinquantenaire (the 50-year jubilee) of the Belgian nation. At Léopold II's insistence, a military parade ground was transformed into a park to house the exhibition halls.

Since 1880 the halls have had a varied history and today they house three major museums. This is a pleasing park of sandy walkways shaded by mature trees. Sadly, however, it has never been the same since the Avenue J. F. Kennedy surfaced in its midst.

Pavillon Horta N6

Also known as the Edicule Lambeaux, this was designed by the young Victor Horta in 1889, when he was working closely with his Neoclassically oriented master, Alphonse Balat. It is, in effect, a straightforward Neoclassical temple, with a few streamlined refinements, and was built to house a series of remarkable relief sculptures called *Les Passions Humaines* by Jef Lambeaux

La Joyeuse Entrée

Avenue de la Joyeuse Entrée near the Parc du Cinquantenaire is named after an ancient tradition. From earliest times the rulers of Brabant were acclaimed by their subjects in a procession known as the Joyeuse Entrée, during which representatives of the people offered their assent to their new ruler in exchange for his undertaking to protect their liberty and privileges. It served as a kind of charter and constitution, and remained a valid benchmark of government until the end of the 18th century. The tradition is still maintained: after making his vows to Parliament, the new king performs the Joyeuse Entrée by greeting the public throngs before the Palais Royal in a prolonged bout of handshaking.

(1852–1908). Lambeaux applied the same graphic realism as his contemporary, Rodin – with the result that the sculptures earnt a reputation for being shocking. The Musées Royaux d'Art et d'Histoire run occasional tours during the summer months.

Just behind the Pavillon Horta is the **Grande Mosquée de Bruxelles**, one of the few purpose-built mosques serving Brussels' large Muslim population.

Arcade du Cinquantenaire O7

The original plan was designed by the architect Gédéon Bordiau (1832–1904). The rudiments of his concept have survived, although today's triumphal arch was added in 1905 to mark Belgium's 75th anniversary. The copper-green quadriga on the top of the arch is by Thomas Vinçotte (1850–1925), offi-cial sculptor to Léopold II: if it looks familiar, no doubt it reminds you of the more famous Brandenburg Gate in Berlin, created over a hundred years earlier. In Léopold's Brussels, originality was not a criterion.

Hall Bordiau O7

To the left of the arch is the sole survivor of the pair of exhibition halls designed by Bordiau – a huge canopy of glass and blue-painted castiron, and a monument to 19th-century industrial ingenuity. Its twin

Flemish Tapestry

Flemish tapestry has been celebrated since the 14th century and was a product of the woollen textile industry upon which Flanders thrived. It was a prized commodity in the Middle Ages, and when the wealthy feudal aristocracy moved around their estates, they took their valuable tapestries with them, partly to act as insulation in the draughty castles. When John the Fearless, Duke of Burgundy, was negotiating with the English in 1411 and 1416, he used tapestry as a bargaining counter, such was its currency.

Subsequent dukes encouraged the establishment of a Flemish tapestry industry, and during the 16th century the workshops of Bruges, Antwerp and particularly Brussels grew in stature.

The great artists of the day turned their hand to designing for the tapestry workshops. Bernard van Orley, who brought the Italian Renaissance to Brussels, is celebrated for his designs. When Pope Leo X wanted tapestry for the Sistine Chapel, it was to Brussels that he sent designs commissioned from Raphael. This had a radical effect on the tapestry world, which set about imitating fine art. Rubens and Jordaens also produced tapestry designs in the next century. The industry thrived until the 18th century, but lost ground when the Baroque period was replaced by more austere Neoclassicism.

stood on the other side of the arch but was destroyed by fire in 1946; rebuilt in a different, but sympathetic style, it now forms part of the Musée Royaux d'Art et d'Histoire.

Musées Royaux d'Art et d'Histoire O7–8

*Entrance in right-hand wing, near the Av des Nerviens, **t** 02 741 7211, **e** info@kmkg-mrah.be, **w** www.kmkg-mrah.be; **metro** Merode or Schuman; **tram** 81 and 82; wheelchair accessible. **Open** Tues–Fri 9.30–5, Sat and Sun 10–5. The Salle aux Trésors is open 10–12 and 1–4 (restricted to 50 visitors at a time); **adm** €4.*

Since its foundation in 1835, this museum, officially known as the Musée du Cinquantenaire, has accumulated many historical and anthropological artefacts, from Phoenician glass to Art Nouveau sculptures.

It has recently been transformed from a lifeless exhibition into one of Europe's truly great museums. The exhibits have been beautifully rearranged in well-lit cases, and redistributed in a way that makes full use of the grandeur of this extraordinary building, with its palatial halls, separated by sweeping marble staircases and courtyards filled with greenery. (Bordiau was also the architect of the sumptuous Hôtel Métropole, *see* p.216.)

You cannot hope to see everything. The best policy is to decide what you want to see, then use the confusing colour-coded map of the museum's three levels to plan your route. Note that **La Salle aux Trésors** (Treasure Room) has limited opening hours, so head here first if open. Dramatically lit in a darkened circular room with massive pillars, like a crypt, it contains a superb collection of medieval treasures – gilded and bejewelled reliquaries and medieval church treasures, ivories, jewellery and textiles.

Particularly worth seeking out are the 'Arts Décoratifs' of the Middle Ages, Renaissance and Baroque periods on **Level 1**. This includes superb Brussels tapestries designed by Bernard van Orley (c. 1499–1541), a remarkable collection of carved, painted and gilded retables (altarpieces) for which Brussels was famous, as well as church treasures and reliquaries, and fragments of medieval houses.

Level 1 also includes a display of 19th-century furniture, in particular some superb examples of the Empire style – the form of Neoclassicism favoured by Napoleon. In **La Salle Wolfers** Art Nouveau and Art Deco artefacts are displayed in glass-fronted cases from the Magasins Wolfers, designed by Victor Horta in 1909. Art Nouveau had a special line in sensuous female statues for the mantelpiece, made of ivory, silver and bronze – a theme later given a more overtly erotic twist by Art Deco designers. *Le Sphinx Mystérieux*, a helmeted female bust, could be seen as an icon of the age.

Lastly, don't miss the **Musée Boyadjian du Cœur** (Boyadjian Heart Museum). Dr Boyadjian, a leading contemporary heart surgeon, was interested in the heart as a symbol, and his extensive private collection was later donated to the museum. The role of the heart in Christian symbolism can be traced to the piercing of Christ's side by the soldier at Calvary; the flaming heart denotes fervent devotion and is the symbol of charity.

Musée Royal de l'Armée et d'Histoire Militaire O6–7

3 Parc du Cinquantenaire, under the arch, to the left, t 02 737 7811, e christine.van.ever broeck@klm-mra.be, w www.klm-mra.be; metro Merode or Schuman; tram 81 and 82. Open Tues–Sun 9–12 and 1–4.50; adm free.

This is another huge collection, but fairly easy to assimilate in a quick visit. The oldest part of the exhibition (installed in 1923) contains antique, glass-fronted cabinets stuffed with uniforms, weapons, flags and 19th-century military mementoes. Portraits of mustachioed generals, tattered regimental colours and rifles, swords and lances arranged on the walls create the atmosphere of a baronial hall.

Follow signs to the **Section Air et Espace**. In a vast hall built for the 1910 International Exhibition is a jumble of aircraft – from fragile First World War canvas-winged biplanes, to Russian MiGs and a sleek Starfighter. It's a rough and ready display, where children are free to roam and worn airliner seats provide a rest stop. Outside is the **Section Blindés**, a graveyard of tanks and armoured cars.

Autoworld O8

11 Parc du Cinquantenaire, under the arch, to the right, t 02 736 4165; wheelchair accessible; metro Merode; tram 81. Open April–Sept daily 10–6, Oct–Mar daily 10–5; adm €5.

This is a formidable array of over 300 glistening motor vehicles, dating back to the dawn of the combustion engine. There are rickety old horseless carriages, dashing early sports cars, prewar breadvans, tail-finned American gas-guzzlers of the 1950s, and huge limousines. The core of the collection was put together by a single private enthusiast, Ghislain Mahy, but the museum is assisted by state funds.

Atelier de Moulages O8

Beneath Autoworld, t 02 741 7294, e srinkel@ kmky-mrah.be. Open Mon–Fri 9–12 and 1.30–3.45; adm free.

In the vaults is this extraordinary Casting and Moulding Workshop. During the 1880s an exhibition of 5,000 plaster casts of famous statues filled the Hall Bordiau. A workshop supplied copies from the moulds, so the public, government institutions and schools were able to order fine art on demand. The workshop still has about 4,000 moulds, many taken from originals in great art collections around the world. Some are newly created, but others date back to the 19th century. (Their Venus de Milo mould was made in 1893.) In cases where the original has been lost or destroyed, the moulds represent a unique archive.

You can watch the craftsmen produce their pristine-white casts. Behind the workshops are cavernous storerooms where miscellaneous casts are piled high: here cultures and historical ages collide in a surreal encounter between nude Greek athletes, Egyptian cats, busts of 19th-century royalty, Madonnas, horses' heads, Dante and Voltaire, dismembered limbs, Buddhas and death masks.

You can buy casts from the showroom or order from the catalogue. Prices vary according to the size and complexity of the piece: they start at €45; you would need €4,462 for a Victory of Samothrace.

Maison de Paul Cauchie P8

5 Rue des Francs; metro Mérode.

This is a spectacular Art Nouveau façade, brought to life by a gilded mural of maidens in togas painted in a style reminiscent of Alphonse Mucha and Gustav Klimt. The design of the house shows the clear progression towards sterner, more angular shapes that took place after the start of the 20th century under the influence of the Vienna Secession. The emphasis is on strident verticals and horizontals and clean-cut geometric shapes – far removed from the effusion of curves on the Maison Saint-Cyr. This was the private house and only architectural work of its creator, Paul Cauchie, a little-known Neo-Impressionist and Symbolist painter. It was also his studio and workplace, as the inscription by the door implies: '*M. et Mme Cauchie décorateurs: cours privé d'art appliqué*'. They could hardly have made a more convincing advertisement of their skills.

AROUND SQUARE AMBIORIX

A faded elegance hangs over Square Ambiorix, named after a rebel chieftain who wiped out a Roman garrison in 54 BC. Once a fashionable bourgeois suburb, it is now a scrappy patch of greenery with fountains and a lively buzz at any time of day. The area holds some of the city's most extraordinary examples of Art Nouveau and provides a welcome relief from the bleak European quarter to the south. The two areas are linked by Rue Archimède, a little enclave of expats, with restaurants and Irish pubs.

Maison St-Cyr M5

*11 Square Ambiorix; **metro** Maelbeek.*
This extraordinary building takes the Art Nouveau idiom to its ultimate conclusion: the façade is a cascade of looping carved stone, swirling wrought iron and entwined woodwork. Glass occupies almost the entire width of its narrow groundplan, veiled by intricate balustrades and curving balconies. There is barely a straight line in sight.

The overall effect is almost unsettling. Here Art Nouveau drifts towards the sickly, degenerative art deplored by the more functionalist designers of the Arts and Crafts movement and the Vienna Secession. Such

elaborate fantasies, however, were the hallmark of the architect of the Maison St-Cyr, Gustave Strauven (1878–1919). This is his most famous work, all the more remarkable considering that he was just 20 years old when he designed it.

Maison Van Eetvelde L5

*4 Av Palmerston; **metro** Maelbeek. Visitable only through ARAU (see p.60).*
This house was designed by the father of Art Nouveau architecture, Victor Horta (see p.155), in 1895–7. Compared with the Maison St-Cyr, this façade is very strait-laced. However, it is typical of Horta, who applied Art Nouveau sparingly and with rigid discipline. The very restraint of this design, with its cast-iron columns and pronounced horizontals, was novel for the time. Art Nouveau embellishments can be seen in the curved brackets beneath the first-floor projection and the decorative panels between the windows. Horta was particularly renowned for his interiors – in this case an ingenious design arranged around an octagonal well and lit by an overhead glass canopy.

Maison Deprez-Van de Velde L5

*3 Av Palmerston; **metro** Maelbeek.*
Opposite is the Maison Deprez-Van de Velde, also by Horta. It was built at the same time as the Maison Van Eetvelde, and its exterior is even more conventional.

Square Marie-Louise K5

***Metro** Maelbeek.*
Avenue Palmerston leads down to the Square Marie-Louise, effectively a semi-circular park, filled by a large duck pond with a soaring water jet in the middle. The view across the sunken pond and up the sloping avenue to Square Ambiorix shows what the planners had in mind when they laid out this area: green and spacious, it offers one of Brussels' most surprising and elegant vistas.

Outside the Centre

The main sights of Brussels are packed conveniently close to the city centre, but there are a few others that justify a short journey to the outskirts. Some of these are well publicized, such as the Atomium; resembling an outsized model from a physics lab, it has virtually become a city emblem. Others are lesser-known gems, such as the *béguinage* at Anderlecht and the Tour Japonaise and Pavillon Chinois at Laeken.

ST-GILLES AND IXELLES

St-Gilles and Ixelles are two of Brussels' most varied quarters, a maze of streets that converge on countless little squares concealing bohemian bars and Art Nouveau treasures. St-Gilles is distinctly two-faced: the downtrodden and damp lower part to the west was once the centre of livestock-rearing – all pig swill and mud – while up the hill to the east, market gardeners turned a more refined hand to the art of the Brussels sprout. Nowadays the west is a rather downbeat series of neighbourhoods hugging the Gare du Midi. Heading east the streets become pleasant, and finally graceful, as you pass the gentle curves and swirling façades of the Art Nouveau district. This haven of *fin de siècle* architecture continues into Ixelles, a district which combines an arty café scene with the sweet-smelling exotica of **Matongé**, the African enclave.

For a walking tour of this area, which takes in some fabulous Art Nouveau architecture, *see* 'Walks', pp.150–57.

Musée Horta

25 Rue Américaine, t 02 543 0490, e musee .horta@horta.irisnet.be; metro Horta. Open Tues–Sun 2–5.30; closed public hols; adm €5.

Victor Horta built this as his home and studio in 1899–1901, when he was at the pinnacle of his powers. It was bought by the Commune de St-Gilles in 1961, and opened as the Musée Horta in 1969. The interior, which had remained more or less intact, has been carefully restored and is now furnished with pieces Horta designed for the house, as well as for other buildings.

As soon as you walk through the front door, the Art Nouveau motifs in the mosaic flooring and the flowing shapes of the coathooks, hatstand and door furniture tell you that you are entering a manicured environment. As in the jewellery of René Lalique, the glassware of Emile Gallé, or the furniture of Louis Majorelle, the genius of good Art Nouveau design is not just in the grace of these sensuous shapes but in the element of surprise. Look out, for instance, for the ribbed, angular shapes of some of Horta's details, as in the brass, columned pier of the entrance lobby and the supports for the arches in the dining room, which, with a stroke of inventive daring, he lined with white-enamelled industrial brick.

One of the distinctive features of a Horta house is Horta's use of light, particularly in stairwells lit by an overhead canopy of glass.

Here the stairs rise to a crescendo of gold, white and copper beneath the glass canopy, enhanced by pond-shaped mirrors, abstracted floral designs on the walls, and the ribbon-like wrought-iron of the light fittings (originally gas) and banisters. The overall effect is one of comfortable elegance.

Hôtel Hannon

1 Av de la Jonction, t 02 538 4220, e contrety@ hebel.net; metro Horta. Open Tues–Sun 1–6; adm €2.50.

Compared with the Musée Horta, this corner house has a spacious ground plan. It was designed for the engineer Edouard Hannon (1853–1931), who worked his way up the Solvay soda empire. He spent part of his career at a Solvay factory near Nancy, in eastern France, where he saw the work of the great Art Nouveau glass, ceramics and furniture designer Emile Gallé (1853–1904). When Hannon decided to build his hôtel in 1902, he persuaded his friend the architect Jules Brunfaut (1852–1942) to create a wholly Art Nouveau house, and he commissioned Gallé to design the furniture. Following Gallé's death in 1904, Hannon asked Louis Majorelle (1859–1926), also from Nancy, to take his place. This was once one of the great Art Nouveau houses of Europe.

Unfortunately, all the original contents have now been dispersed; the house itself was only saved from destruction by the intervention of the Commune de St-Gilles in 1976, and remained a vandalized wreck until renovation in 1984–8. The house is now a gallery for temporary photographic exhibitions called L'Espace Photographique Contretype.

Hôtel Solvay

224 Av Louise; metro Louise, then tram 94.

This house belonged to Ernest Solvay (1838–1922), a chemist who discovered a way of making soda. In 1894 he commissioned Horta to build and furnish this large private house, which was completed four years later.

Compared to other Art Nouveau buildings, Horta's façades were restrained, but you can detect the spirit of Art Nouveau in the gently curving stonework and in sinuous ironwork of the balcony railings. Note the cast-iron columns that run up the two storeys of the projecting bays, complete with projecting rivets. No attempt has been made to disguise these. On the contrary, Horta has made a virtue of their industrial connotations – a provocative gesture at the time. You can get a sense of what lies inside by peering through the glass front door into the spacious hallway, lit by Art Nouveau lamps.

Hôtel Max Hallet

346 Av Louise; metro Louise; tram 94.

During the 1890s Max Hallet was one of the young intellectuals who set Horta on his way to becoming the father of the Art Nouveau movement. As a member of the newly founded Belgian Workers' Party, Hallet helped persuade the party's executive committee to consider Horta for the commission of the Maison du Peuple in Sablon. Art Nouveau was unofficially adopted as the Socialist style and was applied to new public buildings in Socialist boroughs. Hallet asked Horta to draw up plans for this, his own private house.

Its façade, not completed until 1905, demonstrates the growing simplicity of Horta's later work. The subtle curves of the stonework and iron contrast with the horizontal of the balcony, which cuts right across the building's centre. This classical restraint is ignored on the rear façade, where three bulbous glass structures stand on poles to form a winter garden at first floor level.

Abbaye de la Cambre

Rue du Monastère, t 02 648 1121; metro Louise, then tram 93 or 94. Abbey church open Mon–Fri 9–12 and 3–6, Sat 8–12.30 and 3–6, Sun 9–12.30.

This tranquil quadrangle is formed by a set of 18th-century buildings which once belonged to the Abbaye de la Cambre. They are now home to various government offices, including Belgium's National Geographical Institute. The property nestles in a peaceful wooded hollow and includes a series of duck ponds and a raised formal garden that was originally laid out in the 1720s.

Founded in 1201 as a Cistercian nunnery, the abbey thrived in this valley of the River Maelbeek until the religious disturbances of the 16th century. It was renovated during the 18th century, but was then closed by the French in 1796.

The abbey church is the sole survivor of the medieval monastery; a simple but pretty Gothic church, with a bare stone nave leading up to a semicircular apse decorated with modern stained glass. The nave has an unusual vaulted ceiling lined with wood. The abbey cloister dates from the 14th century.

Musée Constantin Meunier

59 Rue de l'Abbaye, t 02 648 4449, e info@ fine-arts-museum.be, w www.fine-arts-museum.be; metro Louise, then tram 93 or 94. Open Tues–Sun 10–12 and 1–5; closed alternate weekends; adm free, ring the bell for admittance.

The painter and sculptor Constantin Meunier (1831–1905) is best remembered for his bronzes of industrial workers – notably the gaunt forge-workers called *puddleurs* (puddlers), with their round leather hats to protect them from sparks. In his early career, Meunier painted only monastic and religious scenes, but between 1879 and 1881 his visits to the industrial regions around Liège and the coal-mining Borinage district (which also impressed the young Van Gogh at about the same time) left a deep mark. Meunier thereafter became a social realist in the mould of Gustave Courbet and Jean-François Millet. Although he played with Impressionism and pointillism, generally he stuck to his guns throughout a period when other painters were using ever more luminous colours and challenging the very basis of figurative painting. Barring the odd lapse into sentimentality, Meunier's work has a deep sense of conviction, and the power to evoke the hardships of physical labour and the misery of industrial society through which pride and dignity burn like embers.

The museum consists of a collection of Meunier's paintings, drawings and sculpture set out on the ground floor and in his large, north-facing studio to the rear. It includes sketches and trial work on the theme of fecundity for his monument to Emile Zola, which was erected in Paris but destroyed by the Germans during the Second World War. One of his most famous paintings, *Le Retour des Mineurs*, is on show here; look out also for the dramatic preparatory sketch (in the passage to the studio), in which the miners are rendered in skeletal crosshatching and set against a dismal industrial landscape.

Musée Communal d'Ixelles

*71 Rue Jean van Volsem, **t** 02 515 64 21/22, **e** musee.ixelles@skynet.be; **metro** Porte de Namur; **bus** 95 or 96 from the Bourse to Place Raymond Blyckaerts; wheelchair accessible. **Open** Tues–Fri 1–6.30, Sat and Sun 10–5; **adm** free to permanent collection.*

This small, informal gallery is full of delightful surprises. The collection was founded in 1892 and includes minor works by great artists, such as sketches by Rembrandt, Boucher, Fragonard and Delacroix, a tiny self-portrait by Jongkind, 15 original posters by Toulouse-Lautrec, a small Cubist painting in acrylic by Picasso, a watercolour of Cannes by Raoul Dufy, and a painted metal work by Frank Stella. Belgian artists are particularly well represented, with paintings by Léon Frédéric, Magritte and Spilliaert. Two works by Rik Wouters (1882–1916) may help to convince you that he was one of Belgium's most endearing artists: one a painting of his wife Nel in a red hat, the other called *La Vierge Folle* (The Mad Virgin), 1912 – a bronze statue of a nude dancing with energetic

abandon. This sculpture is full of the *joie de vivre* for which Wouters' work is celebrated.

Musée Camille Lemonnier

*150 Chaussée de Wavre, **t** 02 512 2968; **metro** Trône. **Open** Mon–Fri 9–6; **adm** by arrangement only.*

Camille Lemonnier (1844–1913) was one of the founding fathers of the naturalistic novel, an art critic and leading intellectual local to Ixelles. He was influenced by French writer Émile Zola and his best-known novel is *Le Petit Homme de Dieu*, published in 1902. This small museum recreates Lemonnier's writing room, displays manuscripts, gilded books and an impressive collection of late 19th-century artwork, including a Rodin sculpture and portraits by Emile Claus.

UCCLE

Uccle, to the south, is the city's largest commune and one of its most prosperous. The leafy boulevards that link what was once a cluster of villages make this an attractive residential district, though there isn't a great amount here to attract the tourist. Most of the embassies are here, and there's an established community of people who work in the EU quarter. The terrain is undulating and there is lots of greenery, including more than 500 hectares of the Forêt de Soignes, and the Parc de Wolvendael.

Bois de la Cambre

*At the end of Av Louise; **tram** 94.*

This large wooded park formed the northern tip of the Forêt de Soignes until it was annexed to the city in 1842. A favourite spot for walks and picnics, the park includes an artificial boating lake, cafés and a roller-skating rink. A series of roads arc through the wood, so the sound of traffic is never far away. However, this is the city's most accessible escape, and it's not hard to find yourself in a secluded spot with nothing in sight but towering 200-year-old beech trees.

Musée David et Alice van Buuren

41 Av Léo Errera, t 02 343 4851, e museumvanbuuren@skynet.be, w www .museumvanburren.com; tram 23 or 90; bus 60 (passes through Ixelles). Open Sun 1–5.30 and Mon 2–5.30; adm €7.50.

If you enjoyed pottering round the rooms of the Musée Horta, then step forward three decades into this Dutch banker's elegant private house, with gardens, built and furnished in the Art Deco style. Exotic woods and ivory are among the materials integrated into the luxurious interior décor, every last item conforming to the harmony of the design. The house contains a remarkable collection of paintings, including works by Bruegel (a version of the *Fall of Icarus*), Wouters, Van Gogh, and the Sint-Martens-Latem School. The gardens, landscaped by René Pechère (who also designed the Mont des Arts gardens, *see* p.99), contain hundreds of rare trees and a maze.

ANDERLECHT

The name Anderlecht will set bells ringing in the mind of any soccer fan: Anderlecht is one of Europe's premier football teams, and its 28,000-seat stadium in the **Parc Astrid** is situated in the heart of this commune. Anderlecht was once an outlying village of Brussels, clustered around the old and atmospheric Eglise Sts-Pierre-et-Guidon, until the late 19th century when it was radically transformed into an industrialized suburb. However, it still retains the independent atmosphere of a village, and there is a distinct air of prosperity in its many shops and restaurants.

During the 13th century a small *béguinage* was founded in the shadow of the church; this is now a charming small museum. Three

hundred years later the great humanist Erasmus came to live nearby for a brief period, and his house is also a museum now.

Musée des Egouts

Pavillon d'Octroi, Porte d'Anderlecht (on Bvd du Midi), t 02 513 8587; metro Anneessens and 5min walk; tram 18 or bus 47 connects Porte d'Anderlecht with the Place de la Vaillance. Open Wed 9am, 11am, 1pm and 3pm (ring doorbell on southeast side); adm €2.

An exhibition and video of the history of Brussels' sewer system and the fate of the River Senne, which was covered over in the 1860s. The visit includes a descent to see the Senne and a short walk along a main sewer.

Musée Bruxellois de la Gueuze

56 Rue Gheude, t 02 521 4928, e cantillon@ belgacom.net; metro Lemmonier or Midi; bus 47. Open Mon–Fri 9–5, Sat 10–5; adm €3. Guided tour on request, extra €3.

The atmospheric old brewery where Cantillon, one of the great gueuze beers, is made in the traditional way from lambic (*see* p.240 for an introduction to these unique beers). The beer is brewed only in the winter months (approx. 15 Oct–15 May), but there is still plenty to see outside this period. A tasting is included in the price.

Maison d'Erasme

31 Rue du Chapitre, t 02 521 1383, e erasmus huis.maisonerasme@skynet.be, w www .ciger.be/erasmus; metro St-Guidon. Open Tues–Sun 10–5; adm €1.25, plus €0.50 for the loan of an invaluable catalogue (in English) of the 663 exhibits.

In 1521, Erasmus spent five months at this house, as a guest of Canon Wijkman, enjoying the relaxation and country air. 'I would be dead by now had I not left the stench of the city [Brussels],' he wrote in one of his witty letters. The brevity of his stay undermines the museum's claim to be the

Erasmus and Humanism

Desiderius Erasmus (c. 1469–1536) was a great Renaissance scholar, and did much to release intellectual thought from the shackles of Christian dogma and medieval superstition. Born Geert Geerts in Rotterdam, the illegitimate son of a priest, he joined a monastery to pursue a life of learning, taking on the name of Desiderius ('beloved') Erasmus (after St Erasmus). In 1492 he was ordained, but became frustrated with the restricted intellectual life of the priesthood. He went to a college in Paris, where he earned a reputation as an inspired teacher, and began his life of travelling from one scholarly establishment to another, in the Netherlands, Italy and England (Oxford in 1499 and Cambridge in 1509–14).

During his stay in England he became friends with Thomas More, who encouraged him to write his most famous work *In Praise of Folly* (1509), a satire directed mainly against theologians. In 1516 he became adviser to the young Duke of Brabant, shortly to become the great Emperor, Charles V, and wrote *The Education of a Christian Prince* for him. That same year he also published his ground-breaking Latin translation (from Greek) of the New Testament.

Erasmus taught piety, pacifism, equality for women and tolerance, illuminating the world with the torch of humanism. Strictly, humanism referred to a new emphasis on secular studies (the humanities) – informed by the rediscovery of classical literature – as opposed to religious studies. Its development coincided with the growth of universities as the leading centres of education, at the expense of the monasteries. (Erasmus helped to found the famous College of Three Languages at Leuven in 1517–21.) But humanism was also a reassertion of the dignity of human life. Previously the Church alone had controlled moral and intellectual issues; ordinary people were generally classed as sinful and could not hope for anything but eternal damnation. The humanists placed people back at the centre of the stage, offering them the choice of leading moral, Christian lives in return for the opportunity to reassess their world.

This intellectual emancipation required courage, diplomacy and determination, with the powerful forces of the Church and vested political interests ranged against it. The prejudices of Erasmus's detractors were soon confirmed: his attacks on the abuses of the Catholic Church (notably in *Colloquia*, 1519) were considered to have a direct influence on the Reformation which had been set in motion by Martin Luther in 1517.

Although Erasmus distanced himself from the Reformation and contested the theology of Martin Luther, he found himself in the midst of religious controversy. In the latter years of his life he was based in Basle, but was forced to flee to Germany between 1529 and 1536 when religious fanatics made life too hot for him there. He returned to Basle in 1536 and died the following year, aged 67.

'House of Erasmus', but don't let that put you off. Restored in the 1930s, after a century of neglect, it consists of a series of rooms containing a rich collection of books, furniture, paintings and engravings from the life and times of Erasmus. Furthermore, it provides a rare opportunity to see the interior of a 16th-century gabled house. The centrepiece, the Salle de Renaissance, is decorated with embossed Spanish leather wall-hangings – rare today but a common treatment in their time. In the cabinets here you'll find various editions of *In Praise of Folly* and *Colloquia*, as well as a chilling collection of books that have been censored. Sections of Erasmus's work have been ripped out, inked over or scored through; in one case even the genitals of cherubs on a title page have been covered over. There is a list of books dated 1537 in which Erasmus's works have been crossed out by the Inquisition and the following inscription inserted: '*Auctor damnatus: opus vero permissum correctum est*' ('Condemned author: work authorized after correction'). Also in this room is the museum's most remarkable painting: an

Epiphany triptych by Hieronymus Bosch (1450–1516), featuring red-nosed peasant numbskulls gathered around a lowly cowshed in a medieval Flemish landscape.

Eglise Sts-Pierre-et-Guidon

*Place de la Vaillance; **metro** St-Guidon; **bus** 47 from Porte d'Anderlecht. **Open** Mon, Tues and Thurs–Sat 9–12 and 2.30–6, Wed 9–6 (5 in winter), Sun 9–12.*

Place de la Vaillance is a pretty, early 20th-century evocation of a Flemish Renaissance square. The church is one of Brussels' few surviving Gothic churches, a robust piece of late medieval architecture with thick stone walls and a roofline bristling with dragon-like gargoyles. A spire was added in the 19th century – an airy confection of stonework as delicate as Brussels lace. Chapels on this site date back to the 10th century, but this church was designed largely by Jan van Ruysbroeck (architect of the old Hôtel de Ville, *see* p.80) and built between 1470 and 1515. Sadly, the exterior is in such a sorry state that much of it has been fenced off.

Once the streets around this church thronged with horses and cattle, for it was the focus of the cult of St Guidon, whose tomb lies in the 11th-century crypt. Until about 25 years ago, local people still brought their animals to the church at Pentecost and on the saint's feast day (the first Sunday after 12 September) to have them blessed.

The Interior

The interior is cool and dingy, with cylindrical grey-stone columns and shadowy recesses, redolent of its medieval past. To the left of the entrance door is the Chapelle de Saint-Guidon, tacked on to the church in the first half of the 16th century. It was here that pilgrims would bring their *ex voto* offerings to plead for St Guidon's intercession. Further up on the south side of the church is the Chapelle de Notre-Dame de Grâce, which contains a statuette of the Virgin Mary that has been venerated here since 1449. This chapel was dedicated to St Guidon and is decorated with original 15th-century frescoes depicting his life. The pulpit in the nave also takes up the theme of St Guidon, showing him with a full-sized cow and a horse.

The church was once lavishly decorated with early 16th-century wall-paintings, some of which were discovered beneath a layer of whitewash in 1840. In the north wall of the nave is a graphic depiction of the martyrdom of St Erasmus, whose guts were slowly wound on to what looks like a kind of barbecue spit. St Erasmus (also called St Elmo) was an early Christian who became the patron saint of sailors. His symbol was the windlass, and this somehow got translated in the medieval mind into an instrument of torture.

In the north transept there is a 15th-century relief sculpture, which serves as a memorial to Albert Ditmar (d. 1439), doctor to various Dukes of Burgundy.

Béguinage

*Rue du Chapelain, **t** 02 521 1383; **metro** St-Guidon. **Open** Thurs–Mon 10–12 and 2–5; **adm** €1.25.*

This tiny enclave – it's really just two shuttered, red-brick cottages facing each other across a courtyard – is the only surviving *béguinage/begijnhof* in Brussels. Founded in 1252, it had a complement of just eight *béguines*. The tiny rooms have now been set out as a museum, evoking the atmosphere of the *béguinage* when it was in operation, with its minuscule chapel and simple bedroom and kitchen with a cast-iron stove. The first room on the left-hand side contains photographs of Anderlecht in the late 19th century when it was still semi-rural. The attic has been set aside as a local folklore museum. On the right-hand side one room has been arranged as the *béguines'* shop, where they would sell *speculoos* biscuits and festive loaves decorated with plaster discs

The History of Béguinages

Béguinages were communities of single women which developed during the 13th century, mainly in response to the imbalance caused by the Crusades: for several centuries there just weren't enough men to go around. Rather than living in isolation or with married relatives, many unmarried women preferred to join a *béguinage* until a suitable partner turned up. Widows (themselves often young) could also stay in a *béguinage*. By and large, the women came from fairly well-off backgrounds, as they had to pay an entry fee and maintenance. These were pious communities, usually closely connected to a church, but the *béguines* were not nuns. They made simple vows of chastity and obedience to their superiors (the elected *maîtresses*), applicable for the duration of their stay. They led modest but comfortable lives, assisted by servants and estate workers, and spent their time in prayer, in making lace, biscuits and sweets, in looking after the sick in their infirmary, and in distributing gifts to the poor.

The origin of the word *béguinage* remains obscure. One legend recalls a priest from Liège, Lambert le Bègue, who encouraged crusaders' widows to form communities, an idea that spread throughout the Netherlands and Germany. *Béguinages* remained a widespread feature of society in the Low Countries – the larger ones had over a thousand members – until the 18th century, and a few are still in operation. Even when deserted, they have a unique atmosphere of care, moderation and tranquillity.

---

illustrating children's stories. Look out too for the display cabinet devoted to St Guidon (or St Guido, *c.* 950–1012), a local saint celebrated as the protector of stables and cowsheds and the healer of livestock and human contagious diseases. The cabinet contains *ex voto* offerings: miniature cast-iron limbs, wax models of cows and pigs, tin noses.

KOEKELBERG AND JETTE

The uninspiring suburb of Koekelberg stands in the shadow of the controversial Basilique Nationale de Sacré Coeur, the world's fourth largest church. The completion of the Léopold II tunnel, along the route linking the basilica with the Botanical Gardens, is part of a recent wave of construction work around the city's northern approach. Further north is Jette, the green middle-class suburb that was home to René Magritte. These two sights could be combined with a visit to either Anderlecht or the Atomium: use the metro link between St-Guidon, Simonis, Pannenhuis and Heysel.

Basilique Nationale de Sacré Cœur

1 Parvis de la Basilique, t 02 425 8822; metro Simonis, then tram 19. Open Easter–early Nov daily 8–6, early Nov–Easter daily 8–5; adm free. Panorama from dome Mar–Oct Mon–Fri 11am and 3pm; adm €2.50.

The green-copper dome that dominates northwestern Brussels belongs to what is often cited as the city's least loved building. Begun in 1905 (another brainchild of Léopold II) and eventually completed in 1979, it belongs to the 'bring-your-own-spirituality' school of ecclesiastical architecture: if you don't, you'll find it about as inspiring as a public swimming bath. One admirer of this gargantuan building was Victor Horta, who praised its reinterpretation of the Byzantine style, and its Art Deco flourishes.

Musée René Magritte

135 Rue Esseghem, t 02 428 2626; metro Pannenhuis. Open Wed–Sun 10–6; adm €6.

The house where Magritte and his wife lived on the ground floor from 1930 to the mid-1950s was bought in 1994 and has been meticulously restored to show how it looked when they lived there, with other exhibits on the upper floors. The studio where Magritte painted most of his famous works comes as a bit of a surprise – it's small, nondescript and a little dingy. Although Magritte painted for 25 years in this house, there are only a few sketches and letters on display, as well as the trademark bowler hat, pipe and chessboard. It provides an interesting insight into the master of the surreal, not least because the house and its contents are so plain.

LAEKEN AND THE ATOMIUM

Laeken is a breezy parkland district of northern Brussels, synonymous with the extensive domain of the royal palace. The magnificent royal glasshouses (Serres Royales), built during the reign of Léopold II, are open to the public for only a very limited period in spring, but nearby you can see two outstanding monuments to Léopold's more exotic fantasies, the Tour Japonaise and the Pavillon Chinois – vivid flashes of Orientalism in this remote and unlikely corner of the city.

A walk across the Parc de Laeken leads to the Atomium – an eccentric 1950s space-age fantasy which dominates the northern skyline and has the best panoramic view over Brussels. In its shadow lies Bruparck, an ersatz Flemish village of restaurants and boutiques surrounded by a model village, a multiscreen cinema complex and an indoor water complex. The promoters of Bruparck call it 'Europe's leisure capital', but it's not nearly as bad as that.

Notre-Dame de Laeken

Parvis Notre-Dame, t 02 478 2095; metro Boekstael. Open Sun 2–5pm.

Laeken has been the out-of-town residence of the royal family since the days of the first king of the Belgians, Léopold I, and the extraordinary Neo-Gothic church of Notre-Dame de Laeken is effectively the royal chapel. The church was designed after 1853 by Joseph Poelaert (architect of the Palais de Justice, *see* p.107) and completed in 1870. Notre-Dame de Laeken is exceptional for its sheer lumpy quality, which is now accentuated by layers of grime.

Royal Crypt

Open April–Oct Sun 2–5, on the anniversaries of the deaths of King Albert (17 Feb 11–5), King Baudouin (31 July 10–5), Queen Astrid (29 Aug 10–12 and 3–5), Léopold III (25 Sept 10–12 and 3–5), All Saints' Day (1 Nov 10–12 and 3–5), on the journées du patrimoine (2nd weekend in Sept 9.30–5) and during the Fête de la Dynastie (15 Nov 3–5).

This clinical-looking marbled sepulchre under the church contains virtually every past member of the Belgian royal family, from Léopold I to Baudouin I, who was interred here in 1993. The various queens buried in the Royal Crypt include Astrid and Charlotte (1840–1927), daughter of Léopold I and wife of the ill-fated Maximilian, Emperor of Mexico, who was executed in 1867.

Cimetière de Laeken

Open 21 Sept–14 Nov daily 8.30–4.30, 15 Nov–20 Sept Tues–Sun 8.30–4.30.

Walk round the west side of the church, past the solemn monument to French soldiers killed on Belgian soil in the First World War and its flame to the Unknown Soldier, to the entrance to the cemetery. This is one of Brussels' most celebrated necropolises, tightly packed with ornate tombs topped by broken columns, urns, angels and statues of incongruously sensual grieving maidens.

The majority of the tombs near the entrance are late 19th century, many belonging to the great and the good of Brussels' public life. The architects Joseph Poelaert (1817–79) and Alphonse Balat (1818–95) are buried here, as is playwright Michel de Ghelderode (1898–1962). Near the east gate, beyond the remnant of a 13th-century church, is a copy of Auguste Rodin's bronze *The Thinker*, contemplating the tomb

of an art critic called Jef Dillen. Although French by birth, Rodin lived and worked in Brussels during the 1870s.

Parc de Laeken

***Metro** Heysel; **tram** 23.*

This agreeable, undulating park contains two royal palaces, both sealed off from the public and more or less obscured from view: the Stuyvenberg Castle (to the west) and the Belvédère (over the hill to the north).

Pavillon Chinois

*44 Av J. Van Praet. **Open** Tues–Sun 10–4.30; **adm** €2 (or €3 for combined ticket with Tour Japonaise), free first Wed pm of each month.*

Following his visit to the Paris Exhibition of 1900, Léopold II hatched a grand plan of lining this street with exotic architecture for the enlightenment of his nation. He commissioned Alexandre Marcel (1860–1928), a specialist in oriental architecture, to devise the plan. The Pavillon Chinois was designed in 1901–2, and its constituent parts were made in Shanghai over the following two years. The final assembly of the pavilion was completed in 1910, after Léopold's death. Restoration has returned this remarkable

building to its original splendour – an intricate jigsaw of gilded wood, polychrome ceramics, carved screens and balustrades. The equally lavish interior contains a collection of Chinese porcelain and furniture.

Tour Japonaise

*44 Av J. Van Praet. **Adm** as for Pavillon Chinois.*

This complex consists of a set of Japanese halls leading up to the base of the five-tiered tower. The entrance halls are the work of Japanese architects and builders, and were designed and built in Japan and then shipped over for the 1900 Exhibition. They now contain an admirable collection of Japanese samurai armour and weaponry. The staircase is pure, unashamed 'Japanoiserie' – a stunning marriage of Art Nouveau and Japanese design. It includes luminous stained-glass panels by J. Galland based on Hokusai and other Japanese printmakers, and superb chandelier lamps by Eugène Soleau consisting of entwined foliage and glass lampshades in the form of petalled flowers. The tower itself was designed by Marcel along the lines of a 17th-century Buddhist pagoda; today only the lower level can be visited, an impressive room decorated with Japanese lacquer panels.

Serres Royales

*Av du Parc Royale, t 02 513 8940,
e tourism.brussels@tib.be. Open only for
guided tours end April–early May. Exact times
and prices change annually.*

Frustratingly, their tops is all you can see of
the famous glasshouses from outside the
Domaine Royal – a view that gives only a
faint hint of their scale, and not a whisper of
their true magnificence. The Serres Royales
are a complex of 11 huge barrel-vaulted
galleries and glass domes, the largest of
which rises to 25m. This extraordinary 'city of
glass' was built for Léopold II during the
1870s by Alphonse Balat (Victor Horta's
teacher). Inside are extensive collections of
tropical and subtropical plants, some dating
back to the 19th century.

Château Royal

Av du Parc Royale. Closed to the public.

The royal palace was first built in 1782–4 by
the governors who replaced Charles of
Lorraine, Maria Christina of Austria and
Albert of Saxe-Teck. After coming close to
demolition during the French occupation, it
was restored as a personal residence by
Napoleon after 1804. He was here with his
new wife, Marie-Louise, in 1812 when he
received intelligence that Csar Alexander I of
Russia had decided to reject the Continental
System (the blockade of British goods from
Europe). At Laeken, therefore, Napoleon drew
up the resolution to begin his disastrous
invasion of Russia, one of the major factors in
his downfall. A fire in 1890 destroyed a large
proportion of the palace but it was rebuilt
along its original Louis XV lines, with
Neoclassical façades topped by a dome of
black tiles. This is now the royal family's
preferred residence, and they tend to use the
Palais Royal in the centre of town only for
formal occasions.

Monument Léopold

Standing on the crest of a low hill, opposite
the royal palace, is this extravagant piece of
Neo-Gothic erected in 1881 in honour of
Léopold I (r. 1831–65). Having laid solid foun-

dations for the Belgian monarchy, he was the
victim of an unwarranted indignity at his
death. As a Protestant, his funeral was not
allowed to take place inside the church at
Laeken. Léopold's coffin had to be placed in a
cardboard mortuary temple outside the
church, before being transferred to the cellar
which, two years later, was upgraded as the
Royal Crypt. Nearby is the **Belvédère**, home to
the heir to the throne.

Atomium

*Bvd du Centenaire, t 02 474 8977,
e info@atomium.be, w www.atomium.be;
metro Heysel. Open April–Aug daily 9–7.30,
Sept–March daily 10–5.30; adm €5, combined
ticket with Mini Europe €13.50, and with
Océade €15.50.*

The Atomium was designed as the centrepiece of the Exposition Universelle et
Internationale de Bruxelles of 1958 – a showpiece of the then-powerful Belgian metal
industry. During the 1950s the atomic structure was a popular design theme, first seen
on a grand scale at the Festival of Britain
Exhibition of 1951. In 1958 a group of Belgian
designers went the whole hog, creating this
giant-sized version of an iron atom. This is
architectural kitsch on a grand scale, sorely
compromised by the practical necessity of
grounding the structure to earth with fire
escapes. It looks more like a space station
than a conceptual image from particle
physics. To underline the absurdity of its
scale, the Atomium often flies a Belgian
tricolour from its top sphere. Yet the
Atomium is a remarkable thing: with its nine
giant steel balls interconnected by metal
tubes (containing escalators) and rising to
102m, it is the Eiffel Tower of Brussels.

Inside, a glass-topped lift whisks you up the
central shaft to the Panorama at 100m. From
here you can see right across Brussels
(assisted by strategically placed maps) and
look down on the Parc de Laeken and over
Bruparck. Beside Bruparck, at the top of the
Boulevard du Centenaire, is the **Parc des
Expositions**, a huge complex built for

another international exhibition in 1935. To its left is the famous **Heysel football stadium**, a name familiar to all British and Italian football fans, for it was here, in 1985, at the European Cup Final between Juventus and Liverpool, that 'running' (a British football-hooligan expression meaning to charge at opposing fans) by Liverpool fans caused a wall to collapse in the old stadium killing 40 people (39 of them Italians). It has since been renamed Stade du Roi Baudouin.

Bruparck

Bvd du Centenaire t 02 474 8377, e info@bruparck.com, w www.bruparck.com; metro Heysel; wheelchair accessible; adm free to Le Village.

Bruparck was founded in 1987 as a sort of mini theme park. At its heart is Le Village, designed as a traffic-free Flemish town centre, with quaint red-brick, gabled buildings on several levels. These mainly house gift shops and a great variety of pubs and international restaurants. At the centre of Le Village is a children's adventure playground and a small arena where entertainers perform free for much of the year. The general atmosphere is peaceful and cheering. The cafés spill out on to the walkways, with tables under awnings and umbrellas, filling up with waves of visitors as they drift to and from the three main attractions around Bruparck.

Mini Europe

t 02 474 1313, e info@minieurope.com, w www.minieurope.com. Open end Mar–June daily 9.30–5, July–Aug 9.30–7 (Aug Fri–Sun till 11pm), Sept–Dec 10–5; adm €10.50, concs €8.

The Acropolis, the Colosseum, the Leaning Tower of Pisa, the Palace of Westminster, the Eiffel Tower, and much more. Mini Europe contains all the major landmarks of the European Union reduced to one-twenty-fifth of their actual size and surrounded by ponds with electronically operated boats and model trains. However, compared with other model villages, this is rather sparse and, some might feel, overpriced.

Kinepolis

Entrance in Bruparck or from Av du Championnat, t 02 474 2600. Open for performances; adm €6.50 for Imax.

This claims to be the largest cinema complex in the world. It includes the Imax theatre, which has a vast 600 sq m screen and shows short feature films that go for awesome 3D effects. There are a further 24 screens operating a varying programme.

Océade

t 02 478 4320. Open April–Aug Tues–Fri 2pm–10pm, Sat and Sun 10am–10pm, during school hols open daily 10am–10pm; adm €12 for 4 hrs. Discounted tickets available with Mini Europe and Atomium.

An inventive complex of indoor swimming pools (at 28°C), saunas, Jacuzzis, slides, wave machines and spiralling water shoots, designed for both exhilaration and relaxation in a tropical setting, and suitable for children and adults of all ages.

FORÊT DE SOIGNES AND TERVUREN

Palais Stoclet

275 Av de Tervuren; metro Montgomery, then tram 39 or 44 to the Père Damien stop. Closed to the public.

The Palais Stoclet is a classic of modern architecture, designed for a private client by the Austrian Josef Hoffmann (1870–1956), one of the founder members of the Vienna Secession. At first glance you would have said it was Art Deco (post-First World War); in fact it dates from 1905–11. It is all strident verticals and receding rectangles, reminiscent of skyscraper architecture. The only element of decorative whimsy is the four nude male statues, braced to the four winds on the summit. It helps, though, to realize that what you see is actually the back of the house. The story goes that Adolphe Stoclet (1871–1941), a wealthy industrialist, wanted the Avenue de Tervuren to be named after him. When this was refused he decided to turn the back of his new villa to the street.

Musée du Transport Urbain Bruxellois

364 Av de Tervuren; metro Montgomery, then tram 39 or 44 to the Dépôt Woluwe stop. Open April–Oct Sat, Sun and public hols 1.30–7; adm €4 incl. historic tram return trip to Tervuren.

Filling the extensive sheds of this old tram depot are dozens of trams (and some buses), which were essential ingredients in the expansion of Brussels in the 19th century. The first trams were the horse-drawn hippomobiles, introduced in 1835, just after Belgium's first railway, superseded by the electric tram in 1895.

The museum has beautifully restored examples of trams of all ages – including the sleek cream and chrome models of the 1950s and 1960s – plus plenty of tram memorabilia – guaranteed to pluck the strings of nostalgia somewhere along the line.

When the Musée du Transport Urbain is open, the no.44 tram route to Tervuren is also used by a selection of historic trams, which visitors to the museum can (and should) use. The trams leave from the museum forecourt and run to a published schedule. The tram journey takes about 20 minutes each way. These historic trams date from the 1920s, but with their panelling and wooden seats they evoke an even earlier era.

The ticket collector and the driver dress in period uniforms; you can watch the driver working the primitive controls. At the stops the ticket collector signals to the driver with a duck-like horn.

Forêt de Soignes

For Tervuren metro Montgomery, then tram 44; for Abbaye du Rouge-Cloître metro Herrmann-Debroux or tram 34.

A vast beech forest bordering southeast Brussels, covering 4,000 hectares; it is a remarkably wild area given its proximity to the city, and ravishingly beautiful in its golden colours of autumn. There are plenty of good paths for walkers – take your own picnic. A popular starting point is the **Abbaye du Rouge-Cloître**, a former 14th-century monastery at Auderghem. The forest includes two major tree collections, the Arboretum Géographique de Tervuren (Old and New World trees), and the Arboretum de Groenendaal (400 forest species).

Musée Royal de l'Afrique Centrale

13 Leuvensesteenweg, entrance through gates at the back of the building, t 02 769 5211, e info@africamuseum.be, w www.africa museum.be; metro Montgomery, then tram 44 to the Tervuren terminus and a 200m walk; historic tram from Musée du Transport Urbain Bruxellois when it's open. Open Tues–Fri 10–5, Sat, Sun and public hols 10–6; adm €2.

There was once a pleasure palace on this huge domain where Charles of Lorraine liked to hold hunting parties, and other festivities and he died here in 1780. The vast, domed Louis XV-style château that now dominates the park looks as though it might have been built in that era: in fact it was designed expressly as a museum at the end of the reign of Léopold II – at about the same time as the Palais Stoclet. The museum first opened its doors to the public in 1910, a year after Léopold's death.

The Musée Royal l'Afrique Centrale (Koninklijk Museum voor Middenafrika in Flemish) details the history of Belgium's colony in the Congo and contains a large and absorbing collection of historical, anthropological and zoological artefacts: fetishes, jewellery, baskets, weapons, sculpture, masks and headdresses, stuffed wildlife – many of which were collected for the Congo exhibit at the Brussels Universal Exhibition of 1897. Among the most memorable exhibits are an

The Belgian Congo

As a young man, King Léopold II travelled widely, and concluded that Belgium should have colonies, like other great European nations. Conveniently, the British–American explorer Henry Morton Stanley (1841–1904) was available to take commissions. Stanley was a human dynamo, who'd already undertaken ambitious expeditions in Africa.

In 1878, Léopold commissioned him to carve out a territory for Belgium in Central Africa, which Stanley achieved through trade negotiations, outrageous trickery and thuggery. Treaties with local tribes sold trading rights in exchange for land ownership. Bands of ruthless bounty hunters followed, making fortunes from this territory's vast natural wealth in diamonds, gold, timber and fertile soil. By 1884 Belgium controlled a vast territory called the Congo Free State. Leopold was infuriated when the Belgian government would not take responsibility for it (believing that trading agreements were more mutually beneficial than colonial possession).

After 1885 he took it over as a personal fiefdom and netted huge personal wealth. The Belgian nation stepped in in 1908, following mounting European criticism over the tyrannical way the colony was being run. The local people were badly abused, with little intervention by the authorities. There were outbursts of resistance, notably in the 1890s and during the First World War, but these were brutally suppressed.

After the First World War the former German colonies were redistributed among the victor nations, so Belgian power was extended to Ruanda–Urundi (after 1962, Rwanda and Burundi). This was a boom period for Belgian Africa, as planters, merchants and mining interests consolidated their gains; the period was also accompanied by improvements in education, public health, and labour relations. The Belgian population of the Congo's capital, Léopoldville (now Kinshasa), rose to 75,000.

After the Second World War, calls for independence became yet more urgent across Africa; in the Belgian Congo they were accompanied by widespread unrest. As events spun out of control, Belgium dropped the Congo like a hot brick and hastily granted it its independence in 1960. This was followed by a period of violent anarchy and in 1965 General Mobutu seized power; he would cling on to it for the next 32 years. The ruling élite maintained their contacts with Belgium, travelling frequently to Europe for education, banking, business and hospital treatment, but political relations became increasingly strained.

In 1971 the Republic of Congo changed its name to Zaire, and President Mobutu took the name Sese Seko, meaning 'The Warrior Who Knows No Defeat'. As his power became entrenched, so his image began to achieve a Stalinist-like omnipresence. It was international prestige, however, that he sought most of all, and his attempts to obtain it took strange forms, most notably his decision in 1974 to stage and finance the Heavyweight Championship fight between Muhammad Ali and George Foreman.

Despite its natural wealth, Zaire remained an impoverished and troubled country ruled by a tiny but wealthy élite, buttressed by enduring economic and political ties to its old colonial ruler. Belgium's contracts diminished as France and the USA enlarged their influence. Mobutu fell out even with his old friend King Baudouin, and was refused permission to attend his funeral in 1993.

Finally, in 1997 President Mobutu was overthrown by the Alliance of Democratic Forces for the Liberation of Congo Zaire led by Laurent Kabila. The fighting lasted a few months, with the ailing president unable to raise a force. Following peace talks, Kabila was sworn in as President of the Democratic Republic of Congo. Mobutu died in exile a few months later, aged 66, and was buried with little fanfare.

It's a sorry tale, from which modern Belgium would prefer to distance itself, but like all colonial histories it has its powerful legacies of trading and government contacts, intermarriage and immigration, and a rose-tinted nostalgia for a bygone era.

enormous pirogue – a 22.5m-long canoe, big enough for 100 men, hewn out of a single tree; a battered trunk used by Dr Livingstone on his last voyage; the peaked cap of the great adventurer Henry Morton Stanley (*see* 'The Belgian Congo'); an explorer's tin travelling case that doubled as a hip bath; slaving manacles; and a pickled coelacanth (the living 'fossil fish', believed to have been extinct for 70 million years until it was discovered off Africa in 1938). Since the 1960s, various artefacts from the Americas and Pacific Islands have been added to the impressive collection.

After visiting the museum, you can walk down to the lakes at the foot of the park, a place for afternoon strollers, anglers and children feeding the ducks. The thick woods of towering beech trees turn golden brown in autumn – a ravishing spectacle on a bright October day.

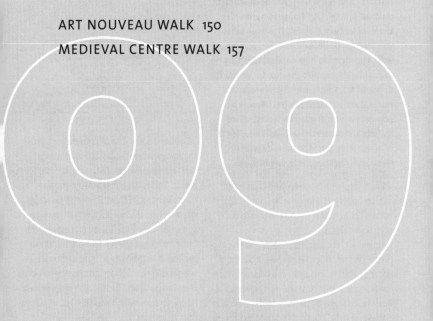

Walks

ART NOUVEAU WALK

Brussels is an Art Nouveau city *par excellence*. In the 1890s this novel decorative style swept through the recently built suburbs like a new religion: no progressive house-owner would consider anything else. Art Nouveau peppers just about every street dating from this era – sometimes in the form of full-blown Art Nouveau *hôtels* (private houses), but more often in small details, such as swirling ironwork railings, curvaceous door handles and hinges, or plaques featuring dreamy maidens with blonde, flowing hair. Even after decades in the doldrums of fashion – and the widespread destruction of much of Brussels' Art Nouveau heritage – there is plenty of it about. This walk takes you through Ixelles and St-Gilles, an area with a particularly high concentration. By no accident, this was also the quarter where the doyen of Art Nouveau architecture, Victor Horta, lived. Art Nouveau has become a popular passion, fuelled by tourist-office leaflets and numerous publications – some of which were timed to coincide with Art Nouveau's declared centenary in 1993.

Start: Intersection of Avenue Louise and Rue Lesbroussart. From metro Louise, take tram 93 or 94 down Avenue Louise to tram stop Lesbroussart.

Finish: It takes 40mins to return to the city centre on foot. Alternatively, walk to metro Porte de Namur. Buses 95 and 96 from Place Raymond Blyckaerts, at the northern end of Rue Malibran, go all the way to the Bourse.

Walking time: About 2.5hrs; add extra time for visiting museums along the route.

Lunch and drinks stops: La Tsampa, *see* p.234; La Quincaillerie, *see* p.234; La Canne en Ville, *see* p.233; L'Amadeus, *see* p.233; Chez Moeder Lambic, *see* p.242; L'Ultime Atome, *see* p.242; Verschueren, *see* p.242.

Note: Don't do this walk on a Monday, when the museums are closed.

From the tram stop at Lesbroussart, cross the busy Avenue Louise and walk a short distance southwards to No.224 Avenue Louise. This is the **Hôtel Solvay**, designed by Victor Horta for Ernest Solvay (1838–1922), a chemist who discovered a way of making soda (still called the Solvay process), which hitherto had only been found naturally in modest quantities as sodium carbonate.

In 1894 Ernest Solvay commissioned Victor Horta to build and furnish this large private house for him, which was finally completed four years later.

Compared with some Art Nouveau buildings in Brussels, Victor Horta's façades were restrained. However, you can certainly detect the spirit of Art Nouveau in the gently curving stonework and in the sinuous ironwork of the balcony railings. Note the cast-iron columns that run up the two storeys of the projecting bays, complete with

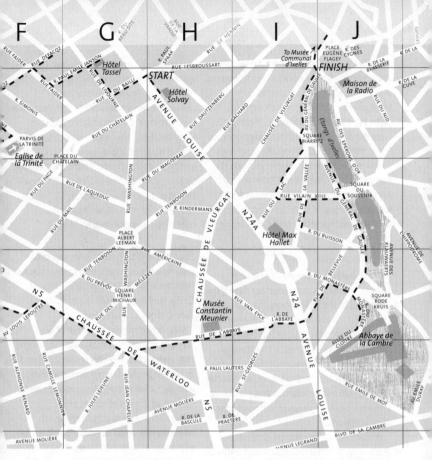

projecting rivets. No attempt has been made to disguise these. On the contrary, Horta has made a virtue of their industrial connotations – a provocative gesture at the time.

Horta was noted above all for his interiors, with their cunning use of light, ingenious configuration of space, and – despite the emphasis on decorative effect – a rigorous functionalism. He liked to design everything down to the door handles and light bulbs. He was given *carte blanche* by Solvay, and so here he worked in marble, teak and mahogany. You can get a sense of what might lie inside by peering through the glass front door into the spacious hallway, which is lit by Art Nouveau lamps.

Retrace your steps, crossing back over Avenue Louise to the Rue du Bailli. Walk down the Rue du Bailli and take the first right into the Rue de Livourne. Take the first right again into Rue Paul-Emile Janson. No.6

is the **Hôtel Tassel**. This *hôtel*, designed and built by Victor Horta in 1893–5, is generally acknowledged as the first building in the world in which Art Nouveau was applied to architecture. It has one of Horta's more exuberant façades, with swirling stonework counterbalanced by the stained glass on the first floor. Here cast iron, exploited for both its structural and its sculptural properties, was left exposed for the first time.

Victor Horta believed that a house '*devait être non seulement à l'image de la vie de l'occupant, mais qu'elle devait en être le portrait*' ('should not just correspond to the lifestyle of the occupant, but should be a portrait of it'). Tassel was a bachelor who liked to entertain; an engineer who belonged to the coterie of the new, liberal and artistically minded industrial class; an enthusiastic amateur photographer; and someone who, as a professor at the Université Libre de

Bruxelles, needed a quiet space for his studies. Horta had to work all these elements into this building, and succeeded triumphantly. However, in the long term these highly individualistic specifications were the downfall of such buildings, because it was difficult to adapt them to other uses.

Walk back up Rue P. E. Janson, crossing the Rue de Livourne. No.23 Rue P. E. Janson has Art Nouveau doors and ironwork. At **No.83 Rue Faider** is one of the city's most delightful Art Nouveau façades. Its undulating stone and ironwork carry the eye upwards from its glass and wooden doors, through the floral motifs in the first-floor windows, to the sensual murals on the upper storey featuring a Mucha-style woman, children and stars. Every detail has been carefully rethought in the Art Nouveau idiom – even the boot scraper and the perversely curved letterbox. Like many Art Nouveau buildings it's been signed and dated like a painting: A. Roosenboom, 1906. Albert Roosenboom (1871–1943) was one of Victor Horta's

Art Nouveau

Art Nouveau was the result of four phenomena which came together during the latter half of the 19th century. The first was the revolution in British design, pioneered in the 1860s by William Morris (1834–96). It stemmed from his disgust with industrial design, which in the mid-19th century was guilty of recycling tired old styles, such as the Neoclassical and Neo-Gothic, and plastering them willy-nilly on mass-produced goods of all descriptions.

William Morris, by contrast, championed the beauty of handmade goods and crafts-manship. Looking back to the guilds of pre-Renaissance Europe, he wanted to elimi-nate the distinction between craftsman, artist, architect and designer. He himself excelled in textile and wallpaper designs; his beautifully balanced, complex patterns, which drew mainly on the organic shapes of plants, were hugely influential in Europe. His ideas were adopted by several design move-ments in Britain, notably the one that, after 1888, was referred to as Arts and Crafts.

After the 1860s Japan began to emerge from a 200-year hibernation and Europe was seized with a fascination for all things Japanese: fans, prints, kimonos, ceramic vases. Japanese design seemed remarkably inventive and original – in its colour combi-nations, its unexpected compositions, and its confident use of asymmetry. For European artists and designers this was hugely eman-cipating. Shops such as Liberty's in London

(founded in 1874) bought large stocks of Japanese goods, which were sold side by side with their own lines of the latest Arts and Crafts products – jewellery, candlesticks, lamps, ceramics and pewterware.

Meanwhile, the development of new building materials, notably cast iron, meant that architects could now create structures in any shape they fancied, and light them with picture windows, glass canopies and decorative screens of leaded glass.

The final phenomenon affecting Art Nouveau was urban development. With the expansion of suburban transport systems – notably the trams and the railways in the case of Brussels – new suburbs mush-roomed. Some 30,000 houses were built in Brussels during the last four decades of the 19th century.

In Belgium this combination of factors led to a search for a brand-new style which would appeal to the acquisitive, newly wealthy middle classes, who were well informed about current trends and had no particular nostalgia for the patrician styles of old. During the 1880s and early 1890s, architects and designers were stimulated by a rash of architectural competitions, and by high-profile art forums, notably Les XX (*see* p.48) and its subsequent manifestation La Libre Esthétique, which directly encouraged dialogue between thinkers, artists, craftsmen and decorators.

At first these craftsmen drew on a broad variety of models ranging from Tuscan villas draughtsmen, but apart from this, he did very little work in the Art Nouveau style.

Turn right up Rue Faider, then right into Rue Defacqz. **No.48 Rue Defacqz** is by Paul Hankar. Paul Hankar (1859–1901), the son of a stonemason, worked for the architect Henri Beyaert (who designed the Place du Petit-Sablon, *see* p.108), before emerging in the 1890s as one of the most prolific architects of the Art Nouveau style. No.48 Rue Defacqz was built in 1897 as the house and studio of the Symbolist painter Albert Ciamberlani

(1864–1956), who is best known for the huge, semicircular mural in the Parc du Cinquantenaire.

This building demonstrates the new-found freedoms which Art Nouveau offered, with its huge round windows on the first floor and its extravagant fish-bone ironwork on the balcony. Although now peeling, the murals on the upper storey – depicting peacocks, fanciful trees and a lightly draped, idealized family – are typical of the soft-focus mood of Art Nouveau figurative painting.

to Moghul palaces, producing what has subsequently become known as the 'eclectic style'. Then, in 1893, a 32-year-old architect called Victor Horta (1861–1947) designed a house for an engineer and professor called Tassel. The Hôtel Tassel, with its organic, flowing shapes in ironwork, stained glass and carved stone, caused a sensation. Many saw it as a monstrosity; others championed it as a masterpiece. Soon Victor Horta was inundated with commissions.

Meanwhile, the message was being spread by other architects and designers, such as Henri Van de Velde, Paul Hankar, Gustave Serrurier-Bovy, Ernest Blérot, Octave van Rysselberghe, and a host of lesser names eager to jump on the bandwagon.

In the early 1890s this new-found passion for curvaceous, swirling design went by various names, including 'Modern Style' and 'Style Anglais'. In 1894 Henri Van de Velde referred to '*un art nouveau*', a term picked up the following year in the name of a new shop in Paris, La Maison de l'Art Nouveau.

Art Nouveau was adopted as a label in both French and English, but it had different names elsewhere: Jugendstil in German and Dutch (after a journal named Jugend), and Stile Liberty in Italy. It was a truly international style, occurring also in the USA, where Louis Comfort Tiffany (1848–1933) became a leading proponent – remembered mostly for his stained-glass lamps.

One of the few countries in Europe that did not get caught up in Art Nouveau fervour

was Britain, still soldiering on with the ideals of more stolid Arts and Crafts design well into the 20th century. There Art Nouveau was restricted to details such as fireplaces and the stained glass in doors. Home-grown talents, such as Arthur Mackmurdo (who had a direct influence on Belgian Art Nouveau) and Charles Rennie Mackintosh (who was much appreciated by the Vienna Secession, led by Gustav Klimt, among others) were largely ignored in their own country.

By the time of the Paris International Exhibition of 1900, Art Nouveau was all the rage on the Continent. That same year Hector Guimard began designing his famous métro entrances in Paris.

Art Nouveau remained a major stylistic force up until the First World War, albeit in an increasingly popularized and watered-down form. After the war, however, it was regarded with some distaste, not simply for being old-fashioned, but because it somehow spoke of the *fin de siècle* decadence that was held responsible for the war. It was ousted by the more strident, angular, Machine Age style of Art Deco.

Only in the hazy, flower-power Romanticism of the late 1960s did Art Nouveau become popular again. By this time many of Brussels' Art Nouveau landmarks had been demolished, or they had decayed beyond recovery. At the movement's height there had been some 2,000 Art Nouveau houses in Brussels; only about half of these have survived today.

Next door, No.50, was also designed by Paul Hankar, in 1898; although radically altered in 1905, it still shows Hankar's imaginative treatment of window space.

It is interesting to compare these with **No.71 Rue Defacqz**, reached by retracing your steps a short way and continuing along the street. This was the house that Paul Hankar built for himself in 1893–4, right on the cusp between his eclectic period – heavily influenced by Beyaert's medieval and Renaissance styles – and Art Nouveau (note the ironwork in the uppermost arches). It has all the imaginative panache of the architecture of the 1890s but lacks the curvaceous and cohesive vision that developed with Art Nouveau.

For a brief change of mood and epoch, take the second left, down Rue de l'Amazone, to a small square called the Parvis de la Trinité. Occupying most of this square is the **Eglise de la Trinité** (*open at irregular hours; while under renovation access is from 54B Rue de l'Aqueduc*). The gable-like façade of this church is a fine example of the transitional period between the Flemish Renaissance and Baroque – a confection of Neoclassical pediments, *œil-de-bœuf* windows and barley-sugar columns. It was built in 1620, but did not arrive here until 1895. It used to belong to a church on Place de Brouckère in the city centre, but when this was condemned to make room for the new boulevard built over the River Senne in the 1870s, parish members raised funds to have the façade rebuilt on this site, where it now seems perfectly at home. The interior of the church, however, is bland and disappointing.

There are several Art Nouveau details in the Parvis de la Trinité. At No.1, the apartments are decorated with Art Nouveau murals; No.6 has Art Nouveau ironwork on the balconies and tilework featuring swallows and a female head in profile.

Walk around the church into the Rue de l'Aqueduc and turn right. You are now crossing from the Commune d'Ixelles into the Commune de St-Gilles, both boroughs created during the late 19th-century building boom. Take the first left into the Rue

Africaine. No.5 has Art Nouveau ironwork at basement level and faded murals on the upper storeys. Take the first right into the Rue Américaine. At 25 Rue Américaine is the **Musée Horta**, an unmissable museum for fans of Horta. Victor Horta built this as his home and studio in 1899–1901, when he was at the pinnacle of his powers. Horta's former home was bought by the Commune de St-Gilles in 1961, and opened as the Musée Horta in 1969. The interior, which had remained more or less intact, has been carefully restored and is now furnished with pieces Horta designed for the house, as well as others from his buildings elsewhere.

As soon as you walk through the front door, the Art Nouveau motifs in the mosaic flooring and the flowing shapes of the coathooks, hatstand and door furniture tell you that you are entering a manicured environment. As in the jewellery of René Lalique, the glassware of Emile Gallé, or the furniture of Louis Majorelle, the genius of good Art Nouveau design is not just in the grace of these sensuous shapes but in the element of surprise. Look out, for instance, for the ribbed, angular shapes of some of Horta's details, as in the brass, columned pier of the entrance lobby and the supports for the arches in the dining room – a room which, with a stroke of inventive daring, he lined with white-enamelled industrial brick. Much of the furniture is in American ash, a pale, matt-surfaced wood far removed from the typically sombre and heavy furniture of the late Victorian period.

One of the distinctive features of a Horta house is his use of light, particularly in stairwells lit by an overhead canopy of glass. Here the stairs rise to a crescendo of gold, white and copper beneath the glass canopy, enhanced by pond-shaped mirrors, abstracted floral designs on the walls, and the ribbon-like wrought-iron of the light fittings (originally gas) and banisters. The overall effect is one of elegance, comfort and uplifting joyousness.

After leaving the museum, continue to the end of the street and turn left and walk

Victor Horta

Victor Horta, the son of a Ghent shoe-maker, had been something of a child prodigy. He attended architecture courses at the Académie des Beaux-Arts in Ghent from the age of 13, and won a gold medal for his work two years later. He spent three influential years as an apprentice in Paris (1878–81) before returning to study at the Académie des Beaux-Arts in Brussels. Here he joined the practice of Alphonse Balat (1818–95), Léopold II's favourite architect, who is best remembered for the huge glasshouses, the Serres Royales in the Parc de Laeken (see p.144). They were exceptional not only for their scale but for the novel way in which the external cast-iron structure was turned into a decorative feature. In 1884 Horta won the Prix Godecharle for architecture (established in memory of the sculptor Gilles-Lambert Godecharle), and the following year he began to design houses on his own account. In 1889 he created the Edicule Lambeaux (now called the Pavillon Horta), a temple-like pavilion in the Parc du Cinquantenaire built to house relief sculptures by Jef Lambeaux. It demonstrates Horta's strong feeling for Neoclassical proportion.

The Hôtel Tassel, built in 1893, was his breakthrough, and for a decade or so Horta reigned supreme in the world of house-design. He was an 'ensemblier' – an architect who conceptualized not only the building but everything within it. It was an exacting task, requiring great imaginative and practical energy from himself and his team of draughtsmen. After 1898 he was working on both his home and the Maison du Peuple (built 1898–9), an ambitious complex near the Sablon, demolished in 1965.

In the early 1900s, however, a new vogue began to take over, led by the architects and painters of the Vienna Secession. Like Mackintosh in Scotland, they adopted a more symmetrical, angular, upright look, prefiguring Art Deco. The Palais Stoclet (see p.145) is the outstanding example of this in Brussels.

The sensuous, organic lines of Art Nouveau began to look outmoded to private clients, and from now on Horta did little domestic architecture. Instead, he concentrated on a number of new department stores, to which he applied his usual attention to detail. These stores included L'Innovation (1900–3), in the Rue Neuve, which was destroyed in 1967 by a horrific fire that killed 251 people; the Magasins Waucquez (1903–6), now the home of the Centre Belge de la Bande Dessinée (see p.119); and the Magasins Wolfers (1909) on Rue d'Arenberg, whose salvaged display cases can now be seen amongst the artifacts of the Musées Royaux d'Art et d'Histoire (see p.130).

During the First World War Horta took part in a conference in London on the reconstruction of Belgium. When the Germans discovered this, he was unable to return, and spent the rest of the war in Britain and the USA. When he came back to Brussels in 1919 he decided to sell his house in Rue Américaine, because the studio was too small for his practice, and its style was now considered old-fashioned. Horta's new style was more akin to Art Deco, and his major projects of the inter-war period included the Palais des Beaux-Arts. As a widely respected figure in the architectural world, holding eminent positions at various institutes, he was made a baron in 1932. He died in 1947.

down the Chaussée de Charleroi to the intersection with the Chaussée de Waterloo. Cross straight over into Avenue Brugmann, which is named after Georges Brugmann (1829–1900), a leading banker of the late 19th century and a generous philanthropist. Continue down Avenue Brugmann to the Avenue de la Jonction. At **Nos.53 and 55**

Avenue Brugmann are two Art Nouveau houses. These were built in 1898 and 1899 respectively, by a little-known architect called E. Pelseneer. No.55 is called **Les Hiboux**, and has murals, round windows and, on the false chimney-tops, sculptures of two owls, which give the house its name.

However, the main reason for coming here is next door, at the corner of the Avenue de la Jonction. This is the **Hôtel Hannon**, which is now a gallery for temporary photographic exhibitions called **L'Espace Photographique Contretype** (*open Tues–Sun 1–6; adm €1.25*).

Compared with the Musée Horta, this corner house has a spacious ground plan. It was designed for the engineer Edouard Hannon (1853–1931), who worked his way up the Solvay soda empire to become one of its big wheels. He spent part of his career at a Solvay factory near Nancy, in eastern France, where he saw the work of the great Art Nouveau glass, ceramics and furniture designer Emile Gallé (1853–1904). When Hannon decided to build his *hôtel* in 1902, he persuaded his friend the architect Jules Brunfaut (1852–1942) to abandon his usual eclectic style and create a wholly Art Nouveau house, and he commissioned Emile Gallé to design the furniture and other accessories. Following Gallé's death in 1904, Hannon asked Louis Majorelle (1859–1926), also from Nancy, to take his place. In other words, this was once one of the great Art Nouveau houses of Europe.

Unfortunately, all the original contents of the house have now been dispersed; the house itself was only saved from destruction by the intervention of the Commune de St-Gilles in 1976, and remained a vandalized wreck until renovation in 1984–8. The architectural rudiments of the house remain, together with the Tiffany-influenced stained glass in the large bow window and the striking set of murals by Paul-Albert Baudouin, a French artist who passionately wanted to revive traditional techniques of fresco painting. The murals in the stairwell and main living room, therefore, are genuine frescoes, painted, like early Renaissance works, directly on to wet plaster.

Leaving the Hôtel Hannon, cross the Avenue Brugmann and walk down the street almost opposite, the Avenue du Haut Pont. Turn left into the Rue Franz Merjay, then first right into the **Rue de la Réforme**.

This is a typical late 19th-century street built for the well-to-do. Its cobbled pavements are overlooked by tall, terraced houses, whose front doors open directly on to the street. The narrow façades created an ideal canvas upon which to apply Art Nouveau style – as can be seen at No.79 (murals under the eaves) and No.74 (iron-work and murals). Turn left when you reach Avenue Louis Lepoutre, then right into the Chaussée de Waterloo. Take the third left, the Rue de l'Abbaye, walk up the hill, and cross the Chaussée de Vleurgat. At 59 Rue de l'Abbaye is the **Musée Constantin Meunier**, the house where Meunier lived at the end of his career (*see* 'Outside the Centre', p.136).

Continue along the Rue de l'Abbaye, then cross the Avenue Louise once more. Take the road that leads to the Avenue Louise at an angle, Rue de Bellevue. **Nos.46, 44 and 42 Rue de Bellevue** were designed by the prolific Art Nouveau architect Ernest Blérot. Ernest Blérot (1870–1957) was both a property developer and an architect. It is reckoned that in just eight years after 1897 he created some 200 houses – of which only 50 have survived. Like many of the Art Nouveau architects he was something of an idealist, believing that everyone should have access to practical and stylish living accommodation. His interiors were left deliberately uncluttered, with the emphasis on light and space. This group of three is typical. The exteriors are all variations on the same theme: brick, curving stonework and murals.

Nos.32 and 30 Rue de Bellevue are also by Blérot, and were built at about the same time. Here he has applied the Art Nouveau style to the traditional terraced house. Take the next right, which leads to **No.30 Rue du Monastère**. This is the earliest house attributed to Blérot, dating from 1897. The ironwork is its most striking Art Nouveau feature on an otherwise subdued building. Note, however, the amount of window space, designed to fill the house with light.

For a time warp, follow the Rue du Monastère down to the **Abbaye de la Cambre** (*see* 'Outside the Centre', p.136). Alternatively, turn left on to the Avenue du Général de Gaulle, which runs alongside the two narrow ponds called the **Etangs d'Ixelles**. There was once a string of ponds that lined the course of the River Maelbeek. The surviving two were bought by the Commune d'Ixelles in 1871 and became the focus of a small park, while the land on either side was developed as a fashionable residential district. Today the ponds have a calming effect, where mothers push prams and infants feed the ducks, and lovers sprawl on the grassy banks behind the stooped figures of fishermen.

Continue up the Avenue Général de Gaulle beyond the Square du Souvenir, which separates the two ponds, to **Nos.38 and 39 Avenue Général de Gaulle**. These are two more houses by Blérot, dating from 1902 and distinguished by the flamboyant ironwork banisters which lead up to the front doors. Blérot frequently worked on pairs of houses, which together form a unity, but each house nonetheless has been treated individually.

Retrace your steps a short way and turn right up Rue Vilain XIIII (sometimes written XIV). This street was named after the statesman Charles Vilain XIIII (1803–78), who as Foreign Minister (1855–7) resisted external pressure to bridle the Belgian press with the famous retort, '*Jamais!*' **Nos.9 and 11 Rue Vilain XIIII** are another pair by Blérot, again dating from 1902, but here the composition includes stained glass and murals. Continue up Rue Vilain XIIII, and take the first left. **No.40 Rue de la Vallée** is yet another Blérot, this time a large, individual *maison de maître*, again 1902. Backtrack to Rue Vilain XIIII, walk up it to the next right, the Rue du Lac. Walk down this to find **No.6 Rue du Lac**.

This is something rather different: an extravagant Art Nouveau façade consisting of sweeping circles of stained glass and a stepped, lit stairway that runs diagonally up to a projecting upper floor. It was designed by an architect called Léon Delune in 1904. Note how the top right-hand corner of the front door cleverly forms a quadrant of one of the circular windows.

Continue down the Rue du Lac to the Avenue Général de Gaulle, turn left and walk up to Place Eugène Flagey. The tiered round tower on your right is the **Maison de la Radio**, the former studios of the two French- and Flemish-speaking broacasting companies RTBF and BRTN. Although one might not call it attractive, this is a classic 1930s Art Deco building, designed by Joseph Diongre (1878–1963), a noted pioneer in the use of reinforced concrete. This 'Usine à Sons' (sound factory) was famous for the acoustic quality of its studios which on completion in 1938 were the most advanced in the world. The great and the good, including Bartok and Stravinsky, passed through its doors. Its strong emphasis on elongated horizontals reflects the influence of cruise-ship design on the architecture of this period and inspired its nickname '*le paquebot*' (steamship). RTBF/BRTN abandoned it in 1995 to an uncertain future, although it has been listed by the World Monuments Fund among the top 100 in its endangered list. Its new owner is the Brussels Transport Authority (STIB), which promises to revive its role as a cherished music venue.

While you're here, you may want to take a detour to the **Musée Communal d'Ixelles** (*see* 'Outside the Centre', p.137).

MEDIEVAL CENTRE WALK

This walk follows a weaving trail around the Grand' Place, through the surrounding medieval streets of the lower town. The main diversions are unusual boutiques, though the route also explores a large section of the historic centre of Brussels, from the intriguing passages around the magnificent main square, to grand 19th-century shopping arcades and the crumbled remains of the city walls.

From the Grand' Place walk east down little Rue de la Colline, one of the many narrow streets laid out in medieval times. On the left you'll pass the **Tintin Boutique**, strategically placed to suck in tourists who stray from the Grand' Place, with Tintin clothes, accessories and the whole range of famous journals. At the end of Rue de la Colline is the arched entrance to the splendid **Galeries Royales de St-Hubert**, a celebrated arcade lined with highbrow shops. Built in 1847, the curved-glass canopy stands 18m tall and stretches more than 200m along the length of the

Galerie de la Reine and the Galerie du Roi, with the smaller Galerie des Princes running off from the intersection. Notice how the Galerie du Roi is slightly offset, so that you can't quite see from one end to the other. The rows of Neoclassical pilasters are decorated in red marble, and the walls have been given a recent lick of cake-icing pink paint. A little way along is **Manufacture Belge de Dentelle**, a long-established lace shop, selling

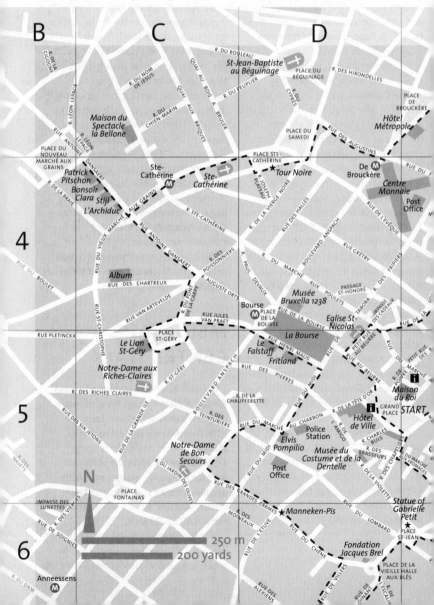

everything from coasters to lace-dressed dolls and parasols. The prices are relatively high, but it is a good place to browse – it's possibly the classiest lace shop in Brussels.

Carry on down past a series of expensive jewellers, a puppet shop and the old-fashioned Taverne du Passage restaurant until you reach the **Arenberg cinema**. Film-maker Louis Lumière held Belgium's first public film showing here in 1896. Today the programme

consists of an eclectic mix of international arty films. If you've the time, hang around to see one of the shorts that are shown regularly throughout the day. In the absence of popcorn, you could pop into **Neuhaus**, opposite the cinema, for a few melt-in-the-mouth pralines. It's a bit like the Gingerbread House inside – piles of edibles, garish colours and the warm stench of chocolate.

Walk through the peristyle that links the three arcades into Galerie du Roi, where you'll find conservative clothes boutiques awash with designer labels, and antiques showrooms that look like royal parlours. Then head back and turn right into the smaller Galerie des Princes. As you walk along take a closer look at the vast amounts of steel needed to support the glass roof, which is only a few metres above your head. On your left you'll find **Tropismes**, one of the most elegant bookstores you're ever likely to visit, the gold-leaf on the walls and ceiling reflected ad infinitum by huge mirrors. Then you might like to stop off for a coffee at **L'Ogenblik**, an informal Parisian-style bistro at the end of Galerie des Princes.

Turn right in to Rue des Dominicains, then left in to Rue de l'Ecuyer briefly, and right again in to Rue Léopold. This takes you past the stage door of **Théâtre de la Monnaie** (the opera house). Have a brief look at the old derelict house on your right. A rash of graffiti lines the boards in front of the house, with messages like '*La qualité est là, mais les sous n'est souvent pas*' (the quality is there, but the cash often isn't). This is where the great

---

Start: The Grand' Place.

Finish: Théâtre Toone.

Walking time: About 3 hours, not including shop, lunch or coffee stops.

Lunch and drinks stops: L'Ogenblik, *see* p.224; Le Métropole, *see* p.232; Le Quai, *see* p.230; Bonsoir Clara, *see* p.230; Le Lion St-Géry, *see* p.238; Le Falstaff, *see* p.237; Fritland, *see* p.225; Plattesteen, *see* p.238; Au Soleil, *see* p.238; Chez Toone, *see* p.237.

Suggested start time: Early morning to avoid the throngs of shoppers and tourists.

French Neoclassical painter **Jacques-Louis David** (*see* p.92) lived during the 18th century.

At the end of Rue Léopold cross straight over onto Rue d'Argent. On the corner is **Sterling Books**, one of Brussels' best English-language bookshops. Walk along Rue d'Argent until you reach the **Place des Martyrs** (*see* p.118), which was completed in 1775. This square, lined with the fresh symmetry of Neoclassical façades, is unlike any other in the capital. It is a quiet place to rest your feet, though there are often film crews and journalists around and about – the headquarters of the Flemish regional government occupies the building at the north end of the square. In the centre is what looks like a simple marble statue repre-senting Belgium ('Belga'); walk right up to it and you will see down into the subterranean mausoleum of the 'martyrs' who gave their lives during the Belgian Revolution of 1830. A row of marble slabs behind a mini colon-nade list the dead.

Leave the square by Rue St-Michel to the west. This leads out on to **Rue Neuve**, the city's counterpart to London's Oxford Street. Lined with mainstream shops and depart-ment stores, it is characterized by the tireless ebb and flow of everyday shoppers and buskers competing to be heard.

Turn left on to Rue Neuve and walk 50 yards then turn right in to **Passage du Nord**. This is another of the capital's 19th-century arcades, built later than the Galeries Royales de St-Hubert (1882) and not on such a grand scale. A series of robed caryatids link the shops on the ground floor with the mezza-nine and the first floor. When the arcade originally opened, the first floor was occu-pied by a number of curiosities, including the 'Fantasies of Nature Room', the 'Amusing Physics Room' and a 'Baby Theatre'. Programmes included shadow shows, puppet shows, dwarf shows and a hypnotism act. Today at No.27 you will find the **Coutellerie du Roi** (founded 1750) selling menacing cutlasses and knives for every conceivable purpose. Next door is another chain of chocolatier Neuhaus. The rest of the

shops in the arcade continue in the main-stream vein of Rue Neuve.

At the end of Passage du Nord, turn left into **Place de Brouckère**, a brash and busy intersection with a hint of Times Square or Piccadilly Circus about it. On your left you will pass the glorious **Hôtel Métropole**. Step inside the attached café resplendent with *fin de siècle* glitter: outrageous chandeliers hang from high ceilings, candelabra sprout from the walls and stained-glass windows refract daylight onto huge mirrors.

At the south end of Place de Brouckère, cross the road on to Rue des Augustins. Walk to the end of the road (towards a large parking sign) and cross over on to small cobbled Place du Samedi. Keep to the left-hand side and follow the road round until you hit **Place Ste-Cathérine**. Directly in front of you is the **Tour Noire**, a defensive bastion that is the best-preserved remnant of the medieval city walls. To your right is the back end of domineering **Eglise Ste-Cathérine**. Walk around the church until you get to the strip of water and fountains that stretch away to the north. This is the site of the capital's old fish market, and the street is now lined with fine fish restaurants. Settle down for a meal at Le Quai, a tiny establish-ment renowned for its lobster.

Continue westwards along the side of Eglise Ste-Cathérine until you reach **Rue Antoine Dansaert** (notice the unusual 'antique' open urinals right up against the side of the church beneath the great flying buttresses). This is the street to head for if you want to add a few truly original (and outlandish) items to your wardrobe. It is the heart of the capital's fashion district, popu-lated by young and wealthy trendsetters. The official sales seasons are in July and January, when you're likely to find some bargains, with prices cut by fifty per cent.

Turn right up Rue Dansaert and – if you can bear the insistent attentions of the staff – traipse around a few of the boutiques. On the left-hand side of the road at No.74 is **Stijl**, a good place to cast an eye over the creations of some of Belgium's most cutting-edge designers. A little further along at No.82 is **Patrick Pitschon**, where you'll find a range of more affordable items. Retrace your steps back along Rue Dansaert, past a string of designer stores and the open-fronted restaurant **Bonsoir Clara** – an eye-catching tunnel of colour lined with long tables. At No.16 is **Le Pain Quotidien**, displaying colourful *tartlettes* and deathly *bombes au chocolat*. A little further down the road is Brussels' longest standing jazz bar, **L'Archiduc** (*open from 4pm*), an Art Deco shrine with an amazing atmosphere.

At the end of Rue Dansaert take the third right on to Rue du Pont de la Carpe, which leads quickly into **Place St-Géry**, an attractive quadrangle surrounded by bars. In the centre of the square is the old **Halles St-Géry**, a small covered market completed in 1881, and now inhabited by an airy café. An odd pyramidal obelisk – transferred at some stage from the Grimbergen monastery – has centre stage inside the old market. Head for the southwest corner of the square and step inside **Le Lion St-Géry**. The pretty courtyard at the rear of this bar reveals a stagnant strip of water that is billed as a remnant of the River Senne, which was covered over centuries ago and now trickles quietly beneath the city.

Leave Place St-Géry by Rue Jules van Praet, which takes you past more bars and a series of ethnic restaurants. At the end is Place de la Bourse. Cross Boulevard Anspach and walk along the right-hand side of **La Bourse**, a grand Neoclassical building that was once the stock exchange. Pop inside **Le Falstaff**, a famous Art Nouveau café with beautiful curves of woodwork designed by an understudy of Victor Horta. Just down from Le Falstaff is **Fritland**, a top spot to sample a cone of double-fried *frites*.

Turn right on to **Rue du Midi**, a busy street lined with philatelists (stamp shops), delicatessens and comic book shops. Brussels is very serious about its trade in stamps, though for the untrained eye, most of the philatelists are much of a muchness. For the collector with plenty of money to spare, dingy William Baeton at No.7 is a hotspot for antique stamps. Another shop to look out for along Rue du Midi is **Elvis Pompilio** (No.60 on the left), a world-renowned hat store for the fanciful exhibitionist.

Meander down **Rue du Marché au Charbon**, an attractive cobbled street lined with bars and restaurants, and look out for the towering comic strip murals outside and opposite the Plattesteen café. Keep going until you reach Au Soleil, a popular and arty café. Turn left here on to Rue des Grandes Carmes and cross Rue du Midi. A little way along is the intersection of cobbled lanes lorded over by the diminutive **Manneken-Pis**, who attracts a thicket of snapping tourists. Remarkably this little bronze statue of a peeing boy has become the symbol of the city. If you are lucky, when you pass by, he may be dressed up in one of his costumes – there are now over 600 of them – which are brought out on appropriate occasions.

Cross over Rue de L'Etuve on to Rue du Chêne. As you approach the top of the hill turn right in to tiny **Rue de Villers** for a brief diversion past a section of the medieval city walls, which stands forlorn like a piece of wreckage rather than a heritage site. Turn left on to Rue de Dinant, which leads down into **Place de la Vieille Halle aux Blés**. Notice the line of gabled baroque houses on the south face of the square. These are former inns from the 17th and 18th centuries, some of which have been restored to house cafés. Continue straight across the square and in to Place St-Jean. Take the second right on to **Rue St-Jean** and walk past the art and music shops. Near the end of the road turn left in to the **Galerie Bortier**, a peaceful little lair of book collectors and students. This small arcade of Parisian inspiration was built one year after the Galeries Royales de St-Hubert and by the same architect, Jean Pierre Cluysenaar. Most of what you see is the result of restoration work from the 1970s – there's a new roof, for example, which maintains the original concept of natural lighting but uses different materials, such as curved panes of glass. Above the shopfronts in the arcade, notice the array of cast-iron figures and motifs – the foliage and grotesques – all of which are originals.

Turn left out of Galerie Bortier on to Rue de la Madeleine, past antiques and bookshops, before taking a sharp left on to **Rue des Eperonniers**. This old cobbled lane is lined with tatooists, jewellers and grungy clothes shops. A little way down on the left is **La Court Echelle**, a magical little boutique selling beautifully crafted dolls' houses with all the furnishings. Keep going, past several entrances to the uninviting **Galerie Agora**, and turn right on to **Rue du Marché aux Fromages**. Now you're back in prettified tourist territory, with mildly tacky restaurants and their hawkers jostling for attention. At the end of the road turn right in to Rue des Chapeliers, which leads you back

to the spacious ease of the Grand' Place once again. Cut diagonally across the square and take Rue au Beurre up to the Eglise St-Nicolas. Turn right into **Petit Rue au Beurre**, where the shopfronts of jewellers are grafted on to the walls of the church. At the end cross Rue du Marché aux Herbes in to Rue de la Fourche, and follow the road round before turning right in to **Rue des Bouchers**. This is the heart of the **Ilôt Sacré**, a tangle of protected medieval lanes thick with tourists. Pick your way past the restaurants and turn right into Petit Rue des Bouchers. Head for **Théâtre Toone** on the left, a puppet theatre established in 1830. Among the repertoire of the wooden and papier-mâché starlets are the works of Shakespeare. Finish the walk with a well-earned beer or two in the puppet-hung bar downstairs.

Day Trips

10

Belgium is a small country, and Belgians think nothing of travelling from Brussels to the coast, or to the valley of the River Semois in the far south, for lunch. The truth is that a guide book to the whole of Belgium could be entitled 'Day Trips from Brussels'. These day trips, however, are all to places lying within 30km of Brussels and are marked on the 'Outside the Centre' map on p.134.

MECHELEN

Of all the Flemish cities, Mechelen is the most charming. It is an unpretentious working town, a cluster of crooked streets centred upon a sprawling marketplace – as much its commercial heart today as in its flamboyant medieval past. Dotted about the city are Renaissance palaces, wizened old abbeys, solid churches – all dominated by the stupendous bell-tower soaring like a vast medieval rocket from St Rombout's Cathedral. Despite its quiet charms, Mechelen tends to be left off the usual tourist trail, perhaps because, the cathedral apart, it cannot boast any high-profile attraction. With its lively atmosphere, prosperous streets and evocative medieval backwaters, it is remarkably unspoilt.

History

Mechelen grew up as a fortified trading centre on the River Dijle (Dyle) in the early medieval period, and became wealthy through its textiles and weaving. It developed into an important administrative centre under the Dukes of Burgundy, and in 1473 Charles the Bold set up the Grand Council here. This was the supreme court of the land, and it remained in Mechelen until the end of the 18th century. When Margaret of Austria, acting as regent for the infant Charles V, became governor of the Netherlands in 1507, she made Mechelen her capital. This was the city's heyday as a European centre of power, culture and learning. However, following Margaret of Austria's death in 1530, the court moved to

Brussels and Mechelen retired from the limelight. Mechelen returned to prosperity in the 17th and 18th centuries, during which it became famous for its lace, tapestry, embossed leather wall-hangings and Baroque woodcarving.

Grote Markt and Stadhuis

The Grote Markt is the largest of the market squares at the centre of the city: no petite Renaissance gem this, but a business-like open space, bordered by picturesque buildings containing restaurants and tea rooms and, on its eastern side, the Stadhuis (town hall). The Stadhuis is made up of two contrasting but adjoining buildings: the plainer 14th-century Lakenhalle (cloth-makers' hall) to the right as you face it, with its squat, unfinished belfry, and the north wing, in 16th-century flamboyant Gothic, flanked by an arcaded walkway. This was originally intended to be the seat of the Grand Council, and building was commenced following designs by the celebrated architect Rombout Keldermans in 1530. However, the project was abandoned in 1543 after the court moved to Brussels, and it was only finally completed to Keldermans' plans in 1911. The **statue** in the middle of the Grote Markt is an unflattering 19th-century impression of Margaret of Austria.

Leading into the Grote Markt from the south is the **Ijzerenleen**, which also serves as a marketplace. It is fronted by the **Oud Schepenhuis** ('old sheriff's office'), a squat gabled and turreted tower built in 1374, which served as the seat of the Grand Council from 1474 to 1618.

St-Romboutskathedraal and Around

Enter by the south door, from the Grote Markt. Open Mon–Sat 9–5.30, Sun 2–5.30.

The real centrepiece of Mechelen is St-Romboutskathedraal. It is named after the

Getting There

By Train

The railway station is a 25min walk south of the town centre. There are direct connections with Brussels Nord, Central and Midi.

By Car

Mechelen (Malines in French) lies halfway between Brussels and Antwerp, just off the A1/E10 autoroute. There is a fair amount of public parking, which is controlled by pay-and-display machines.

Tourist Information

Stadhuis (in the Grote Markt), **t** 015 29 76 55. *Open Mon–Fri 8–5, Sat and Sun 10–12, 2–4.30.*

Festivals

Hanswijkprocessie, *Sun before Ascension Day (May)*. A statue of the Virgin Mary from the Hanswijk Basilica is paraded around the streets, celebrating deliverance from the plague in 1272.

Eating Out

D'Hoogh, *19 Grote Markt*, **t** *015 21 75 53. Open Tues–Fri, Sat evening and Sun lunch.*

Expensive. Fresh, seasonal produce from the market is used to produce the high-quality 'market lunch'.

Brasserie Het Anker, *49 Guido Gezellelaan,* **t** *015 20 38 80. Open daily 11.30am– midnight. Moderate*. Delightful, relaxed bar/restaurant overlooking the courtyard of the Gouden Carolus (Anker) Brewery, to which it belongs. Dishes cooked in beer are a speciality, notably the famous local chicken dish, *Mechelse koekoek* (Mechelen cuckoo).

Mytilus, *23 Grote Markt*, **t** *015 20 19 52. Moderate*. Cosy front-room style restaurant in a corner of the Grote Markt. Fish, lobster, mussels and meat. Menus start at €19.50.

Eat Café, *7 Niewwerk (at eastern end of cathedral)*, **t** *015 34 53 40. Open Tues–Sun. Inexpensive*. Relish a mound of food from a fine buffet of cold dishes, Italian style.

Speelgoedmuseum Café, *21 Nekkerspoel,* **t** *015 20 03 86. Inexpensive*. Attached to the toy museum, access to this café is with a museum ticket only. Dishes include lasagne, waffles and tarts – and you are also welcome to bring your own picnic.

Irish missionary St Rombout (St Rombold), who brought Christianity to this region in the 8th century. The immensity of the interior and its sombre, timeless poise immediately impress themselves upon you. The mighty columns, decked with sympathetic 17th-century statues of the apostles, recede into the soft gloom. The choir has been radically altered by black and white marble Baroque installation around the altar, which was designed by the Mechelen-based sculptor Luc Fayd'Herbe (1617–97).

A treasured collection of **paintings** lines the ambulatory. Immediately to the right of the south door is a *Crucifixion* (1627) by Antoon van Dyck, full of passion and verve. Continuing to the right of the choir, there is a triptych of the *Martyrdom of St Sebastian* by Michiel Coxie (1499–1592), who was born in Mechelen. Another triptych featuring St Luke painting the Virgin is by Abraham Janssens

(1575–1632), an Antwerp painter who might have risen to greater stardom had he not been overshadowed by his famous contemporary Rubens. On the left-hand side of the choir is a triptych of the *Martyrdom of St George (c.* 1588), again by Michiel Coxie, clearly showing the strong influence of his Italian training.

The oak **pulpit** in the nave is a classic piece of 18th-century Baroque woodcarving by the Antwerp sculptor Michiel Vervoort the Elder, and represents the conversion of Saint Norbert (occasioned by a scrape with death when he fell from his horse). Vervoort was noted for his animal sculptures, and if you look closely you can find various small beasts among the foliage, such as a lizard, a snail, a frog and a squirrel.

Near the west door is a model of the cathedral following original plans discovered in Mons. The massive **tower** was going to be almost twice its present size, rising to 167m – the tallest in Europe. Work began in 1452 but stopped in the 1520s. In its present form the tower is remarkable enough: for 87 of its full 97m it rises as a hollow tube, bridged only by six wooden floors, before reaching its lowest stone vault. Depending on the season and the availability of staff, visitors can join a guided tour and climb the staircase of 514 steps to the upper gallery. The tower contains two bronze carillons, one dating back in part to the 17th century – a total of 98 bells, weighing 80 tons. The bells are operated by an ingenious system connected to a keyboard, and concerts are given on Monday evenings during the summer.

If you leave the cathedral by the north door, and turn left into the Wollemarkt, the **bishop's palace** can be seen, a surprisingly secular-looking Neoclassical building (1717) in need of a lick of paint.

Refugie Abdij van Tongerlo
Schoutetstraat. Open Sat only; closed July. Guided tour 10.30am.

This building is now the home of the Gaspard de Wit workshops, royal tapestry manufacturers and restorers. The road leads past further picturesque houses, including the beautiful 16th-century red-brick **Refugie van de Abdij van St-Truiden** (Refuge of the Abbey of St Truiden), a charming stack of stepped gables and steeply pitched roofs.

St-Janskerk
Opposite the *refugie* is St John's Church, a massive edifice in 15th- and 16th-century Gothic with a contrastingly delicate belfry over the crossing. It contains a remarkable triptych of the *Adoration of the Magi* (1619) by Rubens, a fascinating encounter between maternal tenderness and male swagger and power. Isabella Brant, Rubens' first wife, posed as the model for the Virgin.

Museum Hof van Busleyden
Frederik de Merodestraat, t 015 20 20 04. Open Tues–Sun 10–2; adm €2.

This pretty little palace was built in 1503–17 for Hieronymus van Busleyden, a friend of

Erasmus and a councillor to Charles V. It now houses the Beiaard-museum (carillon museum) and the municipal museum, which contains an interesting mixed bag of paintings and sculpture by Rubens, Gaspard de Crayer, Michiel Coxie and others, plus various artefacts such as the old wooden Op Signoorke doll, beloved mascot of Mechelen, which used to be tossed in a sheet at festivals. Its name dates back to 1775 when a man from Antwerp – Mechelen's great rival – was accused of trying to steal the doll. Op Signoorke comes from 'señor', a reference to Antwerp's Spanish connections and once a nickname for the people of Antwerp, used in Mechelen as an expression of contempt.

In the same street is the internationally famous **carillon school**, where people come to learn to play these unusual Flemish bells.

Paleis van Margaretha van Oostenrijk
Keizerstraat. Garden open to the public.

The palace of Margaret of Austria is a fine Renaissance building of the early 16th century, set around a formal garden of clipped box hedges. It was the seat of the Grand Council from 1618 to 1794 and still serves as law courts.

Nearby is **Sint Pieter en Sint Pauluskerk** (Church of SS Peter and Paul), which has a Baroque façade topped by an impressive Jesuit sunburst.

Speelgoedmuseum
21 Nekkerspoel. Open Tues–Sun 10–5; adm €4, children 3–12 €2.50.

The best museum in Mechelen is the toy museum. This major collection of toys takes as its starting point a painting by Bruegel, *Children's Games* (1560), to demonstrate the timeless fascination of toys. There are trains, boats, board games, early Meccano, Fisher-Price, Lego, Barbie and Ken. It is very much a museum designed for children and there's an exhibit devoted to the Brussels-born illustrator Peyo (Pierre Culliford, 1928–92), who in 1957 invented the Smurfs (called Schtroumpfs locally).

Gouden Carolus (Anker) Brewery

49 Guido Gezellelaan, **t** *015 20 38 80. Guided* **tours** *(in groups of 10 or more) April–Sept at 3pm;* **adm** *€3 with one drink.*

This famous small brewery dates back to 1471. It's north of the city close to the atmospheric cluster of streets once occupied by the **Groot Begijnhof** (around the Begijnhofkerk in Nonnenstraat and Hoviusstraat).

LEUVEN

Leuven is famous above all for two things. It is the seat of one of the great, historic universities of Europe – the oldest in Belgium and still the largest, with 23,000 students. It also has the most beautiful Stadhuis (town hall) in the country: like a bejewelled reliquary casket writ large, it is the ultimate example of flamboyant Gothic style. It rather puts everything else in the shade in this compact and user-friendly town, but other highlights include the art museum inside the Sint Pieterskerk, which has a notable collection of medieval and Renaissance painting, and the Stedelijk Museum Vander Kelen-Mertens, which presents a rewarding mixture of furnished rooms, paintings and ceramics. A stroll to the south of the town leads to the picturesque and extensive *béguinage,* the Groot Begijnhof. Leuven is also the home of a well-known beer: the massive, modern Stella Artois brewery can be seen on the Brussels road on the outskirts of the city. The best time to visit is during the university term, when the students animate the streets. Without them the city loses its *raison d'être* and seems a little forlorn.

Getting There

By Train

Trains from Brussels' Nord/Central/Midi take you to the station to the east of the city, about 15 mins' walk from the centre.

By Car

Leuven (Louvain in French) lies 20km to the east of Brussels, just off the A3/E5 autoroute to Liège. Parking in the centre is limited, especially in the busy summer season, and you may need to leave your car on the outskirts – which is still within walking distance of the centre.

Tourist Information

9 Grote Markt, **t** *016 21 15 39. Open March–Sept Mon–Fri 9–5, Sat, Sun and public hols 10–1 and 1.30–5.* Note that a **combinatie-ticket** allows you to see all four of the stedelijk (municipal) museums.

Eating Out

There are numerous restaurants in and around the city centre, including various brasseries and cafés in the Grote Markt itself, and in Muntstraat behind the Stadhuis.

Brasserie Notre-Dame, *Grote Markt,* **t** *016 22 37 62.* **Expensive**. Sleek and buzzing brasserie serving coffee and snack meals. This used to be the venerable coffee house called Het Moorinneken – note the fine bronze bust of a moorish boy over the door.

Sire Pynnock, *10 Hogeschoolplein,* **t** *016 20 25 32. Open Tues–Sun; closed 3 weeks in Aug.* **Expensive**. Serious and inventive *haute cuisine* by a garlanded young chef, with inspired Japanese touches.

Japans Restaurant Fuji, *25 Oude Markt,* **t** *016 22 09 50.* **Moderate**. Japanese food, priced within reach of the students: a four-course set meal for €30.

Kampuchea, *3 S'Meiersstraat,* **t** *016 23 11 21.* **Moderate**. Mouthwatering Cambodian and Vietnamese cuisine, including chicken with ginger, frogs' legs with lemon grass, duck with bananas. Set menus €13.50–33.50.

Restaurant d'Artagnan, *9–11 Krakenstraat,* **t** *016 29 26 26. Open Mon–Sat from 6pm.* **Moderate**. Wooden tables and open kitchen in rooms decked with historic charm. French and Belgian cuisine, with a copious six-course menu (salmon with ginger, lobster with Madagascar pepper) for €32.25.

History

Leuven became the capital of the Duchy of Brabant after 1190 and blossomed with the growth of the Flemish textile industry, swelling to fill two successive rings of town walls. However, the strife between the weavers and the nobles, which affected all of Flanders during the 14th century, was particularly acute in Leuven, and ended up with a defenestration: in 1379 rioters pitched 17 nobles from the windows of the old Stadhuis on to the pikes of the guildsmen below, incurring the wrath and vengeance of the then ruler of Brabant, Wenceslas of Luxembourg. At this point weavers left Leuven in droves, emigrating mainly to England. The town went into a decline and under the Dukes of Burgundy the capital of Brabant was moved to Brussels.

In 1425 a university was founded at Leuven, and in 1517, the great humanist **Desiderius Erasmus** (*see* p.138) and others founded the Collegium Trelingue (College of Three Languages), which encouraged a ground-breaking synthesis of religious and classical studies. However, the rise of Protestantism in northern Europe caused the authorities to retrench; Erasmus's doctrine was condemned, and Leuven became a bastion of Roman Catholic orthodoxy.

The university had a rocky career through the religious disputes of the 16th and 17th centuries. **Cornelius Jansen** (1585–1638) taught here and Leuven became a focus of the subsequent Jansenist movement, which promoted an ascetic way of life and a firm belief in predestination; it was later declared heretical. In 1835 a new Catholic University originally established in Mechelen was transferred to Leuven. Despite a constant power struggle between liberal and conservative Catholics, the university built up noted faculties in science, engineering and the humanities.

Language was a bone of contention throughout most of the last century, resulting in what many look back upon as a regrettable series of events for a great university. During the 19th century all lectures had been in French (except those on theology, delivered in Latin), but riots in the 1920s and disputes in the 1960s resulted in the decision that the university should be split in two. In 1980 the Université Catholique de Louvain transferred to a brand new university city called Louvain-la-Neuve south of Brussels, while the K.U. Leuven (Katholieke Universiteit Leuven) became the exclusive preserve of Flemish speakers.

Stadhuis

*Guided **tours** only which must be booked at least 2 weeks in advance, Mon–Fri 11am and 3pm, Sat and Sun 3pm.*

The pride of Leuven is the magnificent Stadhuis, a spectacular agglomeration of crockets and finials, lace-like balustrades, pinnacles, niches, dormer windows and pepperpot spires, all smothered in carving. There is not a flat surface in sight and, not surprisingly, the building took 30 years to complete. The aim was to outdo Brussels' new town hall – and it succeeded triumphantly. Hundreds of small carvings, mainly of biblical scenes on the theme of sin and punishment, were included as part of the original plan, while some 300 niches remained empty until the larger statues of historical figures and saints were created for them during much-needed restoration that took place in phases between 1828 and 1907. The Stadthuis' paintings and sculpture includes work by Gaspard de Crayer, Constantin Meunier and Jef Lambeaux.

Sint-Pieterskerk

Open Mon–Sat 10–5, Sun 2–5; closed Mon 16 Oct–14 March.

The middle of the rather cramped Grote Markt is occupied by Sint Pieterskerk, built in Gothic style during the 15th century and now with its exterior stonework gleamingly restored. Damaged by fire at the start of the First World War, the choir of this once great church has now become the **Stedelijk Museum voor Religieuze Kunst** (museum of religious art) . The star of the show is **Dirk Bouts** (1415–75), who was born in Haarlem, studied in Brussels under Rogier van der Weyden, then in 1457 moved to Leuven, where he remained for the rest of his career. His triptych of the *Last Supper* (1464–7) is one of the great paintings of the period. The scene is set in a contemporary Gothic hall, and the view glimpsed through the window to the left is probably the marketplace of Leuven. The side panels show a series of biblical scenes set in Flemish landscapes. (These have had a wayward history, having been sold or carried off several times.) A second famous painting by Dirk Bouts is the *Martyrdom of St Erasmus*, in which his intestines are being wound on to a windlass. No one in the scene, not even the saint himself, seems particularly bothered about this; the picture is imbued with a wonderful beatific calm, considered appropriate for scenes of martyrdom at the time. The collection also includes a reduced copy (1440) by **Rogier van der Weyden** (*c*. 1400–64) of his own *Descent from the Cross* (now in the Prado, Madrid), which is filled with a more realistic anguish.

One of the eastern side chapels of the Sint Pieterskerk contains the reliquary shrine to **Fiere Margriet** (Proud Margaret), a local saint. Margaret was servant to an innkeeper, and a witness to his murder, in 1225. The miscreants carried her off, and one attempted to impose his favours upon her ('marry' is the term used in some versions). When she resisted she too was murdered, and her body was cast into the river. The story is told in pictures on the shrine, and also in the neighbouring chapel through a series of paintings by **Pieter Josef Verhaegen** (1728–1811), who lived in Leuven for most of his life and was court painter to Charles of Lorraine.

Stedelijk Museum Vander Kelen-Mertens

Open *Tues–Sat 10–5, Sun and public hols 2–5; adm €5.*

Set in a 17th- and 18th-century private mansion donated to the municipality by the Vander Kelen-Mertens family in 1918, the museum in Savoyestraat presents a series of furnished interiors decorated during the 19th century in retrospective historical styles: hence a Baroque sitting room, with high-backed William and Mary style chairs and *famille-rose* Chinese vases, a Renaissance salon, and a Rococo dining room. The modernized galleries upstairs contain the municipal collection of treasures, acquired mainly through the confiscation of private property by the occupying French Revolutionary Army in the 1790s, and through subsequent donations.

The paintings are primarily by early Renaissance Flemish artists, including **Quentin Metsys** (1466–1530), who is credited with bringing Italian verve to the rather stilted compositions of northern European medieval art. His *Mourning over Christ* has an almost expressionist intensity. The collection includes a splendidly bizarre, Bosch-like *Temptations of St Anthony* (anon.), as well as a fine *Crucifixion* triptych by Michiel Coxie, dated 1571, which shows the kind of flowing Italianate composition that influenced Rubens.

Groot Begijnhof

Namsestraat.

This was once one of the largest *béguinages* in the land (for an explanation of *béguinages, see* p.141), founded in the 13th century. It is now a tidy collection of 72 modest red-brick homes and grassy courtyards, set out along crooked cobbled streets and pathways that crisscross branches of the River Dijle and lead up to an early 14th-century church.

Unfortunately, by the turn of the last century the *béguinage* was in a very decrepit state, and eventually in 1962 it was bought by the university for use as college residences. Since then it has been spruced up and restored, but – alas – some of its character has been lost. The last *béguine* soldiered on through these changes and died in 1988.

WATERLOO

The Battle of Waterloo represents one of the great turning points of European history, when Napoleon's Empire was finally demolished after two decades of tumult and radical change across the continent. For all that, Napoleon remained a great European hero (even today, most Belgians regard the battle as the defeat of Napoleon rather than the victory of Wellington and the Allies).

The significance of the Battle of Waterloo, the romantic tales of bravery and tragedy that emerged from it and Napoleon's enduring fascination made the battlefield a scene of touristic pilgrimage almost before the bodies had been carted off for burial. This accounts to some degree for the strangely amateur and tacky nature of many of the museums connected with the battlefield, but their musty, antique air is part of the unique flavour of the place. The exception is the **Visitors' Centre** at the battlefield site – but even that is barely able to cope with the hordes of tourists who swarm through it. As a result, this can be a disappointing visit unless you know what you are looking at: you have to do a little homework and then let your imagination flow (a useful booklet, called *Waterloo 1815*, can be bought at the Wellington Museum shop, *see* p.172). If you can get away from the crowds it is not difficult to people the landscape with soldiers in your mind's eye.

History

Napoleon, self-proclaimed Emperor of France, had been the master of continental Europe for nearly two decades when he made the fatal decision to invade Russia (from Brussels). His subsequent defeat, forced abdication and confinement to the Italian island of Elba in 1814, however, didn't last for long. Ten months later he marched upon Paris and deposed the unpopular new King Louis XVIII, who fled to Ghent in terror.

The countries of the Alliance of Nations (Russia, the Netherlands, Austria, Britain, Prussia and the other German states) looked on with horror. They declared war, and in April 1815 hastily began to assemble in Brussels, considered a suitable base from which to march on Paris. Wellington, commander of the British, German, Belgian and Dutch troops, had planned to take the initiative, but the quick-thinking Napoleon beat him to it. On 15 June his army of 125,000 men crossed the French border, took Charleroi and came within 25km of the Belgian capital. His strategy was to aim for Brussels, driving a wedge between the British and Field Marshal Blücher's large Prussian force, stationed in eastern Belgium.

The following day, in torrid weather, two preliminary confrontations took place. The Prussians were put to flight at Ligny, to the northeast of Charleroi, whilst in the teeming rain, Wellington's forces were pushed back to the north from Quatre Bras towards Brussels. Sensing his advantage, Napoleon sent Marshal Grouchy at the head of 33,000 men in pursuit of Blücher to prevent the Prussians joining up with Wellington. Meanwhile, Napoleon concentrated his main forces on his old adversary Wellington, whom he had never before confronted directly in battle. Wellington knew that he now had to hold the line before Brussels, and took up a defensible position on a ridge at Mont St Jean.

As a hazy dawn broke on Sunday 18 June, the bedraggled ranks of cavalry, artillery and infantry in their brilliant regimental colours, huge embroidered ensigns held aloft, faced each other across the muddy valley. Napoleon, anxious to begin battle as soon as possible, was persuaded to hold off until the sodden ground could dry out a little. It lost him valuable time. At 1.30pm he launched a massive infantry attack on Wellington's left flank and on the farm in the middle of the field, La Haie-Sainte. Wellington's troops were submitted to countless attacks from the French cavalry, interspersed with repeated bombardments by artillery. They became badly depleted, but held firm. 'Will the English never show their backs?' demanded Napoleon. The battle raged all day, the result held finely in the balance: 'A

Getting There

By Car

The Battle of Waterloo didn't take place at Waterloo at all. In fact the fighting was closer to Braine-l'Alleud, about 4km south of the centre of Waterloo. The battlefield covers a considerable area, so it is best to visit with a car. There are two principal sites: the old inn in the centre of Waterloo where Wellington had his headquarters, now sign-posted the **Wellington Museum**, and the battlefield itself, clearly identifiable from a distance by the **Butte du Lion**, the mound with a statue of a lion on top (follow signs marked 'QG Napoléon' then 'Butte de Lion' to the south of Waterloo on the Charleroi road, the N5). The **Waterloo Visitors' Centre** is clustered around the Butte du Lion.

By Bus

There is a regular bus service from Brussels to Waterloo and the Butte du Lion which departs from Place Rouppe about once every hour. For organized coach trips, ask at the Brussels Tourist Office (*see* p.68).

By Train

Trains leave for Waterloo from Bruxelles Nord, Central and Midi; the station is about 1km from the centre at Waterloo. It is possible to rent **bicycles** at the next station down the track, Braine l'Alleud, under the 'Train et Vélo' scheme.

Tourist Information

149 Chaussée de Bruxelles, **t** 02 354 9910. *Open April–Oct daily 9.30–6.30, Nov–Mar daily 10.30–5.*

A full-scale **re-enactment** of the Battle of Waterloo, carried out by enthusiasts dressed in replica uniforms, takes place once every five years on the Sunday nearest to 18 June. Ask at the tourist office for future dates.

Eating Out

It's all beer and *frites* and tourist menus around the Butte du Lion. In Waterloo itself there is a cluster of more attractive small restaurants in the Passage Wellington.

La Bel Rose, *7 Rue du Couvent, Wellington*. **Expensive**. A more upmarket establishment serving mussels and other Belgian fare.

Le 1900, *26 Rue Rabelais, Louvain-la-Neuve*, **t** *010 45 12 38*. **Moderate**. Worth singling out amongst Louvain-al-Neuve's excellent restaurants for its exceptional atmosphere. It serves coffee, beer and snacks from 8am onwards and boasts an impressive list of dishes: oysters, *bisque de homard*, and venison steaks in bordelaise sauce.

La Fontanell', *27 Av des Eaux Vives, Genval*, **t** *02 652 0381*. **Open** *Thurs–Tues*. **Moderate**. Good Italian restaurant and pizzeria next to the tranquil Lac de Genval.

Le Shangri-La du Lac, *96 Av du Lac, Genval*, **t** *02 654 1244*. **Moderate**. Overlooking the lake, an above-average Chinese restaurant serving dim sum, duck pancakes and other tasty and well-chosen dishes.

Restaurant Victoria, *17 Marcel Félicéstraat, Hoeilaart*, **t** *02 657 0738*. **Open** *Thurs–Mon*. Run by the same family for nearly 40 years, this popular and typically Belgian restaurant serves excellently prepared dishes such as *anguilles au vert* and *entrecôte à l'os*.

damned near thing,' as Wellington later put it, 'the nearest run thing you ever saw in your life.' The roar of cannon fire was deafening: even before news of the battle reached England, the *Kentish Gazette* reported from Ramsgate, over 200km away on the other side of the Channel, that 'a heavy and incessant firing was heard from this coast on Sunday evening in the direction of Dunkirk'. Everything depended on the prompt intervention of Blücher, who was by now within 6km and fighting off a French force sent out to meet him.

At 5.30pm the first of the Prussians reached the field on the French right, and Napoleon threw his remaining cavalry into the fray. However, it was too late: Blücher began to break through. At 7.30pm Napoleon was forced to throw in his élite Imperial Guard, who strode forth courageously, ignoring heavy losses, and pushed through the Allied lines almost as far as the Ferme de

Mont-Saint-Jean. But the Guard was eventually forced to retreat – for the first time in its history – and panic spread among the French. Wellington ordered the counter-attack, riding down the ranks on his chestnut horse Copenhagen and shouting: 'Go on! Go on! They will not stand!' The British and Prussians surged forward in pursuit. Napoleon, staring defeat in the face, had to be bundled into a carriage and whisked back to Paris. He left behind him a field of carnage, where 13,000 soldiers had died and 35,000 had been wounded.

It took days to clear the bodies from the battlefield. Wellington had seen a number of his closest associates killed or fatally wounded, and is said to have broken down and wept as the casualty list was read out to him: 'Next to a battle lost,' he later wrote, 'the greatest misery is a battle gained.'

On 22 June Napoleon abdicated for a second time. The British government decided to hold him captive in perpetuity, exiled to St Helena, a lonely island in the middle of the South Atlantic, where he died in 1821.

The Wellington Museum

Open 1 April–15 Nov 10.30–6.30, 16 Nov–31 March 10.30–5; **adm** €2.

The old Bodenghien Inn at the centre of Waterloo was chosen by Wellington as his headquarters on the night of 17 June before the battle. It's an evocative old building, now converted into a small museum of the history of the town of Waterloo and the battle. Displays include weapons, pieces of uniform, engravings, and the bed in which Sir Alexander Gordon died. To the rear is a modern exhibition with panels giving blow-by-blow plans of various stages of the battle.

La Chapelle Royale

This pretty and unusual Neoclassical church faces the Wellington Museum and was built in 1690 by the Governor General of the Spanish Netherlands, the Marquis of

Castanaga, as an expression of his wish that Charles II of Spain would produce an heir (he didn't). It was deconsecrated by the French revolutionaries and sold in 1799, bought back by the parishioners in 1806 and enlarged in 1823. After 1815 it became a kind of shrine to various British and Dutch officers killed at Waterloo. The domed, circular entrance contains a bust of Wellington and inside the nave are various memorial plaques which make remarkable reading.

The Visitors' Centre and the Butte du Lion

t 02 385 1912, **w** www.waterloo1815.be. **Open** March 10.30–5, April–Sept 9.30–6.30, Oct 9.30–5.30, Nov–Feb 10.30–4; **adm** Lion €1, children €0.50; Lion plus film €7, students €5.50, children €4; Lion plus film plus Panorama €7.50, students €6, children €5.

This is at the heart of the battlefield, 4km south of the centre of Waterloo itself and part of a cluster of attractions that also includes the Panorama and the Waxwork Museum (see opposite). The Visitors' Centre is a modern complex fronted by a brash and shameless souvenir shop. The film is in fact a two-part show. First there is a kind of miniature son-et-lumière based on a model of the battlefield – far from perfect but at least it gives an insight into how the battle developed. Next there is a 15-minute film in which children are seen wandering the battlefield, imagining the battle. The battle scenes used in this come from Sergei Bondarchuk's film Waterloo (1970), and graphically portrays the sheer weight of numbers and the violence of the conflict, which is otherwise hard to picture.

The Butte du Lion is the most prominent monument of the battlefield. Rising 143m and with 226 steps leading up to the top, it was built in 1824–26 and dedicated to the Prince of Orange, who was wounded at the battle. The lion stands at about the mid-point of the Allied lines and the view from the summit offers a magnificent panorama of the battlefield.

Panorama de la Bataille

Open April–Sept 9.30–6.30, Oct 9.30–5.30, Nov–Feb 10.30–4, March 10.30–5; adm €3.

In the latter part of the 19th century there was a vogue for painting large-scale panoramas in circular buildings – a kind of early form of 3D cinema.

The Waterloo Panorama belongs to this tradition: erected in 1912 and painted by a French artist called Louis Dumoulin (1860–1924) and a team of assistants. It measures 110m long by 12m high and consists of a well-executed portrayal of Marshal Ney's attack on the centre of Wellington's army at 3pm.

Musée de Cires

Open April–Sept 9.30–7, Oct 10–6, Nov–Mar Sat and Sun 10–5; adm €1.50.

This oddball waxwork museum contains a few cabinets of military junk, handwritten labels, and astonishingly wooden waxworks (the uniforms, however, are good). It's barely worth the entrance fee, unless you can draw some pleasure from its idiosyncrasy.

Château de Hougoumont

Private property, visitors may walk in the yards but are expected to behave discreetly.

Hougoumont is not really a château but a large and attractive fortified farmhouse – a modest prize considering that 6,000 soldiers died here.

It was defended by the British against persistent attacks from the very start of the battle. Inside the farmyard is a tiny chapel where many of the defenders died.

La Ferme du Caillou

Open April–Oct daily 10–6.30, Nov–March daily 1.30–5; closed Mon if not a public hol, and Jan; adm €1.50.

This farm was Napoleon's base, where he worked out his battle plans on the night of 17 June and morning of 18 June. The house (much altered since 1815) now serves as a Napoleonic Museum, filled with uniforms, furniture, plans and battle mementoes.

Other Monuments and Sites

La Belle Alliance

Napoleon directed the battle from this farm (named after a marriage between a farmer and his servant in the preceding century), which lies a little to the north of La Ferme du Caillou.

Ferme de la Haie-Sainte

This farm stood at the centre of the battlefield and lies on the main Waterloo–Namur road to the south of the Butte du Lion.

Gordon Monument

Just to the north of Ferme de la Haie-Sainte is this single broken pillar. It was erected in memory of Wellington's loyal aide-de-camp, Gordon, who was fatally wounded on this very spot.

Ferme de Mont-St-Jean

Also north on the Waterloo–Charleroi road, is the Ferme de Mont-St-Jean, a farm where British military doctors worked behind the lines in the most dangerous, crude conditions. They did what they could to save the wounded soldiers – without, of course, the aid of anaesthetic.

Monuments to the Fallen

The Ohain road, to the east of the Butte du Lion, was once a deep ditch that formed a part of Wellington's defensive strategy. On either side of the Ohain road are two monuments to the fallen.

To the south is the sober **Hanoverian Monument**, erected in 1818. To the north of the road is the **Monument to the Belgians**. 6,000 Belgian soliders took part in the battle, and some played a decisive role in the defence of La Haie-Sainte and the defeat of the Imperial Guard.

SIX FLAGS BELGIUM

Open *May–June daily 10–6, July–Aug daily 10–9, Sept Sat and Sun 10–6, Oct Sat and Sun 10–8;* *adm* *€28.50, children €14.25, under 1m free, includes the cost of all rides. The vast car park costs an additional €1.50: make a mental note of where you leave your car – the spaces are not numbered.*

Six Flags Belgium is Belgium's premier outdoor amusement park. It offers dozens of rides suitable for all ages – from a gentle, old-fashioned roundabout and track-guided jalopies for the very young, to thrills and spills on high-powered modern roller-coasters. These are laid out in a series of thematic 'villages' joined by a network of tree-shaded walkways, set around a cluster of lakes. Countless souvenir shops, snack bars and restaurants jostle for positions beside the walkways, along with the various stages, marquees and covered halls where animal and circus acts are performed to a posted schedule. The atmosphere is friendly and fun-loving, and Six Flags Belgium can make an enjoyable family day out – provided that you observe some important ground rules. The park attracts as many as 15,000 people a day, resulting in exasperating queues to the best attractions. Avoid weekends in the summer season. Finally, go early: aim to be at the gates for opening time at 10am – there is easily enough in the park to occupy you for a whole day. Take your swimming things and even a change of clothes: many of the rides are water-based and can result in a soaking, which may not be so welcome on a chilly day.

Aqualibi

Open *summer Mon–Fri 6–10pm, Sat and Sun 10–11; winter Wed–Fri 2–11pm;* *adm* *€13.50 for 4 hrs, children under 1.30m €7, under 1.15m free.*

The Six Flags entrance ticket allows you to spend 1½ hours in this adventure swimming centre located at the park gates – although

Getting There

By Car

The Six Flags Belgium amusement park lies just to the south of the town of Wavre, 16km southeast of Brussels. If you are going by car, take the Brussels–Namur motorway (E411) to Wavre, then follow signs from Exit 7.

By Train

Six Flags lies on the railway line linking Ottignies and Leuven, and the nearest station is Bierges, just 300m from the park.

Tourist Information

Six Flags Belgium, **t** 010 42 15 00 or 010 42 17 17.

Eating Out

The park contains numerous restaurants and theme-based snack bars, selling sandwiches, hamburgers, grilled sausages, Chinese food and, of course, *frites*. One of the better options is the branch of famous **Chez Léon**. Prices are high and the quality is not brilliant, so you may prefer to bring a picnic.

you can extend your visit at the extra cost of €2 per half-hour. This complex contains a range of pools of various shapes and forms, including ones with wave machines, and a huge hot-bath and Jacuzzi , plus enormous tubular water chutes and gushing water slides. Six Flag Belgium's own advice should be taken: go to Aqualibi as soon as you reach the park in the morning, as it may become very crowded later on. The sheer weight of numbers can be alarming in the popular chutes. Some of these are for confident swimmers only, and this is not always as clear as it should be from the notices. Once in the chutes it is virtually impossible to beat a retreat, except by being hoicked out igno-miniously by one of the pool attendants.

Bruges

11

The city of Bruges was, like Cinderella, left behind in its medieval rags while the other major Flemish cities joined the ball of industrialization in the 19th century. In 1908 George W. T. Omond wrote: 'Bruges is a city of the dead, of still life, of stagnant waters, of mouldering walls and melancholy streets, long since fallen from its high estate into utter decay.' But just as Cinderella was found by her prince, so Bruges was discovered in the 20th century – by tourism. Travellers, artists and writers became aware of a city preserved in a time warp, its crooked streets, crumbling guildhouses and stone bridges standing over mirror-still canals, reflecting the gables and spires of a medieval skyline.

Bruges has since prospered by its famous charm, and it is now the most visited city in Belgium after Brussels. But there has been a price to pay. The trample of thousands of tourists' feet has gradually smoothed the authentic texture of the city's character. The deadening combination of restoration and tourism is bringing Bruges perilously close to sanitization, to making it into a sterile museum city. As a result of this, some visitors come away sadly disappointed.

This is a shame, for Bruges's charms are real enough. The intimate, pocket-sized city is one of the most remarkable urban heirlooms of Europe, while its two triumphant collections of medieval art would alone justify the visit. Steal away from the main thoroughfares and find a quiet corner, where the old soul of the city still speaks, or marvel as the dawn mists rise off the canals and the setting sun throws the layered architecture into startling relief. Allow Bruges to reveal its famous charms in its own time.

Inset Key

C	Belfort
D	Heilig Bloedbasiliek
F	Oude Griffie
B	Proostdij
A	Provincial Hof
G	Renaissancezaal van het Brugse Vrije
E	Stadhuis
H	Vismarkt

Hotel and Restaurant Key

3	Bauhaus International Youth Hotel
34	't Begijnte
9	De Beurze
19	Den Braamberg
6	Cordoeanier
12	Cornee
7	Het Dagelijks Brood
14	Duc de Bourgogne
20	Den Dyver
11	De Garre
29	Groeninghe
10	Holiday Inn Crowne Plaza

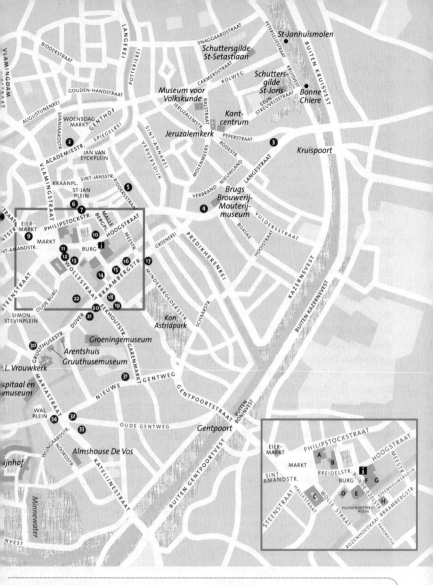

History

Once upon a time Bruges was linked to the sea by a river, the Reie, which led to a deep coastal inlet called the Zwin. It was here that Baldwin Iron-Arm, the first Count of Flanders, decided to build a castle to protect the coast from Viking raids, and gradually the town developed around it, thriving on the trade that came on the Reie and to Damme on the Zwin. As with the other Flemish cities, textiles were the key to Bruges's early prosperity, closely linked to the wool trade with England, which was held to be the source of the finest grade of wool. In 1093 Robert the Frisian made it the capital of the Duchy of Flanders, and by the 13th century Bruges was one of the wealthiest cities of northern Europe and a major player in the Hanseatic League, the powerful association of north European trading cities – Bruges even claims to have had the first stock exchange in Europe (at 35 Grauwwerkersstraat). When Philip the Fair, King of France, came to the city on a state visit in 1301, his wife Joanna of Navarre was so startled by the wealth and luxurious clothes of the inhabitants that she made her famously catty remark: 'I thought I alone was Queen, but I see that I have 600 rivals here.'

But this prosperity was achieved against a backdrop of political strife. Flanders was a duchy of France, a status supported by the French-speaking patricians, called the *leli-aerts* (after the *fleur de lis* or lily, the French royal emblem). The Flemish masses, as well as many leading merchants, however, were proudly Flemish and had acquired a considerable amount of autonomy over the years. Called the *clauwaerts* (from the claws of the Flemish lion), they lived in constant tension with their French overlords. The purpose of Philip the Fair's visit in 1301 was to reassert French authority over the city.

Insulted at being asked to foot the bill for his ostentatious reception, the citizens of Bruges mounted a *clauwaert* revolt in 1302, the so-called 'Bruges Matins', massacring 2,000 French troops and anyone who was unable to pronounce in convincing Flemish the shibboleth 'Schild en Vriend' (shield and friend). This in turn led to widespread rebellion and, six weeks later, the famous Flemish victory over the French at the Battle of the Golden Spurs (see p.29). But after this brief spell of independence the French regained control. Their policy of crushing suppression led to a period of instability and confusion throughout Flanders, and coincided with the outbreak of the Hundred Years' War, and a mass emigration of weavers to England.

The situation was only resolved in 1384 when Philip the Bold, Duke of Burgundy, inherited Flanders. Under the Dukes of Burgundy Bruges entered its second great period of prosperity, particularly during the reign of Philip the Good (1419–67). It was also a dazzling period for Flemish art, with the likes of Jan van Eyck (1390–1441), Hugo van der Goes (?1435–82) and Hans Memling (1430/5–94) among the inhabitants.

Two factors brought about Bruges's decline after the 15th century: the Zwin was virtually silted up by 1550, cutting off the city's vital access to the sea, and the general collapse of the Flemish textile trade. During the next century Bruges became the focus of revolt, both of the iconoclasts, and of the 'Gueux', the rebels fighting against Spain. From this time on the city slowly slid into a forlorn state of decay.

However, by the mid-19th century Bruges's hidden charms had been discovered by the more sanguine tourists, some on their way to visit the battlefield of Waterloo. The city appealed in particular to medievalists consumed by the Neo-Gothic vogue of the period, and British enthusiasts helped to coax the people of Bruges into beginning the renovation.

The Boudewijn Canal was completed in the early 20th century, and now Bruges's thriving industrial sector (well away from the historic city) produces glass, electrical goods and chemicals – but it is tourism that is the mainstay of its modern prosperity.

Getting There

By Car

Bruges is 100km northwest of Brussels, connected by the E40/A10 autoroute. It's a small city with a limited capacity for traffic. Use one of the well-organized car parks in the south and west of the city (around €6 per day). The largest are the underground car parks at 't Zand and near Katelijnepoort. There are others close to the city centre (under the Novotel for around €9 per day) but these fill up quickly at busy times.

By Train

The railway station to the south is about 20mins walk from the city centre. There's a direct train link from Brussels (Gare du Nord/Centrale/Midi) via Ghent.

Getting Around

Bruges' **bus service** (€1 single, €3 for day pass) links the centre with outlying districts, such as 't Zand. **Taxi** ranks are at the railway station and the Markt, or call **t** 050 33 44 44 or **t** 050 38 46 60. Bruges is a pleasant place to cycle, and the station offers **bicycles for hire**. Other bike-hire shops are in the centre: 't Koffieboontje, 4 Hallestraat; and Eric Popelier, 26 Mariastraat.

A **boat trip** on the canals (30mins) is a picturesque, very popular, introduction to the city. All the starting points are along the canal connecting the Minnewater to the Burg (*available daily 10–6 March–Nov; Dec–Feb weekends, school and public hols only; adults €5, children €2.50*). **Horse-drawn carriages** depart from the Markt: March–Nov 10–6, €25 per carriage for 35 mins.

Tourist Information

11 Burg, **t** 050 44 86 86 (**w** *www .bruges.be; open April–Sept Mon–Fri 9.30–6.30, Sat and Sun 10–12 and 2–6.30; Oct–March Mon–Fri 9.30–5, Sat 9.30–1 and 2–5*). There's also an office at the railway station (*similar hours, closed Sun*) offering a guide service (€25 for 2 hrs), or join the daily summer guided tour, starting at 3pm at the Burg tourist office (€3 per person, children under 14 free). Note that many museums have 'family tickets' which offer discounts.

Guided tours of the **First World War battle-fields** and other outlying attractions are offered by Quasimodo, run by Lode and Sandi Notredame, 7 Leenhofweg, 8310 Brugge 3, **t** 050 37 04 70, **f** 050 37 49 60. €38 incl. lunch.

Internet

Bruges Online, 67 Katelijnestraat, **t** 050 34 93 52. A public e-mail and internet service.

Festivals

Heilig-Bloedprocessie (Procession of the Holy Blood) takes place annually on Ascension Day. Following an 800-year-old tradition, the holy relic is paraded through the streets in a pageant which is both religious and light-hearted. Tickets for the grandstand are available from the tourist office from 1st March onwards.

Reiefeest (Festival of the Canals) takes place once every three years (2004, 2007) in the last week of August – a historic pageant along the illuminated waterways.

Praalstoet van de Gouden Boom (Pageant of the Golden Tree) occurs every 5 years in late August (next in 2006). The spectacular marriage of Charles the Bold to Margaret of York in 1468 is celebrated with a costumed procession and tournament.

December is a particularly attractive time to visit Bruges, with a **Christmas market** in the centre of town, a temporary ice rink in the Markt, and stalls selling mulled wine.

Shopping

The main shopping district, to the west around Steenstraat and Zuidzandstraat, is upmarket and tasteful. **Lace** is a famous Bruges product, and there are good shops in Breidelstraat, between the Markt and Burg, and a lively **fish market** (Vismarkt, *see* p.183).

Where to Stay

De Orangerie, 10 Kartuizerinnenstraat, 8000 Brugge, **t** 050 34 16 49, **f** 050 33 30 16, **w** www.hotelorangerie.com. Sumptuous, former 16th-century convent, with canalside breakfast terrace and 19 rooms. €200–300.

De Tuilerieën, 7 Dijver, 8000 Brugge, t 050 34 36 91, f 050 34 04 00, w www.hoteltuilerieen.com. Pampered luxury in a 15th-century town house on the Dijver canal. With swimming pool. €220–335.

Sofitel, 2 Boeveriestraat, 8000 Brugge, t 050 44 97 11, f 050 44 97 99, w www.sofitel.com. Modern, behind a façade of a 17th-century monastery. 15mins walk from the centre. Has a swimming pool. €180–220 excl. breakfast.

Die Swaene, Steenhouwersdijk (Groenerei), 8000 Brugge, t 050 34 27 98, w www.dieswaene-hotel.com. Restored 15th-century mansion close to the Vismarkt. €160–200.

De Snippe, 53 Nieuwe Gentweg, 8000 Brugge, t 050 33 70 70, f 050 33 76 62, e de.snippe@flanderscoast.be. A hotel-restaurant with celebrated cuisine (see opposite). The 18th-century house has been sympathetically restored to comfortable elegance. €145–200.

Holiday Inn Crowne Plaza, 10 Burg, 8000 Brugge, t 050 44 68 44, f 050 44 68 68, w www.crowneplaza.com/bruggebel. Sleek modern hotel, with swimming pool and client parking. €140–375; children free if sharing a room with parents.

Pandhotel, 16 Pandreitje, 8000 Brugge, t 050 34 06 66, f 050 34 05 56, w www.pandhotel.com. 18th-century burgher's house converted into an elegant hotel that's close to the city centre. €135–300.

Park Hotel, 5 Vrijdagmarkt ('t Zand), 8000 Brugge, t 050 33 33 64, w www.parkhotel-brugge.be. Comfortable modern hotel located on 't Zand. €110–135.

Novotel Zuid, 20 Chartreuseweg (Sint-Michiels), 8200 Brugge, t 050 40 21 40, f 050 40 21 41, w www.novotel.com. Commendable modern family hotel situated in woodland, 4km south of the city, and with an outdoor pool. Near the A17 motorway but fitted with double glazing. €110–125.

Jan Brito, 1 Freren Fonteinstraat, 8000, Brugge, t 050 33 06 01, f 050 33 06 52, w www.janbrito.com. 19th-century splendour in a 16th-century mansion. €100–195.

Duc de Bourgogne, 12 Huidenvettersplein, 8000 Brugge, t 050 33 20 38, f 050 34 40 37, e duc.bourgogne@ssi.be. Hotel/restaurant in an historic house with good restaurant (see opposite). Only 10 rooms. €100–135.

Ibis Brugge Centrum, 65A Katelijnestraat, 8000 Brugge, t 050 33 75 75, f 050 33 64 19, e h1047@accor-hotels.com. Large modern hotel, close to the Begijnhof. €80–100.

Patritius, 11 Riddersstraat, 8000 Brugge, t 050 33 84 54, f 050 33 96 34. Spacious, central old mansion with few frills. €70–100.

't Putje, 31 't Zand, 8000 Brugge, t 050 33 28 47, f 050 34 14 23, e hotelputje@hotelputje.com. Clean, friendly, modernized hotel near the 't Zand, 15mins walk from centre. €70–85.

Campanile, 20 Jagerstraat, 8200 St Michiels, t 050 38 13 60, f 050 38 45 42. Family-run hotel south of the station. €70.

Groeninghe, 29 Korte Vuldersstraat, t 050 34 32 55, f 050 34 07 69. Atmosphere of a private home, not far from Sint-Salvator-kathedraal in the west. €65–70.

Cordoeanier, 16–18 Cordoenierstraat, 8000 Brugge, t 050 33 90 51, f 050 34 61 11, e info@cordoeanier.be. Small hotel, good value for its central position. €57–67.

Youth Hostels

Bauhaus International Youth Hotel, 135–137 Langestraat, 8000 Brugge, t 050 34 10 93, f 050 33 41 80, e info@bauhaus.be. 81 beds, 20mins walk from the centre. €11.50 pp.

International Youth Hostel, 143 Baron Ruzettelaan, 8310 Assebroek, t 050 35 2679, f 050 35 3732. Modern youth hostel, located in Assebroek, a suburb to the east. €11.50 pp.

Passage, 26 Dweerstraat, 8000 Brugge, t 050 34 02 32, f 050 34 01 40. 50 beds, stone's throw from Sint-Salvator-kathedraal. €11 pp.

Snuffel Sleep In, 47–49 Ezelstraat, 8000 Brugge, t 050 33 31 33, f 050 33 32 50, e snuffel@flanderscoast.be. Cheap lodgings close to centre. Easygoing regime. €11.50 pp.

Bed and Breakfast

The tourist office publishes a list of approved accommodation. Double rooms are available centrally for €35 upwards, family rooms sleeping 4 for €60–110.

Eating Out

Expensive

Den Braamberg, *11 Pandreitje*, *t 050 33 73 70*. *Open Mon and Wed–Sat 12–2 and 7–9.30; closed 2 weeks in July*. Award-winning restaurant in 18th-century house. Lunch €45.

Den Dyver, *5 Dyver*, *t 050 33 60 69*. *Open Fri–Tues 12–2 and 6.30–9.30, Wed and Thurs 6.30–9.30pm*. Historic backdrop for dishes with beer – a place of pilgrimage for enthusiasts. €40.

De Karmeliet, *19 Langestraat*, *t 050 33 82 59*. *Open Tues–Sat 12–2 and 7–10, Sun 12–2pm*. Top Belgian restaurant, with 3 Michelin stars. Chic, set in a patrician house with outside terrace. Lunch €50.

De Snippe, *53 Nieuwe Gentweg*, *t 050 33 70 70*. *Open Tues–Sat 12–2.30 and 7–9.30, Sun and Mon 7–9.30pm*. Hotel restaurant in a tastefully renovated *maison de maître*, serving superb *haute cuisine française*. Lunch €38; four-course evening menu €71.

Duc de Bourgogne, *12 Huidenvettersplein*, *t 050 33 20 38*. *Open Mon–Sat 12–2.30 and 7–9.30*. Classy hotel-restaurant in a former palace gatehouse, with canal views. Gastronomic menu at €33 upwards.

Patrick Devos, *41 Zilverstraat*, *t 02 33 55 66*. *Open Mon–Fri 12–1.30 and 7–9, Sat 7–9pm*. Much fêted restaurant in an elegant turn-of-the-century house with garden; French cuisine with an ingeniously light touch. Lunch €42, gourmet menu at €59.50.

Tanuki, *1 Oude Gentweg*, *t 050 34 75 12*, *w www.tanuki.be*. *Open Wed–Sun 12–2 and 6.30–9.30*. Japanese *teppanyaki*, *tempura*, *sashimi* and sushi overlooking a Japanese garden. Menus €13 (lunch) to €50.

De Visscherie, *8 Vismarkt*, *t 050 33 02 12*. *Open Wed–Mon*. Fish gastronomy of high renown, overlooking the fish market. Recommended is the *waterzooi van de Noordzee*. €30 plus.

De Watermolen, *130 Oostmeers*, *t 050 34 33 48*. *Open Thurs–Tues 12–9.15*. Bistro with terrace in the south, specializing in fish. €24.

De Witte Poorte, *6 Jan van Eyckplein*, *t 050 33 08 83*. *Open Tues–Sat 12–2 and 7–9; closed 2 weeks in Feb and last 2 weeks of June*. Specialist in Belgian cooking of exceptional quality. Lunch €28.50.

Moderate

't Begijntje, *11 Walstraat*, *t 050 33 00 89*. *Open Thurs–Sat, Mon and Tues 12–9.30, Wed and Sun 12–2pm*. Charming, family-run restaurant serving home-cooked Flemish food. Menus €22–38.

Cornee, *2 De Garre*, *t 050 33 95 88*. *Open Thurs–Tues*. Friendly and intimate restaurant down a tiny alleyway off Breidelstraat. French and Belgian cuisine (eels in green sauce, dishes with *witloof*, etc.). Lunch €25.

De Lijnwaadmarkt, *3 Wollestraat*, *t 050 33 43 13*. Atmospheric restaurant offering well-cooked standards at affordable prices.

Maria van Bourgondië, *1 Guido Gezelleplein*, *t 050 33 20 66*. *Open Thurs–Tues 9am–11pm*. Solid Belgian cooking – soup, ham, pâté, *vlaamse stoofkarbonaden* (beef stew in beer), *waterzooi* – in a comfortable town house with an open fire. Lunch €16.

Pietje Pek, *13 Sint-Jacobstraat*, *t 050 34 78 74*. *Open Thurs–Mon 5.30–11pm*. Atmospheric, family *bistrot* specializing in fondues (meat, cheese). 'Eat-as-much-as-you-like' fondue around €23; children under 10 can share with adults for free.

't Pallieterke, *28 't Zand*, *t 050 34 01 77*. *Open Mon–Sat*. Pleasant, friendly French-style restaurant and tearoom serving mussels, game, fish and *waterzooi*. Menus €13.50–24.50.

Inexpensive

De Beurze, *22 Markt*, *t 050 33 50 79*. *Open daily 9am–11pm*. Laid-back *bistrot* with wooden tables and open fire. Mussels, grilled fish and meat. Lunch €14.75.

De Garre, *1 De Garre*, *t 050 34 10 29*. *Open Mon–Fri 12–2, Sat–Sun 11am–1am*. Cosy *staminee* (pub) of low beams and exposed brick. Good beer and light snacks.

Het Dagelijks Brood, *21 Philipstockstraat*, *t 050 33 60 50*. *Open Mon and Wed–Sat 7–6, Sun 8–6*. Upmarket sandwiches and salads €3.75–7.75.

THE CENTRE

Markt

The old marketplace is at the very heart of the city – once the scene of great trade fairs, medieval jousts and public executions. This is a good place to start, although architecturally it is somewhat disappointing, flanked by 17th-century gabled houses that have been much altered. However, it is still a working market square: there has been a Saturday market here since AD 958.

On the eastern (lower) side is the **Provinciaal Hof**, the imposing provincial government building. It was built in Neo-Gothic style between 1881 and 1921 on the site of the old Waterhalle, a covered hall over the river where cargoes of market goods were unloaded from flat-bottomed barges. In the centre of the square is a statue (1887) by Paul de Vigne of Pieter de Coninck and Jan Breydel, leaders of the 1302 rebellion against the French. On the west side, at No.16, on the corner of Sint-Amandstraat, is the step-gabled **Craenenburg**, now a café, with a Neo-Gothic façade dating from 1955. This was once a grand private house where Archduke Maximilian was held prisoner in 1488. On the opposite corner is the **Huis Bouchotte**, with the oldest genuine façade of the Markt, dating from the late 15th century. Charles II of England lived here during his exile in 1656–7.

The most arresting feature of the Markt is the **Belfort** (*open daily 9.30–5; adm €2.50*). Bruges's belfry is one of its great landmarks, which for centuries served as a watchtower, clock tower and symbol of Bruges's independent spirit. It is a remarkable hybrid building, with three main tiers rising to 83m through a series of architectural styles. There used to be an additional spire, but this was destroyed by lightning in 1741. You have to be fit to climb the 366 steep and narrow steps to the top (only 70 people are allowed into the Belfry at a time – come early to avoid the crush). Close to the top is the splendid automatic clock carillon, installed in 1748, which rings the 47 bells on the quarter hour like a giant musical box, and the room where the *beiaardier* (carillon player) has his keyboard to play the carillon bells directly. It's worth waiting to hear it chime.

Burg

If the Markt is the centre of Bruges, the Burg is its historical heart. This small square boasts a handful of the city's most impressive civic buildings, and its most atmospheric church. From the Breidelstraat entrance, to your left is the **Proostdij** (Provost's House), a grey-stone Flemish–Baroque building (1662), with an elaborate entrance crowned by blind Justice. A stone model of the destroyed church of St Donatian (or Donatus), where Jan van Eyck was buried, is nearby.

On the right-hand flank, in the centre, is the **Stadhuis** (*see* opposite), with its tall Gothic windows and pepperpot ornamental towers. To its right is the **Heilig Bloedbasiliek** (*see* below), built of grey stone with golden figures and ornate ogive arches. Left of the Stadhuis is the **Oude Griffie** (Old Recorder's House), pierced by the arched entrance to an alleyway, also surmounted by a statue of blind Justice. A Gothic and Renaissance building (1534–7), it was later an annexe to the 18th-century **Gerechtshof** (lawcourts, used until 1984) next door.

Heilig Bloedbasiliek

There are two separate parts to the small 'Basilica of the Holy Blood'. The lower church is known as St Basil's Chapel after the relic (four vertebrae) of St Basil the Great, brought back from Caesarea in the Holy Land in 1099. The tone of the 12th-century chapel is bleak and thoroughly medieval: you could imagine crusaders clanking around here, haunted by distant memories of Jerusalem.

Up a splendid, broad, spiral staircase, built in 1523, is the Chapel of the Holy Blood, a 15–16th-century addition, destroyed by the French in the 1790s but rebuilt and richly decorated in the 19th century. The relic of the

Holy Blood – apparently blood washed from the body of Christ by Joseph of Arimathea – was, according to tradition, given to Derick of Alsace, Count of Flanders, in 1148, during the Second Crusade. When it arrived in Bruges in 1150, the dried blood in its rock-crystal phial suddenly became liquid again. The phenomenon was repeated every Friday, and became the focus for fervent devotion and miraculous healings. It is still displayed in the chapel on Fridays (*8.30–11 and 3–4*) – but it hasn't liquified since 1325. The **Schatkamer** or Treasure Chamber (*open April–Sept 9.30–12 and 2–6, Oct–March 10–12 and 2–4; adm €1*), contains an elaborate gold reliquary made by Jan Crabbe in 1617 (used in the Heilig-Bloedprocessie on Ascension Day) with a large diamond said to have belonged to Mary Stuart. There are also two fine paintings by Pieter Pourbus (1524–84).

Stadhuis

12 Burg. **Open** *daily 9.30–5; adm €4, ticket also valid for Museum van het Brugse Vrije.*

The town hall, the oldest and finest in Belgium, dates originally from 1376 to 1420. Heavily restored over the centuries, it is part medieval, part 19th-century medieval fantasy and part modern renovation. The medieval statues of the count and countess of Flanders between the windows were pulled down by French Revolutionaries in 1792, and replaced in modern times.

The Gothic Hall on the upper floor still has its original vaulted wooden ceiling, dating from 1385. It has been beautifully restored, so that the decorated vault keys (illustrating scenes from the New Testament) and consoles next to the walls (illustrating the twelve months of the year and the four elements) can be seen in their full splendour. The walls are stunningly decorated with scenes from Bruges's history, richly painted in 1895 by Albert and Julien Devriendt.

Renaissancezaal van het Brugse Vrije

Open *April–Sept 10–12.30 and 1.15–5, Oct–March 10–12.30 and 2–5; adm €2.50 which also includes entry to the Stadhuis.*

This room is part of the 14th-century Schepenzaal, where aldermen of the Brugse Vrije used to meet. Beyond the main hall is the Renaissance Hall, with a huge oak and black marble chimneypiece (1529–33), a robust and sensuous installation designed by Lancelot Blondeel (1496–?1561) and sculpted by Guyot de Beaugrant (d. 1551). It is a monument to the ruler of the day, Charles V, whose oak statue appears in the centre, flanked by his two pairs of grandparents, Maximilian of Austria and Mary of Burgundy (left), and Ferdinand of Aragon and Isabella of Castile (right). Charles' prominent codpiece makes it clear that this is a work about fertility and lineage. Most remarkable is the condition of the chimneypiece after over 450 years.

Vismarkt, Groenerei and Rosenhoedkaai

The archway and vaulted passage beneath the Oude Griffie in Burg leads to Blinde Ezelstraat (Blind Ass Street – probably a reference to a tavern, since disappeared), and immediately you cross the main canal on one of the Bruges's many bridges. The number of bridges in Bruges is said to have earned the city its name (*brug* means bridge in Flemish). But the more probable theory is that the name is derived from the Norse word *bryggia*, meaning a landing place.

You are now in one of the most picturesque parts of Bruges. On the other side of the bridge is the old **Vismarkt** (*Braambergstraat, open daily*) or fishmarket, erected in 1826, where fish is still sold. The street that follows the canal to the left leads to the **Groenerei**, which offers some of the most famous views of the Burg, the Belfort, and the fetchingly crooked houses that overlook the canal. On the right-hand side (Nos.8–12) is an old almshouse, De Pelikaan, dated 1714. West of the Vismarkt is the picturesque **Huidenvettersplein** (Tanners' Square), in the middle of which stands a statue of two lions (1925), emblems of the tanners' guild. It leads to the **Rosenhoedkaai**, which offers views of the Belfort in one direction and Onze Lieve Vrouwekerk in the other.

Groeningemuseum

12 Dijver, **t** *050 44 87 11.* **Open** *Wed–Mon 9.30–5; adm €6.*

This surprisingly modern building houses one of Europe's most dazzling collections of medieval art. Almost everything in it is of outstanding quality. It's a delight – provided that you can stomach the subject matter of so many of the exhibits: gruesome martyrdom painted with loving attention to every horrific detail.

The great star of the collection is **Jan van Eyck**'s *Madonna with Canon van der Paele* (1436), a large work filled with stunning detail. The Madonna sits enthroned with Christ on her knee, while Canon van der Paele (who commissioned the work) kneels to her left, spectacles in hand. Behind him is St George, his patron saint, kitted out in a full set of ceremonial armour, and opposite him is St Donatian dressed in sumptuous vestments. This is not simply a religious work, but a portrait of living people, surrounded by the kind of luxurious setting that existed in Burgundian Bruges: note the oriental carpet, and the African parrot held by Christ.

St Luke Drawing a Portrait of Our Lady, by van Eyck's pupil **Roger van der Weyden**, is in its way another snapshot of contemporary life: the Virgin gives her breast to a rather starved-looking baby Jesus, surrounded by Renaissance textiles and architecture. **Dirk Bouts** is represented by a triptych featuring the Martyrdom of St Hippolytus. This is upstaged only by *The Judgement of Cambyses* (1498) by **Gerard David** (?1460–1523), the last great artist of the Bruges school. It depicts the corrupt judge Sisamnes being flayed alive with surgical precision by knaves in boots and cloaks; Cambyses, king of Persia in the 6th century BC, and other surrounding figures, including a mangy dog, are painted in great detail and look entirely unconcerned.

A series of panels depicting the legends of St Ursula, by the Master of the Legends of St Ursula, is dated to before 1482. St Ursula, daughter of a king of Britain, escaped to Rome to avoid being married against her will, accompanied by a retinue of virgins. All were murdered later in Cologne, simply because they were Christian.

Hans Memling is represented by the large and impressive Moreel triptych (1484). Willem Moreel, burgomaster of Bruges, is depicted in the left-hand panel, his wife in the right and, in the centre, Saints Christopher, Maurus and Giles. The painting shows the greater confidence in figure work, in the use of perspective and scale, that Memling brought to Bruges.

Other highlights include a nightmarish *Last Judgement* by **Hieronymus Bosch**; the *Allegory of the Peace of the Netherlands* (1577) by **Pieter Claessens the Younger**; and the startling portraits of Archduke Albert and Isabella the Infanta by **Frans Pourbus the Younger** (1569–1622). Further works are from the late 19th and early 20th century.

Arentshuis/ Brangwynmuseum

16 Dijver, **t** *050 44 87 63.* **Open** *April–Sept Wed–Mon 9.30–5, Oct–March Wed–Mon 9.30–12.30 and 2–5; adm €2.*

This rewarding little museum, housed in an 18th-century Neoclassical mansion, contains a set of paintings, prints, furniture and carpets donated to Bruges in 1936 by Frank Brangwyn (1867–1956). This British artist was born in Bruges, and later trained in the workshop of William Morris. He was associated with Siegfried Bing in Paris at the outset of the Art Nouveau movement – but he always held a deep affection for the city of his birth.

Onze Lieve Vrouwekerk

Mariastraat. **Open** *April–Sept Sun–Fri, Oct–Mar daily.*

This is Bruges's most imposing and endearing church, built over some 200 years from 1220. Its soaring, pinnacle-like tower, at 122m, is one of the highest in Belgium. The cream-painted interior has a bold simplicity, with hefty columns and black and white flag-stones. This austerity is offset by outbursts of massive baroque ornament in the side chapels, and in the exuberant pulpit (1743) by **Jan Garemijn**, decked with cherubs and a depiction of Wisdom sitting on a globe.

At the head of the southern aisle, protected by a glass screen, is one of Bruges's great treasures: the *Madonna and Child* (1504–5) by **Michelangelo**, one of the very few Michelangelo sculptures outside Italy, and the only one to leave Italy during his lifetime. Originally intended for the cathedral of Siena, it was acquired (and donated) by Jan van Moscroen, a wealthy merchant. It has twice been carried off as war booty.

The Museum

Open April–Sept 10–12 and 2–5, Oct–March 10–12 and 2–4.30; adm €2.

The main altar sits oddly in the middle of the church; the choir behind it is now a museum. The main exhibits are the elaborate tombs of Charles the Bold and his daughter, Mary of Burgundy. Mary's feet rest on a pair of dogs, the symbol of fidelity, and Charles' rest on a lion, the symbol of strength. Also in the choir is a fine altarpiece by **Bernard van Orley** (1499–1541), and paintings by Pieter Pourbus, including a *Last Supper* (1562).

Memlingmuseum

38 Mariastraat, t 050 44 87 70. Open April–Sept Thurs–Tues 9.30–5, Oct–March Thurs–Tues 9.30–12.30 and 2–5; adm €2.50.

There are just six works by the Flemish master Hans Memling (1435–94) in this museum, occupying a chapel in the old Sint-Janshospitaal. The most famous work in the collection is the Ursula Reliquary. Just one metre long, made of gilt wood, it contains a dozen or so small painted panels that tell in vivid and beautifully rendered detail the story of St Ursula (*see* opposite). The *Mystic Marriage of Saint Catherine* (1479) also demonstrates Memling's sparkling attention

to detail, with baby Jesus sliding a ring onto the finger of St Catherine (with the broken wheel on which the Romans attempted to martyr her), while St Barbara reads a book beside her. St Catherine is believed to symbolize Mary of Burgundy, and St Barbara her mother, Margaret of York. Commissioned for this chapel, the wings show the two St Johns (patrons of the hospital), with John the Baptist spurting blood after decapitation, and St John the Divine (the Evangelist) on the island of Patmos, to which he was exiled.

Gruuthusemuseum

17 Dijver. Open Wed–Mon 9.30–5; adm €3.

The old 15th-century Gruuthuse mansion, much restored, now contains a splendid collection of all the kinds of things that enriched the lives of the merchant classes of Bruges. Most of the objects are solid and util-itarian, but beautifully crafted and often charmingly decorated – weapons, kitchen implements, Delftware, linenfold cupboards, leather trunks, clocks, scales, spinets and hurdy-gurdies, textiles and lace. There is also a guillotine with a genuine French Revolutionary pedigree.

Sint-Salvator-kathedraal

1 St Salvatorskof, t 050 33 61 88. Open April–Sept daily.

Squat and built of yellow brick, this gloomy church only inherited the role of cathedral in 1834 after the destruction of Saint Donatian in 1799. Its roof and tower were rebuilt, after a fire, to a curious Neo-Romanesque design by a British architect, Robert Chantrell. The interior contains an elaborate pulpit (1778–85) by Hendrick Pulincx, and some large religious paintings by the Antwerp painter Erasmus Quellinus (1607–78), an assistant to Rubens. There is also a series of Brussels tapestries, dating to around 1731. The cathedral museum (*open Mon–Fri 2–5, Sun 3–5; adm €1.50*) includes works by Dirk Bouts and Hugo van der Goes. The most arresting feature of the church, however, is the remarkable baroque organ (1682), a mighty confection topped by angels and cherubs playing celestial music.

SOUTH BRUGES

Begijnhof

1 Wijngaardplein, **t** *050 36 01 40.* **Open** *daily; museum open Mar–Nov Mon–Fri 10–12 and 1.45–5, Sat and Sun 10–12 and 1.45–5.30;* **adm** *€2.*

The south of Bruges relaxes into a pretty network of tree-shaded canals. The Begijnhof has occupied its site since 1235, and today it appears like an island, accessed by a bridge and a gatehouse (dated 1776). The small museum in the church contains mementoes of the Begijnhof.

Minnewater

Just south of the Begijnhof, the Minnewater ('lake of love') was once a hive of activity as ships from all over the world jockeyed for position among the quays. Today it's a quiet backwater, enjoyed by strollers and swans, and has good views of the city spires.

Boudewijn Park

Off the A17, **t** *050 38 3838.* **Open** *May–Aug daily 10–6, Easter 10–6, Sept Sat and Sun 10–6;* **adm** *all-in tickets €14.50 for adults, €12.50 for children under 12, children under 1m free.*

Just to the south of Bruges, is this large amusement park with numerous rides including a big wheel and water shoots, crazy golf and a large dolphinarium.

EASTERN BRUGES

Brugse Brouwerij-Mouterijmuseum ('De Gouden Boom')

10 Verbrand Nieuwland. **Open** *April–Sept Wed–Sun 2–6;* **adm** *€2.50 (includes free drink).*

This museum contains artefacts relating to the city's breweries. Beer has been brewed in Bruges for centuries, and the city still has several well-known breweries. De Gouden Boom (next door) produces the excellent Brugse Tripel, and the **Straffe Hendrik** brewery in Walplein produces a beer ('Strong Henry') which is only sold locally (*guided tours only, 10–5; adm €3.50*).

Ghent

12

Of all the great Flemish cities, Ghent wears the robes of its prosperous and noble past with the most dignity. Stately step-gabled façades line the tranquil canals, while the pinnacled and gilded spires of its great monuments shape the skyline.

A number of Ghent's museums surpass expectations – notably the Museum voor Sierkunst (decorative arts), Museum voor Volkskunde (folk museum) and Bijlokemuseum (a rich historical ragbag). Its *begijnhof* (*béguinage*) is one of the most charming and evocative in Belgium. And there is a dazzling jewel in this crown: within its fine cathedral is one of the great masterpieces of European art, Jan van Eyck's *Adoration of the Mystic Lamb*.

A day trip to Ghent would allow you to see its main attractions, but a weekend break would reveal more of its majestic heart. As night falls the atmosphere relaxes in expectation of pleasure, and the welcoming lights of the numerous bars and excellent restaurants – many housed in centuries-old historic buildings – glow across the canals and in the recesses of the crooked streets.

History

Ghent grew up around two 7th-century abbeys, those of St Baaf and Sint Pieter, built among a group of 30 or so islands scattered across the marshy ground where the Rivers Lys (Leie) and Lieve converge before joining the River Scheldt just to the south. (The name Ghent may well derive from the Celtic word *ganda*, meaning 'confluence'.)

Ghent became rich from the cloth trade and in the 13th century forged a canal link with Bruges. At the start of the Hundred Years' War, however, the Count of Flanders, Louis de Nevers, sided with France; the effect was to throttle trade with England, the supplier of wool to the cloth trade. The merchants of Ghent, led by the patrician brewer Jacob van Artevelde (1287–1345), were powerful enough to go their own way and negotiated an alliance with the King of England, Edward III (r. 1327–77), which the English were able to enforce militarily.

It was the start of a troubled history for Ghent, a city which, despite its calm face today, has always had something of a reputation for independence and revolt.

Ghent even continued to resist during the peaceful Burgundian period, until, after five years, it was forced to surrender in 1543. Philip the Good, Duke of Burgundy, made the leading citizens parade out of the city gates dressed only in their shirts. Ghent soon settled the score, by forcing Mary of Burgundy to sign (in the Sint-Jorishof, now a hotel) the Great Privilege, granting considerable autonomy to the city.

As England began to dominate the cloth trade, Ghent turned its trading skills to grain. In 1547 a canal was cut from Ghent to Terneuzen, giving Ghent direct access to the North Sea. As Bruges foundered, Ghent prospered, becoming the most powerful city of the Low Countries.

Hotel and Restaurant Key

3	Amadeus
27	Aparthotel Castelnou
17	Brooderie
6	't Buiske Vol
22	Chez Jean
15	Het Cooremeterhuys
23	Cour St-Georges
5	De Draecke
9	Dulle Griet
11	Eetcafé Belvu
24	Flandria
26	Flor
16	Guido Meerschaut
19	Hotel Gravensteen
25	Ibis Kathedraal
18	Jan Breydel
4	't Kattenhuis
8	Keizershof
1	't Klokhuys
14	De Kruik
21	Het Pand
20	Patachon
7	De Pepermolen
10	Pink Flamingo's
12	In de Raeve
13	Sofitel
2	Togo

PATERSHOL

Museum voor Volkskunde

Gravensteen

GELDMUNT

ST.VEERLEPL.

Museum voor Sierkunst

BURGSTRAAT

St.Michielsbrug

St. Niklaaskerk

Het Pand

ZWARTEZUSTERS STR.

GEBR. VANDEVELDE STRAAT

KOOP HANDELSPL.

COUPURE RECHTS

COUPURE LINKS

Bijlokemuseum

Lele

IZERLAAN

Citadelpark

Museum voor Schone Kunsten

Museum van Hedendaagse Kunst

Plantentuin Universiteit Gent

KORENLEI

KRAANLEI

OTTOGRACHT

BIBLIOTHEEKSTR.

VRIJDAGMARKT

STEENDAM

ONDERSTRAAT

Stadhuis

GOUDEN LEEUWPL.

Belfort

St. BAAFSPL.

St-Baafs-kathedraal

LIMBURGSTR.

Duivelsteen

HENEGOUWENSTR. VLAANDE-

BRABANTDAM

LAMMERSTR.

BAGATTENSTRAAT

ST. PIETERSNIEUWSTRAAT

MUINKKAAI

Kon. Albertpark

FRANKLIN ROOSEVELTLAAN

GR. VAN VLAANDERENPLEIN

RENSTR.

ST. ANNAPL.

LANGE VIOLETTENSTRAAT

TWEEBRUGGENSTRAAT

Klein Begijnhof

ZUIDPARKLAAN

DAMPOORTSTR.

HAGELANDKAAI

SCHOOLKAAI

VOORHOUTKAAI

Station Ghent-Dampoort

St. Baafsabdij

GANDASTR.

KOEPOORTKAAI

FERDINAND LOUSBERGS KAAI

KASTEELLAAN

HUBERT FRERE ORBANLAAN

CH. DE KERCHOVELAAN

OVERPOORTSTR.

KONING LEOPOLD II LAAN

E. CLAUSLAAN

300 metres
300 yards

N

Getting There

Ghent is 50km northwest of Brussels, along autoroute E40. By train, it is 40mins from Brussels. The main station (Gand-Sint-Pieters) is 2.5km south of the centre, with connecting trams (1, 11 and 12) and taxis.

Getting Around

Ghent has a good **bus and tram** network. Maps are available from the ticket office on the Korenmarkt, at the western end of Sint-Niklaaskerk. **Driving** is complicated by a one-way system around the centre, and the presence of trams. Electronic noticeboards on main roads into the centre indicate free parking spaces (€1.25/hr). Car parks are situated in St Michielsplein, just west of the centre, around the Kouter, to the south of the centre, and in the Vrijdagmarkt to the north.

Boat trips on the canals depart from the Graslei and Korenlei. The city centre trip lasts about 30mins (April–Nov 10–7; €3 per person for an open boat). **Horse-drawn carriages** make half-hour trips around the main sights, starting at Sint-Baafsplein (Easter–Sept/Oct 10–7; €20 per carriage).

Tourist Information

Beneath the Belfort, **t** 09 225 36 41, **w** www.gent.be. **Open** April–June 9–8, July–Nov 9.30–6.30, Nov–Mar 9.30–4.30. Not a great source of literature, but staff are on hand to answer questions. Most practical information is available in a single pamphlet on the city, called simply 'Ghent'.

Festivals

The **city illuminations** create a spectacular sight. Many monuments are lit up nightly from May to October, and on Friday and Saturday for the rest of the year.

Ghent's most spectacular festival is its flower show, the **Gentse Floraliën**, at the Flanders Expo (huge international trade fair centre) in late April, every 5 years.

The Flanders-wide **Festival van Vlaanderen** is a major European festival of classical music that takes place annually from April into the autumn. Not to be confused with the annual **Gentse Feesten** (Ghent Festivities); a variety of processions, street theatre and musical events held in early July.

Shopping

The main shopping districts are south of the Belfort, down Mageleleinstraat and Volderstraat, along Koestraat, around the Kalandenberg square, and along the Lange Munt north of the Groentenmarkt. A market is also held on Fridays (7–1pm) and Saturdays (1–5pm) in the large Vrijdagmarkt.

Where to Stay

Sofitel, *63 Hoogport, B-9000 Gent,* **t** *09 233 3331,* **f** *09 233 1102.* Smart, modern hotel in the historic city centre. €146–233.

Hotel Gravensteen, *35 Jan Breydelstraat, B-9000 Gent,* **t** *09 225 1150,* **f** *09 225 1850.* Elegant 19th-century 'Second Empire' town house. Close to the city centre. €118–138.

Cour St-Georges, *2 Botermarkt, B-9000 Gent,* **t** *09 224 2424,* **f** *09 224 2640.* Dated 1228, this is one of the oldest hostelries in Europe. Neo-baronial in style, with unspectacular rooms. Good restaurant. €86–105.

Aparthotel Castelnou, *51 Kasteellaan,* **t** *09 235 0411,* **f** *09 235 0404.* Modern hotel with spacious one-bedroom apartments; €90 for two with breakfast. Inexpensive restaurant and private parking (small charge).

Ibis Kathedraal, *2 Limburgstraat, B-9000, Gent,* **t** *09 233 0000,* **f** *09 233 1000.* Very central, well-run but straightforward international-style hotel. Limited parking on site. €80.

Flandria, *3 Barrestraat,* **t** *09 223 0626,* **f** *09 223 7789.* Modest, agreeable family-run hotel with 22 rooms, near the centre. €47.

De Draecke, *11 Sint-Widostraat (Gravensteen),* **t** *09 233 7050,* **f** *09 233 8001.* Youth hostel, €10–15.

Bed and Breakfast

A list of selected accommodation, including full descriptions, is published by GGG (Gilde der Gentse Gasten Kamers), 81 Baliestraat, B-9000 Gent, **t** 221 2054. Many are handsome, central *maisons de maître,* and cost around €40 per night for two.

Eating Out

Expensive

Chez Jean, *3 Catalioniëstraat*, *t 09 223 3040*. *Open Tues–Sat*. Stylish restaurant, in a gabled house dated 1634 serving seasonal food, such as pheasant in *millefeuille* pastry with endives. Five-course menu €18.50.

Guido Meerschaut, *3 Kleine Vismarkt*, *t 09 223 5349*. *Open Tues–Sat and Sun pm; closed 3 weeks in Sept*. Modern restaurant run by a master-fishmonger; delicious fish at sensible prices. Main courses for €10–25.

Flor, *10 Grote Huidevettershoek*, *t 09 223 8919*. Hotel restaurant in a former textile factory overlooking the canal, with open-view kitchen. Three course menus for €34.

Het Cooremeterhuys, *12 Graslei*, *t 09 223 4971*. *Open Mon, Tues and Thurs–Sat; closed for 4 weeks in July–Aug*. Elegant restaurant in a fine old guildhouse overlooking the Graslei. Sophisticated French cuisine, with main courses for €18.50. Lunch €24.50.

Het Pand, *1 Onderbergen*, *t 09 225 0180*. *Open Mon–Sat*. Stylish restaurant on upper floor of a former monastery. Expect gastro-nomic excursions based on ingredients such as lobster and goose liver. Menu €55.

Jan Breydel, *10 Jan Breydelstraat*, *t 09 225 6287*. *Open Mon pm–Sat*. Genteel, parti-tioned *fin de siècle* setting for *haute cuisine française*. Two-course menu for €40–50.

Cour St-Georges, *2 Botermarkt*, *t 09 224 2424*. *Open Mon–Sun am; closed 3 weeks in July–Aug*. Baronial décor for a famed hotel/restaurant serving a mixture of adventurous French cuisine and good-quality, robust Belgian cooking. Four-course menu at €38.

't Buiske Vol, *17 Kraanlei*, *t 09 225 1880*. *Open Mon, Tues and Thurs–Sat*. Inventive *haute cuisine française*, in a beautifully deco-rated canal house. Menu from €25.

Moderate

Amadeus Sparerib Restaurant, *8 Plotersgracht*, *t 09 225 1385*. A home-like setting in the Patershol district; hefty portions. Three-course menu with ribs €17.

De Kruik, *5 Donkersteeg*, *t 09 225 7101*. *Open Mon–Wed and Fri–Sun am*. Excellent French cuisine (notably fish), served with the chef's choice of wine for an astounding €35 all-in.

De Pepermolen/Moulin à Poivre, *25 Kraanlei*, *t 09 224 2894*. *Open Thurs–Tues*. Sociable canal-house restaurant. Choose anything from a *magret de canard, sauce aigre-douce* to a slab of Scotch beef.

In de Raeve, *2 Schepenhuisstraat (off Onderstraat)*, *t 09 223 3103*. *Open Tues–Sat*. Elegant meat and fish dishes cooked with panache on an open grill. Main courses about €12.50.

Patachon, *24 Korenlei*, *t 09 225 8902*. *Open Thurs–Tues*. In a medieval undercroft. Mussels, squid and salmon at good prices.

't Kattenhuis, *30 Drabstraat*, *t 09 224 3188*. *Open Wed–Mon*. Cat-themed décor. French cuisine, meats and *brochettes* (€16) grilled over an open fire.

't Klokhuys, *65 Corduwaniersstraat*, *t 09 223 4241*. *Open Tues–Sun and Mon pm*. Modern brasserie, in an old, gabled building in Patershol, serving tasty dishes such as eel and lamb chops cooked with basil. €22 plus.

Togo, *Coco de Mer, 19 Vrouwebroersstraat*, *t 09 223 6551*. *Open daily 11.45–2 and 6.30–1*. African dishes, such as stew with dried prawns and manioc for €13.50.

Inexpensive

Brooderie, *8 Jan Breydelstraat*, *t 09 225 0623*. *Open Tues–Sat 7.30am–6pm, Sun 9–6*. Bakery selling delicious cakes, crusty loaves and healthy lunches for around €7.50.

Dulle Griet, *50 Vrijdagmarkt*, *t 09 224 2455*. *Open Mon–Sun am*. Candlelit bar, dripping with beer-drinkers' mementoes. 250 varieties of beer – claims to be a *bieracademie*.

Eetcafé Belvu, *2 Kammerstraat*, *t 09 224 2314*. *Open Sun pm–Tues and Thurs–Sat*. Belgian and Italian dishes. €10.

Keizershof, *47 Vrijdagmarkt* *t 09 223 4446*. *Open Mon–Sat*. Popular tavern serving beers from the barrel and good home-cooked food.

Pink Flamingo's, *55 Onderstraat*, *t 09 233 4718*. *Open Mon–Sat*. No food, but a spendidly oddball café/bar with kitsch décor.

The citizens earned an ancient nickname in 1540. Growing weary of the Holy Roman Emperor Charles V's taxes, they rebelled – and many were ruthlessly hanged, earning them the name *stroppendragers* ('noose bearers'). The event is still recalled in folk processions, such as the Gentse Feesten. This tragedy helped to shape Ghent's outlook through the turmoil of the Counter-Reformation, during which the city suffered at the hands of the Inquisition.

From 1576 Ghent was under Dutch rule, after William of Orange, Stadholder of the Protestant Netherlands, pushed his army southwards and took the city. This forced the treaty known as the Pacification of Ghent, by which Philip II of Spain undertook to withdraw his troops from the 17 United Provinces of the Netherlands, and to grant them religious freedom. This lasted for just under ten years, and for a time Protestants dominated the city council. But in 1585 Alexander Farnese, Duke of Parma, retook Ghent on behalf of Philip II and he pushed the border back to more or less the current frontier with the Netherlands.

After 1648 the Netherlands sealed off the Scheldt estuary, cutting off one of Ghent's two vital canal links to the coast, which crippled their trade. The fortune of the city was only released from this stranglehold by the actions of the French Revolutionary Army in 1794.

Ghent's subsequent revival is largely attributed to a merchant called Lieven Bauwens (1762–1822), who in 1800 managed to smuggle a Spinning Jenny out of England. He set up a cotton-spinning business of his own, and by 1810 cotton had boomed into an industry employing some 10,000 workers. Trade in linen also grew: the River Leie became known as the 'Golden River', because the quantities of flax treated on its banks stained it yellow.

Ghent's industry has continued to thrive; textiles still play an important role, now supplemented by chemicals and steel. The old canal to Terneuzen was enlarged in the 1820s and again in the 1960s. Today Ghent's port constitutes the second largest port in Belgium after Antwerp. Ghent is also the capital of the province of East Flanders.

THE CENTRE

Sint-Baafskathedraal

*St Baafsplein. **Open** 8.30–6; closed (except for worshippers) Sun am and ecclesiastical festivals; **adm** free.*

Ghent's cathedral, one of the finest in Belgium, was named after the city's most cherished early-Christian saint, St Bavo (or Bavon). The present cathedral was founded originally in the 10th century as a church dedicated to St John the Baptist, but was rebuilt in Gothic style over nearly three centuries, from 1290 to 1569. It was renamed after St Bavo in 1540, when Charles V had the old Sint-Baafsabdij pulled down in order to build a castle on the site.

The great treasure of the cathedral is the *Adoration of the Mystic Lamb*, displayed in a rather cramped room to the left of the west (main) door to the cathedral (*adm €2.50*). It is a large polyptych of twelve panels, painted by Jan van Eyck between 1426 and 1432. Given that this is one of the earliest known oil paintings, the proficiency with which the new medium was used is astonishing.

In the nave of Sint-Baafskathedraal is a fine pulpit (1741–5) by Laurent Delvaux (1696–1778) made of an unusual mixture of oak and marble – Baroque, but with a Rococo lightness of touch.

The stark beauty of the 13th- and 14th-century choir, built of grey-blue Tournai stone, has been compromised by the monumental 18th-century Neoclassical screen erected in its midst to draw focus to the altar; this altar was designed by Hendrik Verbruggen (creator of the extraordinary pulpit in the cathedral of Brussels) and shows the *Apotheosis of St Bavo*.

The ambulatory of Sint-Baafskathedraal has been divided up into a series of atmospheric dimly lit chapels, one of which (to the left of the altar) contains *The Vocation of St Bavo* (1623/4) by the master painter Pieter Paul Rubens.

Belfort

***Open** 10–1 and 2–6 daily; **adm** €2.50, children under 15 free.*

The belfry of Ghent is one of the city's great landmarks. It rises majestically to the gilded copper dragon at 91m, and has a weather-vane that can trace its history back to 1377, set above a crescendo of black-tiled pinnacles and rooftops, dappled with gilded crockets. Built originally between 1380 and 1381, it was heavily restored in the 19th century.

It used to contain an alarm bell called Roeland (it was said to have the tongue of the chivalric hero Roland), which was removed on the instruction of Charles V because the bell had been used to call the citizens of Ghent to revolt in 1540.

Today the tower contains not only its clock, but also a 52-bell carillon, 37 of which date back to 1660. (*Carillon concerts: mainly in the summer, Fri and Sat 11.30am–12.30; also 9–10pm Sat July and Aug.*) Visitors can reach the parapet at 65m by lift, from where there are good views of the city.

Stadhuis

*1 Botermarkt, **t** 09 266 5211. **Open** May–Oct Mon–Thurs. Guided **tours** on certain days only (check with tourist office); English tours at 3pm from the tourist office beneath the Belfort; **adm** €2.50.*

This imposing town hall has three faces: you can see two of these faces by standing at the corner of the Botermarkt and Hoogstraat. Overlooking Hoogstraat is the flamboyant Gothic façade (1518–60). Overlooking the Botermarkt is the newer, more restrained Renaissance façade of 1581, which reflects the cooler outlook of the then Protestant administration. The third façade is a complex of antique wonky rooflines which can be glimpsed only from the Gouden Leeuwplein.

Still serving as a centre for city administration – and still the focus of the occasional demonstration – the interior mainly dates from the restoration that took place after 1870. However, among the rooms is the 16th-century Pacificatiezaal where the Pacification of Ghent was signed.

Sint-Niklaaskerk

***Open** Tues–Sun 10–5, Mon 2–5.*

This fine church, built mainly in the 13th century in what is known as Scheldt Gothic, is currently emerging from two decades of renovation, and the entrance for the time being is on the southern side. It has an atmospheric interior, with plain walls and columns of nibbled stone set against concertinaed ranks of dressed-stone buttresses and side chapels and the elegant curvature of the Gothic arches. This was once the church of the guilds (St Nicholas was the patron saint of merchants). The astonishing Baroque altarpiece, which blocks off almost all the east end with its statues, ornate pediment and candy-twist columns in black and white marble, centres on a painting by Niklaas de Liemakere (1601–46), a pupil of Rubens. It shows the appointment of St Nicholas (far left) as Bishop of Myra.

Sint-Michielsbrug

This bridge is Ghent's most famous view-point, and justly so. To the east is the spectacular line-up of the towers of Sint-Niklaaskerk, the Belfort and Sint-Baafskathedraal. To the north of Sint-Michielsbrug, is the city's beautiful stretch of canal, with the Graslei to the right and the Korenlei to the left.

Graslei and Korenlei

The waterway (the canalized River Leie) leading between these two quays was at the heart of the old port of Ghent. The **Graslei** on the eastern side is a fetching jumble of step-gables, stone carving and ranks of elegant windows. The buildings go as far back as the

12th century, added to over the next 500 years, but are mainly Flemish Renaissance in style. From north to south, they are as follows. The building with high pinnacles topped by gilded gryphons is the **Gildehuis van de Metsers** (Guildhouse of the Masons), built in 1521. Next is the 15th-century **Korenmeterhuis** (Guildhouse of the Grainmeasurers). Grain was stored in the building next door, the broad-fronted **Korenstapelhuis**, built originally in 1130. Beside this is the minuscule gabled **Tolhuisje** (1682), the customs house. Then follows the broad **Gildehuis der Graanmeters** (Grainmeasurers – their second house on this frontage), built in 1698 and decorated with escutcheons. The last, and the finest of the buildings, is a beautifully designed Renaissance house (1531), with an elaborately sculpted gable and a façade filled with windows; over the doorway is a relief sculpture of a ship. This is the **Gildehuis der Vrije Schippers** (Free Boatmen), a symbol of the power of the boatmen who had the monopoly for shipping grain and other goods in and out of the city.

Museum voor Sierkunst

5 Jan Breydelstraat, t 09 267 9999. Open Tues–Sun 9.30–5; adm €2.50, children €1.25.

This museum of the decorative arts is one of the most rewarding and delightful in Belgium. It is set out in a series of rooms in a grand 18th-century town house built for a wealthy family of cloth merchants called De Coninck, and has an excellent collection of antique furniture, arranged according to function and date. The modern annexe contains a superb collection of modern design, from Art Nouveau to Postmodernism.

The suggested route through the museum takes you initially past rooms of 17th–19th furniture and artefacts. It then leads to the lower floor of the modern section, and here the real feast begins. There is Art Nouveau glassware, perfume bottles by **René Lalique**, furniture, textiles and a 1925 version of the Wassily Chair, the first to be made of tubular steel, by **Marcel Breuer**. There is also a 1929 version of the X-frame Barcelona Chair by **Ludwig Mies van der Rohe**.

Look out for the work of the British designer **Christopher Dresser**, a leading campaigner for industrial design against the tide of the Arts and Crafts movement. The collection has been kept fresh by some skilful buying which demonstrates vividly how Postmodernism has the same kind of appeal, élan and shock that Art Nouveau and Art Deco both had in their day.

Het Gravensteen

Sint-Veerleplein. Open April–Sept daily 9–6, Oct–March daily 9–5, last entry 45mins before closing; adm €5, children €2, under 12s free.

This grim and muscular fortress comes as something of a shock after the more dainty Gothic architecture of Ghent's other prominent monuments. Its name means 'Castle of the Counts', and it was built in 1180 by Philip of Alsace, Count of Flanders, on the site of the original 9th-century castle of Baldwin Iron-Arm. Restored with a decidedly heavy hand, it is at its best when seen from a distance over the water of the River Lieve.

Museum voor Volkskunde

t 09 223 1336. Open April–Oct Tues–Sun 10–12.30 and 1.30–5.30, Nov–March Tues–Sun 10–12 and 1.30–5; adm €2.

There are numerous folk museums in Belgium, but they don't come much better than this one in Ghent. It is housed in a dainty little cluster of whitewashed almshouses dating originally from 1363. Not all almshouses (also referred to as hospices) were created as acts of pure charity: the Rijm family was forced to fund this one as a form of punishment in settlement of a bitter dispute with a rival family, the Alijns. It contains an impressive collection of furniture, toys, dolls, tools, and so on. There is also a **puppet theatre** where marionette shows are regularly performed.

SOUTH GHENT

Bijlokemuseum

Open *daily 10–1 and 2–6;* **adm** *€2.50, children €1.25.*

This rich and pleasantly unfocused historical museum is housed in the Abdij (Abbey) van de Bijloke, which can be reached from the city centre by walking along the picturesque canals on the Recollettenlei and Lindenlei. The abbey itself is a beguiling set of red-brick buildings designed in a traditional Flemish style.

The museum is casually set out in the cloisters and former dormitories of the abbey. It contains a vast array of historical objects of all kinds, some of high quality: furniture, paintings, donated collections of Chinese ceramics and costumes.

Museum voor Schone Kunsten

Citadelpark, t 09 222 1703. **Open** *Tues–Sun 9.30–5;* **adm** *€2.50, children €1.25.*

The grand Neoclassical entrance to this museum, built in 1902, and Ghent's long artistic tradition promise much, but this municipal gallery of fine art is, alas, faintly disappointing. The collection, however, is punctuated by a few treasures which will make the journey from the centre of the city worthwhile.

The early section, from the Flemish primitives to Pieter Paul Rubens, contains one outstanding piece, the *Bearing of the Cross* by **Jeroen (Hieronymus) Bosch** (1450–1516), who worked in 's-Hertogenbosch in the Netherlands and whose imagery was immensely influential even in his own day. Christ, painted with a sublime expression of suffering and inner peace, is surrounded by a dense throng of grotesque degenerates, many of whom exhibit the kinds of piercings that would be the envy of any modern punk.

Other notable works include *The Virgin with a Carnation* by **Rogier van der Weyden**

(*c.* 1400–64); a *Pietà* by **Hugo van der Goes** (*c.* 1435–82), and two pieces by **Pieter Bruegel the Younger** (1564–1638), after originals by his father. There are four market scenes by the Antwerp painter **Joachim Beuckelaer** (1530–74), and a splendidly sensual *Jupiter and Antiope* by **Antoon van Dyck** (1599–1641), in which a crusty old supreme god is about to furnish the sleeping object of his passion with twins.

Among the 19th century paintings, there is the *Reading by Emile Verhaeren* by the Ghent-born painter **Théo van Rysselberghe** (1862–1926). A founder member of Les XX in Brussels, Rysselberghe adopted the Pointillist style of Seurat and Signac in the 1880s and 1890s and developed it as a technique for landscape, interiors and portraits. The postimpressionist **Henri Evenepoel** (1872–99) is represented by his striking *L'Espagnol à Paris*. There is a winter scene by the 'Luminist' **Emile Claus**, and also a large social-realism work entitled *The Funeral Dinner* by **Léon Frédéric**.

There are also works by **James Ensor** (a typically bizarre *La Vieille Dame aux Masques*, 1899), **Léon Spilliaert** and, from the 20th century, **Rik Wouters**, plus works by the idiosyncratic Flemish Expressionists **Jean Brusselmans** (1884–1953) and **Edgar Tytgat** (1879–1957).

Not unnaturally, a special emphasis is given to the artists associated with the **Sint-Martens-Latem School**. (Sint-Martens-Latem is a small village on a strikingly pretty stretch of the River Leie, *see* p.196.) The school centred around the Symbolist poet **Karel van de Woestyne**, and the sculptor and painter, **George Minne** (1866–1941). This collection includes work by **Gustave van de Woestyne** (1881–1947), **Valerius de Saedeleer** (1867–1941), **Gustave** (1877–1943) and **Leon de Smet** (1881–1966), and the remarkable **Constant Permeke** (1886–1952), a chief figure in Flemish Expressionism.

The gallery also has the marble version of **George Minne's** *Fontein der Geknieden* – sculptures of six contemplative, naked boys kneeling around a fountain.

Museum van Hedendaagse Kunst

Open daily 10–6; adm €2.50, children €1.25.

The museum of contemporary art contains the largest collection of modern paintings and sculpture in Belgium, founded in the 1950s. The permanent collection includes not only work by post-1945 Belgian artists – such as the participants of **La Jeune Peinture Belge** and **Cobra** (*see* p.50) – but numerous pieces by leading figures of the international art scene, such as **Francis Bacon**, **Andy Warhol**, **Joseph Beuys**, and **Gilbert and George**. The museum's temporary exhibitions are generally major events.

Klein Begijnhof

Entrance on Lange Violettenstraat. Open daily; gates close at 9pm.

Of the many *béguinages* (*see* p.141) in Belgium, this is one of the most charming, with its neat and peaceful lines of little red-brick houses set around an open area of grass and trees and a Flemish–Baroque chapel. Founded in 1234 by Joanna of Constantinople, patroness to numerous early *béguinages*, it has changed little since the 17th century. There have been no *béguines* at the Klein Begijnhof for some years, however, and the houses are slowly being converted for secular use.

OTHER ATTRACTIONS

Groot Begijnhof

One of the largest *béguinages* in Belgium, situated a couple of kilometres to the east of the centre of Ghent, between E. van Arenbergstraat and Schoolstraat (look out for the needle-like spire of the church), it is not quite what it seems: it was in fact built in 1874 to house *béguines* from the St Elizabeth Begijnhof, founded in 1234. It is a fair recreation of a medieval *béguinage* – but somehow lacks soul. It is still home to a couple of *béguines*, but most of the houses are now rented out to families.

Sint-Martens-Latem

Sint-Martens-Latem is a village famous for the school of artists which assembled here at the turn of the century (*see* p.195). At Sint-Martens-Latem itself you can see the **Museum Gevaert-Minne** (*open Easter–30 Sept Thurs–Sat 2–6, Sun 10–12 and 2–6, Oct–Easter Wed–Sun 2–5; adm €1.50*), which displays work by Edgard Gevaert and George Minne. At nearby Deurle there are three museums. The **Museum Dhondt-Dhaenens** (*open Wed–Fri 2–5, in summer 2–6, weekends 10–12 and 2–6, closed Dec–15 Feb; adm €1.25*) contains a private collection of work by various members of the school. **The Museum Gustave de Smet** (*opening hours and adm charges as for Museum Gevaert-Minne above*) shows the artist Gustave de Smet's work in his former home; and finall, there's the **Museum Leon de Smet** (*open Easter–30 Sept daily, except Tues 2–6, Oct–Easter by appt only call **t** 09 282 8693; adm free*).

Antwerp

13

A bitter wind, straight off the North Sea, hurries down the wide estuary of the River Scheldt, rattling the old store-sheds that line the riverside quays, and briskening the heartbeat of this invigorating city. Once, upon this wind, came Antwerp's fortunes: goods from around the world were brought and traded with products from the whole of northern and central Europe. Antwerp was one of the great cities of the continent: proud, powerful and adventurous.

This is the city where Rubens lived and worked, the brightest star in a galaxy of artistic talent. The manifestations of the city's artistic tradition can be seen in the city gallery (one of the great collections of art in Belgium), in many of the churches and in a handful of small, charming museums.

The tradition lives on. Antwerp has earned a name for itself as a city where things are happening.The city's strength has today been rekindled by new industry and the mighty, sprawling docks to the north of the city centre. Antwerp is awakening from a period of neglect and is in tune with the new Europe. Its recent successes in the fashion world are a symbol of its new mood, with clothes designed by, among others, Dries van Noten, Ann Demeulemeester, Martin Margiela and Raf Simons.

There is something in the air in Antwerp: go on a Friday or Saturday night and the streets positively zing. Youthful crowds pack out the bars and cafés hosting live music; literary cafés hum to earnest debate; and families fill the numerous restaurants that serve anything from steaming casseroles of mussels and Japanese *sashimi* to some of the most recherché cooking in Belgium.

You could not possibly expect to get a feel for all of this in a day. Spend a weekend or more in Antwerp if you can. If a day is all you have, the chapter should help you to judge which of the many and varied attractions on offer are the most rewarding – and they are not all what the tourist guides would have you believe.

History

The key to Antwerp's history and fortunes is access to the North Sea, which lies 88km to the north along the broad and deep River Scheldt (Schelde in Flemish, Escaut in French). Over the centuries this access, however, has been at the mercy of politics.

Frisian seafarers were the first to make a base here, as early as the 2nd or 3rd centuries AD, and over the following centuries it became a settlement of the Franks. Under

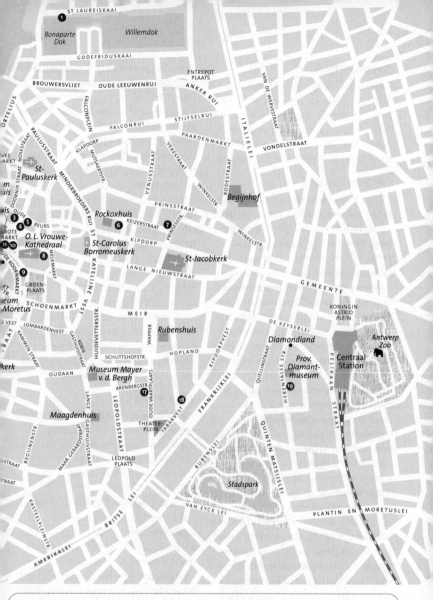

Hotel and Restaurant Key

17	Alfa	12	P. Preud'homme
2	Antigone	17	Prinse
16	Cammerpoorte	13	La Rade
1	Diamond Princess	4	Satsuma
19	Eden	3	Sjalot en Schanul
18	Ibis	14	De Stoemppot
9	Kartini	8	Het Vermoeide Model
5	Marrakech	10	Villa Mozart
11	't Ogenblick	6	De Witte Lelie
		15	Zuiderterras

Getting There

Antwerp is 45km north of Brussels and connected by the E10 autoroute. **Trains** from Brussels arrive at the spectacular Antwerpen Centraal station. Antwerp has an **airport** at Deurne, in its southwestern outskirts, with direct flights from London and Amsterdam.

Getting Around

To get to the centre by **car**, follow the signs to Stadhuis and Schelde. There are plenty of paying **car parks** around the old quayside sheds along the River Scheldt, close to the centre, and a number of underground car parks in convenient places (€12 per day).

Antwerp has an efficient **public transport system** (called De Lijn) consisting of trams, buses and the underground Premétro tram line. A 'Netplan' of the system is available from the tourist office (*see* below) and main stations. **Taxis** are available from designated taxi ranks, or by calling **t** 03 238 9825.

Horse-drawn carriages make tours of the centre, starting from the Grote Markt (*April–Oct daily 11–7, Easter–June and Sept–Oct weekends only 12–6*). You can also take **boat trips** on the River Scheldt. The Flandria line (**t** 03 23 31 00) offers 50min excursions from its quay beside the Steen (*Easter period and April–Oct; adults €5, children under 12 €2.50*). You can also take a 2½-hr boat excursion to the **Port of Antwerp** (*Easter period at 2.30; May–Aug daily 10 and 2.30; Sept weekends only Sat 2.30, Sun 10 and 2.30; adults €10, children under 12 €6.50*), or visit the port by car (*see* p.210).

Tourist Information

15 Grote Markt (corner of Wisselstraat), **t** 03 232 0103, **f** 03 231 1937 (**open** *Mon–Sat 9–5.45, Sun 9–4.45*). Selection of brochures, city maps, and a hotel reservation service.

Shopping

The main shopping street is the **Meir**. The eastern end, leading into Leysstraat and Teniersplein, includes some grand 19th-century Neo-Baroque buildings, now occupied by boutiques and department stores. This procession continues eastwards along De Keyserlei up to Antwerpen Centraal Station. Pelikaanstraat, south of the station, is at the heart of the **diamond district**. There are varied **markets** on Theaterplein at the weekends, and on Wednesday and Friday mornings there's an antiques and jumble market at the Vrijdagmarkt, outside the Museum Plantin-Moretus (*see* p.206).

Antwerp's famed **fashion** is to be found south of the Groenplaats (south of the cathedral). Dries van Noten (*16 Nationalestraat*) has a Modepaleis, and Louis (*2 Lombardenstraat, **t** 03 232 9872*), stocks Ann Demeulemeester, Martin Margiela and Raf Simons. Closing Date (*15 Korte Gasthuisstraat, **t** 03 232 8722*) stocks Walter van Beirendonck's Wild and Lethal Trash line. Further down the street the Nieuwe Gaanderij Arcade is packed with fashion shops. Coccodrillo (*9A–B Schuttershofstraat, **t** 03 233 2093*) sells fashionable shoes.

Where to Stay

De Witte Lelie, *16–18 Keizerstraat, B-2000 Antwerp, **t** 03 226 1966, **f** 03 234 0019, **w** www.dewittelelie.be*. Delightful city hotel. Coolly elegant décor and antique furniture, plus numerous discreet touches of luxury. €168–223.

Alfa, *30 Arenbergstraat, B-2000 Antwerp, **t** 03 203 5410, **f** 03 233 8858, **w** www.alphahotels.com*. Stylish, modern hotel, but a bit characterless. 20 mins' walk from the centre. €135–175.

Villa Mozart, *3–7 Handschoenmarkt, B-2000 Antwerp, **t** 03 231 3031, **f** 03 231 5685, **w** www.bestwestern.com*. Small, tasteful hotel of just 25 Laura-Ashley-decorated rooms, opposite the cathedral. €112–160.

Prinse, *63 Keizerstraat, B-2000 Antwerp, **t** 03 226 4050, **f** 03 225 1148, **e** hotel-prinse@skynet.be*. Converted 16th-century mansion. Historically poor, but quiet, comfortable and fairly central. €105–150.

Antigone, *11–12 Jordaenskaai, B-2000 Antwerp, **t** 03 231 6677, **f** 03 231 3774*. Well-appointed hotel (IKEA meets Art Deco) overlooking the River Scheldt. €87–107.

Diamond Princess, *Bonapartedok, St Laureiskaai, 2000 Antwerp 1, t 03 227 0815, f 03 227 1677*. A 'flothotel' – hotel and restaurant on converted ship. Napoleon's dock is somewhat forlorn. €77–115.

Eden, *25–27 Lange Herentalsestraat, 2018 Antwerp, t 03 233 0608, f 03 233 1228, w www.diamond-hotels.com*. Minimalist hotel in the diamond district. €72–100.

Ibis, *39 Meistraat (Vogelenmarkt), B-2000 Antwerp, t 03 231 8830, w www.ibishotels .com*. Safe if characterless, invigorated by efficient staff. About 20 mins' walk from the centre, overlooking the Theaterplein. €85.

Cammerpoorte, *38–40 Nationalestraat, B-2000 Antwerp, t 03 231 9736, f 03 226 2968*. Modern with adequate rooms. €80–90.

Youth Hostels: Six in the city. Contact *Vlaamse Jeugdherbergcentrale, 40 van Stralenstraat, 2060 Antwerp, t 03 232 7218*.

Eating Out

The area south of the Grote Markt, such as Grote Pieterpotstraat and Oude Koornmarkt, and the Quartier Latin, southeast of the centre (Schutterhofstraat, Kelderstraat, Leopoldsplaats) are good hunting grounds for moderate and lively restaurants.

Expensive

La Rade, *8 Ernest van Dijckkaai, t 03 233 3737. Open Mon–Fri and Sat pm; closed 3 weeks in July*. Superior restaurant, founded in 1949, in the splendid late 19th-century Neo-Renaissance style rooms of an old mansion, overlooking the Scheldt and the Steen. *Haute cuisine française*, elegantly served.

P. Preud'Homme, *28 Suikerrui, t 03 233 4200. Open Feb–Dec*. Elegant venue where well-dressed clients dine on lobster and *haute cuisine* dishes of game and fish. €37–50.

Zuiderterras, *37 Ernest van Dijckkaai, t 03 234 1275*. Overlooks the River Schelde. Elegant French and Belgian cuisine for around €25.

Moderate

Het Vermoeide Model, *2 Lijnwaadmarkt, t 03 233 52 61. Open Tues–Sun*. Tavern ('The Sleepy (Artist's) Model') built into the side of

the cathedral, with a pleasantly antique atmosphere. Grilled fish for €12.50.

Marrakech, *1 Wisselstraat. t 03 231 3092*. Exotic ambience, like the inside of a nomad tent, where hearty plates of couscous are served for €11–15.

Satsuma, *5 Wisselstraat, t 03 226 2443. Open Wed–Mon*. Affordable Japanese restaurant, serving *sashimi* and *tempanyaki*. Seven-course set dinner €31–39; lunch €25.

't Ogenblick, *10–12 Grote Markt, t 03 233 6222. Open Wed–Sun*. Stylish, lively bar, serving inventive light lunches of the freshest ingredients. Main dishes €9–15.50.

Inexpensive

De Stoemppot, *12 Vlasmarkt, t 03 231 3686. Open Wed–Sun; closed Sat lunch*. The place to try out some *stoemp* – traditional Flemish dish of puréed meat and vegetables. *Stoemp* of all flavours for €9.

Kartini, *61 Oude Koornmarkt, t 03 226 4463. Open Tues–Sun evenings*. Indonesian restaurant serving authentic dishes, including a 12 course Rijsttafel Kraton for €37.

Sjalot en Schanul, *12 Oude Beurs, t 03 233 8875. Open daily 9am–8pm*. Combination of greengrocer and relaxed café. Vegetarian dishes and light salads from €11.

Entertainment and Nightlife

Antwerp is famous for its vigorous club scene. Fashions change, but here are a few names to start with. They open at about 10, get going around midnight and don't close until 4am. Entry is usually about €6–10.

Café d'Anvers, *15 Verversrui, t 03 226 3870. Open Fri–Sun*. Old warehouse, very big and dark, popular venue for house music.

Le Palais, *12 van Ertbornstraat, t 03 233 3515*. Large disco, formerly Jimmy's.

Paradox, *25 Waalse Kaai*. Club-discothèque famous for its regular parties.

Red and Blue, *13 Lange Schipperskapelstraat*. House and soul music. Entry before midnight free, thereafter €6.

Zillion, *4 Jan van Gentstraat, t 03 248 1516. Open Thurs–Sat 10pm*. Vast disco: 3 floors and 10 bars. House/techno on Thurs, top international DJs on Fri and Sat.

pressure of Viking raids the Frankish Empire was carved up by the Treaty of Verdun in AD 843. Antwerp, on the eastern bank of the river, became part of Lotharingia (Lorraine) while the rest of Flanders formed part of the French-dominated West Francia, accounting for a different and less traumatic medieval history than that of Bruges and Ghent.

In 1106 Antwerp became part of the Duchy of Brabant, which also included Brussels. It developed as a thriving trading city, Brabant's main port, with wool and textiles its staple commodities. A series of ramparts called vesten was built around the port, the positions of which are still remembered in street names such as Steenhouwersvest, Lombardenvest and Sint-Katelijnevest.

Two centuries on, and Antwerp was seized by Louis de Male, the acquisitive Count of Flanders (in 1357). Through the marriage of Louis' daughter Margaret to Philip the Bold, Duke of Burgundy, both Flanders and Brabant were united as they became part of the powerful Duchy of Burgundy. During this Burgundian era the city's star shone. Foreign merchants moved on to Antwerp as Bruges declined, and by the end of the reign of Charles V (Holy Roman Emperor 1519–56) the population of the city had reached 100,000. Antwerp was the trading capital of Europe, and an intellectual and cultural centre.

The city had achieved remarkable wealth by 1550, but with it came an opening chasm between rich and poor and rapidly deteriorating political stability. The prosperous, cosmopolitan and liberal atmosphere in the city had proved fertile ground for the rise of Protestantism, which led to increasing strife as the Spanish authorities attempted to impose the Catholic faith. This flared up in angry bouts of iconoclasm, notably in 1566, when the cathedral was wrecked.

The religious strife continued. From 1568, William of Orange, leading the Protestant United Provinces of the Netherlands, was at war with Spain in a campaign to oust them from the Low Countries. Antwerp's wavering stance resulted in the Spanish Fury of 1576, where troops who had been deployed by the

Duke of Alva to intimidate the city mutinied and ran amok. Much of the city was torched; 8,000 people lay dead, and many of its leading citizens fled.

The following year William took Antwerp and set up his headquarters in the city. Eight years on, in 1585, the Spanish under Alexander Farnese, Duke of Parma, laid siege. The siege lasted for a year. When the Spanish built a bridge to close off the Scheldt from the sea, at last, Antwerp capitulated. The terms of peace were not harsh, but Philip II insisted that Antwerp was to be a Catholic city. Once more, thousands of Protestants left to settle in the United Provinces, halving the population, and a blockade of the Scheldt mounted by the Dutch and the English, lasting 24 years, brought the city to its knees.

In 1609 the Twelve Years' Truce, signed by the United Provinces and Spain, offered some relief. Antwerp's faltering economy began to recover as it reasserted its role as a regional trading centre. The more stable political situation also gave rise to an unprecedented cultural flourish, focusing particularly on Pieter Paul Rubens, who achieved international celebrity. Antoon van Dyck, Jacob Jordaens and Frans Snyders worked with him in his studio at various times, and the city was also home to David Teniers the Elder and the Younger, Pieter Bruegel the Younger and Jan Bruegel, and the sculptor Artus Quellinus the Elder. But in 1648 Antwerp's Golden Age came to a sticky halt. Spain was now in conflict with France, which was an ally of the United Provinces. To concentrate his fire on France, Philip IV of Spain signed the Peace of Münster, which granted formal recognition to the United Provinces. The United Provinces – which held the territory on both sides of the Scheldt to the north of Antwerp – also demanded the right to close off the Scheldt estuary to shipping, and Spain, with other fish to fry, acquiesced.

It was a disaster for Antwerp, which was effectively throttled by the agreement. The port slid into disuse and despair, and 150 years passed before the stranglehold was lifted, after the French Revolutionary Armies overran the Austrian Netherlands in 1794 and the United Provinces in 1795. The French opened up the Scheldt to Antwerp shipping – but Europe was at war.

In 1803 Napoleon described the state of Antwerp: 'It is little better than a heap of ruins. It is scarcely like a European city. I could almost have believed myself this morning in some African township. Everything needs to be made – harbours, quays, docks; and everything shall be made, for Antwerp must avail itself of the immense advantages of its central position between the North and the South, and of its magnificent and deep river.' Napoleon also recognized Antwerp's strategic potential as 'un pistolet braqué sur le cœur de l'Angleterre' (a pistol pointing at the heart of England), and made a start, by building new naval dockyards to the north of the city centre.

After Napoleon's fall in 1815 Belgium was handed over to the Dutch, and Antwerp suddenly found itself at the heart of the new United Kingdom of the Netherlands. When the Dutch had to abandon Belgium following the Revolution of 1830, it was particularly reluctant to give up Antwerp. It was only in 1832 that the Dutch garrison laid down its arms, when French troops came to the assistance of the Belgians in a punishing struggle.

By 1863 tolls imposed by the Netherlands on traffic through the Scheldt had been lifted. The city's trade had already reawakened: a railway link, the 'Iron Rhine', between Antwerp and the great Rhine port of Cologne had been opened in 1843, and by the latter half of the 19th century, Antwerp rated as the third largest port in the world, after London and New York.

Since then, the success of the city as a centre for trade has barely faltered. Antwerp's modern port (to the north of the city, well away from the centre) is the second biggest in Europe after Rotterdam, with over 120km of docks and a workforce numbering 75,000. With a population of over half a million, Antwerp is also Belgium's second largest city. It basked in the attention

received in 1993 as European Cultural Capital, and has grand plans for the future.

THE CENTRE

Grote Markt and Stadhuis

*Stadhuis open for **tours** Mon, Tues, Thurs and Fri 11, 2 and 3, Sat 2 and 3.*

The central square of Antwerp is one of the most attractive in Belgium, flanked by ornate guildhouses and the famous **Stadhuis** (town hall). Built in 1564, the Stadhuis was designed by the architect and sculptor Cornelis Floris, or Floris de Vriendt (1514–75). His training in Italy is apparent in this building, in the mathematical distribution of windows as well as in the Renaissance flair of the centre-piece. Completed in 1565, it was burnt out during the Spanish Fury of 1576, but restored after 1579. The interior was totally renovated in the 19th century, largely in retrospective historical styles.

The northern side of the square, and the southeastern side facing the Stadhuis, are flanked by lines of old **guildhouses**, crowned by gilded symbols. No.5, 'De Mouwe', was the guildhouse of the coopers (1579); No.7, the 'Pand van Spanje' (1582), was the house of a guild of crossbowmen and is surmounted by a statue of St George and the Dragon (by Jef Lambeaux, *see* below); No.38 (on the southeast side) is 'De Balans' (1615), guildhouse of the drapers; and No.40, 'Rodenborch', was the guildhouse of the carpenters.

Onze Lieve Vrouwe Kathedraal

*t 03 213 9940. **Open** Mon–Fri 10–5, Sat 10–3, Sun and religious hols 1–4; **adm** €2.*

The largest Gothic cathedral in Belgium it may be, but the approach to it through a web of medieval streets gives it a charming, human scale. The earliest parts of the building date from 1352, but the cathedral took nearly three centuries to build, and was not completed until 1521. The first phase was designed by Jan Appelmans; in the last phase the main designers were the influential late Gothic architects Herman de Waghemakere (1430–1503) and his son Domien (1460–1542) and Rombouts Keldermans (1487–1531).

When completed, the cathedral was the richest of the Low Countries. The interior was a dazzling treasure trove, glittering with the dozens of shrines and retables set up by the city's guilds. Many of these, however, were destroyed in a fire in 1553; the building was later sacked by iconoclasts in 1566. The cathedral was stripped of its surviving treasures during the French occupation after 1784. Only a part of its original collection of works of art were recovered from France after 1815.

Despite this history, the cathedral still contains a remarkably rich collection of paintings and sculpture, set against the elegant simplicity of the Gothic architecture, which has an untypically wide and spacious groundplan with seven aisles.

It is famous above all for its paintings by Pieter Paul Rubens, notably the pair of powerful triptychs of *The Raising of the Cross* (1610) and *The Descent from the Cross* (1612) flanking the choir on either side of the transept. The former is a painting of dynamic anguish and tumult; the latter is filled with deep compassion and silence, made all the more heart-rending by the images of the pregnant Madonna and the baptism of Christ on either side. Further works, *The Resurrection* (1612) and, at the altarpiece, *The Assumption of the Virgin Mary* (1626), are not of the same stature.

Etnografisch Museum

19 Suikerrui. **Open** *Tues–Sun 10–4.45;* ***adm*** *€4.*

African masks, drums for New Guinea, a Maori war-canoe, an Inuit child's kayak, Indonesian jewellery, pre-Colombian American pottery, Japanese paintings, Tibetan Buddhas – these are just some of the hundreds of varied objects representing over a century of collecting, housed since 1988 in a new museum on three floors. The Central Africa collection is particularly strong.

Steen and the Nationaal Scheepvaartmuseum

Steeplein, **t** *03 232 0850.* **Open** *Tues–Sun 10–4.45; adm €4.*

The Steen, the powerful old fortress at the river's edge, was built between the 10th and 16th centuries, originally as the residence of the Margrave of Antwerp – although legend said it was home of the giant Antigon. It was used as a prison until 1823, then rescued from that role and heavily restored in the late 19th century. It is now home to the National Maritime Museum. This contains an interesting and well-presented collection of ship-orientated artefacts, including numerous superb models of ships, plus a collection of barges and other small vessels.

Vleeshuis

38–40 Vleeshouwersstraat, **t** *03 233 6404.* **Open** *Tues–Sun 10–4.45; adm €7.50.*

In a forgotten corner of central Antwerp, cheek by jowl with the small red-light district of Burchtgracht, is one of the city's most impressive buildings. This is the Butchers' Hall, the guildhouse and meatmarket of the Guild of Butchers, designed in Gothic style in 1503 by Herman de Waghemakere (one of the architects of the cathedral). Its walls, step-gables and the five hexagonal turrets running up the sides are built in alternating layers of stone and brick – reminiscent of streaky bacon. An atmospheric vaulted passageway leads beneath the western wall into Burchgracht, which follows the line of the old castle moat.

The Butchers' Guild was a powerful institution. The large and robust meat hall inside was for decades the only place in Antwerp where meat could be sold – the steps up to the entrance were called the Bloedberg ('Blood Hill') because of this trade.

The butcher's hall, and other rooms accessed from it, now contain a rewarding collection of historical odds and ends: medieval sculpture, paintings, musical instruments (including 17th-century harpsichords made in the famous Ruckers workshop of Antwerp), and the mummy of a 10th-century BC Egyptian singer.

Sint-Pauluskerk

Veemarkt. **Open** *May–Sept daily 2–5;* **adm** *free.*

This strange, hybrid church, with a Flamboyant Gothic body dating from 1517 and a Baroque spire dating from 1679, rises out of a cluster of buildings (some of which are attached to it) in an attractive quarter of alleyways, small shops and atmospheric bars. The Baroque interior, with its elaborately carved wooden stalls, is an expression of a bold architectural style that sang of the triumph of the Counter-Reformation over iconoclasm. It contains a remarkable collection of paintings, including the series of 15 on the Mysteries of the Rosary (1617–19), by various artists such as Cornelis de Vos (*Nativity, Presentation at the Temple*), David Teniers the Elder (*Gethsemane*), Rubens (*Flagellation*), Van Dyck (*Bearing of the Cross*), and Jordaens (*Crucifixion*).

Sint-Carolus Borromeuskerk

t 03 233 0229. **Opening** *times vary, see schedule on entrance;* **adm** *€12.50. Guided* **tours** *by arrangement, .*

The façade of this church, overlooking Hendrik Conscienceplein, represents one of the great monuments of Jesuit Baroque architecture – a birthday cake of sculpture, pineapples and pepperpot domes, disposed with an elegant pace and rhythm (tradition holds that it was designed by Rubens). The church was built in 1615–21 and dedicated to **St Charles Borromeo** (1538–84), a church reformer who attempted to address the abuses of the Catholic Church in the face of the rising tide of Protestantism.

In 1620 the Jesuits asked Rubens to create three altarpieces and 39 ceiling paintings for the church. But in 1718 a fire caused by lightning destroyed the lot. Given this history, it is barely surprising that the interior is disappointing, although it contains fine late-Baroque woodwork installed after 1718, and a Lady Chapel which survived the fire.

Rockoxhuis

Open *Tues–Sun 10–5;* **adm** *€2.50.*

Nicolaas Rockox (1560–1640) was mayor of Antwerp during many of its years of revival in the early 17th century; he was also a noted humanist, philanthropist and art collector, and a friend and patron of Rubens. The ground floor of his large house, set around a courtyard garden, was converted during the 1970s into a gallery to house a handsome collection of paintings, tapestries and antique furniture from the era. There are sketches and paintings by all the Golden Age Antwerp artists – Rubens, Van Dyck, Jordaens and Frans Snyders, plus work by the preceding generation, including Joachim Beuckelaer and Pieter Bruegel the Younger.

Sint-Jacobskerk

73 Lange Nieuwstraat, t 03 232 1032. **Open** *April–Oct daily 2–5, Nov–Mar 9–12;* **adm** *€2.*

Rubens lies buried in a family chapel in this yellow-sandstone church, designed in late-Gothic style during the 15th and 16th centuries by Herman de Waghemakere and his son Domien, and subsequently by Rombout Keldermans. It stands on the site of a chapel built for pilgrims on their way to Santiago de Compostela (hence the connection with St James), and became the church of the patricians of the city. The interior is one of the richest in Antwerp and contains the tombs of wealthy Antwerp families and numerous works of art. There are sculptures by Hendrik Verbruggen, Artus Quellinus and Luc Fayd'Herbe; and paintings by Bernard van Orley, Otto Venius (Rubens' master), Rubens himself, Jordaens and Van Dyck.

Museum Plantin-Moretus

*22–23 Vrijdagmarkt, t 03 221 1450. **Open** Tues–Sun 10–4.45; **adm** €2.50.*

This is one of the most celebrated museums of Antwerp. In principle it has the ingredients for a fascinating visit – a 16th-century patrician house, set around a courtyard straight out of a painting by a Dutch master, original furnishings, and the workshop and book collection of one of the great masters of early printing, Christopher Plantin. Somehow, however, it contrives to be somewhat dull and cheerless. A little background information helps bring it alive.

On the ground floor are a pair of grand 16th- and 17th-century reception rooms, hung with tapestries and paintings, including some portraits and *The Lion Hunt* by Rubens. A door leads out into the pretty Renaissance courtyard, off which is a series of small rooms, including one that in the 17th century was a bookshop. A passageway leads to the printing workshop, a large room crammed with old printing presses, the earliest of which may date from Plantin's day.

Upstairs a series of rooms leads through various displays which demonstrate the scope of the Plantin family's printing achievements. These include the Polyglot Bible; engravings by Rubens; maps by Gerard Mercator (1512–94) and other early maps showing the Americas gradually being filled in as explorers and traders reported back their discoveries; and a priceless copy of Gutenberg's 36-line Bible. The upper floors

Plantin, Gutenberg and the Invention of Movable Type

European printing was launched with a bang in 1455 when the workshop of Johann Gutenberg in Mainz, Germany, produced the 42-line Bible, a printing masterpiece at virtually the first attempt. Gutenberg, although he did not invent printing, is however credited with putting together the elements that made book printing in Europe not simply possible, but economically attractive. The most important of these elements was movable type, whereby Gutenberg cast individual letters in metal, then assembled them into words. This method of printing soon caught on across Europe, and remained the standard process of printing for some four centuries. Successive printers, however, developed printing as an art in its own right. One of the most influential figures in this process was Christopher Plantin (c. 1520–89).

Plantin was French by birth, but in 1546, after training as a bookbinder, he moved to Antwerp, which had become one of the Low Countries' great centres of printing. Paid a substantial sum as compensation or hush-money in a case of mistaken identity, he bought his first press, and thereby began a career as a printer. He gradually acquired more presses and other printing enterprises, until in 1576 (when he moved into this house) he was in control of 22 presses, three times as many as any of his rivals.

At that time printers were also publishers, and some of the greatest and most influential works of the day were produced by Plantin. His greatest achievement was the eight-volume *Polyglot Bible* (1568–72), a bible printed in five parallel languages (Latin, Greek, Hebrew, Syriac and Chaldean), with extensive notes and glossaries.

The *Polyglot Bible* was to have been sponsored by King Philip II of Spain, and so was named the *Biblia Regia*. Philip failed to advance any of the promised money, however, in 1570 he appointed Plantin as printer to the court and gave him the monopoly for publishing liturgical books for Spain and the Spanish colonies. This may well have had a ironic twist, for Plantin was probably a Protestant.

After Plantin died in 1589 his son-in-law, Jan Moerentorff (1543–1610), known as Moretus, took over the press. The business was passed down through eight generations until 1875, when Hyacinth Moretus allowed the house and workshops to become the museum that we see today.

are the most atmospheric, with a suitably dingy library lined with august leather-bound tomes, and a printers' workroom where the type was cast.

Rubenshuis

9–11 Wapper, t 03 201 1555. Open Tues–Sun 10–4.45; adm €5.

Pieter Paul Rubens (1577–1640) was the outstanding painter of Antwerp during a Golden Age of exceptional artistic endeavour (*see* p.47 for a brief account of his life and achievements). This was the house that he bought in 1610, when he was already a wealthy man, and in the service of the Archduke Albert and the Infanta Isabella as court painter. Over the next 17 years he trans-formed it into a kind of Italian villa.

The house had an illustrious past. Rubens was the centre of an elevated artistic circle that included his associates Antoon van Dyck (1599–1641) and Jacob Jordaens (1593–1678). His noble patrons, including Marie de Médicis (Queen of France) and George Villiers, Duke of Buckingham – also visited Rubens in this house. It later fell into sad neglect, and was only saved after 1937, when it was bought by the city and underwent massive renovation. The paintings and furnishings are designed to evoke Rubens' epoch, but are not his own. The Rubenshuis is considered a premier tourist sight of Antwerp, and its rooms become inundated with visitors.

There are a few highlights, including Rubens' large and high-ceilinged studio, now used as a concert hall. The court outside is separated from the small garden by a magnificent Baroque portico, with elaborate stonework designed by Rubens (the statues of Mercury and Minerva on the parapet are modern replicas). The dining room contains a self-portrait (1625–8) by Rubens, and an example of the still lifes which made the name of Frans Snyders (1579–1657). In the Kunstkammer, where Rubens would have displayed the pride of his large personal collection of paintings, is the intriguing *Gallery of Cornelis van de Geest* by Willem van Haecht, a contemporary of Rubens. The painting depicts Isabella and Albert admiring the art collection of a wealthy Antwerp merchant and shows who were considered the most collectable artists of the day: Jan van Eyck, Albrecht Dürer, Pieter Bruegel the Elder, Quentin Metsys, Rubens and Frans Snyder all feature.

Museum Mayer van den Bergh

Open Tues–Sun 10–4.45; adm €4.

This is the most charming and rewarding of Antwerp's small museums – an Aladdin's cave of paintings, antique furniture and coins and much else. These were all the private possessions of Fritz Mayer van den Bergh (1858–91), who devoted himself to collecting.

The most famous painting of the collection is by Pieter Bruegel the Elder (*c.* 1525–69): *Dulle Griet* (Mad Meg) portrays this medieval allegory of disorder as an armed woman running from a burning town on which she has vented her rage. She is surrounded by a world turned upside down and inhabited by hybrid monsters and visual puns. Bruegel was based in Antwerp from about 1551 to 1563, when he moved to Brussels. The painting dates to about the time of this move and may be a comment on the political and religious troubles that had begun to engulf the Low Countries.

EAST OF THE CENTRE

The Diamond District

It is claimed that 85 per cent of the world's uncut diamonds are traded through Antwerp, and most of these are cut and polished in this city where, it is said, Lodewijk van Bercken developed the art of diamond polishing in 1476. Diamonds are big business, worth seven per cent of Belgium's total export earnings. The bulk of the business is carried out in a square mile area, to the southwest of the Centraal Station.

Provinciaal Diamantmuseum

31–33 Lange Herentalsestraat. **Open** *daily 10–5;* **adm** *free except for special exhibitions, which cost €5.*

This museum provides a good introduction to diamonds through photographic panels, models and exhibits. It shows how diamonds are found, explains their natural structure, and how they are cut and shaped. To get an idea of the scale of the diamond trade, go to **Pelikaanstraat**, where there are dozens of jewellery and gold shops beneath the railway arches. There is nothing fancy about the diamond business here: they stack 'em high and sell 'em cheap. Notices in the windows boast 'Diamond-setting in 15 minutes!'

SOUTH OF THE CENTRE

Koninklijk Museum voor Schone Kunsten

1–9 Léopold de Waelplaats, **t** *03 238 7809; wheelchair accessible.* **Open** *Tues–Sun 10–5;* **adm** *€4, concs €3, free Fri.*

Antwerp's Royal Museum of Fine Art is housed in a overgrand Neoclassical temple, built in 1878–90, topped by female charioteers (by the Antwerp-trained sculptor Thomas Vinçotte), and standing in forlorn grounds. Don't let this put you off, for what lies within is an outstanding collection of north European painting containing numerous treasures. The collection is divided into two parts: the Old Masters of the 14th–17th centuries are in the grand marbled galleries on the upper floor; the 19th–20th century collection is on the ground floor. To see the two collections in chronological order, head first for the upper floor.

Outstanding works from the early collection include **Jan van Eyck**'s unfinished

portrait of *Saint Barbara* (1437), sitting with a book on her lap in front of a Gothic cathedral under construction. The crystal-sharp triptych, the *Altar of the Seven Sacraments* by **Rogier van der Weyden** (*c.* 1400–1464), illustrates the seven key sacraments of the Christian Church (Baptism, Confirmation, the Eucharist, Penance, Orders (being ordained), Matrimony and the Extreme Unction), all being played out around a crucifixion set in a Gothic cathedral. A delightful triptych by **Hans Memling** (1430/5–94) portrays Christ surrounded by angels and angelic musicians.

The 15th-century collection is particularly strong. This was a period when Italian painting was beginning to influence Flemish art, through artists such as **Bernard van Orley** (1492–1542), whose *Last Judgement and Seven Acts of Mercy* contains figures in a Neoclassical setting. Compare this, however, with *The Entombment of Christ*, a magnificent triptych which shows the greater asssurance of the Antwerp painter **Quentin Metsys** (1460–1530). In the left-hand panel Herod is portrayed as a self-centred epicure, while Salome toys idly with St John the Baptist's head; in the right-hand panel St John the Evangelist looks beatific as he is being boiled in a cauldron while eager peasants stoke the fire – grim subjects, but rich in detail and full of vigour.

One of the great figures of 16th-century Antwerp was **Frans Floris** (1519/20–70), brother of Cornelis Floris, the architect of the Stadhuis. Both travelled to Rome in 1540–5, where Frans was deeply impressed by the work of Raphael and by Michelangelo's *Last Judgement* (which he witnessed being unveiled). However, his paintings (such as *Fall of the Rebel Angels* and *Banquet of the Gods*), sensual and powerfully imagined though they are, never quite match his ambitions to rival the Italians.

The centrepiece of the 17th-century collection is the area devoted to **Pieter Paul Rubens** (1577–1640); this being his city, the rooms promise much, but are disappointing. (The collection of the Musées Royaux des Beaux-Arts in Brussels [*see* p.91] is far more impressive.) However, there are two classic Rubens here: the *Enthroned Madonna and Child* surrounded by saints has a typically dynamic composition, which leads the eye from the base of the painting up in to the heavens; and *Adoration of the Magi* is a masterpiece of composition, with at least four main centres of focus, in which swaggering kings, camelriders and helmeted soldiers are stopped in their tracks by the sight of the Holy Child.

In a period of numerous stars illuminated by Rubens' talents, probably his most celebrated contemporary was **Antoon van Dyck** (1599–1641), who for a while worked with him as an assistant. He was famous as a portraitist, particularly at the court of Charles I in London, where he spent much of his later career after 1632 and where he died. But he was a painter of considerably wider skills, as his intense *Lamentation of Christ* demonstrates. After the deaths of Rubens and Van Dyck in 1640 and 1641 respectively, **Jacob Jordaens** (1593–1678) – who had worked alongside Rubens for 20 years – was considered the greatest painter of Antwerp. In a Rubens-like composition, his *Martyrdom of Saint Apollonia* shows the saint having her teeth extracted with a pair of pliers. Jordaens is well known for his voluptuous paintings of fertility and fun, of which *As the Old Sang, the Young Play Pipes* (1638) is a famous example – a cosy middle-class family concert around a table of snacks, which are being eyed up by the dog.

The museum virtually dismisses the 18th century and early 19th century to launch into an excellent late 19th- and 20th-century collection. Just about every major figure in Belgian art since 1850 is represented: **Emile Claus, Théo van Rysselberghe, Léon Spilliaert, Henri Evenepoel, Henry van de Velde** (painter turned Art Nouveau designer), artists of the **Sint-Martens-Latem School** (*see* Ghent, pp.195–6), Flemish Expressionists **Jean Brusselmans** and **Edgard Tytgat, René Magritte, Paul Delvaux** and the artists of **Cobra** including **Pierre Alechinsky**. It is worth looking out in particular for the work of

James Ensor (1860–1949), including the *Oyster Eater* of 1882, a watershed date when he began to pursue his idiosyncratic course. Never has oyster-eating been portrayed with such a pungent subtext of sensual pleasure.

There is also a major collection of work by **Rik Wouters** (1882–1916), the best known of a group called the Brabant Fauvists. Wouters' paintings are colourful, but judiciously balanced and full of light and joyousness. *Woman Ironing* (1912) is one of his best-known works, a wonderfully spontaneous domestic portrait of his wife Nel, whom he married in 1905 and who was virtually the only model for his paintings and sculptures (for which he is equally celebrated).

Léon Frédéric (1856–1940) was an enigmatic painter who succeeded in spanning the chasm between socio-realism and Symbolism with paintings of great power and a technical polish. *Les Enfants Wallons, ou Les Boëchelles*, an affectionate portrait of two peasant girls, is a fine example of this. The Belgian artist **Alfred Stevens** (1823–1906), by contrast, was famous for his portraits of women of both high society and the *demi-monde* of the Second Empire in Paris, where he settled and became an associate of Manet. One of his famous works is *Parisienne Sphinx*, a brilliantly executed portrait, full of spontaneity and sensual mystery.

The collection also includes some interesting pieces by foreign artists, including **James Tissot**, and the *Potato Digger* by **Van Gogh**, painted in 1885 when he was living in the depressing mining district of the Borinage in southern Belgium.

Provinciaal Museum voor Fotografie

Waalse Kaai. Open Tues–Sun 10–5; adm €2.50, free Fri.

This modern museum tracks the history of photography on two floors in a series of well-explained exhibits. (A thorough catalogue to the exhibits, in English, is available free of charge from the reception desk.) The exhibition begins with the very first experiments in photography by its pioneers in the 1820s and 1830s: Joseph Niéce, Louis Daguerre and William Henry Fox Talbot. It includes beguiling landscapes and portraits by Julia Margaret Cameron, who saw the artistic potential of photography in the 1860s. The work of the great American photographers such as Edward Steichen, Alfred Stieglitz, Edward Weston and Ansel Adams is also represented in the collection, and there are numerous classic photographs by other greats: Henri Cartier-Bresson, Brassaï, Robert Capa, Irving Penn et al. A large collection of cameras traces the technical development of photography, and includes some interesting oddities, such as miniature spy cameras built into cigarette lighters and watches.

The second floor is devoted to photography that has attempted to portray the world in more than two dimensions – as in the stereoscopes that became all the rage in the late 19th century. The exhibition also has some of the earliest colour photographs, dating to 1907, and follows the evolution of the moving image.

THE PORT OF ANTWERP

The massive port of Antwerp lies to the north of the city. It is not so much attractive as impressive, and you can tour the harbour by boat (see p.200), or by car, following signs marked Havenroute, a 65km round trip (details are available from Antwerp tourist office, see p.200).

The port, consisting of over 120km of docks, is in fact built inland from the river, and connected to it by seven sea locks. At night the entire scene goes through a magical transformation, as millions of lights on ships and industrial plants convert a grim sterile world into an unearthly fairy-tale landscape.

Where to Stay

As a major centre for business and tourism, Brussels has scores of hotels, ranging from extremely inexpensive – and very central – youth hostels to venerable old luxury hotels of the highest standard. In the middle range there are some agreeable family hotels and dozens of good establishments of the international, 'I-could-be-anywhere' sort: a little soulless they may be, but by and large they are competitively priced and efficiently run by staff who manage to welcome their endless turnover of guests with a smile.

Reservations may not always be essential but they are certainly advisable at busy times of the year – such as during the school holidays in the summer, around Easter and Christmas/New Year, and at weekends between May and September. It is so simple to make a reservation – by telephone or fax – that there seems little point not reserving in advance if you can. Almost all reception staff speak good English – or certainly enough English to take a reservation. You may be asked to send a deposit or give a credit card number to secure the reservation but this is not always the case. You can also make reservations, free of charge, through the central hotel organization, Belgian Tourist Reservation (*BTR, Bvd Anspach 111 BF, 1000 Bruxelles*, **t** *02 513 7484*, **f** *02 513 9277*). If you arrive in the city without a hotel reservation, the tourist office in the Grand' Place (*see p.68*) can offer advice and make reservations for you in return for a small fee.

The hotels in this list have been divided into five categories based primarily on price. These ratings are not the same as the official star ones, which are based on facilities rather than character and comfort. The prices indicated below are for a double room for one night; a light 'continental' breakfast is often included in the overnight price – it is worth establishing this when you make your reservation, as breakfast can otherwise add €6–20 to the bill. Prices are marginally cheaper for single travellers, who will probably occupy double rooms anyhow.

Note that many of the larger hotels frequently offer special discounts for weekends and off-season stays: ask about these if telephoning in advance. Also be aware that some smaller hotels (usually in the one-star category) don't accept credit cards.

These days almost all hotel rooms in Brussels – except the very cheapest – have their own *en suite* bathroom – sometimes squeezed into a space about the size of a telephone kiosk. Most also have a television and telephone, and perhaps a small fridge with minibar.

Price Categories

Price categories are based on the price of a double room:

luxury	over €300
expensive	€140–300
moderate	€80–140
inexpensive	€50–80
cheap	under €50

Around the Grand' Place

Luxury

Amigo D5
1–3 Rue de l'Amigo, 1000 Bruxelles, **t** *02 547 4747*, **f** *02 513 5277*, **e** *hotelamigo@hotelamigo.com*, **w** *www.rfhotels.com*; **metro** *Bourse*.
Elegant modern hotel on the site of an old prison. One of the most Belgian in character, the building is 1950s, but furniture, tapestries, paintings and even some of the floor pavings are antique.

Le Dixseptième E5
25 Rue de la Madeleine, 1000 Bruxelles, **t** *02 502 5744*, **f** *02 502 6424*, **e** *info@ledixseptieme.be*, **w** *www.ledixseptieme.be*; **metro** *Gare Centrale*.
Elegant and charming hotel with 24 rooms occupying the 18th-century residence of the Spanish ambassador. Sympathetically restored in old French style with chandeliers. Comfortable, quiet, stylish but distreet.

Royal Windsor E5
5 Rue Duquesnoy, 1000 Bruxelles, **t** *02 505 5555*, **f** *02 505 5500*, **e** *resa .royalwindsor@warwickhotels.com* **w** *www.warwickhotels.com*; **metro** *Gare Centrale*.
Supreme and showy first-class elegance, all highly modern, though there has been considerable effort to capture 19th-century England in the décor. Some of the 266 rooms are a little on the small side.

Expensive

Aris E5
78–80 Rue du Marché aux Herbes, 1000 Bruxelles, **t** *02 514 4300*, **f** *02 514 0119*, **e** *stephane.debruyn@ advalvas.be*, **w** *www.arishotel.be*; **metro** *Bourse*.
Comfortable modern and clean, but somewhat lacking in character. There are 55 rooms, most of which are a decent size and quite airy.

Bedford C6
135 Rue du Midi, 1000 Bruxelles, **t** *02 507 0000*, **f** *02 507 0010*, **e** *hotelbedfordb@paphost.eunet .be*, **w** *www.hotelbedford.be*; **metro** *Anneessens*.
Stylish modern international hotel; member of the Best Western chain.

Carrefour de l'Europe E5
110 Rue du Marché aux Herbes, 1000 Bruxelles, **t** *02 504 9400*, **f** *02 504 9500*, **e** *carrefour@sabena hotels.com*, **w** *www.sabenahotels .com*; **metro** *Bourse*.
Central hotel built in 1992 with a gabled exterior and international-style comfort inside. To its advantage, less obviously a business hotel compared to the Ibis or Novotel hotels next door.

Floris Grand' Place E5
6–8 Rue des Harengs, 1000 Bruxelles, **t** *02 514 0760*, **f** *02 548 9039*; **metro** *Gare Centrale*.
Set on a small side road just off the Grand' Place, you can't get

much closer to the heart of Brussels. It is newly refurbished so that it now has four-star facilities, but space is still limited. This is a decent option for a few days in Brussels if your priority is to be central and comfortable without paying the earth.

Novotel of Grand' Place E5
120 Rue du Marché aux Herbes, 1000 Bruxelles, t 02 514 3333, f 02 511 7723, e h1030@accor-hotels .com, w www.accorhotel.com; metro Gare Centrale; wheelchair accessible.
Modern hotel dressed in a Flemish-style exterior; efficient, international, and a cut above its neighbour, the Ibis. Makes an effort to be family orientated.

Moderate

Arlequin D–E4
17–19 Rue de la Fourche, 1000 Bruxelles, t 02 514 1615, f 02 514 2202, e reservation@arlequin.be, w www.arlequin.be; metro De Brouckère.
Friendly modern hotel in the thick of touristic Brussels. Recently refurbished, there are 92 decent rooms, some of which have a view of the Grand' Place. Panoramic views of the old town from the breakfast room.

Ibis E5
100 Rue du Marché aux Herbes, 1000 Bruxelles, t 02 514 4040, f 02 514 5067; metro Gare Centrale; wheelchair accessible.
Central, efficient, smart-but-no-frills hotel – and competitively priced. With this worldwide chain don't expect to be surprised, pleasanty or otherwise.

La Madeleine E5
22 Rue de la Montagne, 1000 Bruxelles, t 02 513 2973, f 02 502 1350, w www.madeleine-hotel.be; metro Gare Centrale.
Agreeable smallish hotel with smallish rooms; not all are *en suite*. Clean and simple. The façade of the hotel is listed but inside it has been recently refurbished. Close to the Grand' Place.

Matignon D4
10–12 Rue de la Bourse, 1000 Bruxelles, t 02 511 0888, f 02 513 6927; metro Bourse.
A well-positioned reasonably priced hotel with 37 small but pleasant rooms. The 19th-century façade hides the fact that the interior is modern. There is an affiliated Parisian-style brasserie on street level.

Mozart E5
23 Rue du Marché aux Fromages, 1000 Bruxelles, t 02 502 6661, f 02 502 7758, e hotel.mozart@skynet .be, w www.hotel-mozart.be; metro Gare Centrale.
Try to avoid being allocated a room which overlooks the noisy street below full of kebab shops – but then again it's all part of this hotel's eccentricity. The tacky neon sign of a piano (in fitting with the street outside) conceals the elegant touches of the interior design.

St-Michel E5
15 Grand' Place, 1000 Bruxelles, t 02 511 0956, f 02 511 4600, e hotel saintmichel@hotmail.com; metro Gare Centrale.
This family-run hotel could not be more central. Every room is different, furnished with character, and some (more expensive) overlook the Grand' Place itself. The front rooms are definitely more attractive but can be very noisy.

Inexpensive

Barry B6
25 Place Anneessens, 1000 Bruxelles, t 02 511 2795, f 02 514 1465, e hotel.barry@skynet.be; metro Anneessens.
Right next to the metro station, and just a short walk from the Grand' Place, this is not a bad choice for a budget hotel. However, this area is on the fringes of old Brussels' charm with shabby Boulevard Lemmonnier on either side of the square. There are also rooms for groups of three or four.

Les Eperonniers E5
1 Rue des Eperonniers, 1000 Bruxelles, t 02 513 5366, f 02 511 3230; metro Gare Centrale.
If you can cope with sharing a bathroom, this is worth a try. It's always busy with backpackers. *En suites* cost a bit more.

La Vieille Lanterne D6
29 Rue des Grandes Carmes, 1000 Bruxelles, t 02 512 7494, f 02 512 1397; metro Gare Centrale.
A tiny pension with only six rooms, just round the corner from the Manneken Pis and above a souvenir shop; all the rooms have showers. It's good value and you'll definitely have to book.

Cheap

La Légende D5
35 Rue du Lombard, t 02 512 8290, f 02 512 3493, e hotel_lalegende@ hotmail.com, w www.hotella legende.com; metro Bourse.
Set around a courtyard, this is a basic but convenient option, slightly removed from the bustle. On the cheaper side of moderate, rooms fill up quickly here so book in advance.

Marolles and Sablon

Luxury

Brussels Hilton F8
38 Bvd de Waterloo, 1000 Bruxelles, t 02 504 1111, f 02 504 2111, e brunitwrm@hilton.com, w www.hilton.com; metro Louise; wheelchair accessible.
Ugly modern monolith, but comfortable and with splendid views; noted not only for its service but also for the standards of its restaurants.

Jolly du Grand-Sablon E7
2–4 Rue Bodenbroeck, 1000 Bruxelles, t 02 518 1100, f 02 512 6766; metro Gare Centrale or Porte de Namur.
Member of the Jolly chain, with the advantage of its location off the Place du Grand-Sablon.

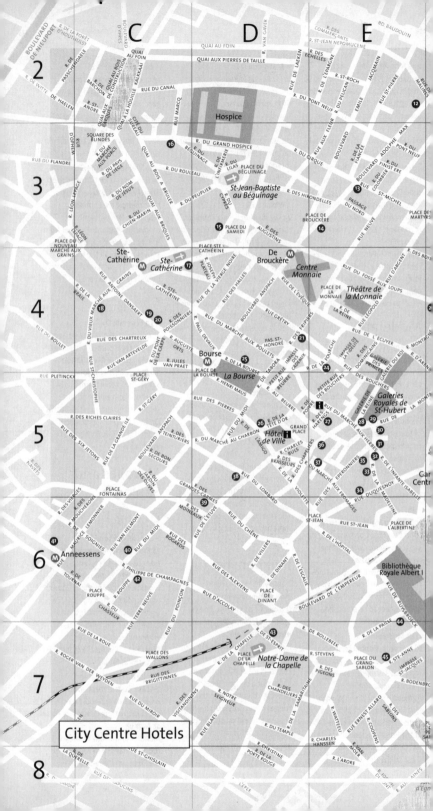

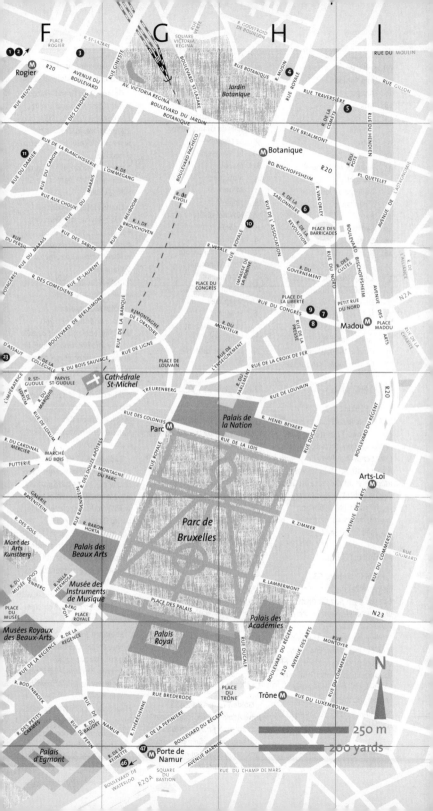

Map Key

44	Alfa Sablon	4	Grand Hôtel Mercure
26	Amigo	47	Hôtel Chambord
28	Aris	14	Hôtel Métropole
24	Arlequin	30	Ibis
10	Astoria	17	Ibis Ste-Catherine
15	Astrid	45	Jolly du Grand-Sablon
18	Atlas	38	La Légende
43	Auberge de Jeunesse Bruegel	29	La Madeleine
6	Auberge de Jeunesse Jacques Brel	8	Madou
		25	Matignon
41	Barry	37	Mozart
40	Bedford	16	Noga
20	La Bourse	32	Novotel of Grand' Place
46	Brussels Hilton	21	Opéra
31	Carrefour de l'Europe	19	Pacific
5	Centre Vincent Van Gogh	22	Radisson SAS Hotel
1	Comfort Art Hotel Siru	34	Royal Windsor
9	Du Congrès	3	Scandic Hotel
33	Le Dixseptième	2	Sheraton Towers
35	Les Eperonniers	11	Sleep Well
27	Floris Grand' Place	36	St-Michel
13	Golden Tulip Atlanta	7	La Tasse d'Argent
23	Golden Tulip Grand' Place	12	Vendôme
		39	La Vieille Lanterne
		42	Windsor

Expensive

Alfa Sablon E6–7

2–8 Rue de la Paille, 1000 Bruxelles, t 02 513 6040, f 02 511 8141, e alfa .sablon@alfahotel.com; metro Gare Centrale or Porte de Namur.
A stylish attractive hotel with 32 rooms just off the Place du Grand-Sablon. Lots of contemporary art on the walls add colour and warmth to the modern décor. This is a quiet, civilised place.

Moderate

Hôtel Chambord G8

82 Rue de Namur, 1000 Bruxelles, t 02 548 9910, f 02 514 0847, w www.hotel-chambord.be; metro Porte de Namur.
Modern hotel where the emphasis is on business travellers' needs. Unusual position on the edge of the upper town, which makes it handy for Avenue Louise, the Sablon and the Coudenberg museums, as well as an easy walk to the Grand' Place.

Inexpensive

Windsor C6

13 Place Rouppe, 1000 Bruxelles, t 02 511 2014, f 02 514 0942; metro Anneessens.
Quiet, modern, clean, comfortable – a small hotel of just 25 rooms, but with a warm welcome that sets its apart.

Cheap

Hôtel Galia C8

15–16 Place du Jeu de Baulle, t 02 502 4243, f 02 502 7619; metro Porte de Hal.
Located in the heart of the Marolles district, with clean, simple accomodation.

North Central Brussels

Luxury

Golden Tulip Atlanta E3

7 Bvd Adolphe Max, 1000 Bruxelles, t 02 217 0120, f 02 217 3758, e info@ gtatlanta.goldentulip.be, w www .goldentuliphotels.nl/gtatlanta; metro De Brouckère.

Good, well-appointed and central hotel, part of an established chain.

Golden Tulip Grand' Place F4

15 Rue d'Assaut, 1000 Bruxelles, t 02 501 1616, f 02 501 1818, e info@ gtgrandplace.goldentulip.be, w www.goldentulip.com; metro De Brouckère.
Modern, no-nonsense hotel, close to the cathedral; part of the City Hotels chain.

Grand Hôtel Mercure H2

250 Rue Royale, 1210 Bruxelles, t 02 220 6611, f 02 217 8444, e h1728@accor-hotels.com, w www.mercure.com; metro Botanique.
Superlative luxury hotel with a royal theme and a gym.

Hôtel Métropole E3

31 Place de Brouckère, 1000 Bruxelles, t 02 217 2300, f 02 218 0220, e info@metropolehotel.be, w www.metropolehotel.com; metro De Brouckère.
Brussels' grandest old hotel: marbled halls and palm court – the picture of Belle Epoque elegance encountered only on film sets; expect to pay at least €320 for a room.

Radisson SAS Hotel F4

47 Rue du Fossé aux Loups, 1000 Bruxelles, t 02 219 2828, f 02 219 6262, e info@bruzh.rdsas.com, w www.radisson.com/brussels.be; metro De Brouckère.
The most impressive modern hotel in Brussels, with atrium containing waterfalls and fountains. Very polished service – as you come to expect from this chain – and super-luxurious, with prices to match (much cheaper weekend rates).

Sheraton Towers F2

3 Place Rogier, 1210 Bruxelles, t 02 224 3111, f 02 224 3456, e ireservations.brussels@sheraton .com, w www.sheraton.com/brus-sels; metro Rogier.
Huge, top-quality international hotel, as the name would suggest, with a swimming pool on the 30th floor – but it's on the margins of the decidedly iffy Gare du Nord district.

Expensive

Astoria H3

*103 Rue Royale, 1000 Bruxelles,
t 02 227 0505, f 02 217 1150, e h1154
@accor-hotels.com, w www
.sofitel.com; metro Gare Centrale.*
Ranked alongside the Hôtel
Métropole as a grand old hotel of
Brussels – timeless elegance,
originally opened in 1908 and
superbly renovated.

Atlas C4

*30 Rue du Vieux Marché aux
Grains, 1000 Bruxelles, t 02 502
6006, f 02 502 6935, e info@atlas-
hotel.be, w www.atlas-hotel.com;
metro Bourse/Ste-Cathérine.*
The décor at this modern 88-room
hotel is a bit bland but there's
private parking and the rooms are
a decent size; six have kitchenettes. Caters mainly for a
business clientele.

Comfort Art Hotel Siru F1–2

*1 Place Rogier, 1210 Bruxelles, t 02
203 3580, f 02 203 3303, e art.hotel
.siru@skynet.be, w www
.comforthotel/siru.com; metro
Rogier.*
'Art hotel', with every room stylishly decorated by work of
contemporary Belgian artists – a
lively and commendable concept
with mixed results. For the more
aesthetically adventurous.

Moderate

Astrid D3

*11 Place du Samedi, 1000 Bruxelles,
t 02 219 3119, f 02 219 3170,
e astrid@switchon.be, w www
.astridhotel.be; metro Ste-
Cathérine.*
In an enclosed square just off
Place Ste-Cathérine, this modern
hotel is a good base for exploring
the fish market restaurants and
some of the bars and designer
boutiques around Rue Dansaert.
There are 100 rooms, not particularly characterful, but the staff are
helpful. Guests are usually businessmen or older tourists.

Du Congrès H4

*42 Rue du Congrès, 1000 Bruxelles,
t 02 217 1890, f 02 217 1897,*
*e hotel.congres@busmail.net,
w www.hoteldecongres.com;
metro Madou.*
A friendly welcome in a fine
maison de maître with *fin de siècle*
touches. The recent renovations
here have vastly improved the
hotel, and it now combines
modernity with an old charm;
there's also a garden.

Ibis Ste-Cathérine D4

*2 Rue J. Platteau, 1000 Bruxelles,
t 02 513 7620, f 02 514 2214, e h1454
@accor-hotels.com; metro Ste-
Cathérine.*
Comfortable, modern, if somewhat characterless hotel, in a
good location close to all the
attractions of the city centre.

Noga C3

*38 Rue du Béguinage, 1000
Bruxelles, t 02 218 6763, f 02 218
1603, e info@nogahotel.com,
w www.nogahotel.com; metro Ste-
Cathérine.*
Welcoming hotel in a quiet street.

Scandic Hotel F2

*20 Place Rogier, 1210 Bruxelles, t 02
203 3125, f 02 203 4331; metro
Rogier.*
Smart, friendly hotel converted in
functional modern style, behind
an Art Deco façade of the 1930s.

Vendôme E2

*98 Bvd Adolphe Max, 1000
Bruxelles, t 02 227 0300, f 02 218
0683, e hotel-vendome@hotel-
vendome.be, w wwwhotel-
vendome.be; metro De Brouckère
or Rogier.*
The rates vary here depending on
the time of year; in the low season
it's a reasonable modern 106-
room hotel convenient for the
shops on Rue Neuve. Rooms are on
the large side, pleasant and functional, designed to meet business
travellers' needs.

Inexpensive

La Bourse C4

*11 Rue Antoine Dansaert, 1000
Bruxelles, t 02 512 6010, f 02 512
6139; metro Bourse.*
This budget hotel is right in the
thick of hip Brussels, among the
area's designer shops, bars and
fish restaurants. All rooms have
private showers/bathrooms. Suits
younger travellers who want to
make the most of the area.

George V B5

*23 Rue 't Kint, 1000 Bruxelles, t 02
513 5093, f 02 513 4493, e george5
@skynet.be, w www.george5.com;
metro Bourse.*
A friendly family-run hotel in a
renovated 19th-century *maison de
maître* on a quiet street. As the
name suggests some of the décor
is old English style, but it's not too
imposing. Triple and quadruple
rooms available.

Madou H4

*45 Rue du Congrès, 1000 Bruxelles,
t 02 217 1890, f 02 217 1897, e hotel
.congres@busmail.net, w www
.hotelmadou.com; metro Madou.*
Clean but slightly shabby hotel
opposite and owned by Hôtel du
Congrès, caters for those needing
a cheaper option. It only has nine
rooms but all of these have
shower and toilets.

Opéra D4

*53 Rue Grétry, 1000 Bruxelles, t 02
219 4343, f 02 219 1720, e hotel
.opera@skynet.be; metro De
Brouckère.*
Despite the low prices you can
hook up your laptop here; there's a
modem in each room. In a bid to
appeal to as wide a range of
customers as possible, there are
triple and quadruple rooms.
Finally, you can have breakfast
served in your room at no extra
charge, providing a touch of
romance in what is otherwise a
straight forward hotel.

Cheap

Pacific C4

*57 Rue Antoine Dansaert, 1000
Bruxelles, t 02 511 8459; metro
Bourse.*
'Clean and cheap' declares the 3rd-
generation owner of this utterly
charming, central hotel – but it is
much more than this. More like a
private home, every room has
bags of old-world character, down
to the original 1910 plumbing. A
full breakfast (included) is served

in an authentic Art Nouveau-style restaurant.

La Tasse d'Argent H4
48 Rue du Congrès, 1000 Bruxelles, t/f 02 218 8375; metro Madou.
Another small hotel on Rue du Congrès, with eight rooms, even cheaper than Madou. It's nothing special but an option for those on the tightest budget. All the rooms have bathrooms and the price includes breakfast.

Quartier Léopold

Luxury

Clubhouse Park P7
21–22 Av de l'Yser, 1040 Bruxelles, t 02 735 7400, f 02 735 1967; metro Mérode.
Business hotel in a renovated town house on the other side of the Parc du Cinquantenaire from the main EU buildings.

Europa Intercontinental K6
107 Rue de la Loi, 1040 Bruxelles, t 02 230 1333, f 02 230 3682, e bruha@interconti.com, w www.interconti.com; metro Maelbeek.
Conveniently located modern hotel, near the EU and run with aplomb by staff who know what the business community needs.

Montgomery Off maps
134 Av de Tervuren, 1150 Bruxelles, t 02 741 8511, f 02 741 8500, e hotel@montgomery.be, w www.montgomery.be; metro Montgomery.
New, very splendid hotel with 65 richly upholstered rooms and suites, furnished in antique style of various inspirations; fax machine and video in every room.

Stanhope H7
9 Rue du Commerce, 1000 Bruxelles, t 02 506 9111, f 02 512 1708, e summithotels@stanhope.be; metro Arts-Loi.
Sumptuously elegant hotel with fifty rooms, that are decorated in the refined style called *à l'anglaise*; strategically placed between the main EU buildings and the city centre.

Swissôtel J8
19 Rue de Parnasse, 1050 Bruxelles, t 02 505 2929, f 02 505 2555, e emailus@swissotel.com, w www.swissotel.com; metro Trône.
A new, glittering addition to this respected international chain with a beautiful indoor swimming pool, sauna and large fitness centre (free for guests). Special weekend rates (Fri, Sat, Sun) which include a buffet breakfast.

Moderate

Lambeau Off maps
150 Av Lambeau, 1200 Bruxelles, t 02 732 5170, f 02 732 5490, e hotellambeau@skynet.be, w www.hotellambeau.be; metro Montgomery.
This agreeable hotel is family-run and is mainly a business hotel, given its address east of the parliament buildings. Good service, satisfactory rooms and easy to reach on the metro.

Inexpensive

Armorial Off maps
101 Bvd Brand Whitlock, 1200 Bruxelles, t 02 734 5636, f 02 734 5005; metro Montgomery or Georges Henri.
For something a little different, at surprisingly low prices: an atmospheric *maison de maître* with just 15 individually furnished rooms; to the east of the Parc du Cinquantenaire.

Derby Off maps
24 Av de Tervuren, 1040 Bruxelles, t 02 733 0819, f 02 733 7475; metro Montgomery.
Popular, straightforward business and tourist hotel to the east of the Parc du Cinquantenaire.

St-Gilles and Ixelles

Luxury

Barsey Mayfair I14
381–383 Av Louise, 1050 Bruxelles, t 02 649 9800, f 02 640 1764, e reservations@mayfair.be,
w www.mayfair.be; metro Louise, then tram 93 or 94.
Classy hotel with interior design by Jacques Garcia, it's style is a combination of clean Neoclassical and the lusciousness of the French Second Empire. The hotel is as unusual as it sounds, with good weekend rates.

Bristol Stéphanie F10
91–93 Av Louise, 1050 Bruxelles, t 02 543 3311, f 02 538 0307, e hotel_bristol@bristol.be, w www.bristol.be; metro Louise, then tram 93, 94.
Has recently come under Norwegian management and has been entirely refurbished. Well run and comfortable, there are Scandinavian touches in some of the décor but the overall feel is of corporate sophistication.

Conrad International F10
71 Av Louise, 1050 Bruxelles, t 02 542 4242, f 02 542 4200, e bruhc_gm@hilton.com, w www.brussels.conradinternational.com; metro Louise, then tram 93 or 94.
Super-luxurious modern hotel in a cocktail of architectural styles designed to impress (though it's grandeur, however well intended, could seem a little false to some). There is no denying the first-class facilities available to guests, including access to a health and fitness club. Good cheaper weekend rates.

Expensive

Capital H13–14
191 Chaussée de Vleurgat, 1050 Bruxelles, t 02 646 6420, f 02 646 3314, e hotel.capital@skynet.be; tram 93 or 94.
Pleasant, modest and friendly new hotel; no extras, but comfortable rooms and efficient, helpful staff.

Four Points H11
15 Rue P. Spaak, 1000 Bruxelles, t 02 645 6111, f 02 646 6344, e reservations.brussels@sheraton.com, w www.fourpoints.com;, metro Louise, then tram 93 or 94.
Spacious and comfortable accommodation in a recently renovated hotel. Some of the rooms are apartment-style, in that they have

kitchenettes and slightly larger beds that are designed to improve the quality of a longer stay in the hotel.

Hôtel Floris Louise F10
59–61 Rue de la Concorde, 1000 Bruxelles, t 02 515 0060, f 02 503 3519, e florislouise@busmail.net; metro Louise; tram 93 or 94.
A small but smart hotel with 29 rooms just off Avenue Louise. Modern and tasteful, it offers most of the services you would expect from a modern international hotel.

Meliá Avenue Louise F10
4 Rue Blanche, 1000 Bruxelles, t 02 535 9500, f 02 535 9600, e melia.avenue.louise@solmelia.com, w www.solmelia.com; metro Louise; tram 92 or 94.
This elegant hotel is part of the Boutique hotel chain; yet another option off Avenue Louise. The fresh flowers throughout and the open fireplace in the reading room are charming touches, but the real attraction here are the rates in July and August when reduced weekend rates are offered all the time.

Tulip Inn Delta F10
17 Chaussée de Charleroi, 1060 Bruxelles, t 02 539 0160, f 02 537 9011, e sales@tibrussels .goldentulip.be; tram 91 or 92; wheelchair accessible.
Functional, with all mod cons, if short on character; one of the City Hotel chain.

Moderate

Agenda F11
6 Rue de Florence, 1000 Bruxelles, t 02 539 0031, f 02 539 0063, e louise@hotel-agenda.com, w www.hotel-agenda.com; metro Louise; tram 93 or 94.
A relaxed hotel which caters well for families. With three family rooms on offer and kitchenettes available on request. It's in a good position with bright, well-sized rooms, pleasant modern décor and a warm and friendly atmosphere.

Argus F9
6 Rue Capitaine Crespel, 1050 Bruxelles, t 02 514 0770, f 02 514 1222, e reception@hotel-argos.be, w www.hotel-argos.be; metro Porte de Namur.
Just off Avenue Louise this quiet and pleasant hotel offers clean modern rooms. The simple décor works well in the somewhat limited space.

Inexpensive

De Boeck's F11
40 Rue Veydt, 1050 Bruxelles, t 02 537 4033, f 02 534 4037, e hotel .deboecks@euronet.be; tram 93 or 94.
Boasting a richly coloured entrance hall this town house hotel is an elegant bargain. The rooms don't live up to the downstairs but they're perfectly decent and the overall impression is that thought and care has gone into this place.

Duke of Windsor E10
4 Rue Capouillet, 1060 Bruxelles, t 02 539 1819; tram 91 or 92.
A tiny hotel with just five decent rooms. Maintains a strictly non-smoking policy.

Hôtel Rembrandt G10
42 Rue de la Concorde, 1050 Bruxelles, t 02 512 7139, f 02 511 7136; metro Louise; tram 93 or 94.
This *résidence* is an unexpected haven of tranquillity off the busy Avenue Louise. The china teapots in the entrance hall are just part of a décor which is classy but quaint. Rooms range from the simple shower only to a plush top-floor suite.

Sun G9
38 Rue du Berger, 1050 Bruxelles, t 02 511 2119, f 02 512 3271, e sunhotel@skynet.be; metro Porte de Namur.
Unfortunately the Rue du Berger is rather run down – so much so it's quite a surprise to find this modern well-run hotel here. It has 22 rooms all with shower or bath facilities, so what what it lacks in its environs it makes up for in good value and comfort.

Cheap

Les Bluets D10
124 Rue Berckmans, 1060 Bruxelles, t 02 534 3983, f 02 543 0970, e bluets@eudoramail.com, w www.geocities.com/les_bluets; metro Hôtel des Monnaies.
This 19th-century home has been converted into an extraordinary guesthouse hotel. It is brimming with old paintings, figurines and plants; the bedrooms remain airy despite having been treated to a similar excess of decoration; no walls or surfaces have been left bare, even the caged birds in the breakfast room and little conservatory are a multitude of breeds and colours. If you like minimalism this isn't the place for you, otherwise you might just love it. Non-smokers only.

Apartment Hotels

There are several of these in Brussels: by providing bedrooms with small kitchens attached they combine the advantages of self-catering with hotel service, and are particularly useful for families. Apartment hotels are available for stays of just one night, but prices become increasingly competitive the longer the stay. There are over twenty apartment hotels in the city.

City Garden K6
59 Rue Joseph II, 1040 Bruxelles, t 02 282 8282, f 02 230 6437; metro Arts-Loi.
Well-appointed, business-orientated apartment hotel, with special rates for minimum one-month stays.

Euro-flat L5–6
50 Bvd Charlemagne, 1000 Bruxelles, t 02 230 0010, f 02 230 3683; metro Maelbeek or Schuman.
Hotel also offering apartments, with rates for the week or month.

Orion C3
51 Quai au Bois à Brûler, 1000 Bruxelles, t 02 221 1411, f 02 221 1599; metro Ste-Cathérine.

Apartment hotel in the old fish-market district close to Place Ste-Cathérine; small but adequate accommodation, special rates for the week or month.

Bed and Breakfast

It is possible to find accommodation in family homes in Brussels, staying on a bed-and-breakfast basis. The conditions vary from household to household, of course, but it can be a remarkably cheap alternative to hotels (around €35–70 per night for two) and can, if successful, provide a rewarding insight into Belgian life. Some of the addresses in Brussels are extremely well located. Details change from year to year, so cannot reliably be published here. There is a useful booklet called 'Bed and Breakfast: Benelux Guide', which is given away free by some of the Belgian tourist offices abroad (*see* p.68). Alternatively, apply directly to the publishers, Taxistop (*28 Rue Fossé aux Loups, 1000 Bruxelles*, **t** *02 223 2310*). Alternatively you could apply to Bed & Brussels (*2 Rue Gustave Biot, B-1050 Bruxelles*, **t** *02 646 0737*, **f** *02 644 0114*, **e** *bnbru@ ibm.net*, **w** *www.bnb-brussels.be*).

Youth Hostels

There are five main youth hostels (*auberge de jeunesse/jeugdherberg*) in the city. Prices per head per night range from about €7–16, depending on the number of beds in the room. Auberge de Jeunesse Jacques Brel, the Vlaamse Jeugdherberg Bruegel and Sleep Well are all located close to the centre and represent outstanding value for money. You don't really have to be a youth, by the way; young at heart will do.

Auberge de Jeunesse Bruegel D7
2 Rue du St-Esprit, 1000 Bruxelles, **t** *02 511 0436*, **f** *02 512 0711*, **e** *jeugdherberg.bruegel@ping.be*; **metro** *Gare Centrale*.
In a prime position at the foot of the Sablon district, off Rue de la Chapelle. Here you have to be a member of the International Youth Hostel Association, but you can join while you're there.

Auberge de Jeunesse Jacques Brel H3
30 Rue de la Sablonnière, 1000 Bruxelles, **t** *02 218 0187*, **f** *02 217 2005*, **e** *brussels.brel@laj.be*, **w** *www.laj.be*; **metro** *Botanique*; wheelchair accessible.

Centre Vincent van Gogh (CHAB) I2
8 Rue Traversière, 1210 Bruxelles, **t** *02 217 0158*, **f** *02 219 7995*, **e** *chab @ping.be*, **w** *www.ping.be/chab*; **metro** *Botanique*.
Close to the Jardin Botanique. The biggest youth hostel in Belgium.

Génération Europe Off maps
4 Rue de l'Eléphant, 1080 Bruxelles, **t** *02 410 3858*, **f** *02 410 3905*; **metro** *Comte de Flandre*.
In Molenbeek, west Brussels, a 20-minute walk from the city centre.

Sleep Well F3
23 Rue du Damier, 1000 Bruxelles, **t** *02 218 5050*, **f** *02 218 1313*, **e** *info@ sleepwell.be*, **w** *www.sleepwell.be*; **metro** *Rogier or De Brouckère*. Booking advised.
Remarkably stylish 'youth hotel', that's friendly, very central and very inexpensive. Monastic accommodation in rooms with up to six beds; shared bathrooms and dining facilities. Some youth hostel rules apply, such as no access to rooms during the day; no linen (sheets can be rented).

Eating Out

It is now a well-known secret that Belgium's food ranks among the best in Europe – and that even the French are prepared to admit it. Belgium – and not just Brussels – has an armful of garlanded restaurants over which even the most hardened international gastronomes will bill and coo. You can eat extremely well in Belgium but, more importantly, it is almost impossible to eat badly. Since virtually everyone in the entire nation is an expert on food, restaurants that dare to serve sub-standard fare simply cannot survive. Belgians have a great enthusiasm for eating out. This means that decent restaurants are well patronized and are able to keep their prices competitive. Standards are invariably high – in the humble *friterie* on a street corner as well as at the dizzying pinnacles of *haute cuisine*.

The foundations of this impressive tradition are laid by the quality of produce. Everyone in the food production chain takes immense pride in their profession, and they are likewise held in high regard by their clients, provided that the Belgians' fastidious standards are met. Butchers' shops, often family-owned, are run by white-coated staff who will advise customers and discuss their needs – and weather their criticism if ever they should fall below expectations. *Pâtisseries* offer an array of glistening *tartes aux fruits*, light and fluffy *tartes aux fromage*, elaborate gâteaux and chocolate extravaganzas. Good pastries are considered an inalienable part of Belgian living, and *pâtisserie* has been raised to an art form; even run-down urban districts have a *pâtisserie*, sometimes striking an incongruous note of luxury. The preoccupation with quality extends even to the large supermarket chains, such as Delhaize and GB, where standards are almost as good as in the numerous specialist high-street, family-run concerns. All the while, a fair amount of Belgium's food is grown in the back yard, where small *potagers* are coaxed into producing immense quantities of nutrition from tightly packed rows of carrots, sprouts, beans, *endives*, artichokes, asparagus, celery and tomatoes.

Some Belgian Specialities

Belgian food is solidly northern European, hearty and copious – with a touch of genius that lifts it above the ordinary. Clearly it is closely allied to French cuisine, but its most famous dishes are still firmly rooted in burgher traditions and by and large the Belgians have little patience with the over-priced preciousness to which *la haute cuisine française* can so easily fall victim.

A famous anecdote about Victor Hugo speaks of these differing traditions. Eating in a Brussels restaurant during his exile in Belgium after 1858, Hugo was addressed by a fellow customer. 'I can see you must be French,' he said, 'from the amount of bread you eat with your meal.' 'I can see you must be Belgian,' retorted Hugo, 'from the amount you eat!'

Steak and chips is virtually the national dish. The steak will be first-class (perhaps a huge *entrecôte à l'os*, or a melt-in-the-mouth *filet pur*) and the chips, of course, have no rival in Europe (*see* p.223). *Moules et frites* (mussels and chips) comes a close second. No dainty soup bowls scattered with mussels here, but a kilo per person, which comes in a casserole the size of a bucket. *Moules marinière* is the standard preparation: cleaned live mussels are cooked on a bed of sweated celery, onion and parsley until the shells open. Few elaborations improve on this formula.

Most restaurants offer French-style cuisine, but in down-to-earth establishments, heartier northern dishes will also feature on the menu. On the lighter side you may find delicately flavoured soups, such as *soupe de cresson* (watercress); excellent fish – in particular, turbot, flounder, plaice, monkfish and bream; tasty, substantial salads, such as *salade Liégeoise* (a warm salad of green beans or *salade frisée* and bacon pieces); and *steak à l'américaine* (or *américain préparé*), raw minced steak with capers, chopped raw onion, Worcestershire sauce and a raw egg. Typically Belgian dishes often crop up on menus. The most famous is *waterzooi*, a soothing soup-like dish in which chicken is cooked with cream and vegetables. The *waterzooi* formula has recently been applied to fish. *Carbonnades flamandes*, another classic Belgian dish, is a hearty, sweetly flavoured beef stew cooked in beer.

Pork is important, and there is a wide variety of pork products, such as *andouillettes* (rich sausages made of offal) and the excellent *boudin blanc* and *boudin noir* (soft meat and blood sausages). Game (*gibier*) in season includes pigeon, hare, pheasant and venison, often made succulent with berries, raisins or braised chicory. Look out for unusual seasonal vegetables, such as salsify and *jets de houblon* – hop shoots, served in spring with a peppery cream sauce and poached eggs.

Belgian food is to some extent regional, but the country is too small to make any great issue of this. Nonetheless, the origins of famous regional dishes are respected: if you want the best *waterzooi* you have to go to Ghent. For the best seafood head for the coast. Eels are seldom better than around the lakes of Overmere, east of Ghent, where the great speciality is *paling in 't groen* (called *anguilles au vert* in French). This is a kind of stew, in which substantial chunks of eel are cooked in handfuls of chervil, sorrel and parsley. The Ardennes region is famous for its game dishes, and also for its cured *jambon d'Ardennes*. Abbeys like

Chimay, Orval and Maredsous, produce their own brands of cheese as well as beer (see pp.240–41), and there are numerous other provincial cheeses, such as Herve, Limburger and Boulette de Romedenne. Brussels, too, claims its own cuisine, often presented under picturesque *bruxellois* titles. The most famous dishes include *bloedpens* (blood pudding), *carbonnades* cooked with the local *lambic* or *gueuze* beer, and various vegetable and meat purées known as *stoemp*. *Choesels* is a celebrated dish made of seven kinds of offal cooked in *lambic*. The crucial ingredient is beef pancreas and it has to be eaten as fresh as possible – traditionally on the day of slaughter.

Belgian biscuits are almost as famous as their chocolates. These include the crumbly, buttery biscuits of the kind made by Dandoy in the suitably named Rue au Beurre adjacent to the Grand' Place. The southern Belgian town of Dinant is famous for its fancy biscuits called *couques* (the most elaborate are intended to be hung on walls, not eaten), while *speculoos*, a hard, buttery biscuit, is a well-known speciality of Flanders. A box of wafer-thin almond biscuits produced by Jules Destrooper makes a good present. At the other end of the scale, you can sink your teeth into a luscious, freshly cooked *gaufre* (waffle) sprinkled with icing sugar.

Chips

If you want a quick snack in Belgium, you could do worse than stopping at a *friture/frituur* van and ordering a cone of chips (French fries). Belgian chips – *frites/frieten* – are quite simply the best: no thicker than your little finger, served piping hot, golden brown and *croustillantes*, or crispy. The traditional accompaniment is a dollop of mayonnaise. One of the reasons Belgian *frites* are so good is the choice of potato – usually a sweeter one such as Bintje, and old enough to have the

right quantity of starch. Belgians bring critical appreciation to their potatoes, just as they do to any other aspect of food: hang the shelf life. Take, for instance, the Saint-Nicholas, a delicious, waxy potato with a yellowish hue and an aromatic, nutty flavour; this potato is not just a lump of carbo-hydrate filler but a vegetable of great distinction.

Belgium, in fact, has a close connection to the history of the potato in Europe. After Sir Walter Raleigh brought the tuber back from the Americas in the 16th century it was virtually forgotten, but a Flemish botanist called Charles de l'Ecluse, working in Emperor Maximilian II's gardens in Vienna, saw its potential and kept it in cultivation. Over 100 years later it still hadn't caught on: it was a food of last resort, fed to farm animals, prisoners and soldiers. It was growing in the province of Hainault by 1715, and came into its own after a wheat-crop failure in 1739–40, whereafter it supplanted cereals as a staple until the growth of grain imports from Canada and the USA in the late 19th century.

So what is the secret of making good Belgian chips? First select an appropriate potato variety; cut the potatoes to size, keeping them fairly thin. Lastly, fry them *twice*: the first time so that they are cooked but not brown; then, after allowing them to cool, cook them a second time until golden brown and *bien croustillantes*!

Chicory

The French-speaking Belgians call them *chicons*, the French call them *endives*, the Flemish call them *witloof*, the English-speaking world refers to them as chicory in the UK and Belgian endives in the US – a suitably mysterious confusion for this bizarre little vegetable. Chicory consists of a head of firm, bullet-shaped leaves – white, yellow and pale green – with a crunchy texture and a distinctive, bitter flavour. It is often eaten raw, in

salads, but with simple cooking, chicory is transformed in to one of the most delicious and surprising of Belgium's foods. Melt some butter in a saucepan, drop in a handful of chicory, put on the lid and cook very slowly until it has collapsed into its own aromatic juices and transmogrified into a sweet, succulent delicacy. Chicory wrapped in slices of ham and baked in a cheese sauce (*chicons gratin*) is a classic, warming Belgian dish.

Chicory is essentially a winter crop. The roots of the *chicorée* lettuce are replanted and allowed to shoot, but are kept in the dark to make the shoots white. The process was apparently discovered by accident in about 1840 by the head gardener at the botanical gardens of Brussels, who was simply trying to overwinter some rootstock. He kept the shoots in the dark by gently piling up the earth over them, and this is the method still used in the *potagers* today. Commercial growers, however, use darkened sheds and hydroponics to maintain a thriving export industry.

Eating Out

There are over 3,000 restaurants in Brussels, and you can bet that 95 per cent of them are good. Given this *embarras du choix*, how do you decide where to eat? The Bruxellois have the same problem: most of them end up with their own selection of favourite restaurants, usually near where they live – why go further when excellence is on your doorstep? Here are a few tips to avoid disappointment. Look out for busy restaurants, patronized by locals; avoid restaurants that appear to cater mainly for tourists. Don't be afraid to ask for recommendations – all Belgians are experts on food and only too happy to advise. Newspapers and magazines, such as *Le Soir* and *The Bulletin*, have regular restaurant reviews, which are reliable guides.

Restaurant hours are generally 12–2.30 and 6–10.30 or 11, although many of the smaller *bistrots* and brasseries serve *cuisine* non-stop from about 11am to midnight. Many restaurants are closed for Saturday lunch and on Sunday, and some shut down completely in July or August. Always phone first to check opening times. It's advisable to make a reservation for the more upmarket establishments. There are restaurants to suit all palates and appetites; menus at the door will show what's on offer. The fixed-price *menu du jour* or *plat du jour* is often a bargain, and you will find that even luxury restaurants usually feature a cheaper menu at lunch time. Many cafés serve a limited range of light dishes for lunch and supper, and bars may offer '*petite restauration*' – snacks of sandwiches, *croque monsieur* (grilled cheese and ham on toast), *toast cannibale* (raw minced steak on toast) and so forth. Such food is usually also available in the *estaminets* – a class of rare, old-world taverns celebrated for their antique clutter and relaxed atmosphere. Some food shops and *pâtisseries* have tables and chairs where you can sit and eat a snack: *dégustation* (sampling/tasting) at a specialist food shop can often end up as a full-scale meal.

Belgian food has few exotic influences, but if you fancy something a little different there are a fair number of restaurants offering foreign food: North African, Japanese, Thai, Indian, Italian and Spanish. Many of these are extremely good – they have to be, to survive in this competitive gastronomic world!

Value Added Tax (TVA/BTW) at 21 per cent is generally already included in the price of restaurant meals. In principle, if you eat in a restaurant you must insist on a VAT receipt and take this out of the restaurant with you. VAT officials may demand to see your receipt, and failure to produce one

can entail a fine, and a penalty for the restaurant owner. However, this recently introduced, uncharacteristically officious regulation appears to have had little impact in Belgium.

Price Categories

It's very difficult to give a hard and fast guide to prices. You can eat relatively cheaply at expensive restaurants if you stick to special *prix fixe* menus. The price categories used here indicate the cost of a three-course meal (without wine), for one person, from the à la carte menu.

expensive over €40
moderate €20–40
inexpensive up to €20

Around the Grand' Place

Restaurants

Expensive

Le Cerf E5
20 Grand' Place, t 02 511 4791; **metro** *Bourse.* **Open** *Mon–Fri noon–3 and 6–11.30; closed mid-July–mid-Aug.*
A very decadent-looking place on the eastern corner of the Grand' Place, with claret upholstery, portraits on the walls and antler-rimmed chandeliers. The food here is highly rated (and you pay for it), with Belgian specialities as the mainstay. Try the lobster with *morel* (an edible fungus).

La Maison du Cygne C5
2 Rue Charles Buls or 9 Grand' Place, t 02 511 8244; **metro** *Gare Centrale.* **Open** *Mon–Fri noon–2.30 and 7–11, Sat 7–11pm; closed 3 weeks in Aug.*
Sumptuous and justly famous restaurant in one of the Grand' Place guildhouses, serving top-notch French cuisine at equally grand prices.

L'Ogenblik E4
1 Galerie des Princes, t 02 511 6151; **metro** *Bourse.* **Open** *Mon–Sat noon–2.30 and 7–midnight.*

Friendly, stylishly low-key brasserie serving elegant – if pricey – dishes of scallops, *gâteau de homard*, wild duck, game.

Moderate

Aux Armes de Bruxelles E4
13 Rue des Bouchers, t 02 511 5598, **w** *www.armesdebruxelles.be;* **metro** *Bourse.* **Open** *Tues–Sun noon–11.*
Sophisticated busy traditional Belgian restaurant, with impeccable service. The pick of the bunch among the dozens of tourist restaurants in the Ilôt Sacré quarter.

't Kelderke E5
15 Grand' Place, t 02 513 7344; **metro** *Gare Centrale.* **Open** *daily noon–2am.*
Medieval cellar setting for authentic shoulder-to-shoulder dining. Hearty *bruxellois* food at reasonable prices.

Rôtisserie Vincent E4
8–10 Rue des Dominicains, t 02 511 2303; metro Gare Centrale. **Open** *daily noon–2.45 and 6.30–11.30; closed mid-July–mid-Aug.*
Bruxellois atmosphere in a colourfully tiled restaurant entered through the steaming kitchen and fronted by what looks like a butcher's window. Good, solid Belgian cooking; *menu du patron* at €25–35.

Taverne du Passage E5
30 Galerie de la Reine, t 02 512 3732, **w** *www.tavernedupassage.com;* **metro** *Gare Centrale.* **Open** *daily noon–midnight; closed Wed and Thurs in June and July.*
Classic old-style restaurant, where smartly-attired, elderly ladies speak in hushed voices over crisp linen. Specializes in Belgian cuisine, such as *andouillette grillée* and *waterzooi*.

Inexpensive

Al Barmaki E5
67 Rue des Eperonniers, t 02 513 0834, metro Gare Centrale. **Open** *Mon–Sat 7pm–midnight.*
A dimly lit Lebanese restaurant with lanterns and mosaics and tasty Middle Eastern offerings

that are guaranteed to fill you up. A good cheap alternative to the plague of *moules et frites* places in this area.

Le Cave de Yasmina E5
9 Rue du Marché aux Fromages, t 02 512 8340; metro Gare Centrale. Open Mon–Sat 6pm–3am.
This is best of the gaudy restaurants that line this lively tourist-packed street, with Tunisian specialities served until the early hours.

Chez Léon E4
18 Rue des Bouchers, t 02 511 1415; metro Bourse. Open Sun–Fri 11.30am–11pm, Sat 11.30am–11.30pm.
The jam-packed, multistoreyed original (which was founded in 1893) of what has now become a small chain, specializing in *moules et frites* and other Belgian standards. Tourists enthuse, but the Bruxellois remain sniffy and unimpressed.

Restaurant Chez Patrick D5
6 Rue des Chapeliers, t 02 511 9815; metro Gare Centrale. Open Tues–Sun noon–2.30 and 7–midnight.
Admirably down-to-earth Brussels-style bar/restaurant, that's located just off the busy Grand' Place.

Taï Hon E5
45 Rue des Eperonniers, t 02 514 5058; metro Gare Centrale. Open Tues–Sun 11–3 and 6–11.

Couples' City

For a special evening out, when money is less of an object (or you'd like to pretend that it is), try one of the following restaurants, picked for their intimate atmosphere or stylish food and décor: **L'Amadeus** (metro Louise; *see p.233*), **La Belle Maraîchère** (metro Ste-Cathérine; *see p.230*), **Comme Chez Soi** (metro Anneessens; *see p.229*), **Du Mim** (metro Gare Centrale; *see p.228*), **L'Ecailler du Palais Royal** (metro Gare Centrale; *see p.229*), **L'Estrille du Vieux Bruxelles** (metro Gare Centrale; *see p.229*), **Les Foudres** (tram 90 or 23; *see p.233*).

Tiny, but deliciously authentic Taiwanese restaurant which succeeds at putting freshness and fervour back into traditional Chinese cooking. Lunch time *plat du jour* for €6.

Zebra C5
35 Place St-Géry, t 02 511 0901; metro Bourse. Open daily 11.45am–2am.
Trendy café/bistro in the most booming part of the city. Brick walls, candlelight, jazz music. Inexpensive tasty snacks; nice terrace in summer.

Cafés

L'Albertine E5
53 Rue de la Madeleine, t 02 513 5671; metro Gare Centrale. Open daily 7.30am–8pm, Sept–Easter closed on Sun.
This functional little café/bar with fixed formica tables and mirrored walls is a good place for a cheap snack away from the tourist din of the Grand' Place. From a generous menu, *croque monsieur*, omelette, spaghetti and a wide range of beers are served to a mainly older local clientele. Very well positioned between the Mont des Arts, the Grand' Place and the Gare Centrale.

Café des Halles St-Géry C5
1 Place St-Géry, t 02 502 4424, metro Bourse. Open daily 10am–3am.
Like London's Covent Garden, the Halles St-Géry used to be a food market. Now it hosts exhibitions mainly dedicated to urban environmental issues. The café, serving drinks and snacks, occupies the bright open space in the centre; a good place to settle on a rainy day.

Le Chapeau d'As D5
36 Rue des Chapeliers, t 02 511 2708; metro Gare Centrale. Open noon–midnight.
An airy traditional-style café with brass fittings and brightly painted wildlife on the walls and ceiling. Worth trying for its Belgian beers and inexpensive food (lasagne for around €7).

La Fleur en Papier Doré D6
55 Rue des Alexiens; metro Anneessens. Open daily 11am–1am.
Splendid old *estaminet*, once the meeting place of the Belgian surrealists and a favourite haunt of Magritte's. Good beers from the barrel, plus light snacks and sandwiches from around €5.

Fritland D5
10 Rue Henri Maus; metro Bourse
A top class *frites* stall with a wide range of mayonnaise – essential for that authentic Belgian *frites* experience. Conveniently situated on Henri Maus street (on the corner of the Bourse).

La Roue d'Or D5
26 Rue des Chapeliers, t 02 514 2554; metro Gare Centrale. Open daily 12.30pm–midnight.
An old brasserie with elaborate chandeliers and a high painted ceiling. Seafood and traditional Belgian cuisine are standard and are served at lunch and dinner. Despite being only a few strides from the Grand' Place, this restaurant escapes the daily lunch time tourist mayhem.

Coudenberg and Parc de Bruxelles

Restaurants

Expensive
Maccan F7
93 Rue de Namur, t 02 513 0696; metro Porte de Namur. Open Mon–Sat noon–2.30 and 7–10.30.
Entered through the marbled hallway of an upper-crust delicatessen, this is a shrine to fish.

Relais de Caprices F6
1 Rue Ravenstein, t 02 512 7768; metro Gare Centrale. Open Mon–Fri noon–2pm, Sat noon–2 and 7–midnight.
Attached to the 15th-century Hôtel Ravenstein, which is a remnant of the palace where Henry VIII's fourth wife Anne of Cleves (aka the 'Flemish Mare') was born. The restaurant serves traditional Belgian cuisine, a little over-priced, though it's well

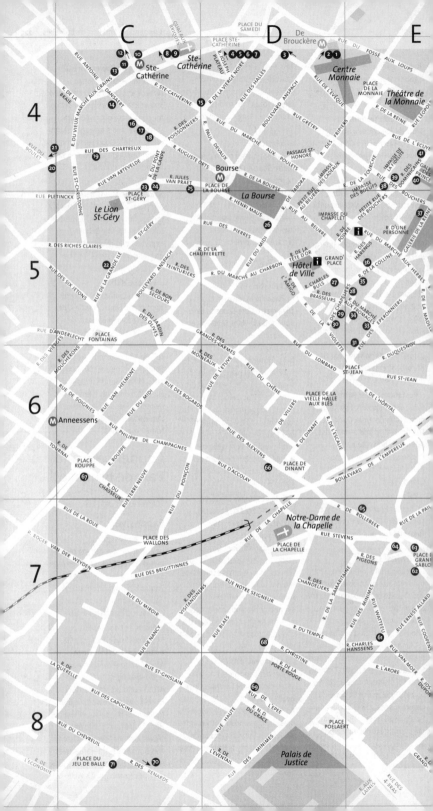

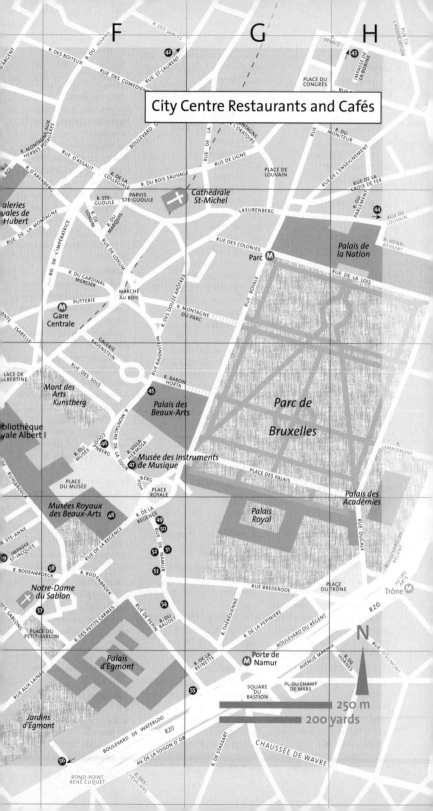

City Centre Restaurants and Cafés

Map Key

32	L'Albertine
4	Les Algues
38	Aux Armes de Bruxelles
19	Arteaspoon
22	Les Ateliers de la Grand Ile
31	Al Barmaki
9	La Belle Maraîchère
68	Le Bermuchet
16	Bonsoir Clara
6	La Boussole
42	Brasserie Horta
69	Brasserie Ploegmans
23	Café des Halles St-Géry
63	Café Leffe
11	Café de Markten
61	Café Le Perroquet
34	Le Cave de Yasmina
36	Le Cerf
30	Le Chapeau d'As
55	Les Chevaliers
39	Chez Léon
57	Chez Marius en Provence
64	Chez Richard
67	Comme Chez Soi
1	Le Corbeau
46	Le Coudenberg
20	Den Teepot
58	L'Ecailler du Palais Royal
62	L'Entrée des Artistes
65	L'Estrille du Vieux Bruxelles
66	La Fleur en Papier Doré
26	Fritland
3	Friture Ste-Cathérine
49	Au Jour le Jour
59	La Kartchma
18	Kasbah
35	't Kelderke
51	The Lunch Company
54	Maccan
56	La Maison du Bœuf
27	La Maison du Cygne
12	La Marée
7	La Marie Joseph
2	Le Métropole
47	Du Mim
48	Musée d'Art Ancien Cafeteria
14	Neos Kosmos
44	The New Cambridge
50	New York
40	L'Ogenblik
53	Pablo's
17	Le Pain Quotidien
60	Le Pain Quotidien
52	Passatempo
5	Persepolis
25	Phat-Thai
10	La Piazetta dei Latini
8	Le Quai
45	Relais de Caprices
28	Restaurant Chez Patrick
41	Rôtisserie Vincent
29	La Roue d'Or
71	De Skieven Architek
21	In 't Spinnekope
33	Taï Hon
37	Taverne du Passage
15	Au Thé de Pékin
43	De Ultieme Hallucinatie
13	La Villette
70	't Warm Water
24	Zebra

positioned (and the only approachable restaurant) in the Mont des Arts area.

Moderate

Au Jour le Jour F7
*4 Rue de Namur, t 02 502 8000;
metro Porte de Namur. Open Mon–
Fri 11.45–3 and 7–10.30, Sat 7–10.30.*
Low lights, friendly service and a faithful following of *habitués* for dishes such as *carpaccio* and *cuisse de canard à l'Ardennaise*; lunch menu at around €10.

Pablo's F7
*51 Rue de Namur, t 02 502 4135;
metro Porte de Namur. Open
Mon–Sat noon–3 and 6–midnight,
Sun 6pm–midnight.*
Upbeat Mexican restaurant with a bar the size of a bowling alley.

Tacos, enchiladas, arroz con pollo, etc., with pitchers of *margaritas.*

Inexpensive

The Lunch Company F7
*16 Rue de Namur, t 02 502 0976;
metro Porte de Mamur. Open daily
11–6.*
A chic and refined salad and sandwich bar that serves Fortnum & Mason teas. Perfect choice for relaxing afternoon tea.

The New Cambridge I4
*Corner of Rue Louvain and Rue du Nord; metro Madou. Open Mon–Fri
7am–6pm.*
Large modern and attractive tavern which greets the lunch time invasion with wholesome Belgian and Italian *plats du jour* for €8 or less.

Cafés

Le Coudenberg F6
*68 Coudenberg, t 02 512 4896;
metro Gare Centrale. Open daily
11am–8pm.*
Given its position right by the Whirling Ear sculpture on the Mont des Arts, this café/bar is somewhere to rest your feet away from the crowds after a museum visit. It's nice and quiet, there's lots of Belgian beer to choose from and if you've got a hunger on you, they'll cook you up steak and chips.

Du Mim F6
*6th Floor, 2 Rue Montagne de la Cour, t 02 502 9508; metro Gare Centrale. Open Tues–Sun 9.30am–
4.30pm.*
This has to be one of the best daytime café experiences in Brussels. Perched near the summit of the Mont des Arts, at the top of one of Brussels' most prominent Art Nouveau buildings (the renovated Magasins Old England), it is the perfect place to acquaint yourself with the city – there are skyline views right across the lower town and out as far north as the Atomium and Parc de Laeken. Although you can visit the café separately, it is actually part of the Musée des Instruments de Musiques (MIM). Light lunch (tarts, quiches) is the mainstay, along with a decent selection of beers and wines. If the weather is fine, sit up on the roof terrace.

**Musée d'Art
Ancien Cafeteria** F7
*Musées Royaux des Beaux-Arts, 3 Rue de la Régence; metro Porte de Namur or Trône. Open Tues–Sun
11am–4.30pm.*
Stylish museum cafeteria serving light refreshments at rather inflated prices.

New York F7
*8 Rue de Namur, t 02 511 2757;
metro Porte de Namur. Open Mon–
Sat 7am–7pm.*
A snack place, offering tasty sandwiches, pizza and basic lunch dishes for around €5.

Passatempo F7

32 Rue de Namur, **t** *02 511 3703;* **metro** *Porte de Namur.* **Open** *Mon–Sat 9am–4.30pm.*

A stylish Italian *vini e cucina*, where you can either sit at a stool with a glass of wine and a few delectable morsels from the deli, or settle down to a generous Italian lunch.

Marolles and Sablon

Restaurants

Expensive

Chez Marius en Provence F7

1 Place du Petit-Sablon, **t** *02 511 1208;* **metro** *Porte de Namur.* **Open** *Mon–Sat noon–3 and 6.30– midnight; closed public hols.*

Stylish, much-loved restaurant specializing in southern French food and famous for its *bouillabaisse*. Prices can escalate to €100 or more, but there are set menus at around €40.

Comme Chez Soi C6

23 Place Rouppe, **t** *02 512 2921;* **metro** *Anneessens.* **Open** *Tues–Sat noon–2 and 7–10; closed July.*

Owned and run by Pierre Wynants, one of Europe's most fêted chefs, this is Brussels' premier restaurant – but with just 40 places you need to book weeks in advance. Exquisite concoctions of snipe, eel, truffle, lobster, all beautifully presented. Expect no change out of €150.

L'Ecailler du Palais Royal F7

18 Rue Bodenbroeck, **t** *02 512 8751;* **metro** *Gare Centrale.* **Open** *Mon–Sat noon–3.30 and 7–11.30; closed public hols and Aug.*

One of Brussels' most celebrated fish restaurants: classy and welcoming, with absolutely *comme il faut cuisine*. Bargain *plat du jour* at €32.

L'Estrille du Vieux Bruxelles E7

7 Rue du Rollebeek, **t** *02 512 5857;* **metro** *Gare Centrale; tram 92, 93 or 94.* **Open** *daily noon–midnight.*

Built on top of the old town ramparts, this 16th-century red-

brick house with a secluded courtyard provides a cosy setting for an elegant restaurant. If you really cannot decide which of the hearty Belgian dishes to go for, you can lump six of them together on one plate for €30 (though you only get a small taster of each dish).

La Maison du Bœuf F8

Hilton Hotel, 38 Bvd de Waterloo, **t** *02 504 1334;* **metro** *Louise.* **Open** *daily noon–3 and 7–11.*

Its high standards of Belgian and French cuisine have earned this restaurant a seriously good reputation. On the first floor overlooking the Jardin d'Egmont.

Moderate

L'Entrée des Artistes E7

42 Place du Grand-Sablon, **t** *02 502 2161;* **metro** *Porte de Namur or Gare Centrale; tram 92, 93 or 94.* **Open** *daily 8am–2am.*

This French brasserie can be a pleasant spot to while away a bit of time on the Place du Grand-Sablon. The lunch menu (typical French fare), which is decent value in comparison to many of the cafés across the square, ensures a clutter of business lunchers around 1pm.

De Skieven Architek C8

50 Place du Jeu de Balle, **t** *02 514 4369; bus 48.* **Open** *daily 6am–1am.*

Welcoming modern bar/café with a sense of history (see p.104). Sandwiches, home-baked pastries, Belgian *plats du jour* (€10) and evening meals available.

Inexpensive

Le Bermuchet D8

198 Rue Haute, **t** *02 513 8882;* **metro** *Porte de Namur or Gare Centrale; tram 92, 93, 94.* **Open** *Mon–Fri noon–2.30 and 7–11.30, Sat 7–11.30pm, Sun noon–2.30pm.*

A truly relaxed and relaxing French bistro in the heart of Marolles – part of a new wave of establishments that are giving a hip edge to this otherwise rough-and-ready district. Predictable mix-and-match *brocante* feel to

the décor, behind a blue-washed façade. Though the menu is not huge, the bistro grub is tasty and excellent value, while the service is charming.

Brasserie Ploegmans D8

148 Rue Haute; bus 48. **Open** *daily 11am–2am.*

Dingy 1930s wood panelling, gravel-voiced card players and their dogs, pinball machines, and cellar-cool *kriek* and *faro* served from the barrel. You could probably find a more marollien dive than this – but would you want to?

Les Chevaliers F8

138 Bvd de Waterloo, **t** *02 537 0991;* **metro** *Louise.* **Open** *Mon–Fri 11–3 and 6.30–11, Sun 6.30–11pm.*

Above-average pizzas cooked in a wood-fired oven.

't Warm Water C8

19 Rue des Renards, **t** *02 513 9159;* **bus 20, 48.** **Open** *daily 8am–7pm.*

Authentic Marollien café that serves tasty, healthy and inexpensive bruxellois breakfasts (including muesli and yoghurt) and snacks.

Bruxellois' City

If you want to watch the locals as you guzzle *bruxellois* specialities, or you fancy getting in with the trendy crowd, try one of the following restaurants:

L'Amandier (bus 60, 37; *see p.234*), **La Belle Maraîchère** (metro Ste-Cathérine; *see p.230*), **Le Bermuchet** (metro Porte de Namur; *see p.229*), **Bonsoir Clara** (metro Bourse; *see p.230*), **Brasserie Ploegmans** (bus 48; *see p.229*), **Café Le Perroquet** (metro Gare Centrale; *see p.230*), **Chez Marius en Provence** (metro Porte de Namur; *see p.229*), **Chez Richard** (metro Porte de Namur; *see p.230*), **L'Esprit du Sel** (metro Schuman; *see p.232*), **Au Jour le Jour** (metro Porte du Namur; *see p.228*), **Mezzanine** (metro Schuman; *see p.232*), **Le Quai** (metro Ste-Cathérine; *see p.230*), **In 't Spinnekopke** (metro Bourse; *see p.231*), **Au Thé de Pékin** (metro Bourse; *see p.231*).

Cafés

Café Leffe E7
46 Place du Grand-Sablon, t 02 513 1999; metro Porte de Namur or Gare Centrale; tram 92, 93 or 94. Open Mon–Fri 10am–midnight, Sat and Sun 10am–1am.
This café perched at the end of the Grand-Sablon square, is regularly swamped at lunch time. They offer a tasty *plat du jour*, to go with a beer of your choice (or coffee), for €7.50.

Café Le Perroquet E7
Corner of Rue Watteeu and Rue Charles Hanssens; metro Gare Centrale. Open daily 10.30am–1am.
A genuine Art Nouveau setting for the young in-crowd of the Sablon. Simple, wholesome lunch dishes are posted on the blackboard daily, around €9.

Chez Richard E7
2 Rue des Minimes, t 02 512 1406; metro Porte de Namur or Gare Centrale; tram 92, 93 or 94. Open Mon–Wed 7am–2am, Thurs–Sat 7am–3am, Sun 9am–midnight.
A lively little café serving upmarket lunches to local business people (*foie gras*, Jerusalem artichoke). It's a little more relaxed than the other upper-crust lunching venues around the square. It mutates into a fashionable drinking den later in the evening.

La Kartchma E7
17 Place du Grand-Sablon, t 02 512 4310; metro Porte de Namur or Gare Centrale; tram 92, 93 or 94. Open daily 10am–4am.
Squeezed in between a string of other upmarket cafés which line Place du Grand-Sablon, though with perhaps a bit more individuality. It's small inside, with two levels and large Art Nouveau style mirrors. If the weather's good you can sit outside and catch a bit of hackneyed jazz from buskers who prowl the square. It calls itself a cocktail bar (claim a free *tapa* with your drink), though it serves the usual café fare from lunch time

onwards. A little snooty, like all the places round here.

Le Pain Quotidien E7
11 Rue des Sablons, t 02 513 5154; metro Porte de Namur or Gare Centrale. Open daily 7.30am–7pm.
One of the largest of this successful and alluring chain of upmarket sandwich and pastry cafés. Sandwiches made with the best ingredients on excellent bread, eaten on large shared tables in a country-style kitchen. Over the years, Le Pain Quotidien has become something of a Belgian institution.

North Central Brussels

Restaurants

Expensive

Les Algues D3
15 Place Ste-Cathérine, t 02 217 9012; metro Ste-Cathérine. Open daily noon–2.3 and 6.30–10.30. Cash only.
This upmarket restaurant on Place Ste-Cathérine, complete with lobster tanks and tropical fish, makes an excellent choice for a fishy feast. The marble entranceway sets the classical tone. The set menus, at €23.50, offer better value.

Le Quai C3
14 Quai aux Briques, t 02 512 3736; metro Ste-Cathérine. Open Mon–Fri noon–2 and 7–10, Sat noon–2 and 7–11, Sun noon–2pm.
Tiny restaurant with a dozen tables, but it's *the* place to eat lobster in Brussels.

De Ultieme Hallucinatie H1
316 Rue Royale, t 02 217 0614; metro Botanique. Open Mon–Fri 11am–2am, Sat and Sun 8pm–2am.
Famous Art Nouveau restaurant, with chandeliers, fireplace, side cabinets, ceiling mouldings, stained-glass partitions all of the period. It boasts an adventurous menu includes *magret de canard aux figues* and warmed *foie gras* with honey.

Outdoor City
Eating out in the open is an attractive option in a city with so much greenery. Buy some picnic goodies from one of the many fine delicatessens or *pâtisseries* and head for the parks in and around the city centre, or try one of the following restaurants/cafés with outdoor seating:
Fritland (metro Bourse; *see* p.225), **Friture Ste-Cathérine** (metro Ste-Cathérine; *see* p.231), **Gioconda' Store Convivio** (metro Horta; *see* p.233), **Jardin d'Espagne** (metro Schuman; *see* p.232), **La Kartchma** (metro Porte de Namur; *see* p.230), **Le Métropole** (metro de Brouckère; *see* p.232), **Du Mim** (metro Gare Centrale; *see* p.228), **Persepolis** (metro Ste-Cathérine; *see* p.232).

Moderate

Les Ateliers de la Grand Île C5
33 Rue de la Grande Île, t 02 512 8190; metro Bourse. Open Mon–Sat 8pm–dawn.
A raucous Russian restaurant set in an old low-ceilinged foundry with interlinking rooms and specialities from Russia, Ukraine, Siberia, Hungary, Georgia, Iran and the Balkans. The setting, the food, and the line-up of gypsy violinists (and vodkas) will set you up perfectly for an experimental evening.

La Belle Maraîchère C4
11 Place Ste-Cathérine, t 02 512 9759; metro Ste-Cathérine. Open Fri–Tues noon–3 and 6–9.30.
With its elegant late-19th-century air, this is one of the great fish restaurants in Brussels. The changing three-course menu includes such wonders as *saumon braisé au champagne*.

Bonsoir Clara C4
22–26 Rue Antoine Dansaert, t 02 502 0990; metro Bourse. Open daily noon–2.30 and 7–11.30.
Deliciously stylish restaurant in Paul Klee colours with low-key lighting, animated by the in-crowd. Inventive cuisine with lunch menu at around €15.

Brasserie Horta F–G3
Centre Belge de la Bande Dessinée, 20 Rue des Sables; **metro** *Botanique.* **Open** *Tues–Sun 10am–6pm.*
Stylish lunch-spot in the Comic Strip Museum, a popular venue for the design world. Menus at €3–30, and children's menus.

In 't Spinnekopke B4
1 Place du Jardin aux Fleurs, **t** *02 511 8695;* **metro** *Bourse.* **Open** *Sun–Fri 11–3 and 6–11, Sat 6–midnight.*
One of Brussels' oldest *estaminets* (its name means 'at the head of the little spider'), dating back to 1762, it's now a charming restaurant noted for its traditional Belgian cuisine. *Coquilles St-Jacques* (scallops) cooked in Trappist beer. Bargain weekday *plat du jour* at €10.

Kasbah C4
20 Rue Antoine Dansaert, **t** *02 502 4026;* **metro** *Bourse.* **Open** *daily 11–2 and 7–11.*
Wondrously theatrical Arabian Nights setting, under dozens of glowing glass lanterns, with top-notch Moroccan cooking. The *tajine aux pruneaux* (spiced Moroccan stew with prunes, €15) is particularly recommended.

La Marie Joseph C3
47–49 Quai au Bois à Brûler, **t** *02 218 0596;* **metro** *Ste-Cathérine.* **Open** *Tues–Sat noon–3 and 6.30–11.*
A modern fish restaurant in the Ste-Cathérine area with fish tanks, bright walls and contemporary art on display. The menu is extensive and the food is reliable.

Neos Kosmos C4
50 Rue Antoine Dansaert, **t** *02 511 8058;* **metro** *Bourse.* **Open** *Mon–Fri noon–2.30 and 6.30–midnight, Sat 6.30–midnight.*
This is probably the most refined Greek cuisine you will ever eat. Complete with stylish décor and very fashionable clientele.

La Piazzetta dei Latini D3
1 Place Ste-Cathérine, **t** *02 502 5030;* **metro** *Ste-Cathérine.* **Open** *Mon–Sat 11–7.*

A shop and restaurant stocked with Italian goodies. Dishes are displayed on the central buffet with the intention of luring you in to dine. Pastas, wines, oils and liquours are on sale for those who catch the Italian bug and want more.

Au Thé de Pékin D4
16–24 Rue de la Vierge Noire, **t** *02 513 4642;* **metro** *Bourse.* **Open** *daily noon–3 and 7–11.*
Large, better-than-average Chinese restaurant, where the local Belgian Chinese come to eat. Menus upwards of €18.

La Villette C4
3 Rue du Vieux Marché aux Grains, **t** *02 512 7550;* **metro** *Ste-Cathérine.* **Open** *Mon–Fri noon–3 and 7–11, Sat 7–11pm.*
Named after the old slaughter-houses of Paris – boldly advertising that this is a decidedly meat-orientated restaurant in a fish-dominated district. Charming, intimate and stylish. Light meals of salads, *américaine maison* (steak tartare), plus serious steaks to satisfy all waist-lines, although for these less beef-favoured days, the menu features a variety of other dishes, including fish.

Inexpensive

La Boussole C3
61 Quai au Bois à Brûler, **t** *02 218 5877;* **metro** *Ste-Cathérine.* **Open** *Sun–Fri 11.30–3 and 5.30–midnight, Sat 5.30pm–midnight.*
A good place to indulge in the all-important *moules et frites* experience away from the tourist crowds. Other restaurants serve a kilo of mussels; whereas here a kilo and a half of the unfortunate bivalves are dumped into an oven-friendly bucket and brought steaming to your table; you'll do well to get through it all. Otherwise, this standard brasserie is a decent place for an anonymous drink.

Le Corbeau E3
18 Rue St-Michel; **metro** *De Brouckère.* **Open** *Mon–Sat 10am–midnight.*
Salads and *plats chauds* for €7.

Den Teepot B4
66 Rue des Chartreux, **t** *02 511 9402;* **metro** *Bourse/Ste-Cathérine.* **Open** *Mon–Sat noon–2pm.*
This little restaurant is attached to a health food store that sells organic produce (most of which is imported from England). Committed vegetarians can let their hair down and choose anything off the menu, which mainly consists of grains and pulses.

Friture Ste-Cathérine D3–4
Place Ste-Cathérine; **metro** *Ste-Cathérine.* **Open** *Mon–Thurs 11–6.30, Fri and Sat 11–11.*
If you want to try real Belgian chips and mayonnaise from a good outdoor chip-stand, this could be the place. Properly double-fried *frites* €1.25, plus €0.50 for the mayonnaise, or one of the other sauces. Also *boulettes* (€1.25), *brochettes*, *curryworst* and soft drinks, which can be consumed on a bench in the marketplace.

La Marée C3
99 Rue de Flandre, **t** *02 511 0040;* **metro** *Ste-Cathérine.* **Open** *Mon–Sat noon–2.30 and 7.30–10; closed June.*
Charming, family-run fish restaurant with an escalating reputation amongst the locals.

Phat-Thai C4
32 Rue Jules Van Praet, **t** *02 511 8243;* **metro** *Bourse.* **Open** *Wed–Sat and Mon noon–2.30 and 6–midnight, Tues and Sun 6pm–midnight.*
All the rich and zingy Thai staples are on offer here, and at affordable prices. It's far from classy, but with eager-to-please staff, who make this place ideal for an inexpensive binge.

Cafés

Arteaspoon C4
32 Rue des Chartreux, **t** *02 513 5117;* **metro** *Bourse.* **Open** *Mon–Fri 11.30am–6pm, Sat noon–7pm.*
A unique place with the stated aim of marrying culture (fine art) and cuisine. It was conceived by

two art historians and the design of the café incorporates two exhibition spaces for temporary displays. The extensive menu offers a range of dishes, including *tapas, tagine, mandarlata, pissaladière* – all of which are prepared in unusual ways. If you're not wanting to eat, you can relax over a tea or coffee and leaf through some of the newspapers and art publications that hang from a rail.

Café de Markten C4
5 Oude Graanmarkt, t 02 514 6604; metro De Brouckère/Ste-Cathérine. Open Mon–Sat 11am–11pm, Sun 11am–6pm.
Attached to De Markten, the Flemish cultural centre, this is a relaxed place to read or have a bite to eat. The décor is minimal – high whitewashed walls and ventilation piping visible. Good place for a late breakfast; cornflakes, muesli, milkshakes and salads are served.

Le Métropole E3
31 Place de Brouckère; metro de Brouckère. Open Mon–Thurs 9am–1am, Fri and Sat 9am–2am.
One of the grandest cafés in Brussels, dating from 1890. Chandeliered luxury, with wicker chairs on the pavement, perfect for watching the world go by. *Petite restauration* offered at acceptable prices.

Le Pain Quotidien C4
16 Rue Antoine Dansaert; metro Bourse. Open daily 7.30am–7pm.
This branch was the very first of this chain of tasteful sandwich bars founded in 1991 and now something of an institution. Country décor and inventive rustic sandwiches, such as *bœuf au basilique* for around €5.

Persepolis C3
1 Quai aux Bois à Brûler, t 02 218 3278; metro Ste-Cathérine. Open Mon–Sat 11.30–3 and 5–11.
An unusual *friterie* on the corner of the fish market at Place Ste-Cathérine. Kebabs, *frites*, an array of flavoured mayonnaises...and Iranian caviar (for the more delicate palate).

Quartier Léopold

Restaurants

Expensive

Jardin d'Espagne M5
65–7 Rue Archimède, t 02 736 3449; metro Schuman. Open Mon–Fri noon–3 and 7–10, Sat 7–10pm.
An acclaimed Spanish restaurant with an emphasis on adventurous seafood concoctions. The décor is straight-laced and formal, while the garden (with fountain) provides an outdoor option.

Vimar L8
70 Place Jourdan, t 02 231 0949; metro Schuman. Open Mon–Sat noon–2.30 and 6.45–10.45.
A stylish setting of crisp linen for serious fish cuisine. Lunch menu at €24.50.

Moderate

Balthazar M5
63 Rue Archimède, t 02 742 0600; metro Schuman. Open Mon–Sat noon–2.30 and 7–11.
Although the specialities are all French-influenced, the menu here reads like a lucky dip of worldwide cuisine: *sushi, carpaccio,* feta salad, *risotto au citron et vodka,* to mention a few. It's extremely popular at lunch time, so definitely book ahead.

L'Esprit du Sel L8
52 Place Jourdan, t 02 230 6040; metro Schuman. Open daily noon–3 and 7–11.
Stylish backdrop to good Belgian and French cooking, including *salade tiède, waterzooi,* salmon and rabbit. Two-course 'business lunch' from €21.

Mezzanine N8–9
152 Av d'Auderghem, t/f 02 736 6606; metro Schuman. Open Mon–Fri noon–2.30 and 6.30–10.30, Sat 7–11pm.
It is well worth heading out to the Léopold quarter to track down this atmospheric little restaurant. With a sofa area for that predinner drink, an aquarium and two levels of tiled tables and wrought-iron chairs, it's a good spot to drag out the evening. The modern Belgian and French cuisine is daring and beautifully presented; ostrich, duck and exotic stuffed vegetables feature alongside an extensive list of European wines.

Sukhothai N9
135 Av d'Auderghem, t 02 649 4666; metro Schuman. Open Mon–Fri noon–2.30 and 7–11, Sat and Sun noon–2.30pm.
Friendly rattan-furnished Thai restaurant, with the full range of Thai favourites, such as *tom yam koong* (spicy soup with prawns and lemon grass). Lunch menu at around €13.

Taj Mahal P8
12 Av des Gaulois, t 02 703 0681; metro Mérode. Open Mon–Fri 12.30–2.30 and 6–11.30, Sat and Sun 6–11.30pm.
Tandooris and *tikkas* served in the Raj-like splendour of a *tous-les-Louis salon* on the first floor of a *maison de maître.* Set lunch available for €16.

Inexpensive

Bodeguilla M5
65–67 Rue Archimède, t 02 736 3449; metro Schuman. Open Mon–Sat noon–midnight.
A small tapas bar in the basement of the Jardin d'Espagne (*see* above). The perpetual throng of Spaniards instils an authentic buzz to the place. Come here for good-value snacking at about €2.50 per *tapa.*

The Pullman J7
12 Place du Luxembourg; metro Trône. Open Mon–Fri 11am–early hours (varies), Sat and Sun 11am–10pm.
One of a set of unpretentious bars around the Gare du Quartier Léopold. Beer at an honest €1.25; bar food such as *assiette Américaine-frites* (steak tartare and chips, €7.50).

Resto-Snack Cordon-Bleu J6
15a Rue Joseph II, t 02 230 9403; metro Maelbeek. Open Mon–Sat 11am–3pm.
Modest restaurant catering for discriminating office workers.

Sandwiches, and dishes of the day like *chicons au gratin* (€8); *carpaccio* of beef (€10).

Cafés

Le Bentley J7
10 Place du Luxembourg, t 02 230 2083; metro Trône. Open Mon–Fri 11am–midnight, Sat 11am–2am.
An attractive new café/bar opposite the train station, clearly aimed at lunching businessmen. There is modern art on the walls and a fresh look to the décor. Substantial salads and pizzas are the mainstay.

Cafétéria O7
Musée du Cinquantenaire; metro Mérode. Open Tues–Fri 9.30am–5pm, Sat and Sun 10am–5pm.
Elegantly refurbished rooms with rattan chairs and old paintings, serving snacks and more substantial salads (prawn, soused herring) and sandwiches. Eat early: it starts getting busy at midday.

Refresh M5
48 Rue Archimède, t 02 230 6911; metro Schuman. Open daily 10am–7pm.
A café attached to a gift shop serving healthy lunches with a Celtic and Nordic influence (reindeer and mushroom quiche). Traditional Irish breakfast is served on Saturday morning.

St-Gilles and Ixelles

Restaurants

Expensive

Chelsea E11
85 Chaussée de Charleroi, t 02 544 1977, w www.chelsea.be; metro Louise; tram 91 or 92. Open Mon–Thurs noon–2 and 7–11, Fri and Sat noon–2 and 7–midnight.
Set up in the style of a grand old Indian palace, with Rajhastani furniture, oriental rugs and delicate woodwork. Though the décor is arresting, the rooms are a little over-cluttered, as is the menu,

with dishes from around the globe. The specialities are French.

Tagawa H13
279 Av Louise, t 02 640 5095; metro Louise; tram 94. Open Mon–Fri noon–2 and 7–10.30, Sat 7–10.30pm.
First-class Japanese food – *sashimi, tempura* and so on. There's bamboo on the ceiling and cooks prepare the food in front of you. Up to €125 for a full meal, lunch menu at €55–80.

Moderate

L'Amadeus F11
13 Rue Veydt, t 02 538 3427; metro Louise. Open Tues–Sun noon–1am, Mon 6.30pm–2am; closed Aug.
A sophisticated restaurant and wine bar housed in Auguste Rodin's former studio. Ideal for a romantic night out, it boasts a generous wine list and extensive variety of classic and modern dishes. Particularly popular for Sunday brunch.

La Canne en Ville E–F14
22 Rue de la Réforme, t 02 347 2926; metro Horta; tram 92. Open Mon–Fri noon–2 and 7–10.30, Sat 7–10.30pm.
Charming restaurant in three small rooms decorated with 1900s tilework, paintings and walking sticks. Well-known for its first-rate French cuisine. Bargain lunch available for €11.

La Cuisine des Anges G11
13 Rue Defacqz, t/f 02 534 2440; tram 93, 94. Open Mon–Fri noon–2.30 and 7.30–9.30.
A French restaurant popular at lunch time. Decorated in rich terracotta colours with good service, well-presented food and the added touch of palate cleansers between each dish.

Les Foudres Off maps
14 Rue Eugène Cattoir, t 02 647 3636; tram 90 or 23; bus 95 or 96. Open Mon–Fri noon–2 and 7–10, Sat 7–10pm.
A wine-lover's paradise: a restaurant with wine shop attached (a *foudre* is a large wine cask). Excellent, well-balanced cuisine

Vegetarian Restaurants
Meat plays a central role in Belgian cuisine, but vegetarians aren't completely left out in the cold. Belgian chefs have become increasingly aware of the call for lighter dishes, and that sometimes means vegetarian. Even traditional Belgian cooking includes noted vegetarian dishes, such as *flamiche aux poireaux*, a kind of flan filled with leeks in a cream sauce. Egg dishes are excellent and, although vegetarians often get tired of being fobbed off with yet another omelette, omelettes in Belgium are actually extremely good. Asparagus, chicory and hop shoots often feature in meatless dishes. In restaurants, you may fare better if you pick and choose from the edges of the menu, ordering two starters instead of a main course and filling up on delicious, substantial puddings. Foreign restaurants, particularly Italian, Indian and Thai, usually cater more than adequately for vegetarians. There are also several specialist vegetarian restaurants, including **La Tsampa** in Rue de Livourne (*see* p.234), whose inspired cooking has come to the attention even of carnivore gastronomes. Others worthy of a mention include:
Shanti, 68 Av A. Buyl (*see* p.234), **Dolma**, 32a Chaussée d'Ixelles (*see* p.234), **Den Teepot**, 66 Rue des Chartreux (*see* p.231), **Sisisi**, 174 Chausée de Charleloi (*see* p.234), **Gioconda' Store Convivio**, 76 Rue de l'Agueduc (*see* p.233), **Le Pain Quotidien**, 11 Rue des Sablons (*see* p.230), 16 Rue Antoine Dansaert (*see* p.232) and 515 Chaussée de Waterloo (*see* p.234).

and fine wines. Set menus at around €30.

Gioconda' Store Convivio F13
76 Rue de l'Aqueduc, t/f 02 539 3299; metro Horta, tram 81. Open Mon–Sat noon–2.30 and 7–10.30.
An informal Italian restaurant and wine shop on the edge of villagey Place du Châtelain. On summer

evenings it's hugely popular, mainly with a young well-to-do crowd who sit at outside tables to nibble on the tasty selection of antipasti (it's help-yourself, so be sure to pile your plate high).

Le Living Room Off maps
50 Chaussée de Charleroi, **t** *02 534 4434;* **tram** *91 or 92.* **Open** *Mon–Fri noon–3 and 7–midnight, Sat 7pm–midnight.*
International, eclectic menu in a handsome town house, refurbished in a low-lit plush style. Extremely trendy.

La Quincaillerie F13
45 Rue du Page, **t** *02 538 2553;* **tram** *81 or 82.* **Open** *Mon–Fri noon–2.30 and 7–midnight, Sat and Sun 7pm–midnight.*
The name means 'hardware store' and that's what it is – a wonderful, invigorating brasserie installed between the ranks of wooden drawers in an authentic 1900s shop. Well-prepared French cuisine at around €35.

Shanti Off maps
68 Av A. Buyl, **t** *02 649 4096;* **tram** *93 or 94.* **Open** *Tues–Sat noon–2 and 6.30–10.*
A very good quality vegetarian restaurant, with food inspired by the Orient, Africa and southern Europe.

La Tsampa G12
109 Rue de Livourne, **t** *02 647 0367;* **metro** *Louise;* **tram** *93 or 94.* **Open** *Mon–Fri noon–2 and 7–9.30, Sat 7–9.30pm.*
A cut above the average vegetarian restaurant, beautifully set out at the back of a health-food shop. Japanese, Indian and Vietnamese touches add colour to an inventive menu, with main dishes at around €10.

Inexpensive

Dolma I11
329 Chaussée d'Ixelles, **t** *02 649 8981;* **tram** *81 or 82.* **Open** *Mon–Sat noon–2 and 7–9.30.*
Vegetarian restaurant with similar cuisine to Shanti, above. Live jazz, folk and world music on Wed, Fri and Sat.

Les Salons de l'Atalaïde Off maps
89 Chaussée de Charleroi, **t** *02 537 2154;* **metro** *Louise;* **tram** *91, 92.* **Open** *Sun–Thurs noon–2am, Fri and Sat 7pm–2am.*
Once a gigantic auction hall, now refurbished in exuberant oriental style for the chic set. The food is not all that great but the setting is. Ideal for tea and cake.

Cafés

A Malte D10
30 Rue Berckmans, **t** *02 537 0991;* **metro** *Louise.* **Open** *daily 10am–3am.*
Trendy café in a picturesque mixture of oriental, Mediterranean and attic style. Refined snacks at reasonable prices.

Le Pain Quotidien Off maps
515 Chaussée de Waterloo, **bus** *60 or 37.* **Open** *daily 7am–7pm.*
One of a small, stylish chain offering imaginative sandwiches made with hunks of rustic bread (€3–10) and washed down with cider, wine or coffee.

Rick's Café I13
344 Av Louise, **t** *02 647 7530;* **tram** *93 or 94.* **Open** *daily 11am–1am.*
Best of the new American-chic cafés, noted for its weekend brunch.

Sisisi E12
174 Chausée de Charleroi; **tram** *91 or 92.* **Open** *Mon–Fri 10am–2am, Sat and Sun noon–2am.*
A relaxed café/bar close to Musée Horta, serving delicious cakes, wholesome and healthy snacks and herbal teas. Full meals are also available.

Uccle

Restaurants

Expensive

L'Amandier Off maps
184 Av de Fré, **t** *02 374 0395;* **bus** *60 or 37.* **Open** *Mon–Sat noon–2 and 7–10.*
Good French food served amid elegant décor designed by Ralph Lauren: what the Francophones would call *huppé* (very select).

Art Nouveau City

For those who can't stop sightseeing even when they're eating, the following restaurants, cafés and bars are set in lovely Art Nouveau surroundings:
Brasserie Horta (metro Botanique; *see* p.231), **Café Le Perroquet** (metro Gare Centrale; *see* p.230), **Le Falstaff** (metro Bourse; *see* p.237), **Fin de Siècle** (metro Bourse; *see* p.239), **La Kartchma** (metro Porte de Namur; *see* p.230), **Du Mim** (metro Gare Centrale; *see* p.228), **De Ultieme Hallucinatie** (metro Botanique; *see* p.230).

A'mbriana Off maps
151 Rue Edith Cavell, **t** *02 375 0156;* **bus** *60.* **Open** *Mon noon–2.30pm, Wed–Fri and Sun noon–2.30 and 7–11.30, Sat 7–11.30pm; closed Aug.*
Elegant Italian restaurant, one of the best in Brussels. *Carpaccio* €13, grilled prawns, etc. Good-value set menu for €25, including wine.

La Villa Lorraine Off maps
28 Chaussée de la Hulpe, **t** *02 374 3163,* **w** *www.villalorraine.be;* **tram** *365.* **Open** *Mon–Sat; closed last 3 weeks in July.*
Luxurious elegance in this establishment at the edge of the peaceful Bois de la Cambre.

Moderate

Leonardo da Vinci Off maps
6 Rue du Postillon, **t** *02 347 0292;* **tram** *18.* **Open** *Mon–Sat noon–2.30 and 6–11.*
Friendly pizzeria with above-average Italian standards. Lunch menu at around €15.

Anderlecht and Koekelberg

Restaurants

Le Béguinage Off maps
3 Place de la Vaillance, **t** *02 523 0844;* **metro** *St Guidon.* **Open** *daily 11am–2am.* **Inexpensive.**
Stylish, agreeable tavern, serving food all day. *Plat du jour* at about €7.50.

Bruneau Off maps
73–75 Av Broustin, Koekelberg, t 02 427 69 78. **Open** *Thurs–Mon lunch and dinner, Tues lunch; closed Aug.*
Famously luxurious, much-garlanded restaurant, with three Michelin stars. Impressive *haute cuisine française*, and prices to match (€124, but set lunch €44).

In de Stad Brugge Off maps
29a Place de la Vaillance, t 02 521 2429; metro St Guidon. **Open** *daily noon–midnight.* **Moderate.**
Cosy old-fashioned brasserie serving steak and chips at €12.

Laeken and Heysel

Restaurants

Moderate

L'Arbre d'Or Off maps
Le Village at Bruparck, t 02 478 7209; metro Heysel. **Open** *daily 10am–11pm.*
Convincing traditional-style tavern-restaurant serving reasonably priced lunches.

Chez Léon Off maps
Le Village at Bruparck, t 02 478 7267; metro Heysel. **Open** *Sun–Fri 11.30am–11pm, Sat 11.30am–11.30pm.*
A new branch of the famous Chez Léon, serving mussels (€16) and other Belgian standards.

La Ferme du Wilg Off maps
164 Chaussée de Wemmel, t 02 420 5610; tram 19; bus 13 or 14. **Open** *Wed–Sun noon–midnight.*
Delightful converted 14th-century farmhouse (with garden in summer) known for its buffet meals (€12.25) and Scotch beef.

Woluwe St-Lambert, Woluwe St-Pierre and Tervuren

Restaurants

Expensive

3Couleurs Off maps
453 Av de Tervuren, t 02 770 33 21; metro Montgomery. **Open** *Tues–Fri noon–4 and 7–9, Sat 7–9pm, Sun noon–4pm; closed mid Aug–mid Sept.*
Comfortable, elegant restaurant that's justly celebrated for its supreme French cuisine.

Moulin de Lindekemale Off maps
6 Av J. F. Debecker, t 02 770 9057; metro Roodebeek. **Open** *Mon–Fri noon–2 and 6–9, Sat 6–9pm, Sun noon–2pm.*
A well-known restaurant in an old watermill. Even if the interior is not as atmospheric as its 15th-century origins would suggest, its French-style cuisine is supremely judged, backed by excellent service. The four-course set menu at €40 includes wines and is well worth devoting an afternoon to.

Moderate

Le Chalet Vert Off maps
145 Grenstraat (near the Musée de l'Afrique Centrale), t 02 767 7431; tram 44. **Open** *Sat–Thurs noon–midnight.*
French cuisine in a refined yet welcoming atmosphere. Menu €15.

Les Jardins de l'Europe Off maps
Woluwe Shopping Center, 202/98 Rue St-Lambert, t 02 762 6182; metro Roodebeek. **Open** *daily 10am–10pm.*
Busy and comfortable brasserie-style restaurant serving admirable food – far better than you might expect in a shopping centre! *Menus du jour* at €10 and €20.

Nightlife

Bars

As self-proclaimed beer capital of the world, Brussels' bar scene is something that ought not to be missed. The range of different bars and cafés (the two are interchangeable) is staggering, and licensing laws permit them to stay open as late as they like, so they tend to be convivial slow-paced places rather than high-octane beer-slugging conventions. That said, there are over a thousand different types of beer on offer – as well as wines, flavoured vodkas and other spirits – so there's no shame in getting a little fuzzy-headed.

On arrival, the best place to take in the Baroque splendour of the Grand' Place is from one of the grand cafés that occupy the square's old guildhouses, though these tend to be overpriced. Southwest of the Grand' Place is cobbled Rue du Marché au Charbon, which meanders down towards Boulevard Anspach and is lined with bars that come to life later in the day. The area south of Ste-Cathérine, around Place St-Géry, is dotted with hip bars and is particularly in vogue at the moment; the main square in Sablon is ringed by upper-crust establishments; while just down the hill in Marolles you'll find smoke-stained local haunts. It is well worth spending an evening or two out in the laid-back suburbs of St-Gilles and Ixelles, both of which are well endowed with watering holes and trendy hangouts.

Around the Grand' Place

A La Bécasse D4
11 Rue de Tabora, t 02 511 0006;
***metro** Bourse.* **Open** *Mon–Thurs 10am–1am, Fri and Sat 10am–2am, Sun 11am–12am.*
This famous drinking hall is not at all enticing from the outside; but press on past the flashing neon

sign and into a tiled alleyway. At the end is a tiny courtyard where you can drink jug-loads of grog off a beer barrel. Inside it's cosy and convivial. Founded 1793.

Le Booze 'n' Blues C5
20 Rue des Riches Claires, t 02 513 9333; ***metro** Bourse.* **Open** *Tues–Sun 4pm–6am.*
A long bar with bare bricks and blues screaming out from the Juke box in the corner. Cranky bar staff and trendy customers. Live blues is occasionally on show here.

Le Cerceuil E5
10–12 Rue des Harengs, t 02 512 3077; ***metro** Gare Centrale.* **Open** *Sun–Thurs 11am–2am, Fri–Sat 11am–5am.*
This bar is certainly unique. The Jupiler comes in huge skull-shaped mugs that are rattled down on to coffins (which serve as tables). There are also coffins nailed to the walls and hanging from the ceiling; and the music is dark and funereal. It feels like the horror ride at an amusement park. Peculiar and popular with curious tourists, though the beer isn't cheap.

La Chaloupe d'Or D5
24–25 Grand' Place; ***metro** Gare Centrale.* **Open** *daily 9am–1am.*
Celebrated and stylish Grand' Place bar/restaurant, set in the tailors' guildhouse and very popular with well-heeled locals and tourists.

Chez Toone E5
21 Petite Rue des Bouchers, t 02 511 7137; ***metro** Bourse.* **Open** *daily 12–12.*
The lilliputian bar attached to the Théâtre Toone (*see p.248*), with veteran puppets hanging from the ceiling. Though in the thick of touristic Brussels, it's a dim, cosy, characterful place with a good selection of beers.

Le Cirio D4
18 Rue de la Bourse; ***metro** Bourse.* **Open** *daily 10am–1am.*
Classic *fin de siècle* café packed with multiple mirrors, gilt, tourists and well-dressed old ladies with their lapdogs.

Couples' City

For an evening *à deux*, these bars have sophisticated, relaxed atmospheres where you can hear yourself think above the music:
L'Archiduc (metro Bourse; *see p.239*), **Le Bistro des Restos** (metro Horta; *see p.242*), **Café de l'Opéra** (De Brouckère, *see p.239*), **La Chaloupe d'Or** (metro Gare Centrale; *see p.237*), **Fin de Siècle** (metro Bourse; *see p.239*), **Mappa Mundo** (metro Bourse; *see p.238*), **Le Roy d'Espagne** (metro Gare Centrale; *see p.238*), **De Ultieme Hallucinatie** (metro Botanique; *see p.240*).

Coaster C5
28 Rue des Riches Claires, t 02 512 0847; ***metro** Bourse.* **Open** *daily 8pm–6am (or later).*
One of Brussels' committed night spots with an underground ambience, a range of cocktails and malt whiskies, table-football and the city's tiniest terrace.

Le Falstaff D5
19 Rue Henri Maus; ***metro** Bourse.* **Open** *daily 10am–1am.*
Large, classic 1903 Art Nouveau café with sweeping curves of woodwork (by Victor Horta's cabinet maker and decorator) and lots of impressive stained glass. Big mix of customers.

Le Fleur en Papier Doré D6
55 Rue des Alexiens, t 02 511 1659; ***metro** Anneessens.* **Open** *daily 11am–1am (or later).*
One of Brussels' drinking institutions, still riding on the back of its popularity with Magritte and the Dadaists in the 1920s (the walls are coated in Surrealist scribblings and pictures). The clientele is a mix of eccentric locals and tourists. Good beer from the barrel and light snacks.

Goupil Le Fol D5
22 Rue de la Violette, t 02 511 1396; ***metro** Bourse.* **Open** *8pm–6am.*
Probably the most eccentric bar in Brussels. An underground cavern stuffed with a lifetime of collectable clutter; old posters on the walls, Jacques Brel memorabilia

and dog-eared paperbacks on the shelves, LPs hanging from the rafters like roosting bats and an old Wurlitzer Juke box. It's so dark (only a scattering of candles) that you'll have problems reading; so sit back with a glass of fruit wine and absorb the melancholia of old French and Belgian *chanteurs*. Frequented by arty types with time on their hands.

À L'Imaige Nostre-Dame D5
8 Rue du Marché aux Herbes, t 02 219 4249; metro Bourse. Open daily 12–12.30, Wed closes 7.30.
A particularly atmospheric old bar set back from the street, with stained-glass windows and exposed beams. Good range of beers – try the speciality, Bourgogne de Flandres.

Java C5
31 Rue St–Géry, t 02 513 4979; metro Bourse. Open 5pm–dawn.
An attractive and funky little bar just south of Place St-Géry, with giant windows and a V-shaped mosaic-work bar that dominates the space inside. Laid back early in the evening, it fills out later on with young trendies and the tunes become a little harder.

Kafé Kan 'H D6
30 Place de la Vieille Halle aux Blés, t 02 502 0007; metro Gare Centrale. Open Wed 11am–6.30pm, Thurs–Sat 11am–late, Sun 11am–6.30pm.
This trendy bar with big old tables and muralled mirrors is part of the Kan 'H cultural centre. A resident DJ plays on Fridays and there are acoustic concerts on the second and fourth Saturdays of each month. The building is 17th-century and was first used as a sorting office.

Le Lion St-Géry C5
22 Place St-Géry, t 02 513 8600; metro Bourse. Open Mon–Sat 11am–2am (or later).
The back courtyard is one of the main reasons to visit this bar. It's a peaceful spot offering unique access to the remnants of the River Senne, which was covered centuries ago and now trickles

quietly beneath the city. Place St-Géry was once an island in the river. After 10pm the courtyard is closed to drinkers and the bar inside becomes another fashionable late-night drinking spot.

Mappa Mundo C4
2–6 Rue du Pont de la Carpe, t 02 514 3555; metro Bourse. Open daily 10am–3am.
A very fashionable bar which has pride of place on the corner of fashionable Place St-Géry. It's full of oak beams and nooks and crannies where you can hole up for the evening. Upstairs there are views over the square.

O'Reilly's D5
1 Place de Bourse, t 02 552 0480; metro Bourse. Open Mon–Fri 11am–2.30am, Sat–Sun 11am–4am.
A sprawling dingy Irish pub with Irish bar staff and a largely British clientele. Major sporting events are shown on the big screen inside to large crowds. During the day it is a quiet place to put up your feet. Later in the evening, as phantom 'last orders' approaches, expat revellers pack in the pints. Things quieten down again as the night progresses.

P. P. Café C4
28 Rue Jules Van Praet; metro Bourse. Open daily 12–3am.
Brussels' first cinema, the Pathé Palace, refurbished in pre-1940s style. Art Deco bar, velvet cinema seats, film music. Trendy.

Plattesteen C5
41 Rue du Marché au Charbon, t 02 512 8203; metro Bourse. Open Mon–Sat 11am–12am.
Popular with a diverse mix of Bruxellois, who come here to socialise, drink beer and fill up on chips and steak. In summer claim an outside table beneath the towering mural.

Le Roi des Belges C4
35 Rue Jules Van Praet, t 02 513 5116; metro Bourse. Open daily 11am–3am.
In recent years Place St-Géry has become one of the hip places to hang out in the evenings. This is one of the new cafés set up to

accommodate the young (mainly professional) crowd. Downstairs the design is sparse, with a steel spiral staircase leading to a 1970s-theme room upstairs. The usual mixture of Belgian and international drinks is served.

Le Roy d'Espagne D5
1 Grand' Place, t 02 513 0807; metro Gare Centrale. Open daily 10am–1am.
An institution: a wonderfully atmospheric bar/restaurant, with waiters in starched, medieval aprons. You pay for its magnificent position in the Grand' Place.

Au Soleil C5
86 Rue du Marché au Charbon, t 02 513 3430; metro Bourse. Open daily 11am–2am (or later).
From the Grand' Place meander along the curves of Rue du Marché au Charbon and you come to this bright and friendly bar, crowded day and night. It's popular with young arty folk and can get packed at weekends. The bar was formerly a gentlemen's outfitters and has retained many of the shop's original fittings.

Wilde C–D5
79 Bvd Anspach; metro Bourse. Open Mon–Thurs 8pm–4am, Fri–Sat 7pm–5am.
Down from O'Reilly's, this stylish-looking bar takes 1970s London as its theme. Unsurprisingly it is the haunt of Belgian anglophiles rather than Britons.

Marolles and Sablon

Brocante C8
170 Rue Blaes, t 02 512 1343; bus 48 (or 15min walk south of metro Gare Centrale). Open daily 11am–2am.
On the corner of Place du Jeu de Balle and appropriately named (it's full of junk, syphoned off the flea market presumably). Inside you'll be among Marolles' locals playing backgammon, slapping the owner's huge slack-jowled dog and chattering away in Marollien (a Flemish dialect unique to this old artisan quarter). If this is all

too much, you can survey the market from beneath an umbrella on an outside table.

Chez Richard E7

2 Rue des Minimes, t 02 512 1406; metro Porte de Namur/Gare Centrale; tram 92, 93 or 94. **Open** *Mon–Wed 7am–2am, Thurs–Sat 7am–3am, Sun 9am–12am.*
This cramped little café/bar leads a double life. During the day it serves upmarket lunches to local business people; at night it mutates into a drinking den fashionable with rich young people who shout over the music. At night it is a good alternative to the snooty café/bars that line the Place du Grand-Sablon.

CyberTheatre G8

4–5 Av de la Toison d'Or, t 02 512 1406, e cyberbar@ arcadis.be; metro Porte de Namur. **Open** *Mon–Wed 7am–2am, Thurs–Sat 7am–3am, Sun 9–9.*
Futuristic and stylish bar, restaurant and multimedia performance venue, the best among a rash of new cybercafés.

Havana D8

4 Rue de l'Epée, t 02 502 1224; bus 48 (or 15min walk from metro Gare Centrale). **Open** *Tues–Thurs 12am–2am, Fri–Sat 6pm–late.*
This Cuban-themed bar is indicative of the way Marolles is going (as *chichi* establishments begin to set up shop along the rundown streets of this proud working-class district). Bare bricks, simple décor, a special smoking room for the enjoyment of Havana cigars, and an assortment of rum-based cocktails attract a young lively crowd, particularly on Saturday nights.

Indigo C8

160 Rue Blaes; bus 48 (or walk from metro Gare Centrale). **Open** *Wed–Fri 10–3.30pm, Sat–Sun 8.30–5.30.*
Busy, arty, joyous café decorated from head to toe in miscellaneous *brocante* (junk); its walls and furniture are splashed with colour. There's an open terrace to the rear for warm summer evenings.

De Skieven Architek C8

50 Place du Jeu de Balle, t 02 514 4369; bus 48 (or 15min walk from metro Gare Centrale). **Open** *daily 6am–1am.*
Architect is a dirty word in Marolles – thanks to the monstrous proportions of the Palais de Justice which looms over the district, and which forced many locals out of their homes when it was built during the 19th century. This is the most prominent bar on the square, and is particularly popular around lunchtime when the flea market is on. There are snacks, newspapers and a good beer menu.

North Central Brussels

L'Archiduc C4

6 Rue Antoine Dansaert; metro Bourse. **Open** *daily 4pm–6am.*
Authentic Art Deco gem and at the core of Brussels' nightlife. Designed like the interior of a cruise ship, it has remained intact since its opening in the 1930s. Jazz and '30s music only; quality jazz concerts are held irregularly.

La Best Toffe H4

6 Place de la Liberté, t 02 218 1710; metro Madou. **Open** *Mon–Sat 10am–12am.*
Pictures of James Dean, Elvis and Engelbert Humperdinck adorn the walls inside this café/bar, where you'll find an array of locals putting away glass upon glass of beer. Outside (merging with the other three or four cafés), tables sprawl beneath the cover of trees on this leafy little square – a pleasant and unlikely spot that has become *à la mode* with the young business crowd in this area.

Le Bier Circus H4

89 Rue de l'Enseignement, t 02 218 0034; metro Madou. **Open** *Mon–Fri 12–2.20 and 6–12, Sat 6–12.*
A tiny and eccentric bar with 200 Belgian beers on offer, and almost as many beer glasses lining the walls. Give your tastebuds a ride and try some of the brews that are virtually unique to this bar.

Café de l'Opéra E4

4 Place de la Monnaie; metro De Brouckère. **Open** *daily 10am–2am.*
Welcoming 1920s-style café, with pavement terrace over the Théâtre de la Monnaie.

Fin de Siècle C4

9 Rue des Chartreux, t 02 513 5123; metro Bourse. **Open** *Tues–Sun 5pm–1am.*
Behind an Art Nouveau façade and lined with contemporary art for sale, this long bar is a sophisticated drinking spot that is very popular at the weekends.

Greenwich C4

7 Rue des Chartreux, t 02 511 4167; metro Bourse. **Open** *daily 11am–2am.*
There's something special about this old bar; at any hour of day or night a respectful hush prevails as drinkers play chess or get down to some serious reading, and barmaids tiptoe about like library assistants. The walls are wood-panelled, the ceiling high, and the atmosphere – like the beer – cloudy, befuddled and a world apart from the street outside; there's no wonder it was a favourite with Magritte.

Kafka D4

5 Rue de la Vierge Noire, t 02 513 5489; metro De Brouckère. **Open** *daily 4pm–3am (or later).*
A traditional-style *bruxellois* café with rustic décor, worn-out tables and a mixed crowd of French and Flemish speakers. Lots of vodkas.

Loplop Café E4

29 Rue de l'Ecuyer, t 02 512 1889; metro De Brouckère. **Open** *Mon–Sat 9am–4am, Sun 11am–4am.*
The rash of colours on the walls, the clutter, and the wide range of drinks on offer reflect the cosmopolitan clientele at this piano bar in the centre of town. It's a little less hectic upstairs.

La Lunette E4

3 Place de la Monnaie, t 02 218 0378; metro De Brouckère. **Open** *daily 8am–1am (or later).*
An old café/bar with high ceilings, tall mirrors and wood panelling. In

Beer

Belgian beer enjoys an unparalleled reputation. For beer lovers, it is the object of pilgrimage and reverence. For others it can be a revelation. Belgium has some 400 different kinds of beers produced by 115 breweries (in 1900 there were 3,223 breweries). Each has its own distinctive style, and even the ubiquitous Stella Artois and Jupiter, made by the brewing giant Interbrew, are a cut above your average lagers.

A word first of all about how beer is made. The essential ingredient is grain – usually barley, but sometimes wheat. (This explains why beer is the historic beverage of grain-growing northern Europe, just as wine is the drink of warmer climes further south.) The barley is soaked in water to stimulate germination, then dried in a kiln to produce malt. The malted barley is then crushed and boiled before being left to ferment, during which process the natural sugars (maltose) and any added sugars are converted into alcohol. Yeast is the agent of fermentation. Some yeasts rise to the top of the brew, forming a crust that protects the beer from the air; this process creates a richly flavoured 'top-fermented' ale. Other yeasts sink to the bottom to make a lighter, clearer, lager-type 'bottom-fermented' beer. The choice of barley, the preparation of the malt, the quality of the water, and the type of yeast used all influence the final taste of the beer. Hops provide a spicy, bitter tang and may be added at various stages of brewing.

With Belgian beer there is no great concern about whether it is served from the keg or in bottles. Some do come in kegs, but many of the best are bottled. The labels on the bottles give the vital statistics, including the all-important alcohol content. By and large Belgian beer has a higher level of alcohol by volume than equivalent British or American beers. Specialist bottled beers start at about 5%; stronger brews measure 8% or 9%. The maximum alcohol content for beer is about 12% – four times the strength of most lager. Bush beer is one of several brands that claims to be Belgium's strongest beer: one bottle is very pleasant; after two bottles you feel as though your knees have been hinged on backwards. Some breweries (especially the abbeys) classify their beer as double/dubbel (dark and sweet, about 6.6%) or triple/tripel (paler and lighter, but stronger, about 8%). Labels also instruct you about the correct temperature at which to serve the beer and the shape of glass to be used. Every brew is assigned its own glass shape, from tumbler to goblet, and this is something that any bartender instinctively understands. Only in the appropriate glass can the merits of a particular beer be fully savoured.

The most famous bottled beers are those produced by the Trappists – the order of Cistercian monks which observe the strict (these days not quite so strict) order of silence. In the 19th century the monasteries produced beer for the consumption of the monks, but then they began to sell it to the outside world in gradually increasing quantities. Trappist beer has become a major income-earner for the monasteries, produced on a semi-industrial basis, nowadays largely by lay workers rather than monks. Nonetheless, the monasteries retain strict control over their product and have resisted offers of expansion into the large-scale export markets, which would rapidly lap up any increased production. These Trappist beers are top-fermented ales, with extra yeast added at bottling to produce a second fermentation in the bottle. As a result a white sediment forms: allow the beer to stand to let it settle, then when you open the bottle pour the entire contents off all at once to avoid disturbing the sediment (it is not harmful, just rather yeasty).

The most famous Trappist beer is probably Chimay, produced by the abbey of Notre-Dame de Scourmont, which in the 1860s became the first to release its

summer tables stretch out across the Place de la Monnaie to lure shoppers off their aching feet.

A la Mort Subite E4
7 Rue Montagne aux Herbes Potagères; metro Gare Centrale. **Open** *Mon–Sat 11am–1am, Sun 12.30pm–1am.*
This famous bar, designed by Paul Hamesse in 1910 and done up like a Rococo *boudoir*, has had a type of *gueuze* named after it.

De Ultieme Hallucinatie H1
316 Rue Royale; metro Botanique. **Open** *Mon–Fri 11am–2am, Sat–Sun 5pm–3am.*

Famous Art Nouveau bar with beautiful ornate curves everywhere you look. Formal service. Drinks and light meals from the bar; for the restaurant, *see p.230.*

Quartier Léopold

Het Ketje J8
4 Place du Luxembourg; metro Trône. **Open** *Mon–Fri 11am–4am, Sat and Sun 11–9.30pm.*
Ketje is a cherished *bruxellois* term for a young lad – ironic when you take a look at the customers, who've probably been drinking

here since the war. This is a good old regular brasserie that will no doubt outlive the pretentions of the flashy new places that have sprung up to cater for the young beer-thirsty Eurocrats. Simple food served throughout the day.

L'Horloge du Sud J9
141 Rue du Trône, t 02 512 1864; metro Trône. **Open** *Mon–Fri 11am–1am, Sat–Sun 5pm–2am.*
This bar does everything it can to drill home its South American theme (increasingly popular in Brussels): marimbas are scattered about; samba and salsa play in the

beers to the public. Today Chimay is available as 7%, 8% and 9% alcohol by volume as indicated by red, white and blue labels respectively. Kept for several years, Chimay Bleu becomes ever richer, its flavour drifting towards port.

The Trappist abbey of Orval, whose brewery is run entirely by lay staff, produces one brand only, sold in distinctive pear-shaped bottles. This is an excellent pale brew, pitched at a fairly modest 5.2% alcohol. Its distinctive spicy flavour derives from the dry hops added at the end of fermentation. Excellent Trappist beers are also produced in the traditional copper kettles of the abbey at Rochefort, including a power-packed version at 11.3%, while the abbey of Westmalle, near Antwerp, produces famous *dubbel* and *tripel* ales. Only Trappist monasteries are allowed to produce Trappist beer. Other monasteries produce similar 'abbey beers' – sometimes franchising their names to commercial brewers, so the monastery connection may be tenuous. Leffe is an abbey beer now owned by Interbrew, but it is still an excellent brand, with several styles from pale to rich and dark, including the warming Radieuse (8.5%).

For a refreshing change, try the remarkable 'white' beers – *witbier/bière blanche*. The most famous are produced at Hoegaarden, to the east of

Brussels. Hoegaarden (also a brand name) is a wheat beer flavoured with a touch of coriander; it has a delicious peppery tang and a modest alcohol content (5%) – excellent for that jaded moment in the late afternoon. Some *blanche* drinkers even add a slice of lemon to their glass. It is often a little cloudy – don't send it back: that is how it should be! Other good white beers are Brugs Tarwebier and Blanche de Namur.

Numerous beers in Belgium belong to no category but their own. Duvel is a famous brand produced at Breendonk in Flanders – strong (8.5%), pale and with a distinctive hoppy bitterness. De Verboden Vrucht (Forbidden Fruit) is a good strong ale (9%) from Hoegaarden, which benefits from secondary fermentation in the bottle; it has a sumptuous label, portraying Adam and Eve in the Garden of Eden clasping glasses of beer. Bruges has its deliciously spicy Brugse Tripel, which weighs in at 9%. Kwak, from east Flanders, is most readily associated with the large one-litre, trumpet-shaped glasses in which it is traditionally served. There is a knack to drinking from these: novices tend to tip it too fast at a critical moment and get a dowsing. A number of breweries produce special Christmas brews with festive labels, such as Blanche de

Noël and also the power-packed Bush Noël.

Last but by no means least is the family of *lambic* beers, unique to the valley of the River Senne. What makes *lambic* so special is that it is 'spontaneously' fermented by the agency of naturally occurring airborne yeasts – tiny fungi called *Brettanomyces* that are found only in Brussels itself and in the countryside to the west. Fermentation begins within three days, but the beer is allowed to age for a year or more. *Lambic* is a fairly strong (about 5.5%) still beer with a distinctive sour, winey flavour – something of an acquired taste.

Cherries (formerly from the Brussels suburb of Schaerbeek) may be macerated in *lambic* to produce the fruity beer called *kriek*; raspberries are added to make *framboise*; and sugar and caramel are added to make *faro*. Blended *lambic* of different ages is allowed to ferment a second time in bottles to become the slightly fizzy sour beer known as *gueuze*.

These are the really essential flavours of Brussels, and worth seeking out in bars where they are available on tap. Or better still, go to the Musée Bruxellois de la Gueuze (see p.138), housed in the Cantillon brewery in Anderlecht, where *gueuze* is still made on cold winter nights in the traditional manner.

---

background; a variety of rums are served; and the bar is even orientated so that it is south-facing. It is furnished simply, with old wooden tables and chairs dotted around a large space.

James Joyce M5–6
34 Rue Archimède, t 02 230 9894; metro Schuman. Open daily 11am–2am.
One of numerous Irish pubs in the area, quieter than the others and not overly themed, with a pleasant little garden. A good place for a quiet pint in the early evening – if you're not bothered

by the exclusively English clientele, or the businessmen in the corner arguing over the pros and cons of a federal Europe. Even sober, the spiral staircase to the toilets demands concentration.

The Pullman J7
12 Place du Luxembourg; metro Trône. Open daily 7am–12am.
A bar where *'il n'y a pas de clef'* ('there is no key'). In other words, it is always open to serve a cast of characters in a 24-hour slice-of-life drama. These include overalled city workers dropping by at 7am

for *un petit coup*, usually a small beer, to start the day on a good note (this is a dying tradition), and youthful party-goers returning home after late-night revels.

St-Gilles and Ixelles

The Bank G12
79 Rue du Bailli, t 02 537 5265; tram 81, 8 or, 94. Open daily 12pm–1am.
An Irish pub set in an old bank with safety deposit boxes along the walls. Bar staff will serve you

Outdoor City

Late on summer evenings, *bruxellois* move outside and cluster in various of the city's squares and streets:

La Best Toffe (metro Madou; *see* p.239), **Brocante** (metro Gare Centrale, *see* p.238), **Indigo** (metro Gare Centrale; *see* p.239), **James Joyce** (metro Schuman; *see* p.241), **Le Lion St-Géry** (metro Bourse; *see* p.238), **La Lunette** (metro De Brouckère; *see* p.239), **Plattesteen** (metro Bourse; *see* p.238), **Le Roy d'Espagne** (metro Gare Centrale; *see* p.238).

at your table, and it's not as rowdy as the standard Irish pub in Brussels. Guinness and Murphys are served alongside a number of Belgian beers.

Le Bistro des Restos F13
39 Rue du Page, t 02 534 3544; metro Horta, tram 81. Open Mon–Fri 11am–3am, Sat 5pm–3am, closed Sun.
Atmospheric candle-flecked interior, with tables outside in summer. Simple food is served and there is a good range of beers. A good spot to pass an evening in this restful suburb.

Chez Moeder Lambic Off maps
68 Rue de Savoie; metro Horta. Open daily 4–4.
Celebrated bar boasting 1,000 different beers, in the rough-and-ready district of St-Gilles.

L'Esquisse Off maps
80 Chaussée de Charleroi, t 02 534 5659; tram 91 or 92. Open Tues–Sun 7pm–dawn.
A trendy candle-lit bar that attracts a young well-heeled crowd. Plenty of effort has gone into the décor – abstract oil paintings adorn the walls, the glass-topped tables are filled with either maize or dried flowers and, though there's plenty of colour splashed about the walls, there's a warmy, earthy feel to the place. If you're peckish in the early hours, there's a selection of chunky sandwiches and salads.

Les Salons de l'Atalaïde Off maps
89 Chaussée de Charleroi; tram 91 or 92. Open daily 12–3 and 7–12.
Huge auction hall, refurbished in fairylike, exuberant, oriental style with round tables, drapes and attentive service.

L'Ultime Atome G9
14 Rue St Boniface, t 02 511 1367; metro Porte de Namur. Open Mon–Fri 8.30am–1am, Sat–Sun 9am–1am.
A hugely popular café/bar at the heart of suburban Ixelles. Wines and a good selection of beers are available. Hearty food at reasonable prices incites fierce competition for tables during the early evening.

Verschueren Off maps
11–13 Parvis de St-Gilles, t 02 539 4068; metro Parvis St-Gilles. Open Sun–Thurs 8am–1am, Fri and Sat 8am–2am.
Though you won't find any tourists here, this workaday old bar is well known among Bruxellois. It is one of the few places licensed to serve *lambic* from the Cantillon brewery (*see* p.138). The décor is practical and non-descript, and both bar and clientele lack any pretensions. You'll find the bar at the foot of the Église du Parvis.

Zen F13
77 Rue du Page, t 02 538 9931; tram 91 or 92. Open Mon–Sat 5pm–2am.
A tranquil bar in the Châtelain village district of Ixelles, with a regular crowd who stop by for cocktails before a big night out. Relaxed, though not at all traditional in feel.

Clubs

On Fridays and Saturdays the young at heart head for the many trendy bars, then those with energy still to burn dance until sunrise. This is a lively and, by and large, amicable club scene, but it's the people rather than the venues that make it work. Ask around in the livelier bars for tips about which places are currently on form.

Bazaar C8
60 Rue des Capucins, t 02 511 2600; metro Porte de Hal. Open Tues–Sun 8pm–1am.
Chic, atmospheric nightspot, laid-back ethnic music, two bars, restaurant serving exotic dishes (crocodile et al) and a dance floor that avoids the sins of 'tchak-boom-tchak'.

Beursschouwburg C4
22 Rue Auguste Orts, t 02 513 8290; metro Bourse. Open Thurs–Sat 8pm onwards.
A large bar featuring funk and acid jazz music (and occasional live bands). Go late if you want lots of company.

Do Brasil B6
88 Rue de la Caserne, t 02 513 5028; metro Lemonnier. Open Wed–Sat 8–late.
Thumping Brazilian fun: tropical food with flair, and samba music to dance to.

Le Bulex Off maps
24 Rue Mommaerts, t 02 534 2828; metro Ribaucourt. Open first Sat of the month after 10pm.
Famed organizers of wild megaparties, throbbing rhythms and massed fun into the early hours. Venues change so phone first. At weekends use Fiestaphone (*t 02 534 2392*).

Canoa Quebrad C5
53 Rue du Marché au Charbon, t 02 511 1354; metro Bourse. Open Thurs–Sat 10.30pm onwards.
A temple of salsa, samba and merengue, with a small dance floor. When you need to take a break, there are mexican cocktails and a chill-out bar at the back.

Le Fool Moon Off maps
26 Quai de Mariemont, Molenbeek-St-Jean, t 02 410 1003; metro Molenbeek. Open daily 9pm–late.
Safe clubbing territory with house beats on the main floor and hip-hop upstairs. The club is quite a way out of the centre, though, so you'll need a taxi to get you back into town.

Le Fuse C8
*208 Rues Blaes, **t** 02 567 1697;*
***metro** Porte de Hal. **Open** Fri and*
Sat after 11pm.
Hottest techno spot in town,
boasting top DJs from the world
over. Also a venue for live music
during the week.

Le Garage E5–6
*16 Rue Duquesnoy, **t** 02 512 6622;*
***metro** Bourse. **Open** Tues–Sat after*
11pm; Sun is gay night.
Spacious disco with energetic
light show – throbs when the
crowds swell at weekends.

Jeux d'Hiver Off maps
Chemin du Gymnase (Bois de la
*Cambre); **tram** 93 or 94. **Open***
*Thurs and Sat 8–late; **adm** free*
(priority to members).
Disco at the edge of the woods,
next to the Théâtre de Poche,
frequented by the youthful smart
set – BCBG (*bon chic, bon genre*).

Mirano Continental I4
*38 Chaussée de Louvain, **t** 02 218*
*5772; **metro** Madou. **Open** Sat after*
11pm.
A converted cinema, now one of
the city's best and most popular
dance spots.

La Rose C4
*21 Rue des Poissonniers, **t** 02 513*
*4325; **metro** Bourse. **Open** Wed–Sun*
5pm onwards.
A splendidly seedy *café/bar-
dansant* close to the Bourse, with
live band, reflector-globes and
toyboys in flares: weird but pure
Jacques Brel.

Sonik C5
112 Rue du Marché aux Charbon,
t** 02 511 9985; **metro** Bourse. **Open
Wed–Sat 11pm–6am.
An intimate club in the heart of
town with a range of DJs who play
house, techno and drum 'n' bass.

Le Sud E4
*43–45 Rue de l'Ecuyer, **t** 02 513 3765;*
***metro** De Brouckère. **Open** Fri and*
Sat after 10pm.
Pieced together from a set of
abandoned houses around a
covered courtyard, this unusual
disco and bar provides a variety of
ambiences under one roof.

Tour et Taxi Off maps
*5 Rue Picard, **t** 02 420 5505; **metro***
*Ribaucourt. **Open** first Fri of month*
10pm–5am.
Young clubbers flock to the huge
space within this old church for
trance and house, and a great
laser display.

Who's Who Land C6–7
*17 Rue de Poinçon, **t** 02 512 5270;*
***metro** Anneessens. **Open** Fri and*
Sat 11pm–4am.
Top house club. Seriously throbbing spaceship for athletic
oblivion – with a quieter refuge
and bar, and adjoining theatre
into which the party (often 2,000
people) spills on Saturdays.

Entertainment

Brussels has all the mainstream cultural attractions of a large European city – a wide choice of international films, imported rock concerts and jazz venues. It also has an armful of theatres (fine, if you speak the language), some seriously good classical music and the opera of the Théâtre de la Monnaie, which commands considerable international respect. Unique to Brussels are the famous Toone puppets, which are to theatre what the Manneken-Pis is to sculpture.

Listings

The best listings magazine for the English-speaking visitor is the pull-out supplement called What's On (in Brussels and other towns and cities) which comes with the weekly publication The Bulletin (out on Thursdays, €2.50). The magazine itself also contains reviews of what's currently on offer. The most widely available French listings magazine for Brussels is the monthly Kiosque (€1.50). The tourist office also publishes a free guide to the main cultural events in the city. A useful Web site is w www.agenda.be.

Ticket Agencies

Tickets to mainstream events can be booked (for a small charge) through the tourist office in the **Grand' Place, t** 02 513 8940 (see p.68). Other agencies include:

Auditorium 44, 44 Boulevard du Jardin Botanique, **t** 02 218 2735.

FNAC, City 2, 123 Rue Neuve, **t** 02 209 2239.

Info Ticket, t 02 504 0390.

Music

Opera and Classical

Belgium must be the only country in the world that was born out of an opera. A performance at the Théâtre de la Monnaie led directly to the revolution of 1830 (see p.117). La Monnaie/De

Munt is still the jewel in the crown of Brussels' cultural life. Its company is renowned for the high quality of its productions, its inventive staging, and as a nursery for talent (while the big stars, and their big fees, are shunned). Opera tickets may be hard to come by, but there is no shortage of classical music concerts. There are a number of well-established concert halls, but look out also for one-off performances held at other venues, such as the churches (Cathédrale St-Michel, Eglise Notre-Dame du Sablon, Eglise Ste-Cathérine, Eglise des Minimes, and so forth).

Le Cercle E7
20–22 Rue Ste-Anne, **t** 02 514 0353; **metro** Porte de Namur.
Venue for small-scale classical music and jazz concerts in Sablon.

Cirque Royal H4
81 Rue de l'Enseignement, **t** 02 218 2015; **metro** Parc.
Venue for visiting opera companies and dance troupes – as well as rock groups.

Conservatoire Royal de Musique F7
30 Rue de la Régence, **t** 02 511 0427; **metro** Louise.
Brussels' venerable Conservatory, which runs a busy programme, mainly of chamber music.

Maison de la Radio J11
Place Eugène Flagey; **tram** 71 or 94.
Classical and contemporary music concerts in this outlandish 1930s landmark (see p.157). It has recently been bought by the Brussels Public Transport Authority (STIB) with the declared intention of continuing to use it as a music venue after several years in limbo.

Musée Charlier I6
16 Av des Arts, **t** 02 218 5382; **metro** Arts-Loi.
Inspirational turn-of-the-century setting for chamber music.

Théâtre de la Monnaie E4
Place de la Monnaie, **t** 02 229 1211; **metro** De Brouckère.
Brussels' most celebrated theatre, devoted to opera, ballet and

classical music concerts since 1850. Many of the tickets are taken by season-ticket holders, and the rest are snapped up fast – so book early (see also p.117).

Palais des Beaux-Arts G6
10 Rue Royale, **t** 02 507 8220; **metro** Gare Centrale.
This is the home of the Philharmonique and the Orchestre National de Belgique/Het Nationaal Orkest van België, and is also one of the key venues for visiting orchestras.

Jazz, Rock and World Music

Although Belgium does have its own rock culture and some very energetic bands, the world still awaits a Belgian band of truly international distinction, though the meteoric rise of rock band Deus goes some way towards achieving this.

Meanwhile, Brussels attracts many of the major international stars, who seem to respond well to their enthusiastic reception, and to the comparatively modest scale of most of the venues.

Jazz has a loyal and devoted following, and blossoms during the annual three-day Brussels Jazz Rally (end April, early May), when mainly European artists invade dozens of bars and small venues in and around the city centre in a happy festival of drinking and foot-tapping. See also Le Botanique (p.247), Le Cercle and Cirque Royal (see both opposite).

Ancienne Belgique C5
110 Bvd Anspach, **t** 02 584 2400; **metro** Bourse.
Medium-sized venue for blues, rock and pop, in a refurbished variety hall.

L'Archiduc C4
6 Rue Antoine Dansaert, **t** 02 512 0652; **metro** Bourse. **Open** daily 4pm–4am.
This renowned jazz café has been going since the 1930s. There's free entrance to jazz sets every Saturday afternoon.

Dolma H9
329 Chaussée d'Ixelles, t 02 649 8981; tram 81 or 82. Open Fri and Sat 7pm onwards; closed Aug.
Vegetarian restaurant which on Fridays and Saturdays doubles up as a popular venue for jazz, blues, folk and world music.

Fool Moon Off maps
26 Quai de Mariement, t 02 410 1003; metro Molenbeek.
Live dance, rock and world music.

Forest National Off maps
36 Avenue du Globe, t 02 340 2211; tram 52 or 48.
This is the largest and somewhat soulless rock venue in Brussels – an arena for 6,000 adoring fans; also plays host to opera and classical music events.

Les Halles de Schaerbeek I1
22a Rue Royale Ste-Marie, t 02 218 0031; tram 92, 93 or 94.
Formerly the main rock venue. After massive renovation this iron- and glass-covered market has now re-emerged as a key venue for rock, pop and world music.

The Music Village D5
50 Rue des Pierres, t 02 513 1345, w www.themusicvillage.com; metro Bourse. Open Wed–Sat 7.30–late; adm €7.50 (or more depending on band), yearly membership €9.
This jazz lovers' haunt is a relatively new venue, though you wouldn't know it – it has the feel of a long-established place. A long bar runs along the back wall with the stage as the focal point. Tiny nail drawers and spades depicted in the stained-glass façade remain from the time when the building was used as a hardware store.

Sounds H9
28 Rue de la Tulipe, t 02 512 9250; bus 54 or 71.
Jazz, folk, funk and South American.

La Soupape Off maps
26 Rue A. de Witte, t 02 649 5888; bus 71.
A café/theatre which specializes in Belgian singer-songwriters.

Travers H2
11 Rue Traversière, t 02 218 4086; metro Botanique.
One of the key jazz and world music venues, which also hosts occasional theatre.

Cinema

Belgium's domestic film industry has had a small but devoted following among arthouse audiences for several decades, fuelled by such work as the touching semi-Surrealist films of André Delvaux, including *L'Homme au Crâne Rasé* (1965) and *Un Soir, un Train* (1968). In 1992, the joint directors Rémy Belvaux, André Bonzel and Benoit Poelvoorde drew wider attention with their acclaimed art-house movie *Man Bites Dog*.

Since then Belgian directors have won a string of accolades: the iconoclastic Jan Bucquoy for *The Sexual Life of the Belgians* (1994), recommended for its witty and cutting portrait of Belgian family life in its opening sequences; Gérard Corbiau for *Farinelli, Il Castrato* (1994); Jaco van Dormael's *Toto the Hero* (1991) and *The Eighth Day* (1996), both starring the Down's syndrome actor Pascal Duquenne; Alain Berliner's *Ma Vie en Rose*; and Luc and Jean-Pierre Dardenne for *Rosetta*, which won the Palme d'Or at Cannes (1999).

By and large, however, films in Belgium are imported, and the most successful tend to be mainstream Hollywood ones. The new releases are usually shown in their original language (VO or *version originale*) with subtitles in French or Flemish (or both), but older and widely popular films often have the soundtrack dubbed (*doublé*). The *Bulletin* gives listings of performances in English. The web site w *www.cinebel.com* is another useful source.

For a comprehensive programme of classic international films, look out for the programme of the Musée du Cinéma; films shown there usually have the original soundtrack with French subtitles.

Remember that in Belgium (as in France) it is customary to tip the cinema attendant who takes your ticket and may show you to your seat (about 25 cents), although many of the newer cinemas have dispensed with this tradition.

Actor's Studio E5
16 Petite Rue des Bouchers, t 02 512 1696; metro De Brouckère.
Two screens showing off-beat films.

Arenberg-Galeries E5
26 Galerie de la Reine, t 02 512 8063.

Aventure D4
57 Galerie du Centre, t 02 219 1748; metro De Brouckère.

Cinquantenaire Drive-in N7
Parc du Cinquantenaire, t 0900 20 700, w www.dedi.be. Screenings July and Aug at 8pm.
An open-air cinema near the triumphal arch in the Parc du Cinquantenaire. Seating is available for those without a car.

Kinepolis Off maps
Bruparck, t 02 474 2600 or0900 35 241; metro Heysel.
A mega-cinema with 24 auditoriums showing primarily mainstream films, plus the Imax theatre (vast screen with 3D effect).

Movy Club Off maps
21 Rue des Moines, t 02 537 6954; tram 52 or 49.

Musée du Cinéma F6
9 Rue Baron Horta, t 02 507 8370, e museeducinema@ledoux.be; metro Gare Centrale.
Daily menu of classic films, and two performances of silent movies with live piano accompaniment; a ticket of €2 to the museum entitles you to see a film as well. The museum publishes a monthly schedule of films, usually organized around a central theme (*see p.97 for further details and how to book*).

Nova E4
3 Rue d'Arenberg, t 02 511 2774;
metro Gare Centrale.
Old cinema rescued by a young
group of film enthusiasts now
presenting mainly art movies, and
occasional concerts.

Styx G9–10
72 Rue de l'Arbre Bénit, t 02 512
2102; metro Porte de Namur.

UGC–Acropole F–G8
8 Av de la Toison d'Or/17 Galerie de
la Toison d'Or, t 0900 10 440.

UGC–De Brouckère E3
38 Place de Brouckère, t 0900 10
440; metro De Brouckère.
Also a venue for jazz concerts.

Vendôme-Roy G8
18 Chaussée de Wavre, t 02 502
3700; metro Porte de Namur.

Cultural Centres

There are a number of these in
central Brussels as well in the
suburbs. They put on a broad
range of events, such as theatre,
performances by foreign dance
troupes, and concerts (classical,
folk, blues, etc.). The most important are:

Le Botanique H2
236 Rue Royale, t 02 226 1211;
metro Botanique.
The cultural centre for the French
community of Brussels, housed in
the elegant domed glasshouse of
the old botanical garden (*see*
p.122).

Palais des Beaux-Arts F6
23 Rue Ravenstein, t 02 507 8200;
metro Gare Centrale.
The cultural centre designed by
Victor Horta between the wars
(*see p.97*).

Theatre

Brussels has its fair share of
theatres and theatre companies
putting on a spread of plays
ranging from French classics by
Molière, Corneille and Racine, to
Feydeau farces, to modern classics
by Ionesco, Michel de Ghelderode
and the like, and works by

contemporary Belgian play-
wrights. For better or worse,
however, there is no equivalent of
Broadway or London's West End,
dominated by musicals that any
visitor might appreciate. Theatre-
goers in Brussels will need a good
grip of French or Flemish – or of
Bruxellois if they are going to
enjoy that most famous of
Brussels plays, the knockabout
comedy *Le Mariage de
Mademoiselle Beulemans* (1910) by
Frans Fonson and Fernand
Wicheler.

L'Atelier Ste-Anne B8
75–77 Rue des Tanneurs, t 02 548
0260; metro Lemmonier.
Engaging venue for high-quality,
small-scale works.

**Espace Delvaux/
La Vénerie** Off maps
Place Keym (Auderghem), t 02 672
1439; metro Beaulieu.
Specializes in humorous
café/theatre performances.

**Koninklijke Vlaamse
Schouwburg** Off maps
58 Rue Delannoy (Molenbeek), t 02
412 7040; metro Etangs Noir. (Due
to move back to 146 Rue de Laeken
in 2003.)
The main Dutch-language theatre
of Brussels, built in grand
Edwardian style.

Magic Land Theatre
No fixed address.
Unpredictable and inventive
street theatre troupe, worth
looking out for.

Rideau de Bruxelles F6
*Palais des Beaux-Arts, 23 Rue
Ravenstein, t 02 507 8360;*
metro Parc.
Intimate theatre with a respected
and long-established company,
performing classic modern
Belgian work by authors such as
Michel de Ghelderode and
Maurice Maeterlinck, as well as
contemporary work.

La Samaritaine D7
16 Rue de la Samaritaine, t 02 511
3395; metro Gare Centrale.
Warm-hearted café/theatre
currently considered on form.

**Théâtre
de la Balsamine** Off maps
1 Avenue Félix Marchal, t 02 735
6468; bus 29 or 54.
Award-winning theatre
presenting mainly new and experimental plays and dance.

**Théâtre National
de Belgique** F2
Place Rogier, t 02 203 5303,
w www.theatrenational.be;
metro Rogier.
Modern francophone plays, often
by Belgian authors, located in an
ugly tower-block.

Théâtre 140 Off maps
140 Av Plasky, t 02 733 9708;
tram 23 or 90.
For over 30 decades a leading
venue for contemporary theatre
and other performances.

Théâtre de Poche Off maps
1a Chemin du Gymnase (Bois de la
Cambre), t 02 649 1727; tram 93,
94.
Widely respected small theatre
presenting contemporary, often
experimental work in pleasant
woodland surroundings.

Théâtre de Quat'Sous D5
34 Rue de la Violette, t 02 512 1022;
metro Gare Centrale.
Tiny, friendly theatre of 50 seats,
performing mainly modern
French plays.

**Théâtre du
Résidence Palace** K6
155 Rue de la Loi, t 02 231 0305;
metro Maelbeek.
1920s Art Deco theatre, with resident company; dance venue also.

**Le Théâtre Royal
des Galeries** E4
32 Galeries du Roi, t 02 512 0407;
metro Gare Centrale.
A theatre founded in 1847, with a
well-worn tradition of comedies
and melodramas; also shows
more challenging productions.

Théâtre Royal du Parc I5
3 Rue de la Loi, t 02 505 3040;
metro Arts-Loi.
Splendid 18th-century theatre
mounting respected seasons of
plays in French, both classical and
modern (Pagnol, Pirandello,
Ionesco, Ibsen and so forth).

Théâtre Varia K9
78 Rue du Sceptre, t 02 640 8258;
bus 59.
Progressive theatre at the cutting
edge of Brussels' avant garde –
often inspired.

Puppets

The Théâtre Toone is a famous
Brussels institution, with a history
that goes back over 150 years. On a
small stage in a loft off an ancient
alleyway, the great works of
Aristophanes, Shakespeare and
Corneille, as well as more jolly
entertainments, are played out
with characteristic relish and
verve by troupes of large puppets
made of wood and papier-mâché,
manipulated by a few rather
crude strings. No subject is too
elevated for these characters: at
Easter they take on The Passion.
The first Toone theatre was established in 1830 by Antoine Genty
(Toone is a shortened form of
Antoine), and the tradition has
been handed down from generation to generation (though not
always within the family). It
started off in the Marolles, but has
been in its present home
since 1966.

The Toone puppets are famous
for their performances in a
French-based Bruxellois dialect,
and José Géal, who now leads the
20 or so puppeteers in the 7th
generation of this theatre (Toone
VII), is not just a famous face in
Brussels but also a noted expert
on the language. If you want to
hear Bruxellois, or more accurately
the dialect of the Marolles district,
called Vloms, this is the place to
come – although you should note
that for some of the classical plays
only certain performances are in
dialect. Some plays are also
performed in English.

It may seem folksy, something
to take the kids along to, but it is
not. These plays are staged in the
evening for good reason: they are
serious productions, hard to
follow and – so say those who can
follow them – often outrageously
bawdy. However much you can
take in, an evening with Toone VII
is an unmistakably Bruxellois
experience.

For children, there is the Théâtre
Peruchet in Ixelles, a delightful
puppet theatre which stages a
varied programme based on fairy
tales, in a converted farmhouse; it
also has a puppet museum, open
during performances. The Théâtre
Ratinet also puts on puppet
shows for children, mainly new
workings of fairy tales.

Théâtre Peruchet Off maps
50 Avenue de la Forêt, t 02 219
6906; tram 94. Performance times
are erratic and need to be checked
beforehand.

Théâtre Ratinet Off maps
44 Avenue de Fré (Uccle), t 02 375
1563; tram 91 or 92. Performances
in the afternoon.

Théâtre Toone VII E5
Impasse Schuddeveld, 21 Petite Rue
des Bouchers, t 02 511 7137;
metro Bourse. Performances at
8.30pm, not every day.
Reservations by telephone or at
the theatre bar (*estaminet*) after
noon. The Toone puppet museum
is open during the intervals.

Dance

The name Maurice Béjart is still
uttered in hushed and reverent
tones in Brussels. He created his
'Ballet du XXe Siècle' during his
long residence at the Théâtre
Royal de la Monnaie, producing
his own kind of modern-dance
grand spectacle. Like it or loathe it,

Béjart's work laid the foundations
for an enthusiastic appreciation of
modern dance in the city. The
Monnaie's resident ballet is now
directed by Anne Teresa de
Keersmaeker, to considerable
acclaim. *See* Cirque Royal (p.245),
Théâtre de la Monnaie (p.245) and
Théâtre du Résidence Palace
(p.247).

Cabaret and Revues

Cabaret is always a mixed bag,
and no more so than in Brussels. It
ranges from small-scale comedy
pieces, accompanied by singers
and illusionists, to glam shows
just this side of sleaze. If it is true
sleaze you want, follow your nose
around the Gare du Nord.

Le Black Bottom D6
1 Rue de Lombard, t 02 511 0608;
metro Bourse. Shows Mon–Thurs
10.30 and 11.30pm, Fri and Sat
midnight and 1am.
Cabaret and varieties, magicians
and comics.

Chez Flo D5
25 Rue au Beurre, t 02 513 3152;
metro Gare Centrale. Shows
Wed–Sat 8pm.
A ritzy transvestite show with
dinner, the classiest of its kind in
town. All good, clean fun – after a
fashion.

Moustache C3
61 Quai au Bois à Brûler, t 02 218
5877; metro Ste-Catherine.
Fish restaurant with famous
comedy cabaret on Saturdays.

Le Pré Salé B3
20 Rue de Flandre, t 02 513 4323;
metro Ste-Catherine.
Restaurant serving Belgian
cuisine, famous for its jocular
'playback' (mimed) show on
Fridays.

Shopping

What will you take home from your trip to Brussels? Fresh-cream chocolates for the neighbours, a few bottles of Belgian beer? A tablecloth of the finest hand-made Brussels lace? A set of Tintin classics to help improve your French? How about a 19th-century engraving of Brussels, an Art Nouveau lamp, or a party mask of Gilles de Binche?

Remember, the very character of Belgium was forged by the strong traditions of its artisans and traders. Shops and stores are in the mainstream of Belgian life, and the Belgians love to shop. To enhance the feel-good factor for those parting with their money, there are numerous elegantly styled *galeries* – covered arcades filled with shops, as well as restaurants and cafés for those who need refuelling between bouts of spending. You could pass most of the day in one: many Belgians do.

If you are in search of a bargain and local colour, there are several regular markets, although these are not quite the cultural feast that they are in, say, France and Italy. Towards the end of the year the traditional Christmas markets – selling crafts, decorations and seasonal fare – strike an authentic festive note, summoning up childhood memories of Christmas as it used to be.

Many of the supermarkets are vast emporia, selling food, wine and beer (including all the best Trappist beers), plus a huge range of goods such as toys, books, stationery, garden furniture, cheap clothes, anything. They are excellent places to stock up on basics and to gauge the range of goods generally available in Belgium. However, to find the best and largest of them, you will have to travel to the suburbs.

The Shopping Districts and *Galeries*

The *galeries* are the Belgian equivalents of shopping malls, and since the Belgians have been building them since the 1840s they have had plenty of time to perfect the formula. The best have quality written all over them: they entice then flatter the shopper with their style and elegance. Larger modern versions tend to be labelled 'Shopping Centers', and have a more down-to-earth range of shops, but here again architects have wisely developed the theory that the pleasure of the shopper is conducive to good trade.

Anspach Center D4
Bd Anspach and Rue de l'Evêque; metro Bourse.
Busy, glitzy shopping centre, with mainly clothes and accessories – smart, but not exclusive. Connected to the Centre Monnaie, close to the Grand' Place.

Centre Monnaie E4
Place de la Monnaie and Bd Anspach; metro De Brouckère.
Another central shopping centre, along similar lines to the Anspach Center.

City 2 F2
Rue Neuve, off Place Rogier; metro Rogier.
A warren of shops, restaurants and cinemas. Its wide range of quality shops includes the mega book and record store FNAC, and the department store Inno.

Galerie Agora E5
Rue des Eperonniers, Rue de la Colline and Rue du Marché aux Herbes; metro Gare Centrale.
A surprisingly upmarket setting for this bazaar of subculture T-shirts, leather, jewellery, baseball caps, body-piercing, and other forms of alternative exotica, all within a stone's throw of the Grand' Place.

Galerie Bortier E5–6
Rue St-Jean and Rue de la Madeleine; metro Gare Centrale.
A 19th-century *galerie*, now a centre for secondhand books (*see* p.83).

Galerie Louise E9–F8
Av de la Toison d'Or and Av Louise; metro Louise.
Sleek and tasteful, at the upper end of the shopping spectrum – mainly high-class clothing stores and shoe shops. Expensive, but the throngs of customers include many an average Bruxellois(e) out to buy that little number for the coming season (*see* p.107).

Galeries Royales de St-Hubert E5
Rue du Marché aux Herbes; metro Gare Centrale.
The oldest and most elegant of them all: marbled halls and a relaxed café ambience in which to window-gaze at exquisite shoes and clothes in luxurious boutiques, as well as browse around some excellent bookshops (*see* p.84).

Galerie de la Toison d'Or F–G8
Av de la Toison d'Or and Chaussée d'Ixelles; metro Louise.
Often paired with its neighbour, the Galerie Louise, and of matching high standard. Clothes, accessories and much more.

Place Louise and Bvd de Waterloo/Av de la Toison d'Or E9
Metro Louise.
This area is noted in particular for its chic clothes shops, and all the best names in *haute couture* are here, lining a broad avenue busy with traffic. Close at hand are two of the most famous modern galeries, the Galerie Louise and the Galerie de la Toison d'Or.

Rue Dansaert C4
Metro Bourse.
Despite its slightly down-at-heel appearance, Rue Dansaert has, for almost a decade now, been a centre for serious avant-garde fashion in Brussels. The fashion shops include Rue Blanche, Virgin Shoes (with Dirk Bikkembergs

shoes), Kat en Muis children's clothes (with lines by Dries Van Noten) and, in the stretch between Marché aux Grains and the Place du Nouveau Marché au Grains, Nathalie Vincent, Idiz Bogum II (secondhand) and Stijl, which carries many of the great Antwerp names.

Rue Neuve E3
Metro Rogier or De Brouckère.
The best-known shopping street is the Rue Neuve, a thronging pedestrianized thoroughfare within short walking distance of the Grand' Place. It contains many of the large chain stores, plus hundreds of clothing boutiques, record shops, camera suppliers and so forth. Despite its reputation, the Rue Neuve has become a little tawdry.

Woluwe Shopping Center Off maps
Place St-Lambert (Woluwe-St-Lambert); metro Roodebeek.
A huge shopping emporium, an excellent example of its kind. Good restaurants and plenty of parking. You could easily spend a day here.

Antiques, *Brocante* and Fine Art

As everywhere else in Europe these days, antique dealers and *brocanteurs* in Brussels know the value of everything, down to the last bit of junk that deserves no living space at all. There are few bargains here, but at least prices are not always exorbitant. The dealers range from traders in old carpets and bits of typewriter at the Place du Jeu de Balle to the owners of chichi antiques galleries of the Place du Grand-Sablon (the headquarters of the antiques trade), selling genuine Pointillist paintings and beautifully veneered Biedermeier cabinets. Brussels, naturally enough, offers a particularly strong line in Art Nouveau

objects, from door furniture to much sought-after lamps.

The Place du Grand-Sablon is also one of the two main centres for the fine art trade, and home to a number of small art galleries. The other is at the upper end of the Avenue Louise.

Anne de Beaujeu E7
7 Rue des Sablons; metro Porte de Namur.
Fine-quality 19th- and 20th-century furniture, furnishings and ornaments in the heart of the antiques district.

Les Caves de Colette E7
59 Rue des Minimes; metro Gare Centrale.
An antique shop with a lived-in look because it is also Colette's home. A huge cellar, with an open fire, kitchen, beds and 101 other things all for sale.

Cento Anni E7
31 Place du Grand-Sablon; metro Porte de Namur.
Classic, florid Art Nouveau glass and metalware.

Le Grenier de la Bourse C4
2 Rue Antoine Dansaert; metro Bourse.
Brocanteur near the city centre, specializing in metal office furniture of the 1920s, pine, Art Nouveau and anything witty and stylish that takes his fancy.

Philippe Denys E7
1 Rue des Sablons; metro Porte de Namur.
Fine silverware of the streamlined Art Nouveau/Art Deco kind by such luminaries as Jean Puiforcat and Georg Jensen, plus furniture and ceramics of the same era.

Sablon Shopping Gardens E7
36 Place du Grand-Sablon; metro Porte de Namur.
A cluster of some 40 sophisticated antique and art shops.

Au Vieux Magasin J8
39–41 Rue Godecharle; metro Trône.
An Aladdin's cave of appealing junk: ancient biscuit tins, *objets d'art*, furniture, Art Nouveau lamps. Must be a bargain somewhere in all this.

Le Village d'Antiquaires E7
22 Rue Bodenbroeck; metro Porte de Namur.
A warren of 10 dealers at the top end of the Place du Grand Sablon selling 18th- to 19th-century furniture, bric-a-brac, prints and glassware.

W. Sand D5
28c Rue du Lombard; metro Bourse.
A long-established dealer in antique sculptures, musical instruments, jewellery and so forth from Africa and the Orient – an anthropological treasure trove.

Antiques Fairs and Flea Markets

Place du Grand-Sablon E7
Metro Porte de Namur. Held Sat 9am–6pm, Sun 9am–2pm.
A small, well-established and rather upmarket antiques fair: old prints, books, 18th-century furniture, porcelain, Art Deco figurines, bakelite.

Place du Jeu de Balle C8
Bus 48; metro Gare Centrale then 15min walk. Held daily 7am–2pm, bigger on Sun.
The premier flea market in Brussels: hunt for bargains; be astounded at what some people attempt to sell.

Stamps

Brussels is a leading European centre for philatelists. There are numerous stamp shops of all kinds and levels all the way down the Rue du Midi, from the Bourse to the Place Rouppe. Here is just a selection:

Belgasafe D5
24 Rue du Midi; metro Bourse.
One of a cluster at the upper end of the street: mainly modern stamps from all over the world, for the general collector.

Philatelie Corneille Soeteman C6
129 Rue du Midi; metro Bourse.
A major auction house, but also exhibits the crème de la crème for purchase in its showroom.

Williame Baeton D5
7 Rue du Midi; metro Bourse.
August antique stamp dealer and
auctioneer, for the expert whose
passion means spending
serious money.

Books and Music

There are hundreds of bookshops in Brussels, selling primarily
works in French and Flemish, of
course. However, the large
English-speaking community has
given rise to a handful of excellent
English-language bookshops.
Belgium also has a strong music
culture and the wide availability
of recordings reflects this.

**Centre Belge de la Bande
Dessinée** F3
*20 Rue des Sables; metro
Botanique.*
Thousands of comic-strip titles –
in French and Dutch.

English Shop B10, K5
*134 Chaussée de Waterloo and 186
Rue Stevin; metro Louise, Schuman.*
Both branches sell a range of
English books (mainly paper-
backs), as well as English food.

FNAC F3
City 2, 123 Rue Neuve; metro Rogier.
French megastore selling a huge
selection of books (in French,
English and other languages), CDs
and cassettes, and computers.
Also has a ticket agency for
concerts, etc.

Free Record Shop E4
*Gaîté Theatre, 18 Rue du Fossé aux
Loups; metro De Brouckère.*
Impressive recently converted
record, CD and video megastore in
a venerable old music hall.

**Musées Royaux des
Beaux-Arts** F6–7
*3 Rue de la Régence; metro Porte de
Namur.*
Good selection of art books,
particularly on Belgian painters.

Sterling Books E4
*38 Rue du Fossé aux Loups;
metro De Brouckère.*
Centrally located English bookshop (near the Place de la

Monnaie) where prices are
pegged to the sterling cover price
(plus 6% VAT).

**Strathmore
Bookshop** Off maps
*110 Rue St-Lambert; metro
Roodebeek.*
Small but impressive English-
language bookshop.

Tropismes E4
*Galerie des Princes, Galeries St-
Hubert; metro Gare Centrale.*
Famously elegant bookstore, a joy
to browse in. Has some English
titles.

Virgin Megastore D4
Anspach Center; metro Bourse.
CDs, videos, videogames.

Waterstone's E3
*71–75 Bvd Adolphe Max; metro De
Brouckère.*
Two floors of English-language
books, newspapers and magazines.

Chocolates

For the background to Belgian
chocolates, *see* 'Chocolate' box
opposite. The manufacturers
listed below are the best known
and have numerous outlets
throughout Brussels; these are all
branches close to the city centre.

Corné E5
*9 Rue de la Madeleine; metro Gare
Centrale.*
One of the big names in luxury
chocolates.

Godiva E5
*22 Grand' Place and 89 Bvd A. Max;
metro Gare Centrale.*
Celebrated and expensive.

Leonidas D4
*46 Bvd Anspach and 34 Rue au
Beurre; metro Bourse.*
Good value and, in many people's
opinion, the best.

Neuhaus E5, D6, E3, D–E9
*27 Galerie de la Reine, Galeries St-
Hubert, 1 Rue de l'Etuve, 34 Passage
du Nord and 27 Av de la Toison
d'Or; metro Gare Centrale/De
Brouckère/Louise.*
Refined, restrained, perhaps the
place for the chocolate addict.

Wittamer E7
*12–13 Place du Grand-Sablon;
metro Porte de Namur.*
The most celebrated chocolatier in
Brussels. Eat one of their chocolate cakes and you'll see why:
angels will dance on your
tongue.

Clothes and
Accessories

You can buy good-quality
clothing of any kind in any price
range in Belgium – from
American-style children's clothing
in the supermarket to Parisian
haute couture and hot-off-the-
press fashions by the Antwerp Six
(*see* pp.197–210). If you are in
search of a touch of Euro-chic,
have a stroll around Place Louise
and Bd de Waterloo, where you'll
find the likes of Chanel, Hermès,
Giorgio Armani and Gianni
Versace, and take a look at the
adjoining Galerie Louise and
Galerie de la Toison d'Or for lesser-
known names and high-quality
shoe shops. Rue Antoine Dansaert,
close to the Bourse in the city
centre, has a growing reputation
for shops at the sharp end of
fashion; for slightly less-elevated
boutiques, try the Anspach Center
and the Rue Neuve.

Bouvy E9
*52 Av de la Toison d'Or; metro
Louise.*
Famous, elegant sportswear shop
established over half a century
ago: who cares if you can't play
tennis if you look this good?

**Comme des Garçons – Yohji
Yama-moto** B3–4
*6 Place du Nouveau Marché aux
Grains; metro Ste-Catherine.*
Outlet for top couturier Rei
Kawakubo and several Japanese
associates.

Delvaux E3, E5
*22 Bvd Adolphe Max, 31 Galerie de
la Reine in Galeries Royales de St-
Hubert and 27 Bvd de Waterloo;
metro De Brouckère/Gare
Centrale/Louise.*

Chocolate

When it comes to chocolate, 'Belgian' is synonymous with quality – so much so that unscrupulous foreign operators will use the term liberally as a sales tool when their product contains only the merest fraction of Belgian chocolate, or is simply prepared in Belgian style. Imitation may be a form of flattery, but do not be misled: only the Belgians produce the chocolates that are responsible for this reputation. This is partly because freshness counts: Belgian chocolates are sumptuous, fresh-cream confections with a limited shelf life (three weeks or so in the fridge); furthermore, because the Belgians themselves are enthusiastic consumers of handmade chocolate, turnover is high and the price is remarkably low.

Three factors have given rise to the unassailable reputation of Belgian chocolate: the cream fillings, white chocolate, and – most important of all – the quality of the plain chocolate. The Belgians may not have been the first to put fresh cream in chocolates, but they pioneered fresh-cream fillings for the mass market. White chocolate is a comparative newcomer; in fact it is barely chocolate at all, but a milk-based confection mixed with cocoa butter and sweetener. The best plain Belgian chocolate contains a very high proportion of cocoa solids – at least 52%, usually more like 70% (90% is the feasible maximum). These cocoa solids are the crushed and ground product of cocoa beans (usually from South America), from which some of the oily cocoa butter has been extracted. This valuable cocoa butter is later reintroduced to make high-quality chocolate (in poor-quality chocolate, vegetable fat is substituted for cocoa butter and there is also a much lower percentage of cocoa solids). Cocoa butter makes a significant difference, as any chocolate addict will tell you: the natural oils in the cocoa butter evaporate in your mouth, provoking a slight cooling, refreshing sensation.

Leonidas, Godiva, Corné de la Toison d'Or and Neuhaus are the most famous manufacturers in Belgium, but there are many more, some of them tiny individual concerns with just one outlet. Of the big names, Leonidas is probably the cheapest, but this has little bearing on quality: many Belgians actually prefer Leonidas and find the others too rich.

Leonidas appears to produce chocolates on an industrial scale, and has numerous outlets. Some have large counters opening directly onto the street, so that the staff can shovel out boxes of chocolates to passing customers with the minimum of delay. Only in Belgium could chocolates be treated as a kind of fast food. Godiva, however, has the greater international reputation: the company now has 1,400 shops worldwide, selling 120 different kinds of chocolate at the luxury end of the market. Why, you may ask, is a Belgian chocolate company named after Lady Godiva, the nobleman's wife who rode naked through the streets of Coventry in the 11th century? The answer is simply that, in 1929, the founders of the business liked the image, which seemed to represent the qualities of their chocolates: elegant, rich, sensual and daring.

You will find chocolates (or pralines, as they are generically known) on sale everywhere in Brussels. If you want to buy a handful of boxes in a hurry to take home with you, there's a Godiva shop in the Grand' Place (No.22) and a large Leonidas shop at 46 Bvd Anspach, close to the Bourse.

The ultimate sophistication in leather goods.

Dod F12
*89 and 64 Rue du Bailli; **tram** 81.*
These two shops (men's at No.89, women's at No.64) are stacked with cut-price designer wear. Very popular with fashion-conscious locals who want something a little different without breaking the bank.

Dujardin E9
*82–84 Av Louise; **metro** Louise.*
This famous shop sells chic children's clothes, all designed and made in Belgium. Recently rescued from oblivion by Delvaux, it is now housed in a vampishly renovated *maison de maître*.

Elixir J9
*352 Chaussée de Wavre; **metro** Trône or Schuman.*
Off-the-peg women's clothes including designer silkwear and glamorous strappy evening dresses.

Elvis Pompilio D5
*60 Rue du Midi; **metro** Bourse.*
Hats wild and wonderful, stylish and fanciful – just how far can Elvis go? His most extravagant creations are virtually sculptures fashioned in felt. But don't expect any change out of €150. Branches in Antwerp and London.

Les Enfants d'Edouard F10
*175–177 Av Louise; **metro** Louise.*
Nearly new secondhand clothes by top designers.

Idiz Bogum I C8, C4
*162 Rues Blaes, and Idiz Bogum II, 76 Rue A. Dansaert; **metro** Gare Centrale/Bourse.*
Chic secondhand clothes of the 1940s–70s, frequented by fashion-hounds and theatrical costumiers.

Kat en Muis C4
*32 Rue Antoine Dansaert; **metro** Bourse.*
Stylish off-the-peg children's clothes. Knitwear, smocks and winning woolly hats, for 0–14 years. It carries clothes by Dries van Noten.

Naf Naf E3
*42 Passage du Nord; **metro** De Brouckère.*
A representative of the upbeat French chain. One of a cluster of

Belgian Lace

Lace (*dentelle* in French, *kant* in Flemish) was originally made from linen, from the flax fields of central Flanders. It was always a cottage industry, but produced by women from virtually every social rank, notably by the thousands of women living in the *béguinages* of the Low Countries (*see* 'The History of Béguinages', p.141).

Having blossomed in the 16th century, lace remained popular for three centuries, during which time fashion for both men and women included lace collars and cuffs. It was also used to make caps, handkerchiefs, shawls, lappets (ribbon-like hair adornments) and bed linen. The Victorian passion for lace with everything, from underwear to the dining-room table, inspired a latter-day Renaissance, but by this time much of the demand was being met by lacemaking machines. Nonetheless, even in the mid-19th century there were an estimated 50,000 women lacemakers in Belgium, 10,000 of them in Brussels.

Various lace-making techniques have been used over the centuries. In the 16th century, lace-making was essentially a form of embroidery; a hundred years later the dominant technique was needlepoint, which had evolved in Venice. Bobbin embroidery developed during the 18th century in Genoa and Milan and soon spread to the main centres for lace-making elsewhere, notably Brussels and also Mechelen and Bruges. The bobbin technique is the one most widely seen today, but all three techniques survived and were used simultaneously.

Handmade bobbin lace is extremely slow to make, requiring thousands of carefully planned movements of the bobbins and pins. The intricate patterns are created by moving the threads attached to the bobbins around the pins, which are pressed into a cushion. Complex lace calls for over 100 separate threads and bobbins. Not surprisingly, good lace is expensive, and the industry has been undermined in recent decades by cheap imports from the Far East. That said, plenty of good, handmade lace is still being produced in Belgium, available in the more respected outlets in Brussels and Bruges, where the staff will be happy to reassure you of its provenance. Cotton lace is more robust and comparatively cheap; linen lace is much finer, and a larger piece with a complex design can cost thousands of euros.

Collections of lace can be seen in a number of Brussels' museums, notably the Musée du Costume et de la Dentelle (*see* p.82). You can see lace being made at the Louise Verschueren shop in Rue Watteeu in Brussels (*see* p.110), and at the Kantcentrum in Bruges.

---

clothing multiples in and around the Rue Neuve.

Patrick Pitschon C4
82 Rue Antoine Dansaert; **metro** *Ste-Catherine.*
Cutting-edge Belgian designer selling practical and affordable clothes alongside more outlandish creations.

Peau d'Zèbre D5
40 Rue du Midi; **metro** *Bourse.*
Remarkable clothes for younger children, designed and made on the premises. Charming, stylish yet practical, in inspired autumnal colours – russets, greys and blacks. Most remarkable of all, they are incredibly good value: nothing costs more than €50.

Peek & Cloppenburg E3
30 Rue Neuve; **metro** *De Brouckère.*
One of a group of stylish general clothing stores at the lower end of the Rue Neuve.

Prêt à Dancer E3
3 Boulevard Adolphe Max; **metro** *De Brouckère.*

Dance types can be sure to find the hottest fashion gear here. Stretchy flared jazz pants, pumps, as well as innumerable leotards.

Ramon & Vally C5
19 Rue des Teinturiers; **metro** *Anneessens.*
Vintage clothes boutique that has the reputation of always being ahead of things. Great for groovy party wear.

Rue Blanche C4
35 Rue Antoine Dansaert; **metro** *Bourse.*
Outlet for this label, known for its tasteful elegance in a modern idiom.

Stijl C4
74 Rue Antoine Dansaert; **metro** *Bourse.*
Well-established avant-garde fashion boutique in an 18th-century converted butter-wrapping factory, with changing rooms in the carriage block. Stijl has exclusive rights in Brussels over a number of top names, so this is the place to hunt for your new outfit by Dries van Noten, Ann Demeulemeester, Dirk Bikkembergs, Martin Margiela, Raf Simons, or a wedding gown by David Fielden.

Virgin C4, E5
10 Rue Antoine Dansaert and 13 Rue des Eperonniers; **metro** *Bourse.*
Gritty, modish boots and shoes, where black rules. For those who want street cred with style, and are prepared to pay for it. Exclusive retailers for Dirk Bikkembergs' shoes.

Food Specialities

There are hundreds of first-class *traiteurs*, *pâtissiers* and other specialist food producers in Brussels. Below is a list of just a few shops of outstanding quality. Many standard specialities – including Trappist beers, *jambon d'Ardennes*, *saucisses de campagne*, cheeses and so forth – are available from the larger supermarkets, but specialist shops earn their keep by being a cut above the rest in a highly competitive market. For chocolates, *see* p.252.

Bernard F7

93 Rue de Namur; metro Porte de Namur.

Marbled delicatessen on the ground floor of a celebrated fish restaurant, specializing in mouth-watering fish and seafood preparations.

Dandoy D5

31 Rue au Beurre and 14 Rue Charles Buls; metro Gare Centrale.

Famous for its buttery, crumbly biscuits: *speculoos* and also many other specialities.

Dragées Maréchal D5

40 Rue des Chapeliers; metro Gare Centrale.

Fine old store founded in 1848, specializing in the sugared almonds and fancy porcelain containers that are traditionally offered to guests at christenings.

Langhendries E4

41 Rue de la Fourche; metro Bourse or De Brouckère.

Supreme selection of beautifully conditioned French, Italian, Dutch and Belgian cheeses from 'dare you to' strong *crottes* to slabs the size of truck tyres, all presented with the true passion of a *maître-fromager*.

Pandin E4

47 Rue de la Fourche; metro Bourse or De Brouckère.

When you have bought your cheese from Langhendries, choose some pâtés, *charcuterie* or delicious ready-made dishes from this ravishing display of the *traiteur*'s art.

Lace

For a summary of Belgian lace, *see* 'Belgian Lace' box. There are numerous outlets selling lace around the Grand' Place – anything from glass-mats and handkerchiefs to tablecloths. The price varies according to provenance and quality, and there is a fair bit of imported lace, made in the Far East. Good lace shops, such as the ones listed below, should

tell you where the lace is made. You only have to watch it being made to understand why there is no such thing as cheap Belgian lace.

Louise Verschueren E7

16 Rue Watteeu; metro Gare Centrale then 10min walk.

Part exhibition, part shop, and a reliable source for real handmade Belgian lace.

Maison Rubbrecht D–E5

23 Grand' Place; metro Gare Centrale.

Central outlet for good-quality lace, much of it handmade.

La Manufacture Belge de la Dentelle E5

6–8 Galerie de la Reine, Galeries Royales de St-Hubert; metro Gare Centrale.

Expensive, but good.

Markets

For antique and flea markets *see* p.251.

Gare du Midi A9

Metro Gare du Midi. Held Sun morning.

The biggest market in Brussels, filling the Boulevard de l'Europe and selling everything from cous-cous to cars. The bicycle market at the upper end of the Boulevard du Midi is a famous place to pick up a secondhand bike.

Grand' Place D–E5

Metro Gare Centrale. Held Sun 8am–12.30pm.

A well-known market that consists of little more than a couple of stalls.

Parvis St-Gilles Off maps

Metro Parvis St-Gilles. Held Tues–Sun 6am–12.30pm.

A busy food market a short walk from the Porte de Hal. Mainly fruit, vegetables and other necessities, displayed in vivid technicolor – and also some speciality hams and cheeses.

Place de la Duchesse de Brabant (Molenbeek) Off maps

Metro Gare de l'Ouest. Held Tues 8am–1pm.

Horse market, should you wish to buy a horse. Rural Belgium in an urban setting.

Place du Châtelain (Ixelles) G12

Tram 81. Held Wed 2–7pm (and sometimes later).

A charming evening food market (often referred to by the appealing expression *marché nocturne*), where basic groceries and vegetables are sold, along with interesting breads, ready-made pasta dishes and other specialities.

Rue Ropsy Chaudron (Anderlecht) Off maps

Tram 47. Held Sat 7am–1pm and Sun 8am–1pm.

A lively market for pets, poultry and North African food, held in and around the impressive iron-work shelter of a late 19th-century abattoir. The modern slaughter-house next to this old abattoir is still active: hundreds of cattle and sheep are brought here to be sold for slaughter on Tuesdays (cattle, from 6am) and Wednesdays (calves and sheep, from 6pm, summer only) – not for the faint-hearted. Committed carnivores come to eat at the nearby restaurants.

Christmas Fairs

These take place in the run-up to the Fête de Saint-Nicolas (6 December) and Christmas itself (contact the tourist office for dates and times). The best-known are held in the Place du Grand-Sablon, and the Place Cardinal Mercier (Jette). The stalls sell decorations, candles, foods associated with the festive season, hand-crafted gifts, and so on, but their particular appeal is the joyous mood and vivid colour which bring light and warmth to those chill and gloomy December days.

Supermarkets and Department Stores

The leading supermarket chains in Belgium are Delhaize, GB and

Sarma. Smaller branches are found around the city, while in out-of-town sites they can take on gigantic proportions. They not only stock all the basics but also have respectable delicatessen counters as well as books, stationery, cheap clothes and toys.

Cora Off maps

Av Ariane, off the E40 (Woluwe St-Lambert); metro Roodebeek; bus 29.

A vast megastore selling everything. Fill up your car with beer, wine and chocolate. Good also for cheap clothes, shoes, toys and toiletries.

GB F2

City 2 (top of Rue Neuve); metro Rogier.

One of a vast chain of standard supermarkets, specializing in food and drink – good quality and competitively priced.

Inno F2

111 Rue Neuve; metro Rogier.

The best-known department store in Brussels: clothes, sports goods, furnishings and domestic appliances, perfumes, textiles – the great department-store mix.

Toys

You can buy good-quality toys in the department stores and a wide range of cheaper ones in supermarkets. The best specialist toy shops are a model mixture of alluring interior design and childhood magic. They include:

Christiaensen F2

City 2 (top of Rue Neuve), 36 Rue Marché aux Herbes and other branches; metro Rogier/De Brouckère.

Comprehensive selections of international toy brands, anything from Barbie to radio-controlled speedboats.

La Courte Echelle E5

12 Rue des Eperonniers; metro Gare Centrale.

Everything for the doll's house – plus the house itself. A magical world of miniaturization where craftsmanship is the guiding principle.

In den Olifant D–E4

47 Rue des Fripiers; metro De Brouckère.

A branch of this small chain of toy stores known for its tasteful range and sympathetic shop designs. Particularly strong in wooden toys.

Picard D6

71 Rue du Lombard; metro Gare Centrale.

If you're going to a fancy-dress party, look no further – children and grown-ups alike. Fantasy outfits, masks, jokes, tricks, splendidly frivolous accessories, in a carnival of colour.

Serneels E9

69 Av Louise; metro Louise.

Tasteful toys and clothes based on comic-strip heroes such as Babar. Lots of beautifully crafted wooden items, as well as mainstream toys.

Unusual and Miscellaneous

Atelier de Moulages N7

Parc du Cinquantenaire (Rue Nerviens); metro Mérode.

Go home with an authentic plastercast of Léopold II (see p.131).

Beer Mania I9

174 Chaussée de Wavre, w www .beermania.be; metro Porte de Namur.

Over 400 beers are sold here, alongside their matching glasses. If you spend too much the shop will have your beers flown home for you. Beer-tastings are on offer.

La Boule Rouge D5

52 Rue des Pierres; metro Bourse.

Artist's materials of every description in neatly ordered stacks and shelves, the very sight of which is inspiration to pick up a brush and have a go.

Boutique de Tintin E5

13 Rue de la Colline; metro Gare Centrale.

Models, T-shirts, stationery, plus the books themselves, featuring Tintin, Captain Haddock, Snowy et al.

Cartes E3

25 Rue Neuve; metro De Brouckère.

Postcards and greetings cards of all kinds and descriptions, featuring everything from work by classic photographers to filmstars, joyous kitsch and the outrageously lewd.

Espace Bizarre C4

19 Rue des Chartreux; metro Bourse.

Beautiful, stylish Japanese furniture and furnishings (futons, tatamis, etc.), plus work by other leading designers.

Euroline E5

52 Rue du Marché aux Herbes; metro Gare Centrale.

One of several Euro shops, selling postcards, stickers, nailbrushes, flags – and just about anything with a flat surface that can be emblazoned with the bespangled Euro flag.

Lauffer E4–5

59 Rue des Bouchers; metro Gare Centrale.

Equipment for the chef, professional and amateur alike. Ranks of superb knives, glistening steel saucepans, precision-made spatulas, wooden molds for *speculoos* biscuits – you can even buy yourself a full chef's outfit and crown yourself with a genuine *bonnet de chef*.

Service de Chalcographie F6

1 Place du Musée; metro Gare Centrale.

Over 5,000 historical and contemporary prints from the royal library collection of plates (see p.100).

Sports
and Green Spaces

Sports

Athletics

There are two major athletics events held in Brussels every summer: the **Ivo Van Damme Memorial** meeting, where top athletes compete (*end of August at the Stade Roi de Baudouin, 135 Avenue de Marathon; metro Heysel*) and the **Brussels 20km Run**, a scaled-down version of the London Marathon, in which tens of thousands of amateurs (and a few world-class runners) amble their way in and around Brussels (last Sun in May, **t** *02 511 9000* for details).

Cycling

Along with football, cycling is the nation's favourite spectator sport. The **Tour de France** sometimes cuts through Belgium via Brussels; otherwise the annual highlight is the **Ronde van Vlaanderen** (Tour of Flanders), which takes place on the first Sunday of April.

The city's tramlines and its narrow cobbled streets make cycling difficult and potentially dangerous in the centre, though cycle lanes are being introduced over the next few years. Brussels' suburban parks are crisscrossed with pathways and make excellent cycling terrain. The best places to head for are the Bois de la Cambre (*see* p.137) and the Forêt de Soignes (*see* p.146). If you want to escape Brussels completely, the Belgian railways operate a bike-hire scheme, whereby the bicycle (which waits for you at your destination) can be returned to any railway station. Contact your nearest railway station for details (**t** *02 555 2555* for Gare du Midi).

Pro Velvo H8
*15 Rue de Londres, **t** 02 502 7355; metro Trône. Open July–Aug Sun–Fri 10–6, Sat 1–7; Sept–June Mon–Fri 10–6.*
An alliance of Belgian cycling organizations which promotes cycling around Brussels and offers bike rentals and themed bike tours of the city and its surroundings (parks and gardens of north Brussels, Art Nouveau in Ixelles, comic-strip art in the centre, and more).

Football

RSC Anderlecht Off maps
*Stade Constant Vanden Stock, 2 Av Théo Verbeeck, Anderlecht, **t** 02 522 1539; metro St Guidon; tram 56; bus 47 or 49.*
Belgium's top club side, and the only team most visitors have heard of. Book tickets here for a full-on football experience complete with hardcore local support (keep your mouth shut if you're English).

Stade Roi Baudouin Off maps
*135 Av de Marathon, **t** 02 479 3654; metro Heysel; tram 19 or 81; bus 84 or 89.*
Belgium's top football stadium with a capacity of 50,000, built in place of the Heysel stadium, which collapsed after violence during the 1985 European Cup Final. This is the place to come and watch an international match. Tickets can be bought from Maison du Football (*145 Av Houba de Strooper, **t** 02 477 1211; metro Houba de Strooper; tram 18 or 81; open Mon–Fri 9–4*).

Golf

The green suburbs of Brussels and beyond abound in golf courses, though green fees are high and most courses are membership only. Those listed below are suitable for visitors. Otherwise try **w** *www.golfin belgium.be*, a valuable resource.

Brussels Golf Club Academy and Training Centre Off maps
*53A Chaussée de la Hulpe, Bruxelles 1180, **t** 02 672 2222. Open daily 8.30am–11pm. Adm €15–40.*
In addition to a nine-hole course, there's a driving range (with 28 open tees, 12 covered tees) and an open green with bunkers to practise on.

Golf Practice Rhode St-Genese Off maps
*92B Av Brassine, 1640 Rhode St Genese, **t** 02 358 3467. Open winter Tues–Thurs, Sat and Sun 10–6 (summer 10–9), Mon and Fri noon–6 (summer noon–9); adm €12–25.*
This offers only a driving range.

Royal Waterloo Golf Club Off maps
*50 Vieux Chemin de Wavre, 1380 Ohain, **t** 02 633 2866. Open winter daily 10am–6pm, summer daily 9.30am–midnight. Adm €40–60 for weekend rounds.*
Not far from Brussels, a quality club offering two 18-hole courses and a 9-hole course.

Horse-riding

The parks and woodland around Brussels have a good network of bridleways and are ideal for riding. There are dozens of riding schools around town (call the **Fédération Royale Belge de Sports Equestres, t** *02 478 5056* for details). If you want to catch a bit of horseracing the nearest racecourse is the **Hippodrome de Boitsfort**, *51 Chaussée de la Hulpe, 1180 Brussels (call **t** 02 672 1484 for details).*

Skating

Skating (of all kinds) is a popular pursuit in Brussels. There are a number of ice rinks as well as facilities for rollerbladers and skateboarders. The **Bois de la Cambre** (*see* p.137) has a purpose-built outdoor rink for rollerskating and -blading, while the **Mont des Arts** is the place to go with your skateboard.

Forest National Off maps
*36 Av du Globe, **t** 02 345 1611; tram 18 or 52; bus 48 or 54. Open Sept–May Mon–Fri 8.30–4.30, weekends and hols (inc. school hols) 10–6; adm €2.50–5.*
One of the large outdoor ice-skating rinks.

Poseidon Off maps
4 Av des Vaillants, t 02 762 1633;
metro Tomberg. Open Sept–April
Mon–Tues noon–10pm, Wed–Sat
10–10, Sun 10–6.30; adm €4.20,
plus skate rental (ID required).
Another permanent outdoor ice-
skating rink.

Roller Park Off maps
300 Quai de Bietsbroeck, t 02 522
5915; metro Veeweyde. Open
Mon–Thurs 10am–10pm, Fri and
Sat 10am–midnight, Sun
10am–7pm; adm €5.
Offers facilities for rollerblading
and skateboarding for all abilities.

Skiing and Snowboarding

**Parc de Neerpede: Yeti Ski &
Snowboard** Off maps
11 Drève Olympique, t 02 520 7757,
e yeti.ski@pi.be, w www.yetiski
.com; tram 47. Open Sept–Easter
Mon, Wed and Fri 1–11pm, Tues and
Thurs 5–11pm, Sat and Sun
10am–8pm.
A dry-ski slope offering lessons
and rental of ski equipment.

Sports Centres

**Centre Sportif de la
Woluwe** Off maps
87 Av E. Mounier, t 02 762 8522;
metro Crainhem. Call for the varied
opening times.
A large sports centre attached to
the Catherine de Louvain university, with multipurpose gym,
squash and tennis courts, basketball courts, climbing wall, sauna
and Jacuzzi.

**Complexe Sportif du Palais
du Midi** B7
3 Rue Van der Weyden, t 02 279
5954; metro Anneessens. Call for
opening times and prices.
A sports complex in the Marolles
district of central Brussels, with
gym, basketball and pool tables.

John Harris Fitness E4
47 Rue Fossé aux Loups, t 02 219
8254; metro Gare Centrale. Open
Mon–Fri 6.30am–10pm, Sat and
Sun 7am–7pm; adm €75 per
month.

State-of-the-art fitness centre
right in the heart of town. You pay
for it, though.

Swimming

Calypso Off maps
60 Av L. Wiener, t 02 675 4899;
metro Boileau then 10min walk;
tram 94 or 95. Open daily
8am–6pm; adm €2 (extra to sun
yourself in the garden).
An indoor pool north of the Fôret
de Soignes, in Watermael-
Boitsfort.

**Centre Sportif de Woluwe-St-
Pierre** Off maps
2 Av Salomé, t 02 773 1820; tram 39;
bus 36. Open Mon–Sat 8am–7pm;
adm €2.75.
A leisure centre with olympic-size
swimming pool, solarium and
Turkish bath. There are also facilities for squash, basketball and
martial arts.

Océade Off maps
20 Bd du Centenaire, t 02 478 4320;
metro Heysel. Adm €12 (valid 4hrs),
concessions €9.70.
An inventive complex of indoor
swimming pools (at 28°C), saunas,
Jacuzzis, slides, wave machines
and spiralling water shoots in a
tropical setting.

St-Gilles Off maps
38 Rue de la Perche, t 02 539 0615;
metro Horta; tram 48 or 18. Open
Mon–Tues and Thurs–Fri 8am–
10pm, Wed 2–8pm, Sat 9am–7pm.
A fair-sized municipal swimming
pool not far from the centre in the
St-Gilles quarter. Hydrotherapy
available.

Tennis and Squash

Tennis and squash are popular
in Brussels, particularly with the
expat community. A few of the
better clubs are listed below.

Liberty's Off maps
6 Place de l'Amitie, t 02 734 6493.
Open daily 9am–midnight.
One of the largest squash centres,
with 16 courts.

Tennis Montjoie Off maps
91 Rue Edith Cavell, t 02 345 2268.
Open Mon–Fri 8am–11pm, Sat and
Sun 8am–7pm.
An indoor tennis complex.

Wimbledon Tennis Off maps
220 Chaussée de Waterloo, 1640
Rhode St Genese, t 02 358 3523.
Open daily 9am–10pm.
Has 19 outdoor tennis courts and 7
squash courts.

Walking

With the Bois de la Cambre and
the Forêt de Soignes only
15–30mins from the centre of
town (*tram 93 or 94 for Bois de la
Cambre; tram 44, bus 95 or 96 for
Forêt des Soignes*), there are plenty
of opportunities for some serious
walking – and the Bruxellois do
take their walking seriously; most
prefer power-walking to jogging,
and at weekends you'll see them
out in their droves. The forests are
well organised for leisure activities, with bridleways, cycle lanes
and footpaths, though you can
stray off the paths with a map and
compass if you like. If you want to
take a more regimented approach,
there are dozens of companies
that offer walking tours of the city
and its parks (call the tourist information centre on t 02 504 0390 to
find a tour that suits you).

Green Spaces

Bois de la Cambre Off maps
*At the end of Avenue Louise; tram
94. See also p.137.*
A large wooded park that formed
the northern tip of the Forêt de
Soignes until it was annexed to
the city in 1842. A favourite spot
for walks and picnics, the park
includes a large artificial boating
lake, cafés and a rollerskating rink.
On Sundays some of the roads
that arc through the wood are
closed to traffic, for use by cyclists
and rollerbladers.

Etangs d'Ixelles J12–14

*East of Av Louise; **tram** 94 or 90.*

There was once a string of ponds that lined the course of the River Maelbeek. The surviving two (the Etangs d'Ixelles) were bought by the Commune d'Ixelles in 1871 and became the focus of a small park, while the land on either side was developed as a fashionable residential district. In season fishermen line the banks, locals walk their dogs and ducks quack for bread. Just south of the ponds are the pretty terraced gardens of the Abbaye de la Cambre.

Forêt des Soignes Off maps

Metro Montgomery, then tram 44 (towards Tervuren), or metro Herrmann-Debroux; tram 34 (for Abbaye du Rouge-Cloître).

The remains of a primeval beech forest which once covered over 20,000 hectares south of the city centre. Today only 4,360 hectares remain, though this is still a substantial amount of woodland to find in such close proximity to the centre. The park stretches 12km from the Bois de la Cambre to Waterloo and a similar distance from La Hulpe to Tervuren, with sights of interest that include the Abbaye du Rouge-Cloître, with its gardens and ponds, and two arboretums with hundreds of species of trees.

Mont des Arts F6

Metro Gare Centrale.

You're unlikely to miss the Mont des Arts gardens, placed as they are on the hillside between the lower and upper town. The gardens were laid out by French landscape gardener René Pechère in 1956 and consist of a rectangle of neat flowerbeds and fountains. The view from the top, across the gardens and towards the towering spire of the Hôtel de Ville in the Grand' Place, is impressive.

Parc de Bruxelles G6

Off the Rue Royale; metro Parc. Open 6am–9pm.

A quiet place for a stroll in the heart of the city, this park once belonged to the Dukes of Brabant and was famed for its beauty. The park was transformed into a formal garden in the French style in 1835, and retains the straight paths and tree formations from that time.

Parc du Cinquantenaire N7

Metro Schuman or Mérode.

This park is Brussels' grandest, completed in 1880 to host celebrations for Belgium's 50th anniversary. At the eastern end of the park are several important museums: the Musée Royaux d'Art et d'Histoire, the Musée de l'Armée et d'Histoire Militaire and Autoworld. The regal expanse of greenery contains Brussels' own Arc de Triomphe, the Pavillon Horta, and a generous scattering of Neoclassical statues.

Parc d'Egmont F8

Access from Rue du Grand-Cerf and Bd de Waterloo (at the foot of the Hilton and at No.31); metro Louise or Porte de Namur.

This small park was once part of the grounds of the Palais d'Egmont, original built in the 16th century. There's a bronze statue of Peter Pan, an orangery and a former 15th-century well called Pollepel (Cooking Spoon). Nowadays the park wears a slightly forlorn air.

Parc Léopold K8

Metro Schuman, then head down Rue Froissart and turn right onto Rue Belliard.

Tucked behind the Parlement Européen, this park is a welcome relief from the uncompromising presence of the shimmering EU buildings. Landscaped around a lake, the ground rises steeply to the north towards the buildings that form the Institut Royal des Sciences Naturelles, founded by Ernest Solvay at the end of the 19th century.

Parc Roi Baudouin Off maps

Metro Stuyvenbergh; tram 94.

Consisting of three distinct parks in the suburb of Jette north of the centre, the Parc Roi Baudouin is one of Brussels most attractive green spaces. The Dieleghem Wood and the Laerbeekbos are beautiful expanses of 200-year-old beech forest, while the Poelbos is home to nesting kingfishers and rare flora such as a double-leaved orchid and the rare black byrony plant, survivor of an era when the climate around Brussels was subtropical.

Parc Tenbosch G12–13

Off Rue Washington, Ixelles; tram 60. Open until dusk.

Hidden away in the heart of Ixelles (west of Avenue Louise), this little park comes as a pleasant surprise. Formerly the gardens of an old mansion, its winding paths make it seem bigger than it is. The old tennis courts have been taken over by football practice grounds, and there is a new play area for young children.

Parc de Woluwe Off maps

Off Av de Tervuren; tram 44.

This hilly park was designed around the pretty Mellaerts ponds at the end of the 19th century. There are rowing boats and pedalos for hire in the summer and on cold winter weekends the ponds provide a natural setting for ice-skating. This is an ideal spot for a picnic.

Parc de Wolvendael Off maps

Off Avenue Wolvendael; tram 92, 91.

The Parc de Wolvendael can lay claim to being Brussels' most historic piece of parkland; it was first mentioned in 1209, when it formed part of a former manor estate. It contains a small stone château built in 1763, a Louis XVI-style pavilion, some ancient sunken paths and the square tower of a former 15th-century manor house.

Children's Brussels

The first thing you notice about Belgian children is how well behaved they are. Traditionally, Belgium has a comparatively close-knit society, where values are maintained not only by parents or guardians but also through the kindly guidance of ever-present older cousins, aunts, great-aunts and grandmothers. Just about all children go to the local state-run school, which therefore has the strong backing of Belgium's mighty middle classes. If a child is unacceptably disruptive, the parents will soon be under pressure to do something about it. For all that, this is a child-friendly society, where children are broadly welcomed and generally well catered for.

Children below the age of six can travel free on all forms of public transport if accompanied by an adult. On trains, children between the ages of six and twelve can travel free with an adult Mon–Fri after 9am. Entrance to museums and other attractions offer the usual concessions to children.

For children's clothes and toy shops, see the Shopping chapter, pp.249–56.

Babysitting

In the 'Where to Stay' chapter, we list those hotels that offer babysitting. Apply to the Office National de l'Enfance (ONE), t 02 739 3979, for a list of crèches and childcare facilities in your area. City International School, t 02 734 8816, runs a full-time daily crèche.

Otherwise, try one of the following English-speaking agencies:

Bond van Grote en van Jonge Gezinnen
t 02 507 8811.
Association that provides baby or childsitting services in Brussels.

Ligue des Familles
127 Rue du Trône (18), t 02 507 7211, f 02 507 7200, w www.ligues desfamilles.be.

An organisation that provides information on childminding services for children up to six years old.

ULB Service des Etudiants
t 02 650 21 71. Phone Mon–Fri 10am–4pm.
Babysitting service offered by students of the Université Libre de Bruxelles.

Eating Out

Providing children behave, they will be accepted in all restaurants, cafés and bars. Since lunch in Belgium often lasts well beyond the endurance of most children, many parents wisely take toys and colouring kits to the restaurant. In our 'Eating Out' chapter we list those restaurants that supply child's portions and high chairs.

Museums

Centre Belge de la Bande Dessinée F3
20 Rue des Sables, t 02 219 1980; metro Botanique or Rogier. Open Tues–Sun 10am–6pm; adm adults €6.20, under-12s €2.50.
A good place to take kids over the age of six, although it's geared towards adults. There's a library where children can flick through comics to their hearts' content. See also p.119.

Musée du Cacao et du Chocolat E5
13 Grand' Place, t 02 514 2048, w www.mucc.be; metro Gare Centrale. Open Tues–Sun 10am–5pm; adm €4.96, under-12s free.
Traces the making and history of chocolate, with demonstrations and a tasting.

Musée des Enfants Off maps
15 Rue de Bourgmestre, t 02 640 0107, e childrenmuseum.brussels @skynet.be, w www.museedes enfants.be; tram 94 (as far as Jardin de Roi stop); bus 71. Open July–Aug Mon–Fri 2.30–5pm; Sept–April Wed, Sat, Sun 2.30–5pm; May–June Wed and Sat 2.30–5pm; adm €6.25.

Great for children aged 4–10. There are interactive puzzles and educational games, a theatre section with a dressing-up area, a kitchen for supervised baking and a small outdoor playground with animal enclosure.

Musée des Instruments de Musique (MIM) F2
2 Rue Montagne de la Cour, t 02 545 0130, e info@mim.fgov.be, w www.mim.fgov.be; metro Parc or Gare Centrale. Open Tues, Wed and Fri 9.30am–5pm, Thurs 9.30am–8pm, Sat and Sun 10am–5pm; adm €2.48.
Offers a range of musical activities for children including a section called the Garden of Orpheus, which is a 'multi-sensory and playful approach to music'. See also p.94.

Musée du Jouet H3
24 Rue de l'Association, t 02 219 6168, w www.cyber.be/museedu jouet. Open daily 10am–6pm; adm €3.
Crammed with toys of all kinds and ages: dolls, teddy bears, trains, magic lanterns, puppets. Children are genuinely welcome: there is an area where they can play with larger toys, the display cases have steps so that smaller children can see into them, and the top floor can be hired for parties. See also p.121.

Musée Royal de l'Afrique Centrale Off maps
13 Leuvensesteenweg, t 02 769 5211, e info@africamuseum.be, w www.africamuseum.be; metro Montgomery, then tram 44 to end of line. Open Tues–Fri 10am–5pm, Sat, Sun and hols 10am–6pm; adm €2.
A monument to Belgium's colonial past in Central Africa, full of masks and artefacts. Regular educational workshops are on offer for children. On the edge of the Forêt de Soignes, and set in attractive grounds with ponds, gardens and big expanses of grass – a good family day out. See also p.146.

Musée des Sciences
Naturelles K8

29 Rue Vautier, t 02 627 4238, e educakbinirsnb.be, w www .natural.sciences.net; metro Maelbeek. Open Tues–Fri 9.30am–4.45pm, Sat and Sun 10am–6pm; adm €3.72.

In our dinosaur-crazed age, this museum will be popular with the kids; it contains one of the world's finest collections of dinosaur remains. The star exhibits are the 65-million-year-old iguanodons of Bernissart, discovered in Belgium in the 19th century. *See* also p.127.

Musée du Transport
Urbain Bruxellois Off maps

364 Av de Tervuren; metro Montgomery, then tram 39 or 44 to the Dépôt Woluwe stop. Open April–Oct Sat, Sun and public hols 1.30–7pm; adm €4 incl. historic tram return trip to Tervuren.

The museum has beautifully restored examples of trams of all ages. Kids will love the historic tram ride to get there (*see* p.146). The ticket collector and the driver dress in period uniforms; you can watch the driver working the primitive controls. At the stops the ticket collector signals to the driver with a duck-like horn.

Scientastic D4

Bourse Metro station, Level –1, t 02 732 1336, e scientastic@yahoo.fr, w wwwscientastic.com; metro Bourse. Open Mon–Fri 12.30–2pm, Sat, Sun and hols 2–5.30pm; adm €3.97.

A small interactive science museum with hands-on exhibits focusing on the sensory world; you can make your voice sound like a duck or smell your way out of a maze. Its position means it's easy to fit it around any other plans you have for a day in the centre of town.

Outdoor Attractions

With such green suburbs, Brussels offers plenty of parkland in which to entertain children. Of the parks in and around the centre, among the best for children are the **Bois de la Cambre** (*see* p.259), with playgrounds, a boating lake, a rollerskating rink and numerous cafés; **Parc Wolvendael** (*see* p.260)in Uccle, which has crazy golf, an old-fashioned playground, an outdoor café and ponds; and **Parc de Woluwe**, (*see* p.260)which is a good place to fly a kite or hire pedalos.

Manneken-Pis D6

Corner of Rue de l'Etuve and Rue du Chêne; metro Bourse.

The appeal of this little fellow is obvious. Kids may also enjoy his selection of costumes, in the Musée Communal de la Ville de Bruxelles (*see* p.76).

Mini-Europe Off maps

1 Avenue du Football, Heysel, t 02 474 1313, e info@minieurope.com, w www.minieurope.com; metro Hesel; tram 23 or 81. Open April–June 9.30am–5pm, July–Aug 9.30am–7pm, Sept 9.30am–5pm, Oct–6 Jan 10am–5pm; by night: Aug daily until 11pm; adm adults €10.66, under-12s €8.25.

Exact copies of all the great edifices of Europe, but at one twenty-fifth of the size. The children seem to love it. When you've had enough of Europe there's the Atomium (*see* p.144), built in 1958 for the International Exhibition. It's a 300ft lift-ride up to the top sphere, so the views aren't bad. If there is still energy to expend, then there's Océade nearby (*see* p.145), a complex of swimming pools, slides and wave machines that's packed out in summer. On the same site is Kinepolis: an Imax cinema and 28 screens showing mainstream films.

Parc Paradisio Off maps

1 Domaine de Cambron, 7940 Cambron-Casteau, t 06 845 4653, e info@paradisio.be, w www .paradisio.be. By train: Gare Cambron-Casteau (call SNCB on t 02 555 2525 and ask for the special fare package). By car: exit 30 on the E429 motorway. Open daily 10am–6pm (July–Aug 10am–7pm); adm adults €5, 3–15s €3.50.

Set among the ruins of a 12th-century Cistercian abbey near Mons, this wildlife park contains Europe's largest aviary, a tropical greenhouse, an orchid garden and more than 2,500 birds. There are also otters, caimans, meerkats, a children's farm and a large playground.

Six Flags Belgium Off maps

9 Rue Joseph Deschamps, 1300 Wavre, t 010 42 1500. By train: take the Ottignies-Louvain-la-Nieve line to Gare de Bierges. By car: exit 7 (Walibi) on the E411. Open daily 10am–6pm; adm €28.50.

A huge, enormously popular, money-spinning theme park 20km from the centre of Brussels. Formerly called Walibi, the park was reopened in the summer of 2001 as Six Flags Belgium with several new hair-raising rides. Bugs Bunny Land is devoted to younger children, with small safe rides and a water playground. Like any theme park of the moment, though, the queues are abysmal. Attached is Aqualibi (t 010 42 1515; entrance on same ticket), a 'tropical' water park with wave machines and water chutes.

Entertaiment

Théâtre Marionettes
de Toone E5

21 Petite Rue des Bouchers, t 02 511 7137; metro Bourse. Performances daily 8.30pm.

You can make reservations after noon in the bar. There is also a Toone Theatre Museum, with a collection of the distinctive elongated puppets used in the show, but this is only open in the intervals during performances.

Théâtre Peruchet Off maps

50 Avenue de la Forêt, t 02 219 6906; tram 94. Performances Wed, Sat and Sun at 3pm; adm for museum and puppet show €6.

Attached to the International Puppet Museum. Kids can come here to watch some of the exhibits in action.

Gay and Lesbian Brussels

Brussels may not rank as one of the gay centres of Europe, but nonetheless it has an active, if discreet, gay scene.

Information and Organizations

There are two gay listings magazines (all in French), giving details of events, bars, contacts, accommodation and so forth: *Regard*, t 02 733 1024, e regard@euronet.be (every other month; BP 215, 1040 Brussels – apply using address only, without the name *Regard*); and *Tels Quels* (monthly; 44 Rue du Marché au Charbon, 1000 Brussels). *Tels Quels* also has a café and meeting point, 44 Rue du Marché au Charbon (t 02 512 4587; open Thurs–Tues 5pm–2am, Wed 2pm–2am; D5). **A Hirent d'Elles**, 81 Rue du Marché au Charbon, t 02 512 4587, w www.ahirentdelles.org, is a lesbian organization attached to *Tels Quels*.

Another source of information is **Infor Homo**, 100 Av de l'Opale, 1040 Brussels, t 02 733 1024, which also has a Gay Switchboard. Last, but by no means least, the **English-speaking Gay Group** (EGG), t 02 537 4704, e 00522.30@compuserve.com, w www.geocities.com/~eggbrussels, is an informal club for men and women of all nationalities which offers the opportunity to make new friends at relaxed, informal gatherings and monthly parties. It now has a mailing list of 700 members. You can also write to EGG, BP 198, 1060 Brussels 6.

Accommodation

Les Ecrins D3
15 Rue du Rouleau, t 02 219 3657, f 02 223 5740, e les.ecrins@skynet.be, w www.lesecrins.com; metro Ste-Catherine. Inexpensive.
A gay-friendly *fin de siècle* hotel with 11 rooms in the lively Ste-Catherine area. All rooms have private bathrooms.

Eating Out

La Cantina Cubana D6
6 Rue des Grands-Carmes, t 02 502 6540; metro Bourse. Open Tues–Sun 8pm–midnight. Moderate–inexpensive.
From the outside this Cuban restaurant looks a little over-themed. However, the food is excellent; try the vegetarian special, an enormous plateload of exotic and wonderfully prepared vegetables, grains and pulses. Mixed.

Le Comptoir D6
26 Place de la Vieille Halle aux Blés, t 02 514 0500; metro Gare Centrale. Open Mon–Thurs 7pm–midnight, Fri–Sun 7pm–1am. Moderate.
Restaurant above the well-known gay bar of the same name (*see* below), serving modern French and Belgian dishes. Bare-brick walls, platforms and wooden floors lend a warm atmosphere to the place.

Dolores D5
40 Rue du Marché au Charbon, t 0476 530 494; metro Bourse. Open Tues–Sun noon–11pm. Moderate.
A tiny Spanish restaurant and bar that is 'hetero-friendly'.

Le Fils de Jules F13
35 Rue du Page, t 02 534 0057; tram 81, 82 or 91. Open Mon–Sat noon–2.30 and 7–11, Sun noon–2.30pm. Moderate.
Tasty Belgian cuisine in the trendy suburb of Ixelles.

Bars

The main area for gay bars in the centre of Brussels is around the Bourse, along Rue du Marché au Charbon, and southwards down Boulevard Lemonnier.

L'Amour Fou G9
185 Chaussée d'Ixelles, t 02 514 2709, w www.amourfou.com; metro Porte de Namur. Open daily 9pm–3am.
A gay-friendly café with a mainly young crowd. Food available.

L'Arbre à Champagne D6
46 Place de la Vieille Halle aux Blés, t 02 503 2227; metro Gare Centrale. Open Mon–Thurs noon–11pm, Fri and Sat noon–1am, Sun 3pm–1am.
A gay-friendly tearoom and piano bar playing classical music. Light meals available.

Le Belgica D5
32 Rue du Marché au Charbon, t 02 514 0324; metro Bourse. Open Thurs–Sun 10pm–3am.
A long-established bar in the style of a classic Bruxellois café. The crowd is lively and mostly young.

Le Boulev' Art D4
108 Bd Anspach, t 02 512 5362; metro Bourse. Open daily 10am–2am.
A gay bar with snacks and an outdoor terrace.

Chez Maman D5
7 Rue des Grands-Carmes, t 02 502 8696; metro Bourse. Open Thurs–Tues 10pm–3am.
Popular gay and lesbian bar with regular transvestite shows.

Le Comptoir D6
26 Place de la Vieille Halle aux Blés, t 02 514 0500; metro Gare Centrale. Open Mon–Thurs 7pm–midnight, Fri–Sun 7pm–1am.
A trendy bar with attached art gallery on a recently revamped Baroque square tucked behind Place St-Jean.

Le Duquesnoy E6
12 Rue Duquesnoy, t 02 502 3883; metro Gare Centrale. Open Mon–Thurs 9pm–3am, Fri and Sat 9pm–5am, Sun 6pm–3am.
A full-on gay bar that aims to cater for every taste. Divided into three floors, each playing different music.

Gate E4
36 Rue Fossé aux Loups, t 02 223 0434, w www.lets-gate.com; metro De Brouckère. Open Mon–Thurs noon–1am, Fri–Sun 6pm–late.
A lively little bar attracting a younger mixed crowd. Saturday night is for women only.

L'Homo Erectus D5

57 Rue des Pierres, **t** *02 514 7493,* **w** *www.lhomoerectus.com;* **metro** *Gare Centrale or Bourse.* **Open** *daily noon–late.*

A cosy place right by the Grand' Place. It's meant to be mixed, but is predominantly a men's scene.

H2o D5

27 Rue du Marché au Charbon, **t** *02 514 1256;* **metro** *Bourse.* **Open** *daily 7pm–2am.*

A relaxed and sophisticated candle-lit bar right in the heart of the gay district. The late-20s/early-30s crowd is mixed. There is a small menu and food is served until 1am.

The Slave C5

7 Plattesteen, **t** *02 513 4746;* **metro** *Bourse.* **Open** *Mon–Fri 10am–4am, Sat and Sun 10am–6am.*

A leather bar with 'darkroom' and pornography on TV screens. Unsurprisingly, very few people admit to going here.

Tels Quels D5

44 Rue du Marché au Charbon, **t** *02 512 4587;* **metro** *Bourse.* **Open** *Thurs–Tues 5pm–2am, Wed 2pm–2am.*

A café/bar attached to the gay and lesbian information centre, which offers advice on gay rights and publishes a monthly magazine (*see* 'Information and Organizations', *above*). A relaxed atmosphere with organised group discussions.

Clubs

Le Cabaret E4

41 Rue de l'Ecuyer, **t** *02 503 5840,* **e** *bulldog.comm@village.uunet.be;* **metro** *De Brouckère.* **Open** *Sun 11pm–6am.*

Relaxed atmosphere with a mixture of young and older men.

La Démence C8

208 Rue Blaes, **t** *02 511 9789,* **w** *www.lademence.com;* **metro** *Porte de Hal.* **Open** *Sun every three weeks 11pm–7am.*

A very popular gay night on two floors at Le Fuse (*see p.243*). Mixture of house and garage music.

Different D5

112 Rue du Marché au Charbon, **t** *02 514 3064,* **w** *www.bedifferent.org;* **metro** *Bourse.* **Open** *1st Sat of the month 11pm–late.*

A small gay and lesbian club with renowned DJs and a relaxed atmosphere.

D-Light C8

208 Rue Blaes, **t** *02 511 9789;* **metro** *Porte de Hal.* **Open** *last Fri of the month 11pm–7am.*

A lesbian night held on the top floor of Le Fuse (*see p.243*). Trance, garage and mellow house.

Why Not C5

7 Rue des Riches-Claires, **t** *02 512 6343,* **e** *clubwhynot@skynet.be,* **w** *www.welcome.to/whynot;* **metro** *Anneessens.* **Open** *Mon–Thurs 11pm–6am, Fri–Sun 11pm–7am.*

Mostly frequented by young men (with a number of older stragglers), this is the only dance club in Brussels that is open every night.

Wing's D3

3 Rue de Cyprès, **t** *0475 660 990,* **w** *www.brussels.be.org/fy/wings;* **metro** *Ste-Catherine.* **Open** *Fri and Sat 10pm–late, Sun 9pm–late.*

Mixed and rather cliquey club predominantly frequented by women. Saturday is for women only.

Festivals

Belgium has a long calendar of events: some are age-old ceremonies and pageants, widely advertised and drawing large crowds; others are religious festivals, including some of disturbing fervour; others still are entirely local excuses for an annual knees-up and binge. Listed below are the most famous of these, as well as others worth the detour, plus some annual traditions observed among family and friends.

January

Fête des Rois
6 Jan
Epiphany is celebrated with an almond-flavoured cake called the *galette des rois*, which contains a plastic bean. Whoever finds the bean in his or her slice is awarded the paper crown that is sold with the cake.

International Film Festival Brussels
Mid–late Jan
The focus is on Belgian and other European films, with some non-European entries. Various venues. Contact: **t** 02 227 3980, **w** *www .brusselsfestival.be.*

February/March

Carnival
This is the carnival season. Strictly speaking, carnival is a last fling before the beginning of Lent (Latin corruption: *carne vale*, 'farewell to meat'), but carnivals take place in Belgium throughout Lent and even well before it. The most famous one is at Binche, a town in western Belgium between Charleroi and Mons. After a steady build-up on the Sundays preceding Lent, the town erupts into a three-day feast with street dancing and processions, culminating in the parade of the extraordinary Gilles de Binche on Shrove Tuesday. The Gilles (clowns) dress in extravagant medieval motley with bizarre bespectacled masks. In the afternoon they don massive headdresses of towering ostrich feathers, then walk around town

throwing oranges at their friends. The day is rounded off with fireworks and dancing. Parallel pre-Lenten festivities take place in the eastern towns of Eupen (Sat, Sun and Mon) and Malmédy (mainly Sat and Sun).

Easter Sunday
Children look for Easter eggs, which are said to have been hidden in the garden in the early morning by the *cloches de Rome* (the bells of Rome).

May

Brussels Jazz Marathon
Late May
Fans of jazz can enjoy more than 350 musicians performing in clubs, bars and open spaces throughout the city. Contact: **t** 02 456 0486.

20 km de Bruxelles
Annual half-marathon, with participants from all over the world competing through the streets of Brussels. Contact: **t** 02 511 9000, **w** *www.sibp.be/20km/ intro.html.*

July

Ommegang
First Thursday, 9–11pm
Ommegang literally means 'walk-around'. The grand pageant of Brussels, when some 2,000 participants dressed in Renaissance costume – as nobles, guildsmen, mounted soldiers, flag-throwers, jesters, peasants – go on a procession through the Grand' Place before the King and the royal family. The ceremony dates back at least as far as 1549, when it was performed in front of Charles V and the infant Prince Philip; it has now become little more than a costume parade and photo opportunity. Nonetheless, seats are at a premium and have to be booked in advance (from early June onwards) through the tourist office.

Independence Day
21 July
Public holiday marking the coronation of Leopold I. Military

parade and fireworks, among other special events.

July–August

Brussels Summer Festival
A classical-music extravaganza in different venues across the city. Contact: **t** 02 279 6436.

Foire du Midi
Mid-July–3rd week in Aug
The great summer funfair of Brussels fills one side of the Boulevard du Midi between the Porte de Hal and the Place de la Constitution. It brings together a mass of noisy, gaudy attractions, from rifle galleries and halls of mirrors to dodgems and the big wheel. Good-humoured fun for all the family: there are plenty of children's rides, and grown-ups can always retreat to the mass of makeshift bars and restaurants serving seafood, beer and wine at trestle tables (the fair is often seen as the beginning of the shellfish season).

August

Plantation du Meiboom
9 Aug
A deracinated may tree is paraded around the centre of Brussels amid much jollity, then planted at the corner of the Rue du Marais and Rue des Sables. *See* 'Meiboom' box.

Tapis de Fleurs
13–14 Aug
The Grand' Place is covered in an elaborate 'carpet of flowers' (biennial: 2002, 2004, etc.).

September

Journée du Patrimoine
Second Sunday
All kinds of historic houses, private collections, businesses and craft workshops throw open their doors to the public for a day, in celebration of the national heritage. Ask at the tourist office.

November

Toussaint
1–2 Nov
A time when the Belgians honour their dead by tidying up the

Meiboom

In early August the corner of Rue du Marais and Rue des Sables is the scene of the planting of the may tree (*meiboom*), a ceremony that has taken place for close on 800 years. A large, deracinated may tree is paraded joyously from the Place Ste-Catherine to the Grand' Place, then erected on this spot. The story goes that in 1213 a travelling wedding group were attacked by robbers but miraculously escaped unscathed. Believing they had been saved by their patron saint, St Laurent, and overcome by gratitude, they started the tradition of planting the may tree every year on his saint's day, in celebration of summer and survival.

cemeteries and filling them with flowers in preparation for 2 November, known as the Jour des Morts. An estimated 55 million flowers are sold during this period.

December

Fête de St-Nicolas
6 Dec
St Nicholas, a.k.a. Santa Claus, walks the streets and markets and enters schools in his guise as the Bishop of Myra. He is usually accompanied by his jolly sidekick, the blacked-up and decidedly un-PC Zwarte Piet. This is when many Belgian children receive their main Christmas gifts, as well as traditional *speculoos* biscuits.

Réveillon
24 December
Christmas Eve is the main feast-day of Christmas: the centrepiece is a sumptuous evening meal, after which good Catholics stagger off to Mass.

Christmas Day
25 Dec
A day of family visits and more gifts.

New Year
31 Dec
Celebrated by huge crowds gathering in the Grand' Place.

Language

Belgium has two main languages: French and Flemish (a form of Dutch known informally as *Vlaams* in Belgium but which more correctly should be referred to as Dutch or *Nederlands*, the pure form taught in schools). On a language map of Belgium, the border between the French-speaking and the Flemish-speaking parts runs east to west and roughly slices the country in two, with the Flemish speakers to the north and the French speakers to the south. The north is generally referred to as Flanders (Vlaanderen) and the Flemish-speakers (or Dutch-speakers) are the Flemish or Flemings; the French-speaking south is called Wallonia (La Wallonie), which is inhabited by Walloons, a few of whom still speak the dialect form of French called *wallon*. The people of Brussels are 85 per cent French-speaking, but Brussels is not part of Wallonia. The third official language, German, is spoken in the small eastern territories of Eupen, Malmédy and Moresnet ceded to Belgium in 1918 by the Treaty of Versailles.

French was imposed as the language of the ruling classes by the Burgundians in the 14th century, and by the 19th century the French-speaking population held political and economic ascendancy over the Flemish. This equation has changed radically since the Second World War, partly because of the decline of heavy industry in the south and the growing strength of modern light industries in the north, and partly because to succeed in administration it is now essential to be bilingual. Remarkably few French-speakers have made the effort to be conversant with Flemish, while a larger proportion of the Flemish have learned French. The result is that the Flemish have now gained the upper hand in the civil service, as well as in public services such as the post office and railways.

However, many of the Flemish appear to preserve a residual distaste for the French language. When you address a Belgian – particularly a civil servant – in the north of the country or in Brussels, do not assume that he or she will want to speak in French: if you happen to be talking to a Flemish-speaker, you are likely to be met with a decidedly cool response, and would be better advised to start off in English. It may subsequently turn out that French is, in fact, your most effective common language, but at least you will have established the rules of play.

Naturally enough, Flemish speakers in Brussels use the Flemish names for streets and the main sights, and may not volunteer the French equivalent. Hence be ready to be directed to the Grote Markt as opposed to the Grand' Place, the Muntplein as opposed to the Place de la Monnaie, or Nieuwstraat as opposed to Rue Neuve. (For a list of place names in both languages, *see* p.276.)

There is one final complication. The true Bruxellois, whose family has lived in Brussels for generations, may be at home in both Flemish and French, and often occupies a linguistic world somewhere in between, switching from one language to another without even being aware of it. Over time this has given rise to dialect forms of both French and Flemish, generally referred to as *bruxellois*. Although primarily Flemish in origin, *bruxellois* provides a common pool of linguistic inheritance from which both language groups draw, adding spice to their vocabulary. Few people, however, now speak pure *bruxellois*, although efforts are being made to save it from complete extinction. The Toone puppet shows (*see* p.248) are performed in *bruxellois*, for example.

English is not as widely spoken in Brussels – and in Belgium generally – as it is, for example, in the Netherlands. The chances are, however, that in most tourist contexts (hotels, restaurants, museums) the staff will be able to speak English – at least well enough to communicate. Nonetheless, some knowledge of both French and Flemish will inevitably be helpful.

The French spoken in Belgium is very similar to standard French, although the Belgian accent is distinctive – more throaty and rounded, less nasal than Parisian French. There are certain distinctive features – such as the use of *septante* (seventy) and *nonante* (ninety) instead of the standard French *soixante-dix* and *quatre-vingt dix*. The francophone Belgians are also far more casual than the French about the use of *tu* and *vous* (the informal and formal words for 'you').

Flemish Pronunciation

Flemish (*Vlaams*) is a variant form of Dutch (*Nederlands*). Two main problems confront anyone trying to learn even just the rudiments. One is the grammatical structure – although if you know German you will be familiar with the broad pattern of the back-to-front word order. The other problem is pronunciation. It is phonetic language, but you have to begin by shedding any preconceived notion about how written vowels should be pronounced. *A, e, i, o* and u are pronounced in a broadly similar way to English – although the *a* is much throatier and ends up more like the *o* in the English 'odd'.

When it comes to combination vowels, however, any attempt to interpret them in an English or, worse, a French manner, will end in failure. Wipe the slate clean and relearn! Names of places, or familiar words, will often provide useful aids to memory. For instance *huis* sounds similar to the English word 'house', which is what it means (although the 'ow' sound is more complex, making it more like 'ah-oohss').

Combination Vowels

aa like aa in the English 'aard-vaark'; e.g. *waar* (= where; pron. 'wahr')

ae like ar in the English 'part'; e.g. Verhaeren (Belgian poet; pron. 'Verharen')

au like ow in the English 'cow'; e.g. *kabeljauw* (= cod; pron. 'cabbe-lyow')

ee like ai in the English 'hail'; e.g. *een* (= one; pron. 'ayn')

ei like ij (*see* below); e.g *trein* (= train; pron. 'trayne')

eie like ay in the English 'say'; e.g. Leie (name of a river; pron. 'Lay')

eu like the English 'err'; e.g. Leuven (place name; pron. 'Lerven')

eeu ay-ooh; e.g. *leeuw* (= lion; pron. 'lay-oohv')

ie ee in the English 'three'; e.g. *drie* (= three; pron. 'dree')

ieu ee-oo; e.g. *nieuw* (= new; pron. 'nee-oo')

ij like ay in John Wayne; e.g. *wijn* (= wine; pron. 'wayne')

oe like oo in the English 'pool'; e.g. Poelaert (Brussels architect; pron. 'Poolart')

oo like oa in the English 'boat'; e.g. *Te koop* (= For sale; pron. 'Te cope' or 'Te cohp')

ou like oo in the English 'out'; e.g. *zout* (= salt; pron 'zout')

ui like ow in the English 'house'; e.g. *huis* (= house; pron. 'ouse' or 'ah-oohss')

uu like oo in the English 'hoot'; e.g. *Te huur* (= For rent; pron. 'Te ooer', but round your lips, or you risk enquiring about a *hoer*, a prostitute)

Consonants

Most consonants sound the same as they do in English, although some combinations present their own difficulties. Here are some of the more troublesome ones:

ch pronounced like the ch in the Scottish 'loch'.

g pronounced like a gutteral h – something similar to the h in 'hotel' or (again) like the ch in the Scottish 'loch'.

j pronounced like the English y.

v closer to the English f.

w in Flemish is like a soft English w.

sch at the end of a word is pronounced s. At the start of the word it sounds more like sr, with a bit of gutteral throat-clearing.

Basic Vocabulary

Greetings

English/French/Flemish

yes *oui/ja*

no *non/nee*

please
   s'il vous plaît
   alstublieft (abbrev. a. u. b.)

thank you (very much)
   merci (bien)
   dank u (wel), bedankt

hello, good day
   bonjour
   goedendag, or simply *dag*

good morning
   bonjour/goedemorgen

good evening
   bonsoir/goedenavond

good night (at bedtime)
   bonne nuit/goede nacht

goodbye
   au revoir/tot ziens

How are you?
   Comment allez-vous?
   Hoe maakt u het?

How are things?
   Ça va?/Hoe gaat het?

Very well, thank you.
   Très bien, merci./Goed, dank u.

My name is ...
   Je m'appelle .../Mijn naam is ...

mister/sir
   monsieur/mijnheer

mrs/madam
   madame/mevrouw

how much?
   combien?/hoeveel?

I can't speak French/Dutch
   Je ne parle pas français.
   Ik spreek geen Nederlands.

Do you speak English?
   Parlez-vous anglais?
   Spreekt u engels?

a little *un peu/een beetje*

I do not understand.
   Je ne comprends pas.
   Ik begrijp het niet.

I don't know
   Je ne sais pas./Ik weet het niet.

Go away!
   Allez-vous en!/Ga weg!

Where is the toilet?
   Où est la toilette?
   Waar is het toilet?

ladies *dames/damestoilet*

gents *messieurs/herentoilet*

Watch out!
   Attention!/Pas op!

Sorry!
   Pardon!/Sorry!, Het spijt me.

Cheers!
   Santé!/Gezondheid!, Proost!

Countries and Nationalities

I am ... *Je suis .../Ik ben ...*

Britain/British
   Grande-Bretagne, britannique
   Groot Brittannië, Brits

England/English
   Angleterre, anglais(e)
   Engeland, Engels

Scotland
   Ecosse, écossais(e)
   Schotland, Schots

Wales/Welsh
   Pays de Galles, gallois(e)
   Wales, Welsh

Ireland/Irish
   Irelande, irlandais(e)
   Ierland, Iers

America/American
   Amérique, américain(e)
   Amerika, Amerikaan

USA
   Les Etats-Unis
   Verenigde Staten

Canada/Canadian
   Canada, canadien(ne)
   Canada, Canadees

Australia/Australian
   Australie, australien(ne)
   Australië, Australisch

New Zealand
   Nouvelle-Zélande
   Nieuw-Zeeland

South Africa
   L'Afrique du Sud/Zuid Afrika

Belgium
   Belgique
   België/Belgisch

France/French
   France, français(e)
   Frankrijik, Frans

Flanders/Flemish
   Flandre, flamand(e)
   Vlaanderen, Vlaams

The Netherlands/Dutch
   Les Pays-Bas, néerlandais(e)
   Nederland, Nederlands

Numbers

0	zéro/nul
1	un/une/een
2	deux/twee
3	trois/drie
4	quatre/vier
5	cinq/vijf
6	six/zes
7	sept/zeven
8	huit/acht
9	neuf/negen
10	dix/tien
11	onze/elf
12	douze/twaalf
13	treize/dertien
14	quatorze/veertien
15	quinze/vijftien
16	seize/zestien
17	dix-sept/zeventien
18	dix-huit/achttien
19	dix-neuf/negentien
20	vingt/twintig
21	vingt et un/een en twintig
22	vingt-deux/twee en twintig
30	trente/dertig
31	trent et un/een en dertig
40	quarante/veertig
50	cinquante/vijftig
60	soixante/zestig
70	soixante-dix (French)/ septante (Belgian)/zeventig
80	quatre-vingt/tachtig
90	quatre-vingt dix (French)/ nonante (Belgian)/negentig
100	cent/honderd
101	cent et un/honderdeen
200	deux cents/twee honderd

thousand mille/duizend
million million/miljoen
first premier, première/eerste
second deuxième/tweede
third troisième/derde
half un demi/een half
a third un tiers/een derde
a quarter un quart/een kwart

Time

What is the time?
  Quelle heure est-il?
  Hoe laat is het?
today
  aujourd'hui/vandaag
yesterday hier/gisteren
tomorrow demain/morgen
morning
  matin/morgen/ochtend
afternoon
  après-midi/namiddag

evening soir/avond
night nuit/nacht
day jour/dag
week semaine/week
month mois/maand
year an/année/jaar
century siècle/eeuw
early tôt/vroeg
late tard/laat
Monday lundi/maandag
Tuesday mardi/dinsdag
Wednesday mercredi/woensdag
Thursday jeudi/donderdag
Friday vendredi/vrijdag
Saturday samedi/zaterdag
Sunday dimanche/zondag
public holiday jour ferié/feestdag
New Year Nouvel An/Nieuwjaar
Easter Pâques/Pasen
Christmas Noël/Kerstmis

Miscellaneous Small Words

very très/erg, zeer
much beaucoup/veel
too much trop/te veel
little/few peu/weinig
enough assez/genoeg
expensive cher, chère/duur
cheap pas cher, chère/goedkoop
old vieux, vieille/oud
new nouveau, nouvelle/nieuw
little petit/klein
big grand/groot
quickly vite/snel
slowly lentement/langzaam

Directions and Transport

I want to go to ...
  Je voudrais aller à ...
  Ik wil naar ...
Where is ... ?
  Où est ... ?/Waar is ... ?
left gauche/links
right droite/rechts
straight on tout droit/vooruit
near près/dichtbij
far loin/ver
airport
  aéroport/luchthaven, vliegveld
railway station gare/station
platform (five)
  quai (cinq)/spoor (vijf)
ticket billet/kaartje
single/one way
  aller simple/enkel
return/round trip
  aller et retour/heen en terug
car voiture/auto

car hire
  location des voitures
  auto verhuur
driving licence
  permis de conduire/rijbewijs
petrol essence/benzine
petrol station
  station d'essence
  benzinestation
unleaded sans plomb/loodvrij
car park parking/parkeerplaats
diversion
  déviation/wegomlegging
bicycle bicyclette, vélo/fiets

Emergencies

police police/politie
doctor médecin/dokter
dentist dentiste/tandarts
ill malade/ziek
I'm not feeling well.
  Je ne me sens pas bien.
  Ik voel niet lekker.
ambulance
  ambulance/ambulance
hospital hôpital/ziekenhuis
medicine
  médicament/geneesmiddel

Shopping and Services

shop magasin/winkel
bakery boulangerie/bakkerij
cake shop
  pâtisserie/banketbakkerij
grocer
  épicerie/kruidenierswinkel
bookshop librairie/boekhandel
I'm looking for ...
  Je cherche .../Ik zoek ...
pharmacy pharmacie/apotheek
clothes vêtements/kleding
shoes chaussures/schoenen
It's too big/small.
  Il est trop grand/petit.
  Het is te groot/klein.
lace dentelle/kant
bank banque/bank
post office
  bureau de poste/postkantoor
postage stamp timbre/postzegel
letter lettre/brief
postcard
  carte postale/ansichtkaart
air mail par avion/luchtpost

Notices and Labels

closed fermé/gesloten
open ouvert/open

entrance
entrée/toegang, ingang
exit *sortie/uitgang, uitrit*
No smoking
Défense de fumer/Niet roken
street *rue/straat*

Eating Out

The language of cuisine in Belgium is predominantly French. In restaurants in Flanders and Flemish-speaking Brussels, French terms tend to be used for the dishes, but the Flemish terms are used in shops.

General

English/French/Flemish
restaurant *restaurant/restaurant*
to eat *manger/eten*
to drink *boire/drinken*
I would like ...
Je voudrais .../Ik wil graag ...
to pay *payer/betalen*
Could I have the bill, please?
L'addition, s'il vous plaît.
De rekening, alstublieft.
vegetarian *végétarien/vegetariër*
breakfast *petit déjeuner/ontbijt*
lunch
déjeuner
middagmaal, noenmaal
dinner *souper/avondeten*
beer *bière/bier*
wine *vin/wijn*
a bottle of wine
une bouteille de vin
een fles wijn
red wine *vin rouge/rode wijn*
white wine
vin blanc/witte wijn
glass *verre/glas*
coffee *café/koffie*
tea *thé/thee*
milk *lait/melk*
soft drinks
limonades/limonaden
orange juice
jus d'orange/sinaasappelsap
mineral water
eau minérale/mineraalwater
It is/tastes good!
C'est trés bon!
Het smaakt lekker!
soup *soupe, potage/soep*
starter
hors d'oeuvre, entrée
voorgerecht

main course
plat principal, hoofdgerecht
dessert *dessert, nagerecht*
dish of the day
plat du jour/dagschotel
bread *pain/brood*
butter *beurre/boter*
cheese *fromage/kaas*
egg *oeuf/ei*
jam *confiture/jam*
salt *sel/zout*
pepper *poivre/peper*
sugar *sucre/suiker*

Fish

fish *poisson/vis*
bass *bar/loup de mer/zeebaars*
cod *cabillaud/kabeljauw*
eel *anguille/paling*
haddock
aiglefin, églefin/schelvis
herring *hareng/haring*
lobster *homard/kreeft*
mackerel *maquereau/makreel*
monkfish *lotte/lotte/zeeduivel*
mullet (red) *rouget/roodbaars*
mussel *moule/mossel*
oyster *huître/oester*
Pike *brochet/snoek*
plaice *plie/pladijs/schol*
salmon *saumon/zalm*
scallop
coquille Saint-Jacques
Sint-Jacobsoester, Jacobsschelp
shrimp/prawn *crevette/garnaal*
skate *raie/rog*
sole *sole/zeetong*
squid *calamar/calamar, inktvis*
trout *truite/forel*
tuna *thon/tonijn*
winkles *bigorneaux/kreukels*

Meat

meat *viande/vlees*
game *gibier/wild*
beef *boeuf/rundvlees*
chicken *poulet/kip*
duck *canard/eend*
goose *oie/gans*
guinea fowl *pintade/parelhoen*
hare *lièvre/haas*
ham *jambon/ham*
lamb *agneau/lamsvlee*
pheasant *faisant/fazant*
pork *porc/varkensvlees*
quail *caille/caille, kwartel*
rabbit *lapin/konijn*
snails *escargots/escargots, slakken*
veal *veau/kalfsvlees*

venison *cerf, chevreuil/ree(bok)*
wild boar (young boar)
sanglier (marcassin)
wildzwijn, werzwijn
brains *cervelle/hersenen*
leg *gigot/bout*
liver *foie/lever*
kidneys *rognons/nieren*
sausage
saucisse, saucisson/worst

Vegetables

vegetables *légumes/groenten*
aubergine/eggplant
aubergine/aubergine
asparagus *asperges/asperges*
Belgian endive/chicory
chicon/witloof
broad beans *fèves/tuinbonen*
Brussels sprouts
choux de Bruxelles/spruitjes
carrots *carottes/worteltjes*
cauliflower *choufleur/bloemkohl*
chervil *cerfeuil/kervel*
chives *ciboulette/bieslook*
courgette/zucchini
courgette/courgette
fennel *fenouil/venkel*
garlic *ail/knoflook*
green beans
haricots princesse/princesbonen
haricot beans *haricots/snijbonen*
leek *poireau/prei*
mushroom
champignon/champignon
onion *oignon/ui*
peas *petits pois/erwten*
potatoes
pommes de terre/aardappelen
potato chips/french fries
frites/frieten
rice *riz/rijst*
spinach *épinard/spinazie*
tomato *tomate/tomaat*

Fruit

fruit *fruits/fruit, vruchten*
apple *pomme/appel*
banana *banane/banaan*
cherry *cerise/kers*
chestnut *marron/kastanje*
orange *orange/sinaasappel*
peach *pêche/perzik*
pear *poire/peer*
pineapple *ananas/ananas*
plum *prune/pruim*
raspberry *framboise/framboos*
strawberry *fraise/aardbei*

Dessert

cake *gâteau/koek*
cheesecake
  tarte au fromage/kaastaart
tart *tarte/taart*
whipped cream
  crème Chantilly/slagroom
ice cream *glace/ijs*
pancake *crêpe/pannekoek*
waffle *gaufre/wafel*

Preparation

rare *saignant/rood*
medium
  à point/half doorbakken
well done *bien cuit/gaar*
plain (without sauces)
  nature/natuur
minced *haché/gehakt*
stuffed *farci/gevuld*
grilled *grillé/geroosterd*
steamed *à la vapeur/gestoomd*
smoked *fumé/gerookt*

French/Walloon Dishes and Specialities

à l'ardennaise cooked with Ardennes ham (and sometimes cheese)
à la liégeoise cooked or prepared with strips of bacon
à la nage (fish) served in a delicately flavoured stock
américain préparé raw minced steak mashed up with egg yolk, onions, capers, etc.
andouillettes rich sausages made of offal
assiette anglaise a selection of cold meats
bisque de homard thick, creamy lobster soup
blanquette de veau a casserole of veal in a white sauce
boudin/boudin noir sausage/black pudding
boulettes meatballs
brochette shish kebab
caille aux raisins quail cooked with grapes
carbonnades flamandes beef stew cooked with beer
civet (de lapin, etc.) game stew enriched with blood and red wine
cramique raisin bread
croque monsieur grilled cheese (and sometimes ham) on toast

cuisses de grenouille frogs' legs
entrecôte à l'osa huge rib steak
(poissons) en escavèche (cold fish) cooked in a jellied stock flavoured with herbs
faisan à la brabançonne pheasant cooked with braised Belgian endives
flamiche aux poireaux a kind of quiche made with leeks and cream
gratin de/au gratin browned in the oven, usually dotted with butter or cheese
jambon d'Ardennes cured ham (like Parma ham)
magret de canard sliced duck breast
moules marinière steamed mussels, cooked with celery, onions and parsley
moules parquées mussels grilled with garlic butter
navarin d'agneau lamb stew
oiseaux sans tête slices of beef rolled around a meat stuffing
pâté de foie gras rich pâté made from the livers of force-fed geese or ducks
plateau de fruits de mer platter of mixed cold shellfish and other seafood
printanier cooked with spring vegetables
salade liégeoise green salad made with green beans and bacon pieces
salmis (de bécasse) roast meat (woodcock) recooked in a rich wine sauce
sauce béarnaise egg and butter sauce with vinegar, shallots and tarragon
béchamel creamy sauce made with butter, flour and milk
bordelaise rich sauce made with bone marrow and red wine
chasseur 'hunter's' sauce made with wine, mushrooms and onions
hollandaise sauce made with butter, egg yolk and lemon juice
madère sauce made with butter, flour, stock and madiera wine
Mornay béchamel sauce with cheese
mousseline a light, whipped sauce of egg yolk, lemon and butter

Soubise béchamel sauce with onion purée
tartare mayonnaise with mustard, gherkins, capers and green herbs
sole meunièresole fried in butter
steak à l'américaine raw minced steak
steak tartare raw minced steak (steak *à la américaine* is the usual term)
tartare (de thon) raw and minced (tuna)
tarte tatin baked apple tart turned upside-down on a pastry base
(cuisine du) terroir local/regional (cooking)
tartine slice of bread and butter (for open sandwich)
toast cannibal raw minced steak on toast
tourte savoury pie made with meat and vegetables

Flemish Dishes

bloedpens blood pudding
boterhama slice of bread and butter (for open sandwich)
fricandel meatballs
Gentse stoverijrich beef stew from Ghent cooked with beer and mustard
hutsepot hearty stew (perhaps oxtail or pig's trotters) with root vegetables
karbonaden braised beef with onions, usually cooked in beer
paling in 't groen eels in green herb sauce
rijstpap rice pudding flavoured with cinnamon
speculoos hard biscuits made with butter, brown sugar and spices
stoemp mashed potato mixed with vegetable and/or meat purée
waterzooi chicken (now also fish) cooked in a soup-like cream sauce

Bruxellois Dishes and Specialities

boddink a sort of bread-and-butter pudding
caricolles whelks, cockles (any snail-like seafood)
choesels casserole of mixed offal

faro *lambic* beer flavoured with sugar and caramel

gueuze beer made from matured and blended lambic

kipkap jellied meat made of unpopular cuts (ears, tail, cheeks etc)

kriek *lambic* beer flavoured with cherries

lambic beer brewed in the Senne Valley, fermented by natural yeasts

pistolet bread roll

plattekeis fromage blanc (a kind of cream cheese)

smoutebollen deep-fried pastries dusted with icing sugar (fairground food)

A Smattering of Bruxellois

amigo police cell

braderie sale of goods at knockdown prices

brol something worthless, junk

brusseleir a bruxellois (person)

(faire sa petite) commission 'spend a penny'; urinate

dégobiller vomit, throw up

dikenek arrogant know-it-all

drache a downpour

drève/dreef a tree-lined avenue

estaminet a cosy kind of pub

fritkot chip shop or van

impasse alleyway

kaberdoech cabaret, bistrot

ketje young lad

kiekerfretters archaic term, occasionally heard, for Bruxellois people

klachkop bald

maboule mad

manneken/menneke little boy, rascal

pachacroute idle worker, loafer, skiver

patapoef fat

patraque unwell, weak

pei man/person

schieve lavabo idiot (literally, 'twisted/bowed basin')

schieve architek despicable person (*see* p.104)

tof very pretty, good

volle gaz at full speed

zwanze a joke

Place Names

Many places in Belgium have two versions of their name: Flemish and French. Signposts tend to be based on the assumption that you know that Mons is the same as Bergen, or that Mechelen is Malines – which can cause instant panic to the navigator. In this guide we have used French only, but in Brussels all names – districts, streets, institutions – have two versions. Many of these pairs are clearly recognizable as one and the same – others are totally different from each other. Below is a list of the principal cities and towns in Belgium, and some of the place names in Brussels, where the two versions are noticeably different and might cause confusion.

Cities and Towns

French/Flemish/English

Alost Aalst

Anvers Antwerpen/Antwerp

Bruges Brugge

Bruxelles Brussel/Brussels

Courtrai Kortrijk

Gand Gent/Ghent

Louvain Leuven

Liège Luik

Lierre Lier

Malines Mechelen

Mons Bergen

Namur Namen

Ostende Oostende/Ostend

Tongres Tongeren

Tournai Doornik

Veurne Furnes

Ypres Ieper

Zeebruges Zeebrugge

Brussels Place and Street Names

French/Flemish

Berchem-Sainte-Agathe
 Sint-Agatha-Berchem

Botanique Kruidtuin

Bourse Beurs

Forêt Vorst

Gare du Midi Zuidstation

Grand' Place Grote Markt

Ilôt Sacré Vrije Gemeente

Ixelles Elsene

La Hulpe Ter Hulpen

Molenbeek-Saint-Jean
 Sint-Jan-Molenbeek

Notre-Dame-au-Bois Jezus-Eik

Parc du Cinquantenaire Jubelpark

Place de la Monnaie Muntplein

Place Royale Koningsplein

Potagères Warmoesberg

Quai au Bois à Brûler
 Branthoutkaai

Quai aux Briques Baksteenkaai

Rhode-Saint-Genèse
 Sint Genesius-Rode

Rue au Beurre Boterstraat

Rue de Flandre Vlaamsesteenweg

Rue de la Montagne Bergstraat

Rue de l'Etuve Stoofstraat

Rue des Eperonniers
 Spoormakersstraat

Rue du Fossé aux Loups
 Wolvengrachtstraat

Rue du Marché aux Fromages
 Kaasmarkt

Rue du Marché aux Herbes
 Grasmarkt

Rue du Marché aux Poulets
 Kiekenmarkt

Rue Montagne aux Herbes Rue Neuve Nieuwstraat

Sablon Zavel

Saint-Josse-ten-Noode
 Sint-Joost-ten-Node

Watermael-Boitsfort
 Watermaal-Bosvoorde

Woluwé-Saint-Lambert
 Sint Lambrechts-Woluwe

Woluwé-Saint-Pierre
 Sint-Pieters-Woluwe

Index

Numbers in **bold** indicate main references. Numbers in *italic* indicate maps.

Brussels Street Maps

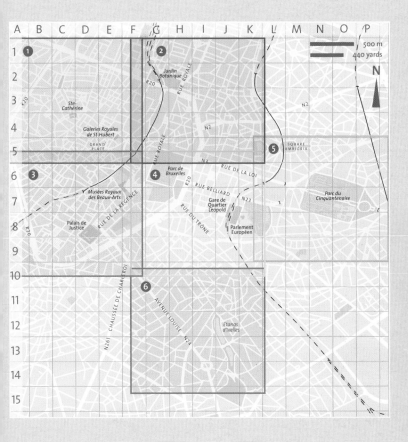

| | | | | | | | | | | | | | | | |
|A|B|C|D|E|F|G|H|I|J|K|L|M|N|O|P|

1 ❶ ❷

500 m
440 yards

N

2 Jardin Botanique
R20
RUE ROYALE

3 R20 Ste-Catherine N2

4 Galeries Royales de St-Hubert N2

5 GRAND' PLACE RUE ROYALE N3 ❺ SQUARE AMBIORIX

6 ❸ Parc de Bruxelles ❹ R20 RUE DE LA LOI
RUE BELLIARD Parc du Cinquantenaire

7 Musées Royaux des Beaux-Arts RUE DE LA RÉGENCE Gare de Quartier Léopold N23

8 R20 Palais de Justice RUE DU TRÔNE Parlement Européen

9

10 ❻

11 CHAUSSÉE DE CHARLEROI AVENUE LOUISE N24

12 N261 Étangs d'Ixelles

13

14

15

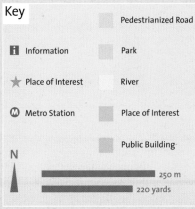

Key

		Pedestrianized Road
🛈	Information	Park
★	Place of Interest	River
Ⓜ	Metro Station	Place of Interest
		Public Building

N

250 m
220 yards

A

1
RUE DU CHOEUR
RUE ADOLPHE LAVALLÉE
RUE COURTOIS
R. DU CHIEN VERT

R. HÉLÈNE RYCKMANS
PARVIS SAINT-JEAN BAPTISTE

2
RUE DU COMTE DE FLANDRE
R. DE LA PROSPÉRITÉ
RUE DE L'AVENIR
R. DARMON
R. HAUBRECHTS

Ⓜ Comte de Flandre
RUE SAINTE-MARIE

R. VANDERMAELEN

3
CHAUSSÉE DE GAND N9
R. DES MARINIERS
R. DU CHEVAL NOIR
QUAI DE HAINAULT

R. DU PÈNE
D'ALOST

BOULEVARD BARTHÉLÉMY
RUE VANDENBRANDEN

4
R. NOTRE-DAME DU SOMMEIL
R. DE LA POUDRIÈRE
RUE DES FABRIQUES
RUE DE LA SENNE

RUE DU CHAR
RUE DU

5
RUE DE L'ABATTOIR
R. ANNEESSENS
RUE CURRENS
RUE DE LA SENNE
RUE CAMUSEL
R. DE LA BUANDERIE
RUE D'ANDERLECHT

B

1
RUE COURTOIS
RUE DES ATELIERS

RUE DU RUISSEAU
RUE DU HOUILLEURS
R. DES HOUILLEURS

2
RUE DE L'AVENIR
QUAI DES CHARBONNAGES
BOULEVARD DE NIEUPORT
R. DE WITTE DE HAELEN
RUE LOCQUENGHIEN
R20

3
RUE DU FLANDRE
RUE DE LA CLÉ
IMPASSE POILS
R. DE LA CIGOGNE
RUE ANTOINE DANSAERT
R. DE LA SERRURE
RUE DU HOUBLON

4
RUE DU GRAND SERMENT
RUE DES MOINES
RUE DU REMPART DES MOINES
RUE DU BOULET
PLACE DU NOUVEAU MARCHÉ AUX GRAINS
RUE DE LA BRAIE

5
RUE PLETINCKX
RUE DES SIX JETONS
RUE DES NAYLTS
RUE DE LA GRANDE ÎLE

C

1
PLACE SAINCTELETTE
R20A
PLACE DE L'YSER
BD. DU NEUVIÈME DE LIGNE
BOULEVARD
BD. DE DIXMUDE
BD. DE DIXMODE
BD. D'YPRES

2
R. DE LA FORÊT D'HOUTHULST
R. DE PASSCHENDAELE
R. DE BARCHON
R. ST. ANDRÉ
QUAI AUX BARQUES
QUAI AU BOIS DE CONSTRUCTION
QUAI À LA HOUILLE
QUAI À LA CHAUX
CITÉ DU SUREAU
R. MARCQ
QUAI

3
★ Monument aux Pigeons Soldats
SQUARE DES BLINDÉS
RUE D'OPHEM
R. DU MARCHÉ AUX PORCS
R. DU PAYS DE LIÈGE
R. DU NOM DE JÉSUS
R. LÉON LEPAGE
R. DU CHIEN-MARIN
QUAI AU BOIS À BRULER
R. DU ROULEA
BEG

Maison du Spectacle la Bellone

4
PLACE DU NOUVEAU MARCHÉ AUX GRAINS
Ste-Catherine
Ⓜ
Ste-Cathérin
Patrick Pitschon
Bonsoir Clara
Stijl L'Archiduc
R. SAINTE-CATHERINE
R. VIEUX AUX GRAINS
Album
RUE DES CHARTREUX
R. DES POISSONNIER
R. AUGUST ORTS
R. DU PONT DE LA CARPE
R. JULES VAN PRAE
RUE ST-CHRISTOPHE
RUE VAN ARTEVELDE

5
PLACE ST-GÉRY
Le Lion St-Géry
Notre Dame aux Riches-Claires
R. DES RICHES CLAIRES
R. SAINT-GÉRY
BOULEVARD ANSPACH
R. DES TEINTURIERS
R. DE BON SECOURS
Notre-Dame de Bon Secours

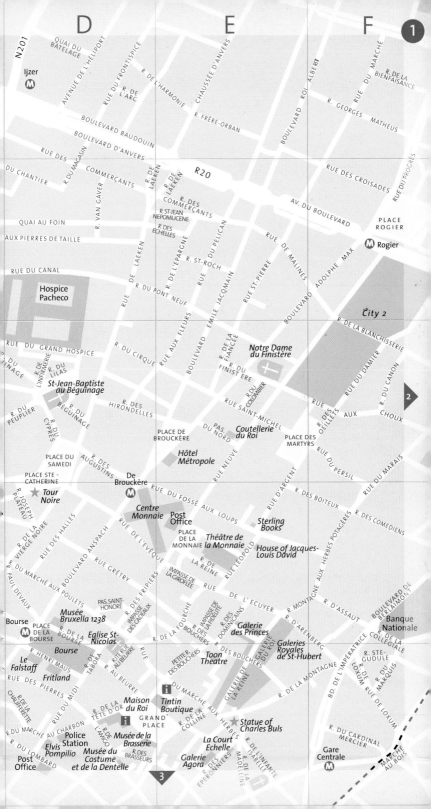

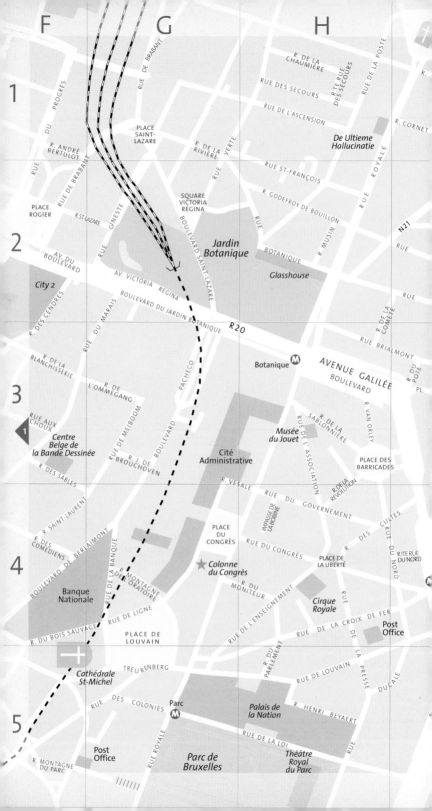

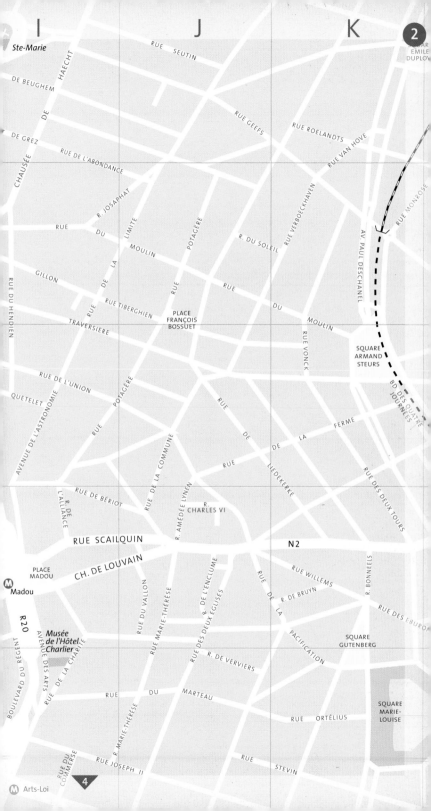

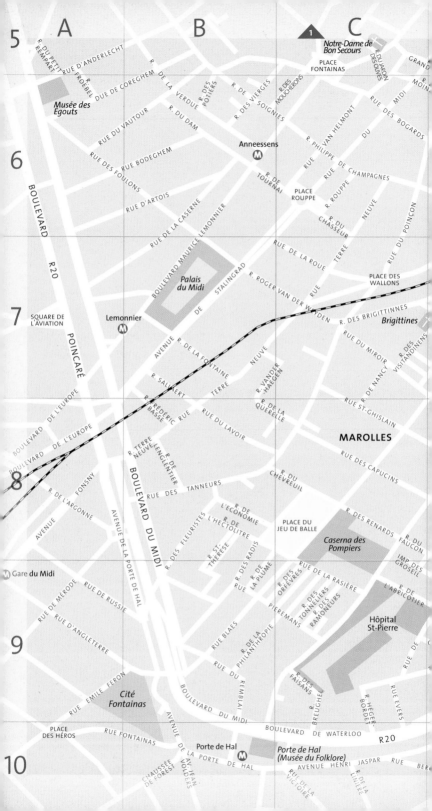

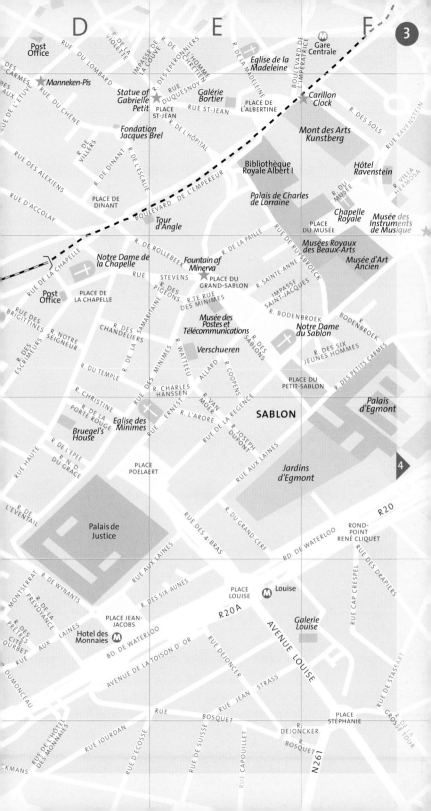

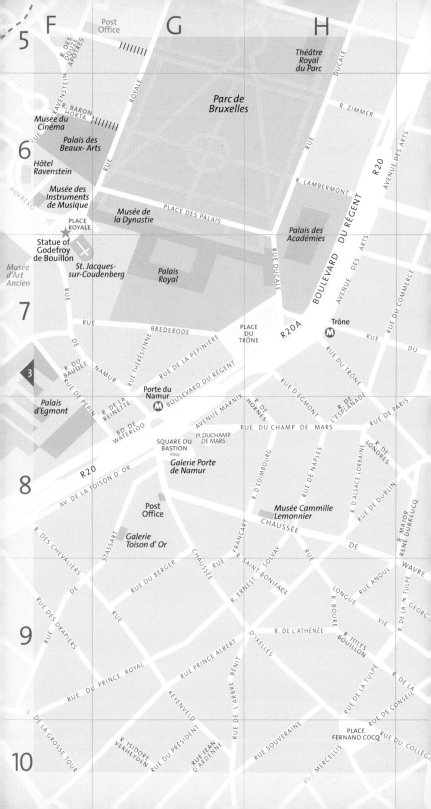

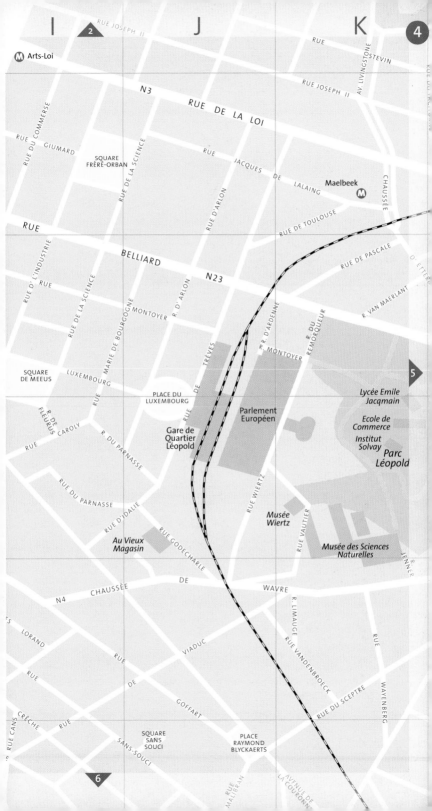

I

J

K

4

RUE JOSEPH II

2

RUE

AV. LIVINGSTONE

M Arts-Loi

N3

RUE JOSEPH II

RUE DE LA LOI

RUE DU COMMERSE

GIUMARD

SQUARE
FRÈRE-ORBAN

RUE DE LA SCIENCE

RUE

JACQUES DE LALAING

Maelbeek

CHAUSSÉE

RUE D'ARLON

M

RUE DE TOULOUSE

RUE

BELLIARD

N23

RUE DE PASCALE

D'ETTER

RUE DE L'INDUSTRIE

RUE

RUE DE LA SCIENCE

MARIE DE BOURGOGNE

MONTOYER

R. D'ARLON

R. D'ARDENNE

R. MONTOYER

R. DU REMORQUEUR

R. VAN MAERLANT

SQUARE
DE MEEUS

LUXEMBOURG

RUE DE TRÈVES

5

R. DE FLEURUS

CAROLY

R. DU PARNASSE

PLACE DU
LUXEMBOURG

Parlement
Européen

Lycée Emile
Jacqmain

Ecole de
Commerce

Institut
Solvay

Parc
Léopold

Gare de
Quartier
Léopold

RUE

RUE DU PARNASSE

RUE D'IDALIE

RUE GODECHARLE

Au Vieux
Magasin

DE

CHAUSSÉE

N4

Musée
Wiertz

RUE WIERTZ

RUE VAUTIER

Musée des Sciences
Naturelles

JENNER

WAVRE

R. LIMAUGE

RUE

LORAND

RUE

DE

VIADUC

RUE VANDENBROECK

RUE DU SCEPTRE

WAYENBERG

CRÈCHE

RUE CANS

RUE

GOFFART

SQUARE
SANS
SOUCI

SANS-SOUCI

PLACE
RAYMOND
BLYCKAERTS

RUE MALIBRAN

AVENUE DE
LA COURONNE

6

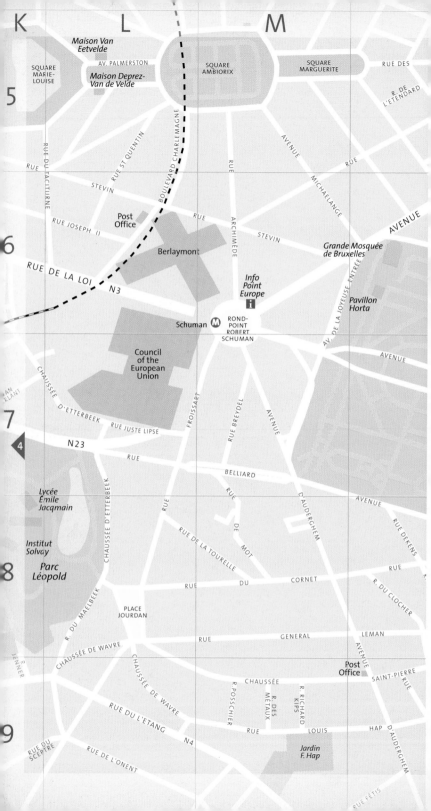

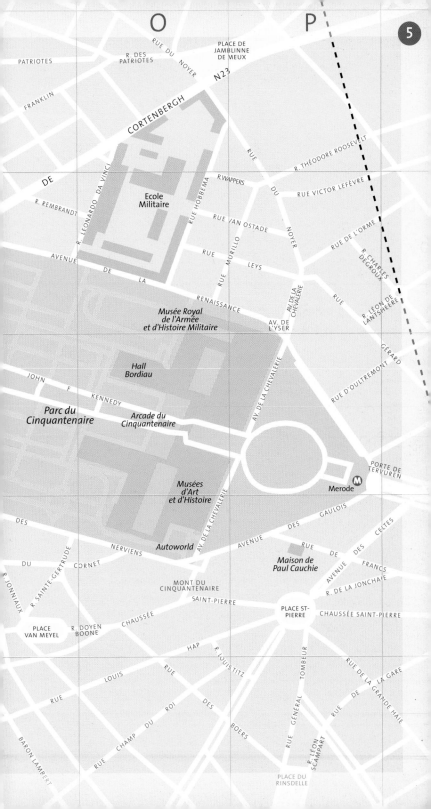

PATRIOTES

R. DES PATRIOTES

RUE DU NOYER

PLACE DE JAMBLINNE DE MEUX

N23

FRANKLIN

CORTENBERGH

RUE THÉODORE ROOSEVELT

DE

R. REMBRANDT

R. LÉONARDO DA VINCI

Ecole Militaire

RUE HOBBEMA

R. WAPPERS

RUE DU NOYER

RUE VICTOR LEFÈVRE

RUE VAN OSTADE

RUE DE L'ORME

R. CHARLES DEGROUX

AVENUE

DE

LA

RUE MURILLO

LEYS

RENAISSANCE

AV. DE LA CHEVALERIE

RUE

R. LÉON DE LANTSHEERE

Musée Royal de l'Armée et d'Histoire Militaire

AV. DE L'YSER

JOHN

F

KENNEDY

Hall Bordiau

AV. DE LA CHEVALERIE

RUE D'OULTREMONT

GÉRARD

Parc du Cinquantenaire

Arcade du Cinquantenaire

Musées d'Art et d'Histoire

PORTE DE TERVUREN

M Merode

DES

NERVIENS

CORNET

AV. DE LA CHEVALERIE

Autoworld

AVENUE

DES

GAULOIS

RUE

DE

DES

CELTES

DU

R. SAINTE-GERTRUDE

R. JONNIAUX

Maison de Paul Cauchie

AVENUE

FRANCS

R. DE LA JONCHAIE

MONT DU CINQUANTENAIRE

SAINT-PIERRE

PLACE ST-PIERRE

CHAUSSÉE SAINT-PIERRE

PLACE VAN MEYEL

R. DOYEN BOONE

CHAUSSÉE

HAP

R. LOUISTITZ

RUE GÉNÉRAL TOMBEUR

RUE DE LA GARE

LA GARE

LOUIS

RUE

DU

ROI

DES

BOERS

RUE

DE LA GRANDE HAIE

BARON LAMBERT

RUE

CHAMP

R. LÉON SCAMPART

PLACE DU RINSDELLE

4

RUE SANS-SOUCI

RUE DU COLLÈGE

R. JEAN VAN VOLSEM

AVENUE DE LA COURONNE

R. DES ARTISAN
R. DU CHÂTEA

RUE MAES

PLACE HENDRIK CONSCIENCE

Musée Communal d'Ixelles

RUE MAES

R. CLÉMENTINE

MALIBRAN

R. JEAN VAN VOLSEM

RUE DU COLLÈGE

RUE

R. ITE RUE MALIBRAN

RUE DILLENS

RUE MARIE-HENRIETTE

RUE WÉRY

RUE DE LA BRASSERIE

RUE DES LIÉGEOIS

PLACE EUGÈNE FLAGEY

R. DES CYGNES

R. DE LA DIGUE

R. DE LA BRASSERIE

R. DE LA LEVURE

RUE DE LA LEVURE

RUE ALFRED GIRON

HARD

Maison de la Radio

R. DE LA CUVE

RUE DU NID

AV. DU GÉNÉRAL DE GAULLE

AVENUE DES ÉPERONS D'OR

CHAUSSÉE DE BOONDAEL

HAUSSÉE DE VLEURGAT

SQUARE BIARRITZ

Etangs d'Ixelles

DU LAC

RUE DE LA VALLÉE

AVENUE

SQUARE DU SOUVENIR

RUE VILAIN XIV

R. VILAIN XIV

DU GÉNÉRAL

AVENUE

Hôtel Max Hallet

RUE DU BUISSON

DE

AVENUE DES KLAUWAERTS

DE

BELLEVUE

RUE DU MONASTERE

RUE DE

GAULLE

SQUARE RODE KRUIS

AV. GÉO BERNIER

L'HIPPODROME

RUE ST-GEORGES

N24

CLOÎTRE

ALLÉE DU

Abbaye de la Cambre

low cost travel to europe

malaga
nice
alicante
rome
copenhagen
faro

go® www.go-fly.com

go enjoy